John Ruskin

A Life in Pictures

John Ruskin

A LIFE IN PICTURES

James S. Dearden
(Companion of the Guild of St George)

Published by
Sheffield Academic Press Ltd
Mansion House
19 Kingfield Road
Sheffield S11 9AS
England

Designed and typeset by Rebecca Mazonowicz
and
Printed on acid-free paper in Great Britain
by Bookcraft Ltd
Midsomer Norton, Bath

British Library Cataloguing in Publication Data

A catalogue record for this book is available
from the British Library

ISBN 1 84127 046 6
ISBN 1 84127 045 8 (paper)

Contents

List of plates

Foreword

In December 1960 I contributed to *Apollo* an article on the dozen portraits of John Ruskin then belonging to the Whitehouse Collection which were housed either in the Ruskin Galleries, Bembridge School, Isle of Wight, or at Brantwood, Coniston. I followed this six months later with a second article, on fourteen further portraits in other collections. Soon afterwards I determined to catalogue all of the portraits, in whatever medium, that I could find. This was later extended to include all known portraits, whether or not it was possible to locate them.

With a few pauses this work has continued ever since, and I am grateful to the publishers for agreeing to publish it to coincide both with the celebrations being planned to mark the centenary of Ruskin's death in 2000, and with the exhibition of portraits to be held in 2000 in Sheffield, Lancaster and Oxford.

In the forty years that it has taken to make this book, I have received help from very many people. Owners of portraits have provided me with statistics relating to them; galleries and sale rooms have helped in the tracing of lost portraits, and in the discovery of new ones; authorities on photography have given advice; and there are few Ruskin scholars in the world who have not been bothered at one time or another for help in connection with portraits. I feel that I will not be the only person who will be glad that the work is finished! To all of these friends – too numerous to mention individually – I express my very grateful thanks.

Without the help of Alan Turvey, another Ruskin portrait-hunter, I would have overlooked several recent works, and I thank him for his help.

I am also grateful to the many owners of portraits, caricatures, busts and photographs – whose names are listed in my Catalogue of Portraits – for allowing me to reproduce the various items in their care. Particularly I am indebted to the Trustees of the Ruskin Foundation at the Ruskin Library, Lancaster University, and Brantwood, Coniston, where are located the largest number of portraits, in the Whitehouse Collection, and from where are also reproduced a large number of the photographs and caricatures. I must also thank all of my friends associated with the Ruskin Library in Tokyo, and the Mikimoto Collection, for help in identifying their various portrait holdings.

I am glad to acknowledge permission to reproduce photographs supplied by the National Portrait Gallery, the Tate Gallery, the Pierpont Morgan Library, the Ashmolean Museum, the Kunstmuseum, Bern, Wellesley College Library, and the Ruskin Museum, Coniston.

Generous support of The Paul Mellon Centre for Studies in British Art, and The Guild of St George, has made it possible for many of the portraits to be reproduced in colour, and I acknowledge their help. I am also deeply indebted to Mrs Sue Wheeler of the Sheffield Galleries and Museums Trust for her help in preparing the manuscript for publication.

J.S.D.

Bembridge, Isle of Wight

Chapter I
'I like to be flattered'

Portrait painters, sculptors, caricaturists and photographers dogged John Ruskin's footsteps from the cradle to the grave and beyond. And for someone who professed a disliking of having his portrait taken, he allowed them to catch him quite often! The present catalogue lists 332 likenesses made between 1822 and 1999.

Since Ruskin died in 1900, it is obvious that some of this number must be based on earlier likenesses. In fact quite a lot of the likenesses listed as having been made in his lifetime were also not 'original', in that they were not taken from life. Nevertheless, the total includes about 118 portraits and busts for which Ruskin sat – either knowingly or unknowingly – as well as some 82 photographs.

The portraits were fairly evenly spaced throughout his life, from 1822 when he posed to Northcote, to 1900 when Cox sketched him in his coffin. The earliest photographs were taken in 1856, with the greatest number being taken between 1882 and 1897. In addition to portraitists and photographers, Ruskin also increasingly attracted the attention of caricaturists as he became a public figure.

Then there are many word-pictures of Ruskin, left both by those who knew him well, and by those who merely admired him from afar. A typical example is the following description of Ruskin as he appeared to those attending his Slade lectures at Oxford in the 1880s.

> The figure of the lecturer was striking, with ample gown – discarded often when its folds became too hopelessly involved – and the velvet college cap, one of the few remaining memorials of the gentleman commoner. The quaintness of his costume – the light homespun tweed, the double-breasted waistcoat, the ill-fitting and old-fashioned frock-coat, the amplitude of inevitable blue tie – accurately reflected something of the originality of his mind and talk. If it were not for the peculiarly delicate hands and tapering fingers, denoting the artistic temperament, the Oxford Professor might well have been taken for an old-fashioned country gentleman. In repose his face was at this time furrowed into sadness; but the blue eyes, piercing from beneath thick, bushy eyebrows, never ceased to shine with the fire of genius...[1]

The first study of the portraits of Ruskin was made by M.H. Spielmann and was published in a two-part article in *The Magazine of Art*,[2] of which Spielmann was editor, in 1891. At this time, both the subject and many of the artists involved were still alive and much of Spielmann's information was derived from interviews or correspondence[3] with them.

Introducing the first of his two articles on the portraits, Spielmann wrote 'Mr Ruskin has no special love of being reproduced: paradoxical as it may sound, his lack of vanity in respect of his own features struck me at once, when we were talking on this subject, as savouring not a little and not unpleasantly, of that very weakness'.[4]

In his second article Spielmann explains that he went to Brantwood, Ruskin's home at Coniston for the last thirty years of his life, to question him about the portraits of himself. 'We were talking about his portraits when he took occasion to tell me, in a sweeping sort of way, that he was dissatisfied with all that had been done of him, and the truer and more candid they were the less he cared for them. "I like to be flattered, both by pen and pencil, so it can be done prettily and in good taste", he said with a candid smile, not at all ashamed of the little confession'.[5]

When Spielmann wrote his biography[6] he distilled and revised most of the material from his two articles into Chapter XIV – 'The Portraits of Ruskin'.

Cook and Wedderburn introduced much information about the various portraits in the introductions to the various volumes of *Works* and they included a catalogue of the portraits[7] in the penultimate volume. Their catalogue listed 69 numbered and several unnumbered portraits, many of which

1 E.T. Cook & A. Wedderburn (ed.), *The Library Edition of the Works of John Ruskin* (London: George Allen, 39 vols., 1903–12) (hereafter referred to as *Works*), vol. XX, p. xxiii.

2 M.H. Spielmann, 'The Portraits of John Ruskin I', *Magazine of Art* (January 1891), pp. 73-79 (hereafter referred to as *Spielmann I*), and 'The Portraits of John Ruskin – (concluded)', *Magazine of Art*, February 1891, pp. 121-26 (hereafter referred to as *Spielmann II*).

3 In 1961, knowing my interest in the subject, Spielmann's son Dr Percy E. Spielmann gave some of these letters to me. After Dr Spielmann's death, many of his papers and those of his father were sold, and other letters relating to the portraits passed to the John Rylands University Library of Manchester, and the Pierpont Morgan Library, New York.

4 *Spielmann I*, p. 74.

5 *Spielmann II*, p. 123.

6 M.H. Spielmann, *John Ruskin* (London: Cassell, 1900).

7 'Portraits', *Works* XXXVIII, pp. 207-13 (hereafter referred to as *Works Catalogue*).

were reproduced in *Works*. Surprisingly, *Works Catalogue* omits a number of portraits. Some of these omissions are minor sketches which the editors possibly considered too inconsequential to list. Others, made without Ruskin's knowledge, were probably unknown to them. But several major portraits including at least two self-portraits and others by Arthur Severn, William Bell Scott, Samuel Laurence and Charles Fairfax Murray are also overlooked. In the case of photographs, Cook and Wedderburn sometimes only list one when they must have known of others taken at the same sitting. And several groups of photographs taken in the 1890s are omitted entirely.

My own interest in the portraits began soon after I arrived at Bembridge School to care for the Ruskin Galleries and the allied collection at Brantwood. In 1960 the first of my two articles on the portraits appeared in *Apollo*.[8] It was devoted to a study of the largest single collection of Ruskin portraits – the dozen then owned by the Education Trust Ltd, and exhibited at the Ruskin Galleries and at Brantwood. The purpose behind its publication was to present to the public a series of portraits of Ruskin, a number of which were hitherto unpublished, in conjunction with notes sketching Ruskin's life as a background.

Having prepared the first article, it occurred to me that a valuable service could be performed by re-cataloguing all of the Ruskin portraits, and recording their present whereabouts. It was therefore decided to expand the first article into a series, rediscovering and dealing with the whole range of Ruskin portraits (as opposed to photographs). The second article duly appeared in June 1961.[9] I decided on a policy of only describing and reproducing portraits whose actual whereabouts were known to me. At that time I knew where fourteen portraits were, in addition to those already dealt with in the first article. Busts, medallions and caricatures were not then included, it being hoped to reserve these for a separate article.

The real task of re-discovering the remaining thirty portraits listed in the *Works Catalogue* had to be started after the second article was published. As the search for the unlocated *Works Catalogue* portraits continued, more and more unrecorded portraits turned up, showing that Cook and Wedderburn's list was really only a starting point in the study of Ruskin portraiture.

The idea for the present book dealing with all known portraits gradually crystallised, and over the years my catalogue has grown from Cook and Wedderburn's original 69 to a present 332. In order to make my own catalogue as complete as possible it has been necessary to abandon my original policy of only writing about portraits whose whereabouts were known. In addition to unrecorded portraits which have been discovered during the research for the book, a number of references to unknown portraits have come to light, the actual portraits themselves still defying discovery.

It is impossible to know how many unrecorded portraits remain to be discovered. Of the portraits listed in *Works Catalogue*, one of the two childhood portraits by James Northcote, three portraits by Thomas Richmond and one each by Andrews and Severn are temporarily 'lost'. The outstanding busts and medallions are those by Munro, Ashmore and Emptmeyer. The original drawings for most of the caricatures have not been found. Four portraits have been found in a negative way! 'The Author of Modern Painters' and the head by George Richmond are, unhappily, believed to have been destroyed in the fire which severely damaged Charles Goodspeed's study. Burne-Jones's beginnings for his portrait, and the full-length clay statue by Boehm were probably destroyed by the artists themselves.

There were certainly more than a dozen portraits in Ruskin's own collection, including the two by Northcote, two by George Richmond, the Millais head and shoulders of 1854 (he gave the Glenfinlas portrait to Henry Acland in 1871), a couple by Arthur Severn, a Collingwood, and several self-portraits. These all came onto the market as a result of the series of sales held in 1930-31 to disperse the contents of Brantwood and the Severns' London home in Warwick Square. These sales led to the temporary loss of several portraits, while others passed into private or institutional hands.

The largest group of portraits is that now in the Whitehouse Collection and divided between the Ruskin Library at Lancaster and Brantwood, Coniston. This collection now totals 33; several of the portraits which have been 'discovered' during the course of work on this book have been presented by their owners to the Whitehouse Collection.

The next largest holding of Ruskin portraits is in the Ruskin Museum, Coniston (eleven), while the National Portrait Gallery has seven and the Ashmolean Museum at Oxford has six.

8 J.S. Dearden, 'Some Portraits of John Ruskin', *Apollo* (December 1960), pp.190-95 (hereafter referred to as *Dearden I*).

9 J.S. Dearden, 'Further Portraits of John Ruskin', *Apollo* (June 1961), pp.171-78 (hereafter referred to as *Dearden II*).

In America, the Pierpont Morgan Library has ten portraits, and there are a number of others in private and public collections.

During the course of portrait hunting a number of likenesses purporting to be Ruskin have turned up, which in my opinion, for various reasons, are not of him. These are all interesting portraits by or attributed to E.M.Ward, Sir John Gilbert, George Richmond and others – but they are not of Ruskin.

In a rather different category are two miniatures. Lot 497 in the Warwick Square sale of 16 July 1931 was catalogued as 'An oval miniature portrait on ivory, "John Ruskin in Middle Age"'. in fact this miniature was probably the one of Ruskin's grandfather which was exhibited at Coniston in 1900 (no. 286) 'Mr John Ruskin of Edinburgh, Mr Ruskin's grandfather – in middle life'. The second miniature was reported to me by the late Helen Viljoen as being in the collection of the late Mrs Atthill, granddaughter of Ruskin's cousin Mary Richardson. The miniature, which shows a figure of about twenty-one years of age, was in a frame on the reverse of which were two locks of brown hair held together by three small seed pearls, and the initials 'J.R.'. The miniature was given by Joan Severn to Mrs Mary Bolding, mother of Mrs Atthill. On inquiry, Mrs Atthill told me that the miniature was not of John Ruskin, but was probably of his father, John James, or more probably of his grandfather, John Thomas (no. 285 in the 1900 Coniston exhibition was '... Mr Ruskin's grandfather, as a young man').

But the picture which has caused the most trouble is the self-portrait of 1861. This was first published in 1893 as the frontispiece to the first volume of W.G. Collingwood's *Life and Work of John Ruskin*. The portrait was excellently reproduced by chromolithography onto a good quality paper. Over the past forty years this reproduction has turned up at least a dozen times, in leading sales rooms and elsewhere, being offered as the original portrait. In fact the original is now in the Pierpont Morgan Library. It is a little faded and the reproduction shows what it must have been like when Ruskin made it.

Although Ruskin was painted by several of the leading portrait-painters of the day – Northcote, George Richmond, Millais, Laurence, Herkomer – it is to be regretted that Burne-Jones's beginnings have not survived, and that the projected G.F. Watts portrait never materialised. Holman Hunt, too, never painted Ruskin. But at least he apparently posed Ruskin for one of the photographs by Hollyer. Hollyer was just one of the excellent early photographers to whom Ruskin sat. Sutcliffe, Downey, Dodgson, Angie Acland and McClelland were others. It would have been interesting to see what Julia Margaret Cameron could have produced, had she photographed Ruskin instead of thumping him on the back! Angie Acland tells the story:[10]

> During the time that Mr Ruskin was with us Mrs Cameron, a very well known artistic portrait photographer of those days, was with us on a visit and the two had frequent skirmishes about photography. I was lying on my couch in the drawing room one day when Mrs Cameron insisted on showing Mr Ruskin some of the wonderful heads of well known people which she had taken. He got more and more impatient until they came to one of Sir John Hershel in which his hair all stood up like a halo of fireworks. Mr Ruskin banged to the portfolio upon which Mrs Cameron thumped his poor frail back exclaiming 'John Ruskin you are not worthy of photographs!' They then left the room. Mrs Cameron wore a red bonnet with strings and when she got very excited she pushed it back and it hung down her back by the strings. Apparently they went out but arrived back to luncheon arm in arm with the bonnet on and peace signed.

The story of Ruskin's portraits embraces not only the story of his life, but also forms an interesting study of the development of portraiture through a hundred and eighty years.

10 S.A. Acland, manuscript autobiography, *Memories of my Eightieth Year* (Oxford, Bodl. Ms. Eng. Misc.) d. 214, fol. 46.

Chapter II
General Physical Appearance

Writing to his brother John in 1850, Thomas Carlyle described Ruskin as 'a small but rather dainty dilettante soul, of the Scotch-Cockney breed'[1] while Tolstoy, bestowing the greatest compliment he could, said 'I like his face. I have seen two portraits, front face and profile, both after he had grown a beard. He was like a Russian peasant'.[2]

In his prime Ruskin was just a little less than six feet tall, though of very slight build and only about ten stones in weight. As Collingwood[3] reminds us, he suffered 'from a weakness of the spine, which during all the periods of his early manhood gave him trouble, and finished by bending his tall and lithe figure into something that, were it not for his face, would be deformity'.

When he first met him in the early 1850s Holman Hunt was struck by Ruskin's great slenderness of build, and in his *Pre-Raphaelitism and the Pre-Raphaelite Brotherhood* he describes Ruskin as he remembered him when they met in Venice in 1869:

> Ruskin was at that time a man of nearly six feet in height, but of great sparseness of limb, which his tailor only partially succeeded in concealing; the colour of his hair was rusty, his eyes were bluish-grey, his complexion pink in hue, and his skin transparent, showing violet veins about the eyes, but the delicacy of the tint of his visage was in part subdued by sun freckles.[4]

Charles Eliot Norton, who visited Ruskin at his home on Denmark Hill in 1869 has left us a description of his friend in an account[5] of an imaginary visit to the Ruskin household.

> ...We should hear Ruskin's quick light step through the hall, and he would come in with the most warmly welcoming smile, both hands outstretched, and most cordial words of pleasure at our coming.
>
> You would be struck at once with the sweetness and refinement of his look, with a certain touch of quaintness in his dress and manner which gives a pleasant flavour to his originality, with the peculiar and sorrowful tenderness of expression in his eyes, with the mobility of his mouth, and with the fine, nervous, overstrung organisation betrayed alike in gait, in carriage, in manner, in expression, in shape and in words. At first, for five minutes perhaps, he would show in your presence as a stranger, a little shyness and constraint, apparent in a want of entire simplicity of manner. But this would wear off quickly and in a quarter of an hour you and he would be on easy terms, and talking as if you had known each other for years.

Norton mentions Ruskin's 'quaintness' of dress. Throughout his early and middle years Ruskin tended to dress in a rather formal manner, though in later years this gave way to a more homespun appearance. But his style of dress did not change greatly throughout his life, so he must have appeared to younger people rather old fashioned. He probably inherited his conservatism of dress from his father, whom A.J. Mumby described in 1863 as 'a dry antique little man in a lean frockcoat of old-world shape'.[6] When the young A.C. Benson saw Ruskin in 1880 he thought he came from a previous century, and Sydney Cockerell, who was at Brantwood at Easter 1887, also noticed the archaic appearance.[7]

> He was fairly tall but his height was already diminished by a little hunch in the shoulders. His hair was dark, long and thick, the beard iron-grey. His head was of the long type. His forehead sloped, and on each side, between his temples and his ears, there was a noticeable depression. He had heavy eyebrows and the bluest of blue eyes. Their colour was repeated with a difference

1 Thomas – John Carlyle, 18 Dec. 1850, Nat. Lib. of Scotland 513.65 quoted in *Rylands Bulletin* vol. 41, no. 1, p. 209.

2 'The Latest from Tolstoy', *Daily Chronicle* (3 August 1903), quoted in *Works* XXXIV, p. 729.

3 W.G. Collingwood, *The Life and Work of John Ruskin* (London: Methuen, 1893), vol. I, p. 94.

4 W. Holman Hunt, *Pre-Raphaelitism and the Pre-Raphaelite Brotherhood* (London: Macmillan, 1905), vol. II, p. 259. *Works* XIX, p. lv, dates this meeting from a letter from Ruskin to his mother as being on 30 June 1869. However, Ruskin was not in Venice but in Verona on that day. The true date of the meeting, as shown by a letter from Ruskin to Joan Agnew, was 31 July 1869.

5 S. Norton and M.A. DeWolfe Howe (eds.), *Letters of Charles Eliot Norton* (Boston and New York: Houghton Mifflin, 1913) I, p. 357.

6 D. Hudson, *Mumby, Man of Two Worlds* (London: Abacus, 1974), p. 166.

7 V. Meynell (ed.), *Friends of a Lifetime* (London: Jonathan Cape, 1940), p. 30.

> in his large blue neckties. (I have one of these and I know nothing that could recall the wearer more completely). His hands were small and delicate (I have one of his little gloves). He wore very old-fashioned clothes – trousers and double-breasted waistcoat of homespun and a long dark coat. Round his neck was a gold chain attached to his watch. He smile was kindness itself, his voice sometimes almost caressing. He could not quite pronounce his R's.

By 1885 Ruskin's weakness of spine developed into a chronic stoop and so he appeared to get smaller. Thanking Spielmann for a copy of his first *Portraits of John Ruskin* article, Joan Severn wrote:[8]

> The only *wrong impression* given, is about Ruskin's *height*! – I grant alas! that in the last 10 years he has stooped so much that he has shrunk into what might be considered by some people a *'little man'* – but 25 years ago! I should certainly have called him *much above* the average height – and as a *young man* he was *well over 5 feet 10 inches*! – indeed almost *5ft 11* & people who knew him *then* would have called him *tall*! – he has the peculiarity of having very long legs – ... I think Ruskin much better looking as an old man – with his beard which is very picturesque and his eyes are as beautiful as ever – and so is his hair!

* * * *

Ruskin's head is undoubtedly the feature which has received the most attention from recorders of his appearance. Spielmann[9] sought the opinion of 'an accredited student of physiognomy' who told him that judged by the shape of his head and face Ruskin belonged to what phrenologists and physiognomists would call the 'eagle tribe' – the aquiline nose denoting sovereignty over men; the projecting brows, perceptiveness with undoubted aesthetic tendencies; the chin a considerable degree of determination to direct his strongly-conceived opinions yet with hardly a corresponding capacity for continuous logical deduction. Writing in the *Phrenological Magazine*[10] L.N. Fowler, (who based his study of Ruskin on photographs) observed that Ruskin's brain was of full size and of peculiar shape, being long, high and narrow. He had a large forehead and 'it is very seldom that even good mechanics or artists measure so much from eye to eye'. Someone who was present at the lecture Ruskin gave in June 1883 in Mrs Bishop's drawing room in Prince of Wales Terrace had noticed that Ruskin's 'thick brown hair was brushed close to his head, which is abnormally flat at the top; so that, at a little distance, he looked like the picture of a hooded Capuchin Friar'.[11]

Ruskin's eyes were bright blue, almost exactly matching the colour of the necktie which he habitually wore. They were very penetrating and searching and have been mentioned by almost everyone who has described Ruskin. Speaking at the Ruskin Centenary Celebrations in 1919 Lord Bryce said that he did not remember another pair of eyes that had impressed him so much, except perhaps those of Garibaldi. A *Daily News*[12] correspondent, writing his personal recollections of Ruskin, said that

> The wonderful eyes were the feature of the face – somebody said they were the bluest eyes in all England and he himself was once moved to pay them some very pretty compliments. They could express anything. I have seen them flash and flame under the overhanging eyebrows, melt into tenderness, sparkle with fun and mischief, and, alas at times grow dim with the deepest sorrow. ... As a lecturer, I suppose it was his wonderful personal magnetism that drew his vast audiences, for as a lecturer, pure and simple, I never could place him in the first rank. The melodious voice that had such a charm in conversation had but small carrying power, it rose into shrillness at times; besides, he disregarded all the rules of oratory... .

At certain periods of his life Ruskin seems to have taken a quite neurotic interest in his eyes, their function and their protection. Charles Fortescue-Brickdale,[13] whose father was a contemporary of Ruskin at Christ Church, records that as an undergraduate at Oxford Ruskin wore 'blue spectacles' – probably sun-glasses – thus earning himself the nickname 'Giglamps'.

Writing to his father on 10 August 1845 Ruskin refers to a pair of dark glasses which he had had made to protect his eyes from the Alpine snow. Above 1000 feet, he wrote from Macagnaga, he found 'snow of the most dazzling kind, not only white but flashing like spar. My spectacles which I had made on purpose at Charing Cross – extra thick, and as black as pitch – served me well. George [his man servant] had a pair too, but

8 Joan Severn – M.H. Spielmann 22 Dec 1890, original in possession of J.S. Dearden.

9 M.H. Spielmann, *John Ruskin*, p. 164

10 L.N. Fowler, 'Phrenological Description of Mr John Ruskin', *The Phrenological Magazine*, vol. 1, June 1880, pp. 169-72

11 *Academy*, 19 Nov 1898, reprinted in *St George* II, p. 55.

12 'John Ruskin, Some Personal Recollections', *Daily News*, 17 Feb 1900, perhaps written by E.T. Cook, editor of the paper between 1896 and 1901.

13 Letter to the Editor of *The Times*, 4 May 1932.

Joseph [Couttet, his guide] had not brought his from Chamouni, and he ... was obliged to walk behind me in my steps, being utterly unable to see'.

Ruskin's diaries are filled, at certain periods, with references to his eyes. Particularly these occur at times of over-work or illness – 1840-41, 1867-68, 1877 and 1886. But in many cases the symptoms seem quite imaginary (though no less worrying) and in any case they are quite in keeping with his over-work and sometimes over-indulgence. For example the 'floating sparks in my eyes' which he noted in 1867[14] may well have been as a result of eating too much fatty food. And he himself ascribed his 'Attack of sight failure after breakfast'[15] on Saturday 17 April 1886 to two eggs eaten for tea on the previous Thursday!

At Fréjus on 22 October 1840 the twenty-one years old Ruskin had written in his diary 'I thank God for giving me a few more such hours and scenes, while my sight is still so far perfect. If it gets weaker, I think I shall stay in Italy or Switzerland. What have I to go home for?' In Rome in December 1840 he noted 'I should write much more here, were it not for my eyes', and on 31 January 1841, 'I must keep my eyes safe if I can'. Perhaps some of his optical trouble in 1841 was due to over-indulgence; 'The things [i.e. spots] are large in my eyes today, especially the right ....' (1 April), and 'I have had these motes in mine eyes a whole year, and they are nothing like beams yet, thank God! Better than they were at Nice considerably'. (26 April).

By 1843 Ruskin had come to accept that over-work caused eye fatigue. 'Hang it, eleven o'clock again – my eyes won't stand this'.[16] 'I've been working desperately hard today, and my eyes are weak – must get to sleep'.[17]

Between 1847 and 1867 the preoccupation with his eyes seems to have waned, but by the end of 1868 Ruskin noted in his diary 'eyes giving me some anxiety'. By now he was almost fifty and may well have been suffering from a simple myopic astigmatism. On 4 January 1872 he told Norton that he had been depressed since the beginning of the year. 'One of the distinctest sources of this depression is my certitude that I ought now to wear spectacles'.[18]

However, Ruskin seems to have postponed the wearing of spectacles for at least another couple of years for at the end of 1873 he was writing to Norton again.

> ... I am surprised to find how well my health holds, under steady press of work; but my sight begins to fail, and I shall begin with spectacles this next year.[19]

On 11 November 1876 he confided to his diary that he was going to write larger and larger because he could see comfortably enough thus, by candle-light, without spectacles – but he determined hence-forward only to write, not read, by candle-light. From this reference to spectacles I infer that Ruskin by now had them – but did not always trouble to use them. And twelve months later, forgetting his resolution, he was 'Much put out by not being able to read now with safety by candle-light'.[20] By 22 January 1878 we know for certain that he had glasses for he noted in his diary that he could not 'read Smith's Dictionary of the Bible even with spectacles'.

Three years later, writing to Dr John Brown, he noticed that the comparative strength of his two eyes, which had always been different, was changing. In 1852 he had told his father[21] that he saw far better and further with the left eye. Now he wrote to Dr Brown[22]

> ... My drawing does not tire me, but the focus of my best farthest-seeing eye has altered more than that of the nearer-sighted, weaker one; and now, in small work, they begin to dispute about where the line is to go, which I am sorry for, but shall take to larger work ...

Curiously, after nearly fifty years of worrying about his eyes, one of the last references to them in his diary is boasting of their strength. 'I see everything far and near down to the blue lines on this paper and up to the snow lines on the [Coniston] Old Man – as few men of my age'.[23]

* * * *

Wilenski reminds us that Ruskin really had excellent health throughout his life, but his mental illness brought on physical distress. We have seen that he had a neurotic preoccupation with his eyes. To a lesser extent he was also obsessed by his teeth, although the condition of them was probably far better than average for the time. His diary only actually records the extraction of five teeth, and serious trouble with toothache in 1841, 1857, 1866-67 and 1883.

14 John Ruskin's diary, hereafter referred to as *Diary*, 9 April 1867.
15 *Diary* 17 April 1886.
16 *Diary* 21 Jan. 1843.
17 *Diary* 11 March 1844.
18 JR – C.E. Norton, 4 Jan. 1872, *Works* XXXVII, p. 47.
19 JR – C.E. Norton, 2 Dec. 1873, *Works* XXXVIII, p. 74.
20 *Diary* 27 Dec. 1877.
21 JR – JJR, 11 Feb. 1852. J.L. Bradley (ed.), *Ruskin's Letters from Venice 1851–52*, (New Haven: Yale University Press, 1955), p. 175.
22 JR – Dr John Brown, 5 August 1881. *Works* XXXVII, p. 373.
23 *Diary* 30 May 1886.

Ruskin first seems to have had serious toothache while under the care of Dr Jephson at Leamington in the autumn of 1841. He was able to relieve the torture with applications of cold water, and rather like the head that one bangs against a wall because it is nice when one stops, 'It is worth a little toothache to know what it is to have rest'. After suffering for nearly a week Ruskin was obliged to have the offending tooth out at 8.30 on a Sunday evening.[24]

There does not seem to have been any more real trouble until the Spring and Autumn of 1857, and then again until November 1861 when there was another week of agony and having to 'stay in to flannel and mustard'.[25] Until he died in July 1866 Mr Rogers of 5 Sackville Street had been Ruskin's dentist. His successor was Alfred Woodhouse of 54 Conduit Street whom Ruskin had to visit soon after Rogers's death, on 10 August 1866, when he 'lost two poor serviceable things'.[26] Perhaps Woodhouse was repairing years of neglect by his patient for there seems to have been frequent attacks of toothache and visits to Woodhouse throughout the rest of the year and up to 19 June 1867 when Ruskin wrote 'At Woodhouse's I hope for last time for a month or two'.

During this period of treatment Woodhouse appears to have been fitting Ruskin for dentures. He had broken an appointment with Woodhouse on 19 January 1867,[27] saying that he was 'very comfortable just now' and afraid that exposure to the weather would cause toothache. But he warned Woodhouse that when he *did* come, 'you will have a good deal to do; for I've been practising with the teeth and I find my long exposed *upper* tooth is of hardly any use and the teeth catch and strain that more than the back ones – on which they grate with a sound of death's head and cross bones, *through* one's meat, – and to my horror, I find that the food accumulates more in *front* from the front teeth not being so much used – so that I could never eat before people ... What did you make me all that

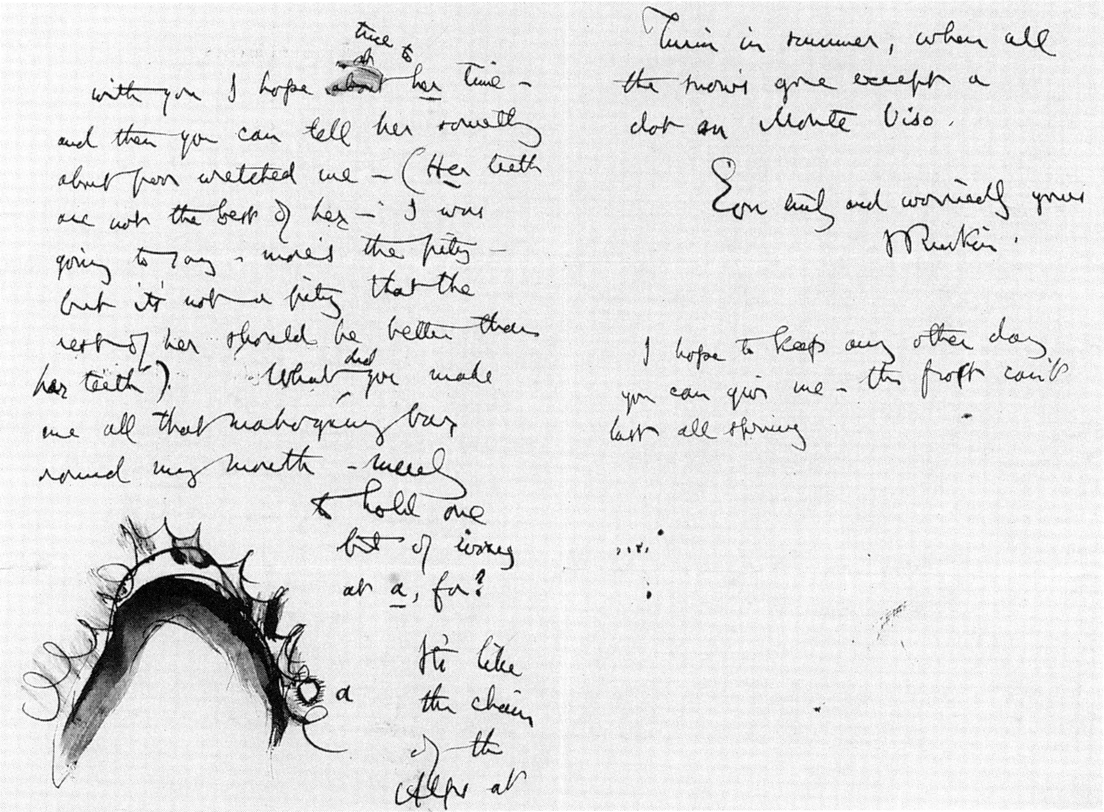
with you I hope true & her time – and then you can tell her something about poor wretched me – (Her teeth are not the best of her – I was going to say – more's the pity – but it's not a pity that the rest of her should be better than her teeth). What did you make me all that mahogany bar round my mouth – merely to hold one bit of ivory at a, for? It's like the chain of the Alps at

Turin in summer, when all the snows gone except a dot on Monte Viso.

Ever truly and worriedly yours
J Ruskin.

I hope to keep any other day you can give me – the frost can't last all spring

Figure 1

24 *Diary* 17 Oct .1841.
25 *Diary* 10 Nov. 1861.
26 *Diary* 10 Aug. 1866.
27 JR – A. Woodhouse, 19 Jan. 1867, Pierpont Morgan Library MA2228.

mahogany bar[28] round my mouth – merely to hold one bit of ivory at *a*, for? [see Figure 1] It's like the chain of the Alps at Turin in summer, when all the snow's gone except a dot on Monte Viso'.

Once his 'teeth [had been] put to such rights as they can take', Ruskin does not appear to have had a great deal more discomfort from them, though on one occasion in 1877 he found 'a good bathe of brandy seemed helpful last night' and in 1887 E.T. Cook noted that he had lost some more teeth. Although he found the mechanics of Woodhouse's profession interesting – 'had a nice lesson in gold-work from Mr Woodhouse' – Ruskin found the *thought* of visiting his dentist as bothersome as most people! 'Set to work to finish *Punch* lecture with prospect of teeth scraping all the afternoon'.[29]

As far as the more visible, outside, of Ruskin's mouth was concerned, he had an accident as a small boy which he was always conscious of, as having changed its shape. He described the event at length in his autobiography, *Praeterita*.[30]

> ...When I was about five years old, having been on amicable terms for a while with a black Newfoundland, then on probation for a watch-dog at Herne Hill, after one of our long summer journeys my first thought on getting home was to go to see Lion. My mother trusted me to go to the stable with our one serving-man, Thomas, giving him strict orders that I was not to be allowed within stretch of the dog's chain. Thomas, for better security, carried me in his arms. Lion was at his dinner, and took no notice of either of us; on which I besought leave to pat him. Foolishly Thomas stooped towards him that I might, when the dog instantly flew at me, and bit a piece clean out of the corner of my lip on the left side ... The bitten side of the (then really pretty) mouth, was spoiled for evermore, but the wound, drawn close, healed quickly; ...

The damaged mouth is not *particularly* noticeable in any of the portraits or photographs. Even his own sketch of his mouth made in March 1861 (No. 54, see Figure 2) does not show the unevenness which troubled him.

Of course for part of his life his mouth was concealed by the moustache and beard that he

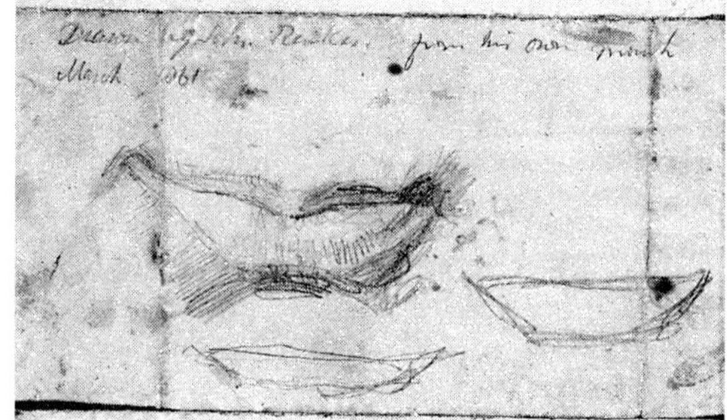

Figure 2

grew, as Edward Burne-Jones observed in a letter to Norton.[31]

> Ruskin flourishes, gave a lecture on Cistercian architecture[32] the other day that was like most ancient times, and of his very best, and looks well – really stronger than for many a year past. The hair that he has grown over his mouth hides that often angry feature, and his eyes look gentle and invite the unwary, who would never guess the dragon that lurks in the bush below.

Ruskin did not grow his beard and moustache until he was about 61 years old. He had, of course, side whiskers by the time Richmond painted him as 'The Author of *Modern Painters*'. But perhaps he had remembered his father's wish, 'I do hope you will always be able to keep a smooth face – for I never see a man (not a Jew or a Soldier) with Hair on his face that I do not set down as an idiot'.[33] This had been written in response to Ruskin's observation[34] that '... it is noticeable that the whisker on my right cheek grows strongly. I have always to cut it – that on the left hardly at all ...'

The beard appeared in 1881 during Ruskin's illness and convalescence and may first be seen in the sketch Ruskin made for the Weblings (No. 161). 'The "Barbe de Fleuve" only came because I was too ill to shave' wrote Ruskin to Chesneau.[35] At first it was neatly trimmed, though perhaps it was allowed to grow a little in the following year. Not until Ruskin's final retirement to Brantwood in 1889 was the beard allowed to grow almost unchecked and the first photographs to show him

28 Ruskin was not inferring that the base of his dentures was made of mahogany but was of a mahogany colour. Up to 1830 all dentures had been carved entirely out of ivory, but in that year Harrington of Portsmouth experimented with softened and moulded tortoiseshell as a base. In 1839 Goodyear invented vulcanised rubber, and this too started to be used in the making of dentures. Both vulcanite and tortoiseshell would be of a brown colour.

29 *Diary* 2 Nov. 1883.

30 *Works* XXXV, p. 67.

31 G. Burne-Jones, *Memorials of Edward Burne-Jones* (London: Macmillan, 1904), vol. II, p. 133.

32 'Mending the Sieve: or, Cistercian Architecture', delivered at the London Institute on 4 Dec. 1882. See *Works* XXXIII, p. 227.

33 JJR – JR, Feb. 1852. Whitehouse Collection, now in the care of The Ruskin Foundation, Ruskin Library, Lancaster University, RF L 4. Hereafter material in this collection will only be referred to by the prefix RF, followed by the catalogue number.

34 JR – JJR, 11 Feb. 1852. Bradley, *Ruskin's Letters from Venice 1851–52*, p. 175.

35 JR – Ernest Chesneau, 30 Jan. 1883, *Works* XXXVII, p. 435.

with the patriarchal beard of his last years are those taken of him in the 'Jumping Jenny' in 1891 (Nos. 232–4).

Ruskin's hair was of a light sandy colour which in 1869 Miss R.J. Roberts[36] thought 'rather long'. Though he noted the appearance of his first grey hair on his mother's birthday, 2 September 1850, when he was only 31, his hair did not in fact lose its colour until he was an old man. It was allowed to grow longer in 1881, probably for the same reason that his beard was grown, and again in 1884 there was another appreciable increase in length. He inherited his bushy eyebrows from his father.

Writing in the *Leeds Mercury*[37] fifteen days after Ruskin's eightieth birthday 'W.H.B.' referred to his hair.

> ... Mr Ruskin still possesses a wonderful wealth of hair. Only four years ago it retained much of its original colour, but now it is for the most part iron grey. Of late his beard has been allowed to grow in all its luxuriance of silvery whiteness. It is a remarkable and venerable face, and long to be remembered for its expression of power, of conquest and of light ... One who knows Mr Ruskin well has assured us that his facial expression has changed greatly in recent years. His features have now an almost spiritual whiteness which was not there only a few years ago.

Cockerell, however, who was at Brantwood only ten weeks before Ruskin died did not consider that the colour of the hair was much changed.

> He looked – shrunken, but very little changed in face since I saw him last in 1892 – his hair still dark and very thick (I have some of it cut in his 80th year), his beard still with a trace of brown.[38]

* * * *

Ruskin clearly inherited the shape of his hands from his father. Both of John James Ruskin's hands are visible in the portrait by George Watson, now at Brantwood (Figure 3), and they can be seen to be delicate and long-fingered. Ruskin's own long-fingered hands may be seen in several of the portraits and photographs. In the 'Author of *Modern Painters*' (No. 15) by George Richmond, the left hand is on his knee while the right wrist rests across his other leg and the hand holds a crayon. The length of the fingers and general smallness of the hands may easily be judged. Richmond's son,

Figure 3

Sir William Richmond, first remembered seeing Ruskin about 1853 and he included in his description a couple of sentences about Ruskin's hands and their gestures.

> I always think that the shape as well as the gestures of hands go far to reveal character; his were singularly long and prehensile, they seemed to search, to find, hold, retain, or give away in harmony with the mutual struggle to convince, going on with his swiftly moving mind ... In this habit of enforcing speech with gesture he was unlike an Anglo-Saxon, the Celtic blood asserted itself.[39]

The hands can again be seen to advantage in one of William Downey's 1863 photographs of Ruskin with William Bell Scott and Dante Gabriel Rossetti (No. 65). The thumb of the left hand, which is grasping Rossetti's arm, hardly reaches to the first joint of the index finger. The right hand which holds the walking stick looks so unusual and

36 E.T. Cook, *Life of John Ruskin*, (London: George Allen, 1911), vol. II, p. 79.
37 'Mr Ruskin at home', *Leeds Mercury*, 23 Feb. 1899.
38 Meynell, *Friends of a Lifetime*, pp. 60-61, 7 Nov. 1899.
39 Sir W.B. Richmond, 'Ruskin as I knew him', *St George* V, p. 287.

skeletal that it might also be malformed. Indeed his right forefinger was damaged in a riding accident when he was a boy and never came straight again.[40]

His hands were very small, as can be seen from one of his gloves now in the possession of Mrs Virginia Surtees. This is a machine-knitted glove of mushroom coloured cotton velour and was given to Mrs Surtees by Sir Sydney Cockerell. Presumably Ruskin's gloves would have been made for him because of the peculiar shape of his hands, but their modern equivalent in size is that of a small man's 8, or perhaps a little smaller.

Ruskin's long fingers must have given him a firm grasp when shaking hands. Collingwood has observed that

> Ruskin's was all finger-grip; long, strong talons, curiously delicate-skinned and refined in form, though not academically beautiful. Those whose personal acquaintance with him dated only from the later years never knew his hand, for then it had lost its nervous strength; and in cold weather – the greatest half of the year in the North – the hand suffered more than the head. But his palm, and especially the back of his hand, was tiny. When he rowed his boat he held the oars entirely in his fingers; when he shook hands you felt the pressure of the fingers, not of the palm. In writing, he held the pen as we are taught to hold the drawing pencil, and the long fingers gave much more play to the point than is usual in formed penmanship.[41]

On his first visit to Brantwood at Easter 1887 Cockerell also noticed the unusual way in which Ruskin held his pen – between his first and second fingers, instead of the more usual way between the thumb and index finger. Many years later Cockerell noticed Joseph Conrad holding his pen in the same way.[42]

Ruskin noticed that his way of holding a pen affected his writing and he seems to have at least tried to change his grip, but apparently without success. He wrote to his father from Florence on 15 June 1845, 'I see my hand [writing] gets worse and worse – it is from my way of holding the pen. I must positively alter it, and hold the right way, for this won't do'.[43] And again from Verona on 7 September 1845, 'As I find it absolutely necessary both for my writing and drawing, to alter the way I hold my pen, you will probably have my letters at present even more illegible than usual'.[44] One of the Barraud photographs of 1885 (No. 217) shows Ruskin seated at a table with his pen poised between the second and third fingers of the right hand. The back of his hand is almost entirely concealed within his starched shirt cuff (Figure 4).

Figure 4

40 *Works* XXXV, pp. 96-97.
41 W.G. Collingwood, *Ruskin Relics* (London: Isbister, 1903), p. 136.
42 Meynell, *Friends of a Lifetime*, p. 34.
43 H.I. Shapiro (ed.), *Ruskin in Italy. Letters to his Parents 1845* (Oxford: Clarendon Press, 1972), p. 115.
44 Shapiro, *Ruskin in Italy. Letters to his Parents 1845*, p. 115.

A.C. Benson, then a boy of 18, noticed Ruskin's hands and cuffs when he visited Eton to lecture on Amiens on 6 November 1880. 'The sleeves were long, and the delicate hands that emerged were enveloped in long somewhat crumpled cuffs...'.[45] In another account he observed that 'the long linen cuffs ... came half over his hands...'[46]

From time to time these cuffs caused Ruskin no little difficulty, as he told Susan Beever:

> Here's your little note first of all. And if you only knew how my wristbands are plaguing me you'd be very sorry. They're too much starched, and would come down like mittens; and now I've turned them up, they're just like two horrid china cups upside down, inside my coat, and I'm afraid to write for fear of breaking them.[47]

H.W. Nevinson, who met Ruskin at Sallenches on 12 September 1888 noted in his diary the appearance of his hands as he approached old age.

> His hands, as one might suppose, are long, thin, delicate, with loose, soft skin in wrinkles of age – just a thought too soft, perhaps...[48]

It is interesting that two sculptors had the idea of modelling Ruskin's hand. Mr Atkinson spent some time at Brantwood in 1881. Many of the casts of plants and leaves which he made at that time are now in the Coniston Museum. He also modelled a bust of Ruskin (Nos. 164–65). But according to Collingwood[49]

> ... the sculptor's chief personal wish was to get a mould of Ruskin's hand. He used to say that there was more in it than in his face; at least it was the most characteristic feature, and representable in solid form, while the face, depending on the bright blue eye and changeful expression, evaded him as it evaded more celebrated sculptors. But Ruskin did not like being oiled and moulded, and though Mr Atkinson made enticing demonstrations on less worthy fingers, till we were all up to our elbows in plaster of Paris, he never to my knowledge won his point.

In the next decade, when the American artist and sculptor Gutzon Borglum visited Brantwood he made sketches of Ruskin, one of which shows the left hand grasping the arm of his study armchair (Figure 5). Later, when Borglum's sketches were translated into a statue, he was so pleased at the way that the hands had turned out that he made a separate model of the left one which was cast as a paper weight (Figure 6).

Thus the hands which wrote and drew so much have been thoroughly recorded by authors, artists, photographers and sculptors.

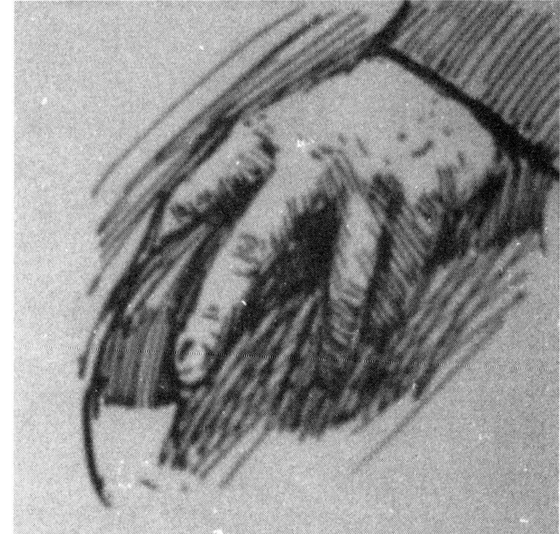

Figure 5

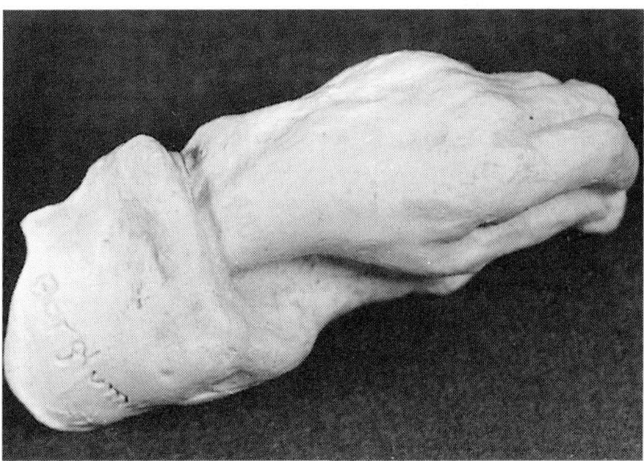

Figure 6

45 A.C. Benson, *Memories and Friends* (London: John Murray, 1924).
46 A.C. Benson, *Ruskin, A Study in Personality* (London: Smith, Elder, 1913), p. 184.
47 19 Dec. 1882. *Works* XXXVII, p. 425.
48 H.W. Nevinson, 'Some Memories of Ruskin', *Ruskin the Prophet* (London: George Allen & Unwin, 1920), p. 154.
49 Collingwood, *Ruskin Relics*, p. 136.

Chapter III
Ruskin's Clothes

If there had never been any portraits of Ruskin, we would still have a very good idea of his general appearance, both from descriptions recorded by those who saw him, and from his clothes or details of his clothing which have survived.

A surprisingly large number of Ruskin's clothes and accessories have survived and several of these items are of considerable value in what they can tell us of Ruskin's appearance and build. The Keswick Museum has the court dress which he wore either in 1838 to attend Queen Victoria's coronation, or to be presented in 1850. In the Whitehouse Collection is the evening dress which he wore towards the end of his life and which he may well have worn when delivering lectures in the '80s. At the Ruskin Museum in Coniston are his last umbrella, a walking stick given to him by Joan Severn and inscribed 'J. Ruskin, C.C.C. 1874',[1] and another stick given to him by Major R.H. Gunning.[2] At Lancaster, in addition to his grandfather's silver mounted and ivory topped cane inscribed 'Sr R.C. to J.T.R., Bowerswell', is a 5' 6" staff with iron point, inscribed on the silver band 'From Prof. Ruskin to G. Mackay, 1889'.

Mrs Surtees has a cravat, handkerchief and glove (referred to elsewhere) which Sir Sydney Cockerell gave to her in 1954.[3] Lord Clark had another handkerchief which he has used to effect during at least one of his Ruskin lectures; yet a third is at Brantwood in company with a blue cravat, a white cravat and a hat. This hat is a light grey trilby with light braid round the edge of the brim and with a matching band. It is very similar to the one worn by Ruskin in some of the late groups of photographs taken with Joan Severn. It is about a size 7 1/8 (Ruskin had long hair at this time, so his head was probably a couple of sizes smaller) and contains the maker's label of Robert Heath, 25 St George's Place, Hyde Park Corner.[4]

Other clothes which are helpful in demonstrating Ruskin's proportions are a collar (at Brantwood) which is size 15 and was made by E. Bennett, 4 Glasshouse St, and an unusual shirt (Whitehouse Collection) which has an attached collar of size 16. The right sleeve is embroidered 'J.R. 12.95'.

On Ruskin's death in 1900, items of his clothing were given to members of the Brantwood staff as keepsakes. The importance of the item appears to have been dictated by the recipient's status in the household. For example, Ruskin's valet, Peter Baxter, received his college cap, gown, hood and surplice,[5] and so on down the scale to shirts or handkerchiefs for parlour or kitchen maids.

But apart from this distribution Ruskin's wardrobe remained more or less intact until the dispersal sales of the houses in 1931. At that time a few items considered to be of interest were included in the sales. Lot 164 at Brantwood was 'Ruskin's shawl', while at Warwick Square lot 455 was 'A pair of John Ruskin's slippers in a bag made by Lady Stansfield', and lot 456 'John Ruskin's dress suit'. Although it was not catalogued, Ruskin's court dress was bought from Brantwood by the Grasmere antique dealer T.H. Telford. It subsequently made its appearance at several Fancy Dress Dances before eventually going to Keswick Museum.

There were two occasions in his life when Ruskin wore court dress and he had a new one each time. Styles in court dress did not vary and it is uncertain whether the Keswick Museum dress dates from 1838 or 1850.

In 1838 Hopkinson, the coach builder of Long Acre, gave Ruskin a ticket for a seat in Poet's Corner at Queen Victoria's coronation. It was towards the end of the university summer term and while John James Ruskin was in London, Ruskin and his mother were still at Oxford. On 22 June J.J.R. wrote to his wife

> I went to Owens[6] and ordered a white satin waistcoat gold sprigs – High Dress Coat bright Buttons – Buy White Gloves at Oxford – Trowsers [sic] also of Owen – a Court White Neckcloth or Black satin will do – or White to come from Keene & Co.[7] ... [8]

1 Exhibited at Coniston 1900, no. 301.

2 Exhibited at Coniston 1900, no. 302.

3 *Ruskin Centenary Exhibition* (1919) p.24, no. 12, and *Ruskin and his circle* (1964) no. 55. The handkerchief is of cream silk 24" x 26", with JR embroidered in red silk on one corner.

4 St George's Place was behind St George's Hospital at Hyde Park Corner. In 1854 Heath's establishment was at 18 St George's Place. By 1864 he had moved to No. 25. By 1884 he had expanded to take in No. 24 as well. He was still at the same address in 1892 though the disappearance of St George's Place by 1899 caused his removal to nearby Knightsbridge.

5 Exhibited at Coniston, 1900, no. 303.

6 Ben Owen of 184 Regent Street had been John's usual tailor since he was a child.

7 Keene & Co. of South Audley Street, another tailor, who had supplied Ruskin's needs for several years.

8 JJR – MR, 22 June 1838, RF L2.

Nevertheless, despite the short notice, all was ready for the coronation on 28 June!

Ruskin next needed court dress again in 1850 and we can follow the arrangements in his wife Effie's letter to her mother.

Thursday 15 June 1850
I had expected to have gone to the first Drawing-room on Thursday but John has done nothing about his dress but shrug his shoulders and I suppose if we get to the second or third we shall do well enough but I am sorry we cannot get to the first.

Wednesday 19 June
I am quite busy preparing for tomorrow. John found from Lord Eastnor[9] that he could not go to the Drawing room without first being presented at the levee on the 3rd of July but he thought it right to go with me as far as the Throne room, therefore Stulz[10] is making his court dress and he will accompany me in it and then wait and bring me home again ... yesterday ... I was running all over the town getting John ruffles, stockings and I don't know what.

Friday 21 June
[After describing their arrival at Buckingham Palace Effie continues]
John left me at the door of the Throne room ... John looked extremely well. He had his hair a little curl [sic] which added to his appearance very much.

Saturday 3 July
John went to the Levee two days ago[11] and got through nicely. Lord Eastnor [his sponsor] gave me many instructions about dressing him properly and said he would not see him until it was over for anything and all the responsibility would fall upon him and he was quite certain the sword would be on the wrong side.

The court dress at Keswick now comprises shoes, knee breeches, swallowtail coat, black silk cockade hat and a white lace cravat. The shoes are of fine black leather lined with blue satin and have steel buckles. They are 11" long and measure from sole to sole over the widest part of the foot 5". The breeches have three steel buttons on each leg. The coat is of the usual court pattern, fastening across the chest with a pair of hooks. There are six steel buttons down the front, three on each cuff, three below the pocket on each side and six on the back. The sleeves are trimmed with lace cuffs. Breeches and coat are made of a very, very dark blue Vicuna type of cloth (Figures 7, 8 and 9).

Before I examined the dress several years ago, my tailor suggested the measurements I should take, and I recorded the following.

Coat
length to natural waist 19½"
waist to tail 20"
total length of jacket 39½"
centre back seam to outside sleeve seam 7½"
outside sleeve 26½"
inside sleeve 21"
back collar seam to front fastening 15½"
width of sleeve at elbow 13½" (at cuff 10½")
across chest 18"

Breeches
side seam 31" to band at knee
leg seam 20½" to band at knee
waist 31"
knee (round band) 13"

Figure 7

9 Charles Somers Cocks, 3rd Earl Eastnor, was a contemporary of Ruskin at Oxford and they remained friends for many years. JJR's diary notes that Lord Eastnor, George Richmond, W. Boxall, Charles Newton, G.F. Watts, and John and Effie had dined at Denmark Hill on 25 June 1850.

10 Stulz of 10 Clifford Street was John's – and *the* – tailor of the day. JJR's accounts show that the suit cost £21 7s.

11 There is some uncertainty about the actual date. In his diary for 3 July JJR recorded 'John presented at court by Lord Eastnor'.

Figure 8

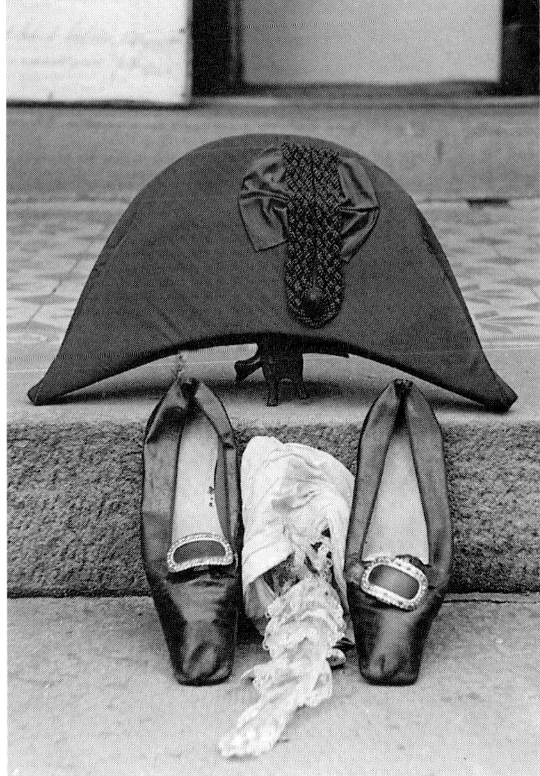

Figure 9

I duly returned to my tailor with the measurements and he looked at them with interest. To the best of his recollection he know nothing of Ruskin's life and had never seen a picture of him – but his first question was 'Was he consumptive'! Ruskin of course had considerable trouble with his chest as a young man. The picture that the measurements conjoured up was of a tall, very slight, flat-chested man with very long arms, legs longer than average, average calves and slender feet.

The evening dress now in the Whitehouse Collection confirms the unusual length of Ruskin's arms and legs. Ruskin was, when this suit was made, probably 5' 10" tall. The inside leg measures 32½" indicating that he had a very long leg and short body. The inside sleeve measurement is 18½", again rather longer than usual for the height. The waist measures 31" – so in the thirty or even forty years spanned by the two suits Ruskin had not put on any weight!

The suit is a three piece. The trousers are made of a much heavier black cloth than the waistcoat and coat. The single-breasted waistcoat has five silk-covered buttons and is decorated with black embroidery. The coat is in no way remarkable.

The various technical statistics of Ruskin's existing clothes do not make exciting reading. However they are worth recording, for they help to build up the picture of Ruskin's physical appearance and to confirm the various descriptions of him.

The modes of dress adopted by Ruskin fall into three fairly distinct categories. In his undergraduate days and just after, he was really quite a dandy; later, and for most of his middle life he dressed in the height of Victorian formal respectability, while in later life he adopted the more comfortable dress of the homespun country squire.

The earliest dress of which we have a record is that in which Ruskin was baptised on 20 February 1819 at his home at Hunter Street, Brunswick Square. This dress was exhibited at the Severns' home at Herne Hill on 7 May 1907[12] and someone who saw it made sketches of it (Figure 10), which are accompanied by the following notes.

12 There was also a meeting of St George's Guild at the Grand Hotel, Trafalgar Square, on the same day. The christening clothes were also included in the 1900 Coniston exhibition (239) and the 1919 Ruskin Centenary Exhibition (p. 15, no. 26). The robe and cap (not the shoes) were included with other Ruskin relics in the sale at Sotheby's on 8 May 1931 (49) but were unsold and seem finally to have passed into the hands of Ruskin's solicitors. After the death of Peter Evans, their ultimate descendant, his widow gave the robe and cap to Brantwood in 1988.

> JR's Christening dress – creamy India muslin with little frills an inch wide. The very narrow bodice (3 inches wide and between 2 sets of 3 bobbins). Shown at Herne Hill May 7 1907 with a dimity hair thread dress – also frilled, and a baby shirt marked a year before his birth in red old fashioned hand marking – each article with inscription by his mother. His baby bands flannel also. His cap – Fine Valencienne insertion about 2 inches wide and real lace insertion between. His night socks all knitted in white wool with a close basket pattern at the top and marked in red.

John James Ruskin's accounts give some idea of the clothes worn by the young Ruskin, and one can occasionally find in them items mentioned in descriptions. A case in point is the description of Ruskin recorded by Mary Richardson in her diary of 16 August 1833. John and his father had walked from Sallenches to see the source of the Arveron, leaving Mary with Mrs Ruskin, to meet them later.

> We asked several people whether they had met two gentlemen, some said 'No', some said 'Yes', one little fellow said he was sure he had seen the gentlemen we were enquiring after; that one of them had a chapeau blanc and that the young gentleman's cap was of velours, which was really the case.[13]

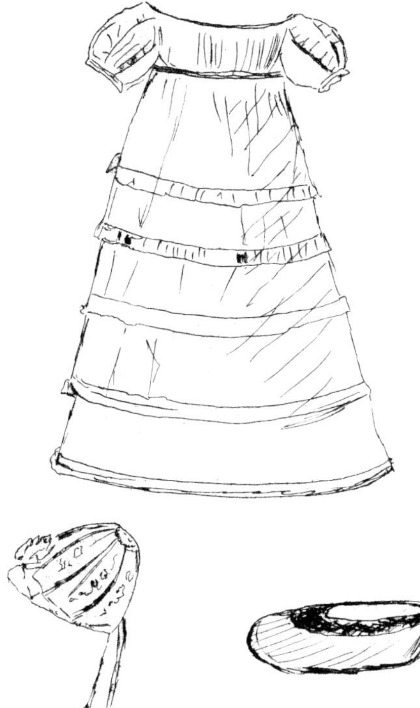

Figure 10

At this time, and until at least 1841, John's clothes came from Owen, while Keene was his shirtmaker. Later the well-known blue cravats came from Geohegan of 178 Regent Street, and in 1870 his bootmaker was Hoby & Co. of 20 Pall Mall. His footwear may have been made by Hoby from a much earlier date, for he is mentioned in a letter of 1840 to Edward Clayton in which Ruskin extols the watercolours of David Cox.

> He is a man of dew: his sketches breathe of morning air, and his grass would wet your feet through, if you were to walk on it in Hoby's best.

Later Ruskin patronised Stulz & Co., the fashionable tailor of 10 Clifford Street. Stulz also supplied John James's clothes and if he did not always appreciate the latest fashion, he certainly knew what he wanted, as Stulz discovered to his cost on at least one occasion.

> Mr Ruskin was obliged to send back a Great Coat to Messrs Stulz & Co. Mr R wanted a travelling coat but as he travels inside he wanted a neat warm but not a heavy Box Coat. This is the heaviest coat he ever tried on and the velvet is put on in such a fashion as if it was an effort to bestow enough – It is in fact a prodigious a most tremendous Coat – The collar is a quarter of a yard deep – and the cut is very strange. In most coats there is an opening – In this the collar seems a mere cut from Lappelle not an opening as & the Lappelle seems ridiculously pointed in place of the form usually seen – Mr Ruskin is very reluctant in questioning Messrs Stulz' taste but the man who made this coat must have a heavy taste – The whole of the velvet must be taken from Breast and Silk or only cloth left and the velvet may do for future collar. The collar is too deep – the coat also will want fitting after velvet is off front. Mr Ruskin regrets ordering double breast and heavy cloth as he fears he will always find the weight intolerable.
>
> Herne Hill, 24 Jany.[1838][14]

13 Transcript in the Whitehouse Collection. The mention of Ruskin's cap is interesting. His father's accounts show that it had cost 28s. in May 1833. The accounts also show that in the 14 years between 1827 and 1840 Ruskin had 46 hats or caps, 9 of them in 1840.

14 JJR – Stulz & Co., RF L 11. JJR's accounts show 'D[ou]ble [Breasted] G[rea]t Coat £8'.

In a letter written in 1837 H.G. Liddell, Dean of Christ Church, describes something of Ruskin's appearance in his undergraduate days.[15]

> ... I am going to drink tea with Adolphus Liddell tonight, and see the drawings of a very wonderful gentleman-commoner here who draws wonderfully. He is a very strange fellow, always dressing in a greatcoat with a brown velvet collar, and a large neck cloth tied over his mouth...

Collingwood tells us that a portrait was once sent to Brantwood of a dandy in a green coat of wonderful cut, supposed to represent Ruskin in his youth, but suggesting Lord Lytton's 'Pelham' rather than the homespun seer of Coniston. 'Did you ever wear a coat like that?' Collingwood asked him, to which he replied 'I'm not so sure I didn't.'

It is in the Chalon miniature (No. 8) and the portrait by Thomas Richmond (No. 14) that we see the undergraduate Ruskin. In the latter, his coat is not of green, nor yet of 'a beautiful blue'. It is a soberly black swallowtail and cut not unlike his coronation coat, but the lapels are gold and red, and he wears a high black neckcloth patterned in red and blue. His trousers are skin-tight and behind him his tasselled cane rests on his stovepipe hat. But two years later, when Thomas's brother George painted 'The Author of *Modern Painters*', Ruskin had begun to adopt the frock coat in which he became a familiar figure for much of his life. In this portrait he wears a red waistcoat, but had probably by now adopted the familiar blue neckcloth.

In early 1849 F.J. Furnivall met Ruskin for the first time and he has left a description of the meeting.[16]

> After a short chat with the wife, I saw the door open, and John Ruskin walk softly in. I sprang up at once to take the outstretched hand, and then and there began a friendship which was for many years the chief joy of my life. Ruskin was a tall, slight fellow, whose piercing frank blue eyes looked through you and drew you to him. A fair man, with rough light hair and reddish whiskers, in a dark blue frock coat with velvet collar, bright Oxford blue stock, black trousers and patent slippers – how vivid he is to me still! The only blemish in his face was the lower lip, which protruded somewhat: he had been bitten there by a dog in his early youth. But you ceast to notice this as soon as he began to talk. I never met any man whose charm of manner at all approached Ruskin's. Partly feminine it was, no doubt; but the delicacy, the sympathy, the gentleness and affectionateness of his way, the fresh and penetrating things he said, the boyish fun, the earnestness, the interest he showed in all deep matters, combined to make a whole which I have never seen equalled.

During their brief married life, Effie took a hand in the selection of Ruskin's wardrobe, as she told her mother in a letter from Venice in 1852.[17]

> He is very nicely dressed just now. I bought him trowers and vest of Turkish 'gane', white crossed with black; it looks so glossy, clean and nice with a blue tie that I shall buy him another set as they are very cheap and nice in comparison with Stulz's...

It was in the following summer that the Ruskins and the Millais brothers spent the disastrous holiday at Glenfinlas. Here Millais painted Ruskin's portrait standing by the waterfall (No. 26) and Ruskin prepared the series of lectures that he was to deliver in Edinburgh that autumn. The first lecture was held on 1 November. It was the first time that Ruskin had lectured and it was to begin a new phase in his career. The reporter from the *Edinburgh Guardian* attended, and has left a description of the event.[18]

> ... After waiting a weary time ... the door by the side of the platform opens, and a thin gentleman with light hair, a stiff white cravat, dark overcoat with velvet collar, walking, too with a slight stoop, goes up to the desk, and looking round with a self-possessed and somewhat formal air, proceeds to take off his greatcoat, revealing thereby, in addition to the orthodox white cravat, the most orthodox of white waistcoats ... 'Dark hair, pale face, and massive marble brow – that is my ideal of Mr Ruskin', said a young lady near us. This proved to be quite a fancy portrait, as unlike the reality as could well be imagined. Mr Ruskin has light sand-coloured hair; his face is more red than pale; the mouth well cut, with a good deal of decision in its curve, though somewhat wanting in sustained dignity and strength, an aquiline nose; his fore-

15 *Works* XXXV, p. lxiii.

16 F.J. Furnivall (ed.), *Two Letters concerning 'Notes on the Construction of Sheepfolds'* (London: T.J. Wise, 1890), p. 8.

17 Effie Ruskin to Mrs Gray, Venice, 23 May 1852; M. Lutyens: *Effie in Venice* (London: John Murray, 1965), p. 316.

18 W.G. Collingwood, *The Life of John Ruskin* (London: Methuen, 1900), p. 142, quotes from the *Edinburgh Guardian*, 19 Nov. 1853. Leon in *Ruskin the Great Victorian* (London: Routledge & Kegan Paul, 1949), p. 189, quotes more of the report.

head by no means broad or massive, but the brows full and well bound together; the eye we could not see in consequence of the shadows that fell upon his countenance from the lights overhead, but we are sure that the poetry and passion we looked for almost in vain in other features must be concentrated there ... Mr Ruskin's elocution is peculiar; he has difficulty in sounding the letter 'R'; but it is not this we now refer to, it is to the peculiar tone in the rising and falling of his voice at measured intervals, in a way scarcely ever heard except in the public lection of the service appointed to be read in churches. These are the two things with which, perhaps, you are most surprised, – his dress and his manner of speaking, – both of which ... are eminently clerical. You naturally expect, in one so independent, a manner free from conventional restraint, and an utterance, whatever may be the power of his voice, at least expressive of a strong individuality; and you find instead a Christ Church man of ten years' standing, who has not yet taken orders ...

Ruskin's parents had obviously been anxious to hear about the lectures and must have asked what their son had worn at his first appearance on a lecture platform. He told them[19]

> My dress at lectures was my usual dinner dress, just what you and my mother like me best in; coat by Stulz. It only produced an effect here, because their lecturers seem usually to address them, and they come to hear, in frock coats and dirty boots.

Tom Richmond must have been in the audience at one of the Edinburgh lectures, and when he dined with the elder Ruskins on 17 November, and again on the 22nd, he must have been closely questioned about the lectures.

> Tom Richmond did not allude to your diction but that you were a gentle creature in appearance not a robustious periwig pated fellow – as many platform people are.[20]

The Ruskins were not keen on their son's embarking on a career as a lecturer and in a letter[21] about now J.J.R. told his son of the serious doubts he was having about John lecturing at the nearby Camberwell Institute. Perhaps it was too close to home for comfort! And incidentally the letter gives an interesting side light on Ruskin's wardrobe.

> I see small bills up through the village with all the Lecturers names – among them Mr White who gets your old Clothes ... Would it not be better to Dykes that you would have lectured with pleasure but that your Father and Mother had insuperable objection to your Lecturing and you yield to their wishes ... You would by Camberwell lecture get approached by many neighbours whom neither you nor your wife would resist [?] and soon find yourself in Hot Water...

Ruskin bowed to his parents' wishes, but accepted the presidency of the Camberwell Institute! He did not lecture there until 1866, two years after his father's death.

Sir Sidney Colvin[22] remembered Ruskin aged about 40 as:

> elegant after the fashion of his time as well as impressive in a fashion all his own. There remains with me quite unfaded the image of his slender, slightly stooping figure clad in the invariable dark blue frock coat and bright blue necktie; of his small head with its strongly marked features, its sweep of thick brown hair and closely trimmed side-whiskers; above all of the singular bitter-sweet expression of his mouth (due partly as I have always understood, to the vestiges of a scar left on the upper lip by a dog's bite in boyhood) and of the intense weight and penetration of his glance as he fixed his deep blue eyes upon yours from under the thick bushy prominence of his eyebrows (these were an inheritance from his father, who had them shaggier and longer than have seen on any other man).

Meanwhile, ten years later, Holman Hunt,[23] meeting Ruskin in Venice, noticed that he was 'faultlessly groomed, and, despite his soft felt hat, was not at all costumed like an art specialist, no passers-by stared at him more that they would have done at any other *forestiere*'.

At this time Ruskin had just been appointed Slade Professor of Fine Art at Oxford. His inaugural lecture was delivered on his birthday in 1870. W.G. Collingwood, who knew Ruskin at Oxford at this period, described him as[24]

> a tall and slim figure, not yet shortened from its five feet ten or eleven by the habitual stoop, which ten years later brought him down to less than middle height; a stiff, blue frock-coat; predominant, half-starched wristbands, and tall collars of

19 JR – JJR, 1 Dec 1853, *Works* XII, p. xxxv.
20 JJR – JR, 6/7 Dec. 1853, RF L 4.
21 JJR – JR, 1 Dec. 1853, RF L 4.
22 S. Colvin, *Memories and Notes* (London: Edwin Arnold, 1921), p. 40.
23 Hunt, *Pre-Raphaelitism and the Pre-Raphaelite Brotherhood*, vol. II, p. 259. The meeting took place on 31 July 1869; see note 14.
24 Collingwood, *The Life and Works of John Ruskin*, vol. II, p. 103.

the Gladstonian type; and the bright blue stock which everyone knows for his heraldic bearing: no rings or gewgaws, but a long thin gold chain to his watch: a plain old-English gentleman, neither fashionable dandy nor artistic mountebank ... there was his face, still young-looking and beardless; made for expression, and sensitive to every change of emotion. A long head with enormous capacity of brain, veiled by thick wavy hair, not affectedly lengthy but as abundant as ever, and darkened into a deep brown, without a trace of grey; and short light whiskers growing high over his cheeks. A forehead not on the model of the heroic type, but as if the sculptor had heaped his clay in handfuls over the eyebrows, and then heaped more. A big nose, aquiline, and broad at the base, with great thoroughbred nostrils and the 'septum' between them thin and deeply depressed; and there was a turn down at the corners of the mouth, and a breadth of lower lip ... And under shaggy eyebrows, ever so far behind – the fieriest blue eyes, that changed with changing expression, from grave to gay, from lively to severe; that riveted you, magnetised you, seemed to look through you and read your soul; and indeed, when they lighted on you, you felt you had a soul of sorts ...

Arthur Severn married Ruskin's cousin Joan Agnew at St Matthew's Church, Denmark Hill, on Thursday 2 April 1871. Ruskin gave away the bride, and later, writing in his Memoir,[25] Severn recalled

The Professor looked quite the bridegroom himself, in a new bright blue stock, very light grey trousers, an almost fashionable frock-coat with a rose in the button-hole, and quite gay in manner.

Soon after the wedding, Ruskin bought his new home, Brantwood at Coniston, and Alexander Wedderburn, who visited him there in 1875, recorded[26] one of the last descriptions of Ruskin as he dressed in his youth and middle age.

Between one and six o'clock, the tourist in the Lakes may see a slight figure dressed in a grey frock-coat (which the people round, ignorant of Ascot, believed unique), and wearing the bright blue tie so familiar to audiences at Oxford and elsewhere, walk about the quiet lanes, sitting down by the harbour's side, or rowing on the water. The back is somewhat bent, the light brown hair, straight and long, the whiskers scarcely showing signs of the eight and fifty summers numbered, and the spectator need not be surprised at the determined energy at which a boat is brought to shore or pushed out into the lake.

Ruskin was about to enter his 'homespun' phase. In the middle of 1876 Egbert Rydings, a Companion of the Guild of St George and disciple of Ruskin's teaching, proposed to start a homespun woollen industry at Laxey in the Isle of Man. The Guild built him a watermill, of which Ruskin was inordinately proud, and eventually Laxey cloth began to be made. At one time Ruskin proposed that a square yard of Laxey homespun of a given weight should be adopted as one of the standards of value in St George's currency. He set the example and had his own grey clothes made of Laxey material. His secretaries, Laurence Hilliard and W.G. Collingwood, followed suit – but as Collingwood commented, the chief drawback to the clothes so made was that they never wore out!

Whitelands College was one of the educational establishments in which Ruskin took an interest at this period. He presented copies of his books to the library at Whitelands and was helpful to them in many other ways. In 1877 the students asked if they could make something for him and a waistcoat was suggested.

My waistcoats are the things most useful to me needing four pockets, and I believe these are more or less constructible by hand. So I shall send one to Miss Stanley, and I've no objection to a little zigzaging or other aculine ornamentation on them, which I shall proudly manifest to beholders when the wind isn't too cold on the hills.[27]

Eventually the waistcoat was finished and in December Ruskin, who was staying with the Severns at Herne Hill, wrote to Faunthorpe,[28] the principal of Whitelands

I chance fortunately to be in town at my pet cousin's, who, as ladies say, is 'dying' to see the waistcoat, so I send my servant over to bring it. I should have come myself had I not been laid up with cold, and shall not be long in writing of its reception to Miss Stanley.

25 J.S. Dearden (ed.), *The Professor* (London: George Allen & Unwin, 1967), p. 36.

26 *World*, August 1877.

27 T.J. Wise (ed.), *Letters from John Ruskin to Rev. J.P. Faunthorpe M.A.* (London: private publication, 1894), vol. I, pp. 8-9; letter dated 2 Oct. 1877.

28 Wise, *Letters from John Ruskin to Rev. J.P. Faunthorpe M.A.*11. 14 Dec. 1877.

But despite his fancy waistcoats and homespun, Ruskin retained his accustomed formal mode of dress in the evenings, or in London. In December 1877 he and Matthew Arnold attended a dinner party.

> Ruskin was there looking very slight and spiritual. I am getting to like him. He gains much by evening dress, plain black and white, and by his fancy being forbidden to range through the world of coloured cravats.[29]

Except for evening wear, of course, Ruskin's ties never varied from his accustomed blue. Canon H.S. Holland was in the party when Ruskin stayed with the Gladstones at Hawarden in 1878 and he thought that his blue stock, collar and frock coat made him look like something between an old fashioned nobleman of the Forties and an angel that had lost its way.[30] Almost all who described Ruskin have dwelt on his tie. H.W. Nevinson, who watched him Sunday after Sunday walk up the Christ Church Choir, marvelled at the length of the blue tie which appeared to be twisted round and round his collar and to prop up his chin.[31] In a later account[32] Nevinson expanded his memories of Christ Church Choir.

> Up that pavement, at all events on Sundays when we were all dressed in white surplices like the angels, a strange figure used to pass and seat himself in a stall behind the row of us on the north side ... I always at on the south side myself, and so could contemplate that strange figure at leisure – the mass of tawny hair, carefully brushed in order; the bright grey, nearly blue, eyes, usually quiet and meditative under tawny and projecting eyebrows; the eagle nose, the long and sensitive mouth, and rather receding chin; the whole face thin, well wrinkled and clean-shaven; the bright blue neck-tie wound two or three times about an upstanding collar, not hanging down over the shirt front, but apparently fastened by some invisible pin; the head inclined a little to the right, owing to the draughtsman's habit of raising the left shoulder; the loose and unfashionable clothes partly concealed by the long black gown; the whole bearing shy ...

Ruskin lectured six times at Eton between 1873 and 1880. On the occasion of his last visit, when he lectured on 'Amiens' on 6 November 1880, he was invited to Eton by the 18-year-old President of the Literary Society, A.C. Benson. A room was made available for Ruskin and here Benson met him before the lecture.

> He was slim in form, but much bowed. He was clean-shaven then, and wore his hair rather long; his whole dress was very old-fashioned to my eyes. He was dressed in evening clothes, and I remember his low-cut waistcoat, his high-collared coat, the long linen cuffs that came half over his hands, his white gloves.[33]

In another account of the meeting in his *Friends and Memories* Benson said that

> The figure before me seemed to have come from a previous century. As I remember, his tight-waisted frockcoat had a velvet collar ... and he showed a soft and many pleated shirt-front over a double-breasted waistcoat. I think he wore a long gold watchguard. His hair was thick and grizzled and grew very full, especially over the forehead: he had large side-whiskers and bushy eyebrows. The face was extraordinarily lined and the big mouth with a full underlip gave him a tenacious and, I thought, rather a formidable air ...

Benson may well have confused Ruskin's dress on this occasion. It is possible that Ruskin was in his frock coat when he arrived at Eton, and subsequently changed into evening dress for the lecture.

When at home at Brantwood, Ruskin delighted in chopping wood on his estate (see Nos. 101–102). His gloves and bill hook are still in the Coniston Museum, and in *A Museum or Picture Gallery*[34] he described the problems he had with his gloves.

> I am always busy, for a good part of the day, in my wood, and wear out my leathern gloves fast, after once I can wear them at all ... I get them from the shop, looking as stout and trim as you please, and half an hour after I've got to work they split up the fingers and thumbs like ripe horse-chestnut shells, and I find myself with five dangling rags round my wrists, and a rotten white thread dragging after me through the wood, or tickling my nose ... I go home, invoking the universe against sewing-machines; and beg the charity of a sound stitch or two from any of the maids who know their woman's art ...

M.E. Sadler first saw Ruskin during his second Oxford period. He attended a meeting at

29 *Letters to Matthew Arnold,* II, p. 141.
30 G. Wyndham (ed.), *Letters to M.G. & H.G.* (privately printed, 1903), p. 124.
31 *Daily Chronicle*, 8 Feb. 1899.
32 Nevinson, 'Some Memories of Ruskin', p. 149.
33 Benson, *Ruskin, a Study in Personality*, p. 184.
34 *Works* XXXIV, p. 258.

University College in the summer of 1881. William Morris was speaking at a protest meeting against the laying of a tramway down the High Street.

> A step below the dais in a little bow-backed chair sat huddled an old gentleman, nameless to me and never seen before. But there was something in him which radiated power. To his quiet venerable shape one's eye kept returning in spite of all the hot words of William Morris. Straight iron-grey hair, large pathetic eyes, now pensive, now flashing, light grey tweed trousers, a double-breasted waistcoat of the same cloth, a tight black frockcoat, and beneath his collar a vast tie of a vivid shameless blue, which made us – who were then wearing russet silk from Liberty – shiver at such a sign of Philistinism. And, at last, he rose, and his voice was magic. This was the man who broke his heart for England.[35]

To the young Beatrix Potter at the Royal Academy of 4 March 1884, Ruskin was almost a figure of fun. He had been in London for some weeks, and wrote in his diary on 6 March 'Yesterday at Kensington Crush, and a little colded, I fancy ...'; meanwhile Beatrix Potter had on the previous day confided to her Journal

> Went for the second time to the Academy and Grosvenor. Saw the pictures better this time. Also saw at the Academy the Duke of Westminster and Mr Ruskin, and at the Grosvenor the Princess of Wales.
>
> Mr Ruskin was one of the most ridiculous figures I have seen. A very old hat, much necktie[36] and aged coat buttoned up to his neck, humpbacked, not particularly clean looking. He had on high boots, and one of his trousers was tucked up on the top of one. He became aware of this half way round the room, and stood on one leg to put it right, but in so doing hitched up the other trouser worse than the first one had been.
>
> He was making remarks on the pictures which were listened to with great attention by his party, an old lady and gentleman and a young girl, but other people evidently did not know him. He armed the old lady in the first rooms, and the girl in the others.

In 1887 Ruskin was not enjoying good health, and he stayed for some time at Folkestone and Sandgate. His valet, Peter Baxter, who was having an unenviable time, had been instructed by Joan Severn to send her daily reports of Ruskin's progress. Poor Baxter was terribly worried by Ruskin's excesses and wrote from the Paris Hotel on 30 August[37]

> ... I had to get in a hair dresser for him to smarten him up as I had not cut his hair fashionable enough, so he just got the first cut or two when the Master jumped up and damd him for his modern style of cutting, ordered him to leave the room ... He is having two new top coats made and five waistcoats the tailor was not to tell me but I seen them this afternoon when he brought them to fit on one is to come down to his feet almost so as the waves can dash against him – without wetting him the other is a short light one ...

The news must have caused consternation at Brantwood. When taxed with his extravagance he sent an estimate of the tailor's bill to Joan Severn.[38]

Four plain, one dress waistcoats	4	10	0
One ordinary coat – say	6	6	0
One greatcoat ? say	7	7	0
One storm coat say	8	8	0
Over-all Donnies ? say	1	1	0
	£28	2	0

> Raven 1 8 0 – trousers & waistcoat
>
> Baxter declares that Miss Anderson[39] must have paid my tailors bill – *He* has no idea of the price of my coats.

35 E.H. Scott, *Ruskin's Guild of St George*, introduction by M.E. Sadler, p. xi.

36 Had Beatrix Potter remembered Ruskin's liking for large blue neckclothes when in *Apply Dapley's Nursery Rhymes* she drew the guinea pig with a big blue cravat of exactly the same shade as Ruskin's and gave him a matching blue book to carry? Amusingly there is a certain similarity between her drawing of the amiable guinea pig and the Brookes painting of Ruskin's be-whiskered face at the Royal Academy in 1887 (No. 224)! I am grateful to Mrs Lightman for drawing my attention to the illustration and the rhyme

> There once was an amiable guinea-pig,
> Who brushed back his hair like a periwig –
> He wore a sweet tie,
> As blue as the sky –
> And his whiskers and buttons
> Were very big.

37 P. Baxter – Joan Severn, 30 Aug. 1887, RF L 63.

38 JR – Joan Severn, 3 Sept. 1887, RF L 48.

39 Sara Anderson was Ruskin's secretary. John Raven was the Coniston tailor who had married Kate Smith, Ruskin's housekeeper.

£28 2s. may not sound a princely sum today, but to put it into context we must remember that just a few months before this Ruskin had agreed with his cook to pay her an annual wage of £25.

Two years later, ill-health finally overtook Ruskin and he retired to Brantwood and remained there until his death in 1900. He was visited in these last eleven years by a flock of admirers and inquisitive visitors. One such visitor who came to Brantwood in 1893 wrote his 'Reminiscences of Ruskin' in the *Athenoeum*[40] fifteen years later.

> Ruskin sat crouched like an old lion in his arm chair ... He was, as always, carefully dressed, with perhaps the extra neatness of an invalid, the historic blue tie showing through his long beard as he stroked and parted it, the eyes shining from under shaggy brows ...

40 *Athenœum*, 17 Oct. 1908.

Chapter IV
The Portraits

1 John Ruskin, aet 3½, 1822, by James Northcote (1746–1831) (Plate 1)

2 Reduced copy of No. 1, by Joseph Arthur Palliser Severn (1842–1931) or William Gershom Collingwood (1854–1932)

3 Reduced copy of No. 1, by unidentified artist

The first portrait to be painted of John Ruskin was that made of him as a small boy by James Northcote. We have Ruskin's word that he was three and a half years old when he sat to Northcote in his studio at 39 Argyll Street. Ruskin's father's diary[1] contains a list of the pictures in his collection, but unfortunately the dates of the family portraits are not recorded. J.J. Ruskin's account books before 1827 are not available so it is not possible to verify the date of the portrait exactly from these sources.

Ruskin devoted some space to describing the painting of this portrait in his autobiography, *Præterita*. After talking about his childhood toys (or lack of them) and pastimes, he goes on to say:

> But the carpet, and what patterns I could find in bed-covers, dresses, or wallpapers to be examined, were my chief resources, and my attention to the particulars of these was soon so accurate, that when at three and a half I was taken to have my portrait painted by Mr Northcote, I had not been ten minutes alone with him before I asked him why there were holes in his carpet. The portrait in question represents a very pretty child with yellow hair, dressed in a white frock like a girl, with a broad, light-blue sash and blue shoes to match; the feet of the child wholesomely large in proportion to its body; and the shoes still more wholesomely large in proportion to the feet.

1

2

1 RF MS 33.

> These articles of my daily dress were all sent to the old painter for perfect realisation; but they appear in the picture more remarkable than they were in the nursery, because I am represented as running in a field at the edge of a wood with the trunks of its trees striped across in the manner of Sir Joshua Reynolds; while two rounded hills, as blue as my shoes, appear in the distance, which were put in by the painter at my own request; for I had already been once, if not twice, taken to Scotland; and my Scottish nurse having always sung to me as we approached the Tweed or Esk, –
>
> 'For Scotland, my darling, lies full in thy view,
> With her barefooted lassies, and mountains so blue'.
>
> the idea of distant hills was connected in my mind with approach to the extreme felicities of life, in my Scottish aunt's garden of gooseberry bushes, sloping to the Tay. But that, when old Mr Northcote asked me (little thinking, I fancy, to get any answer so explicit) what I would like to have in the distance of my picture, I should have said 'blue hills' instead of 'gooseberry bushes', appears to me – and I think without any morbid tendency to think over-much of myself – a fact sufficiently curious, and not without promise, in a child of that age.
>
> I think it should be related also that having, as aforesaid, been steadily whipped if I was troublesome, my formed habit of serenity was greatly pleasing to the old painter; for I sat contentedly motionless, counting the holes in his carpet, or watching him squeeze his paint out of its bladders, – a beautiful operation, indeed, to my thinking; – but I do not remember taking any interest in Mr Northcote's application of the pigment to the canvas; my ideas of delightful art, in that respect, involving indispensably the possession of a large pot, filled with paint of the brightest green, and a brush which would come out of it soppy. But my quietude was so pleasing to the old man that he begged my father and mother to let me sit to him for the face of a child which he was painting in a classical subject; where I was accordingly represented as reclining on a leopard skin, and having a thorn taken out of my foot by a wild man of the woods.[2] (No. 5)

In a letter of 23 February 1822 John James Ruskin wrote from Leicester to his wife: 'I would have asked you to buy a Dog as I do not know exactly what John wants but I could not say I had bought it. I have therefore bought here a Dog and a Sheep for him which I shall try and bring home safe to him'.[3] In the light of this reference it seems that this *may* have been the dog which shares the portrait with Ruskin (especially as there are several sheep in No. 5!). However it is difficult to imagine how John James, travelling by stage coach, would bring a dog and a sheep back to London with him – or indeed where they would have kept a sheep at Hunter Street. Perhaps this dog and sheep were toys.

We do not know the name of the King Charles spaniel in the portrait. It was probably John's first dog. This spaniel was joined in the following year by Lion, the black Newfoundland bought as a guard dog when the Ruskins moved to No. 28 Herne Hill. It was Lion who bit John's lip. Gypsy seems to have replaced Lion by early 1829 and to have been joined by Dash a year later. Dash was another King Charles spaniel which had belonged to Ruskin's Croydon aunt, Bridget Richardson, until her death in 1830. These were the earliest in a long line of dogs in Ruskin's household.

In 1825 John James Ruskin and his wife Margaret sat to Northcote for their portraits. These portraits, together with the portrait of John, used to hang in the family's dining room, and they are listed as being there when John James listed his pictures with their costs and insurance values.[4] John's portrait is recorded in the list as having cost £42. In later years, when Ruskin moved to Brantwood, the portrait occupied an honoured place in the dining room, above the sideboard and flanked by his parents.

Ruskin held the work of Northcote in high regard though he wrote little about him. However, on one occasion when he was showing the portrait of his father to M.H. Spielmann, Ruskin said that he was pleased that his father 'had the good taste and good sense to have his portrait painted by so clever an artist'.[5]

Together with other family portraits the Northcote of John was sold at Sotheby's on 20 May 1931[6] where it was bought for £130 by 'Vokins'. It subsequently disappeared for a number of years and next reappeared in 1950, then owned by Mr Theodore Leavitt, in an exhibition in Buffalo, New York. It was sold in 1951 to the New York dealer H.B. Yotnakparien of 817 Madison Avenue.

Yotnakparien was unable to remember who bought the picture from him but he *did* recall that he had sold it as a 'dog' painting, interest in New York at that time evidently being greater in dogs

2 *Works* XXXV, pp. 21-22.
3 RF L 2.
4 RF MS 33.
5 Spielmann, *John Ruskin*, pp. 161-62.
6 Lot 125.

Figure 11: No. 1 in location. The dining room at Brantwood, c.1890, with the three family portraits by Northcote. The frame to the extreme right of the photograph contains the George Richmond portrait, No. 15.

than in Ruskin! Thus the portrait remained 'lost' for some 36 years, until it reappeared as Lot 57 in Sotheby's sale at Bond Street on 18 November 1987. It was bought by the National Portrait Gallery with grants from the National Heritage Memorial Fund and the National Art-Collections Fund, to be deposited on permanent loan at Brantwood. Following cleaning and restoration it was re-hung in its former position on the dining room wall at Brantwood.

Spielmann refers to a reduced copy of this portrait (possibly by Arthur Severn) hanging in the Severns' house at Herne Hill. This is also mentioned in the *Works* Catalogue and is probably the copy (No. 2) now hanging in the Coniston Museum since it does not appear among the listed pictures in the sale catalogue of the Severns' later home in Warwick Square. Whether the copy is by Severn or Collingwood is difficult to determine. The presence of Collingwood's name and address in the reverse may be an indication of ownership rather than authorship. No. 2, with No. 6, may have originally been made for purposes of reproduction. The tree standing beyond the water in the right middle distance of the original painting is missing in the copy, and this feature makes it possible to recognise which version was used for particular reproductions. Perhaps significantly the only time that both copies were reproduced together was in *The Bookman* of March 1900.

4 John Ruskin, aet c.3½, c.1822, by an unknown silhouettist

4

This silhouette must have been made at about the same time as the Northcote portrait (No. 1). The dog appears to be the same King Charles spaniel of that portrait, and indeed Ruskin appears to be wearing the same clothes, although on this occasion the monstrous hat and cape have been added to the ensemble.

It is difficult to determine exactly what happened to the silhouette after it left Brantwood. Reporting to J. Howard Whitehouse[7] on 1 August 1931 his agent at the Brantwood sale, Ralph Brown explained that various items had been sold privately *before* the sale and he reported that 'six family miniatures and silhouettes' had been drawn to his attention. These were in the hands of the Grasmere antique dealer T.H. Telford. Brown described them as:

Silhouettes	*Ruskin as a boy – signed on the back J* *Ruskin's grandfather – signed on the back J* *Ruskin's mother – by Miers, with the London label*
Miniatures (on ivory)	*Mrs Peter Richardson* *JRS's grandfather and Mrs Catherine?* *Mrs John Ruskin's grandmother*

Brown explained that the three miniatures were 'pencilled indistinctly on the back', and it is evident that he had mistranscribed the inscriptions. Telford would not sell the items individually, and Whitehouse would not pay his price for the collection. However, eventually the group *was* split up and the American Ruskin scholar Helen Viljoen bought:

Miniature of John Thomas Ruskin set in a bracelet c.1764
Miniature of John Thomas Ruskin c.1795
Miniature of John Thomas Ruskin c.1815
Miniature of Catherine Tweddale Ruskin c.1795
Miniature of Mrs Patrick Richardson of Perth, copy by Mrs W.G. Collingwood

All had been included in the 1900 Ruskin exhibition at Coniston (Nos. 282–83, 285–87): all were reproduced in Viljoen's *Ruskin's Scottish Heritage*, 1956, and all but Mrs Patrick Richardson were subsequently included in the Ruskin exhibition which she mounted at Queen's College Library, New York, in 1965.

What happened to the silhouettes is less clear. The silhouettes of John Thomas Ruskin and Margaret Ruskin seem to have disappeared while the Barrow-in-Furness collector F.J. Sharp bought the *present* silhouette – either from the group owned by Telford – or separately from Violet Severn at Brantwood. But it is unclear whether or not the present silhouette and that owned by Telford are one and the same, or whether the Telford silhouette is currently now 'lost'.

On Sharp's death in 1957 the silhouette passed, together with the major part of his collection, to Dr Viljoen. In turn, on her death in 1974 it passed to the present owner, the Pierpont Morgan Library.

The silhouette is inscribed on the reverse by Joan Severn 'Di Pa as a child certified by himself', and by F.J. Sharp, 'Portrait of John Ruskin. The above writing is in the hand of Mrs A. Severn'. Sharp has also written on the reverse of the mount, 'Silhouette Portrait of John Ruskin. The inscription "Di Pa" etc. is in the writing of Mrs Arthur Severn (Joan Ruskin Severn). This is the first, known, portrait of Ruskin'.

I know of no documentary evidence to prove that this is, in fact, the *first* portrait. Clearly, since he owned it, he would have *liked* it to have been, but in the absence of contradictory evidence I am happy to accept Cook and Wedderburn's listing of the Northcote portrait as the first.

7 See J.S. Dearden, *Ruskin, Bembridge and Brantwood* (Keele: Ryburn Publishing, 1994), p. 98.

5 John Ruskin, aet 4, 1823, by James Northcote. 'The Sylvan Doctor'.

6 Reduced copy of No. 5 by Arthur Severn or W.G. Collingwood

As mentioned above, this allegorical painting, sometimes also known as 'The thorn in the foot', was made soon after the earlier portrait by Northcote. John James Ruskin's picture list shows that the cost was £31 10s,[8] and that at one time the picture was hanging in the family's dining room. But by 1900 Collingwood[9] noted that it had been relegated to an outhouse at Brantwood. It was sold at Sotheby's in 1931[10] to 'Parkin' and its present whereabouts are unknown. As is the case with the other Northcote portrait, there is also a reduced copy (No. 6) of the present picture.

5

6

7 John Ruskin, aet c.12, an imaginative portrait by Arthur Severn (Plate 2)

Ruskin began sketching and drawing when he was a small child. He remembered making a drawing of a castle when he was about four but the earliest surviving examples of his art date from 1826 or 1827. By 1831 he was taking drawing lessons. His earliest outdoor sketches were made on a trip to Kent in 1831 or 1832. In 1833 and again in 1835 the Ruskins made continental journeys and by this time John was a dedicated artist. During the 1833 tour, Ruskin has explained in *Præteritea*, his father liked to reach the place where they were going to spend the night early and so would not stop the horses for John to sketch, 'the extra pence to postillion for waiting being also an item of weight in his mind'. Thus most of his sketches on this tour were made from the window of the moving carriage. His 1835 landscapes were made in the style of Turner's vignettes which he had admired in Samuel Roger's

8 RF MS 33.
9 Collingwood, *The Life of John Ruskin*, p. 15.
10 20 May 1931, lot 124.

Italy, while his detailed architectural studies were in direct imitation of the work of Samuel Prout whose work he had seen in *Sketches in Flanders and Germany*. During this tour he was allowed to devote more time to his sketching. It is the young Ruskin of about twelve years old that Severn has portrayed in this imaginative sketch. The subject may be identified by the initials 'J.R.' on the water mug.

7

8 John Ruskin, aet 17, 1836. Miniature portrait by Alfred Edward Chalon (1780–1860) (Plate 3)

This previously unpublished miniature is the first known portrait of the adolescent Ruskin. This is Ruskin the published poet, the writer on geology, the champion of Turner. In 1836 Ruskin was attending the Rev. Thomas Dale's lectures on early English literature at King's College, he was taking watercolour lessons from Copley Fielding and drawing lessons from Charles Runciman. In October he matriculated at Christ Church, Oxford, and in December he took his final examinations at King's College.

In this year, Ruskin's articles 'The Indulation of Sandstone' and 'Observations on the Causes which occasion the Variation of Temperature between Spring and River Water' both appeared in Loudon's *Magazine of Natural History* in September and October. His poem 'The Months' was in the 1836 edition of *Friendships Offering* and he wrote his reply to the Rev. J. Eagles's criticism of Turner for *Blackwood's*.

And he fell in love with Adèle Domecq – who with her family visited the Ruskins at No. 28 Herne Hill.

The circumstances under which the miniature was painted are not recorded. However, in 1836 preparations were being made for Ruskin to go to Oxford in January of the following year. He was to be accompanied by his mother who would live in Oxford during his terms at Christ Church; his father would remain in London or travelling the country in connection with his sherry business, joining his family at Oxford when he had the opportunity. I would suggest that the miniature, in its leather case, was painted as part of these preparations, for John James to have with him during his separation from his family.

Unfortunately John James's usually helpful account books do not help on this occasion, merely recording on 17 October 1837 a payment of £5 for 'John's picture' – more than likely either a picture bought for John, or one of John's own drawings bought by his father. Again, the 1843 Insurance List is unhelpful, only noting '2 miniatures £20'. These could have been any of the portraits listed under No. 4.

The artist, A.E. Chalon, was born in Geneva, the son of a Huguenot refugee who settled in Kensington. He entered the Royal Academy Schools in 1797, first exhibited at the Academy in 1801, was elected an Associate in 1812 and a Royal Academician in 1816. In 1833 he was elected a Visitor to the Life Academy of the R.A. with Eastlake, Turner and Abraham Cooper. With his brother J.J. Chalon, he founded the Sketching Society in 1808. A.E. Chalon was appointed Painter in Watercolour to Queen Victoria and his portrait of her was reproduced on many early issues of colonial stamps. Ruskin does not appear to have referred to him in his writings, but there are a number of references to the work of his brother J.J. Chalon.

8

9–12 John Ruskin, aet 21, 1840-41, by Constantin Roesler Franz (Plate 4)

13 Copy of Franz cameo by The Mikimoto Company

The Ruskins' continental tour of 1840–41 took them to Rome between 28 November and 5 January and it was here that the first portrait to show John as a man was made.

Ruskin had arrived in Rome with a letter of introduction from Henry Acland (a friend made at Oxford) to Joseph Severn. After the initial round of sight-seeing John went to call on Severn who was well-known as the friend of Keats. Severn lived at this time in the Via Rasella and on the first visit, Ruskin missed him, passing Severn and his friend George Richmond on the stairway outside. Severn is said to have observed to Richmond 'that young man has the face of a poet'. Eventually they met and thereafter the Ruskins saw a lot of Severn, George Richmond, and Richmond's brother Thomas who was also with them in Rome.

There are frequent references to the trio in Ruskin's diary. On 12 December 'Interrupted last night by Severn, who came in and chatted till 11 o'clock, cleverish and droll, but rather what I should call a cockney, though he has lived twenty years in Rome: but Cockneyism is in spirit, not habitation'. Ruskin liked George Richmond 'who confirms my first impression of him. He is a most gentlemanly man, and of fine mind. His brother [Thomas] ugly, and disagreeable in manner but clever'.

About 20 December Ruskin caught a fever which kept him indoors for a week. Ruskin's cousin, Mary Richardson, who was travelling with the family, noted in her diary that they all breakfasted together for the first time since John's illness on new Year's morning, and in the evening they 'had Mr George and Mr Thomas Richmond,

10

Mr Severn and Mr Anderson [who had arrived the previous day from Naples] to dinner: a very merry party, Mr Severn told a number of curious anecdotes illustrative of Italian manners ... Again Mr T.R. told very well a story of a clergyman ... much of the point of this story depended on the manner in which it was told, which was admirable'.[11]

Meanwhile George Richmond wrote to tell his wife:

> ... we are going to eat our new year's dinner with Mr & Mrs Ruskin and their son. The latter is very poorly indeed he is a most pleasing man and of considerable power as a poet – with a good notion of art – he was prize poet at Oxford. We have been and are returned from our dinner which regales us highly – for the first time since we left we saw and I partook of a haunch of Mutton – we met Severn there and passed a pleasant evening ... The Ruskins ... are extremely friendly and kind I have promised to pay them a visit for two or three days to paint their son in the summer if all is well. Tell Acland ... that he Mr Ruskin is worthy of being his friend ...[12]

During this stay in Rome Severn and the Richmonds often acted as guides to the studios of fellow artists. Either Severn or the Richmonds may have told the Ruskins of the cameo-cutters of Rome, whom they were to visit. In *Præterita* Ruskin later wrote that one of the 'living arts' of Rome at that time was the cutting of cameos in pink shell, and that 'polite travellers' were expected to take home specimens of the art.

> We bought, according to the custom, some coquillage of Gods and Graces; but the cameo cutters were also skilled in mortal portraiture, and papa and mama, still expectant of my future greatness, resolved to have me carved in cameo.
>
> I had always been content enough with my front face in the glass, and had never thought of contriving vision of the profile. The cameo finished, I saw at a glance to be well cut; but the image it gave of me was not to my mind.

The cameo must have been cut at the end of December 1840, or at the beginning of January, for Mary Richardson, recorded in her diary on 5 January 1841

> ... In the evening the two Mr Richmonds came to tea and spent a couple of hours afterwards in very agreeable conversation. Mr R[ichmond] approved much of a likeness of John taken in cameo by M. Frantz, [sic] of Via Condotti, the likeness strikes us all as being very strong indeed. John only sat for about an hour to have a chalk sketch taken of him, and then for 10 minutes or quarter of an hour, to the artist who cut the cameo.

John James Ruskin later recorded the transaction in his account book,[13] where we discover 'John's profile Rome 63/-. 15 cameos £9 15s'. A little further on in the account book appears another entry: '2 profiles John £5 8s 6d'. This shows that the Ruskins must have decided to have a further two cameos of John cut, probably as gifts for close friends.

The original cameo remained in the Ruskin collection until the Brantwood sales of 1930–31. It was then bought by the late F.J. Sharp. After his death it was acquired for the Brantwood collection where it is now on exhibition.

One of the duplicate cameos was evidently given by Ruskin to Mrs Thomas Hayes (née Sidney). Mrs Hayes and her sister, Lady Edwardes, lived in

11 RF T 49.
12 Letter from George Richmond to his wife, quoted in Sotheby's catalogue, 6 July 1977, lot 291, now at University of North Carolina Library.

13 RF MS 28.

London before they were married, with their guardian, Dr George Grant. Grant was the close friend and physician of the Ruskins, and his step-daughters, Augusta and Emma Sidney, were life-long friends of Ruskin. The cameo that Ruskin gave to Mrs Hayes is still in her family. The whereabouts of the third cameo is not known to me.

Ruskin said in *Præterita* that the image the cameo gave was 'not to my mind'. Writing of it in 1886[14] he said

> I did not analyse its elements at the time, but should now describe it as a George the Third's penny, with a halfpennyworth of George the Fourth, the pride of Amurath the Fifth, and the temper of eight little Lucifers in a swept lodging.
>
> Now I knew my self proud; yes, and of late, sullen; but I did not in the least recognise pride or sulkiness for leading faults of my nature. On the contrary, I knew myself wholly reverent to all real greatness, and wholly good-humoured – when I got my own way. What more can you expect of average boy or beast? ... The George the Third and Fourth character I recognise very definitely among my people, as already noticed in my cousin George of Croydon.[15]

Writing to Joan Severn in the following year,[16] Ruskin said that he had been searching for the cameo in order to show it to Kate Greenaway. On looking at it again, he decided 'The cameo is not quite so ugly as I thought it'.

Mr Ryuzo Mikimoto, a dedicated Ruskin collector, scholar and founder of the Ruskin Society of Tokyo in the 1930s employed several different sculptors to make copies of Ruskin busts for him. He also had a number of medals and other Ruskin keepsakes made by his Mikimoto Company. Bronze casts were made, copying the Franz cameo; these also seem to have been produced by The Mikimoto Company.

14 John Ruskin, aet 22, c.1841, by Thomas Richmond (1802–1874) (Plate 5)

The friendship which Ruskin had formed with the Richmond brothers was to endure for their lifetimes. Both brothers were portrait painters. George was the better known; Thomas, the elder brother, practised for many years as a miniaturist in Sheffield and later in London. He had a large following among hunting men. Between 1833 and 1860 he exhibited 51 portraits in London.

Between them the brothers made seven portraits of Ruskin and two of his wife Effie. The first portrait of the series of John is that painted by Thomas Richmond, and dated by Cook and Wedderburn as c.1841. It shows John as an elegant young man in a dark tail coat. In his hands he holds his gloves while his top hat and cane are on a stone seat behind him. The watch-chain which he wore round his neck can be seen across his gold lapels.

It is interesting to note that John's hair is not parted on its usual side, but the fact that it is also parted this way in the two Northcote and the Laurence portraits, shows that he evidently liked a change every now and again.

The portrait is undated and there is no evidence, other than John's youthful appearance, to show when it was done. Clearly it could not have been done before the winter of 1840–41 for John

14

14 *Works* XXXV, pp. 280ff.
15 Earlier in *Præterita* Ruskin had written, '... George was the best of boys and men, but of small wit. He extremely resembled a rural George the Fourth...'
16 RF L 48.

did not meet Richmond till then. His brother George, and Joseph Severn, returned to England while the Ruskins were still in Rome in early 1841, and thereafter Thomas was their almost constant companion on visits to studios and other outings. But it seems unlikely that the present portrait was done in Rome, for there is no mention of it in Mary Richardson's detailed diary of the tour. It was not until the end of June that the Ruskins returned home, and it seems probable that the portrait was painted soon after that.

Ruskin makes no reference to the Thomas Richmond portraits of himself, but according to Effie Ruskin, both father and son expressed themselves 'delighted' with Richmond's 1851 portrait of Effie. However, privately, the Ruskins were not all that pleased. John James wrote to his son in Venice[17] 'Tom I regret to say cannot hold a candle to George – It is second rate or lower'.

The present portrait of John never seems to have been in the Ruskin collection. An old label says that it was 'purchased at Brighton in 1884'. In 1912 it belonged to William Ward. It subsequently came into the possession of Mrs van Buren Emmons who gave it to the Whitehouse Collection at Bembridge in May 1967.

15 John Ruskin, aet 24, 1843, by George Richmond (1809–1896), 'The Author of *Modern Painters*'

15

In 1843 Ruskin was still unknown, save to a small circle. He had contributed poems to various periodicals and a number of his articles on architecture, natural history and geological subjects had appeared in print. His admiration for the work of Turner had caused him to write the first volume of *Modern Painters* and at the end of 1842 and beginning of 1843 he was busy finishing the manuscript and seeing the book through the press.

We know that the initial arrangement for George Richmond to paint John had been made in Rome in 1840. At the beginning of 1843,[18] the year in which Ruskin took his M.A. at Oxford, his father commissioned Richmond to make a portrait of the young champion of Turner. On 24 February Ruskin recorded in his diary, 'In at Richmond's and had a pleasant sitting'. Further documentation of the portrait is found in the elder Ruskin's account book[19] under 'March 1843' where we read the entry 'John's picture £105'. The picture framer's bill was £9 12s. In May it was exhibited at the Royal Academy where it was catalogued as 'John Raskin Esq.' and although *Modern Painters*, also published in May, was currently causing something of a stir in the art world, there were few to connect it with the 'John Raskin' of Richmond's portrait for the author appeared on the title page of his book as 'A Graduate of Oxford'. The diary entry for 22 May 1843 probably refers to the portrait: 'In at the Royal Academy with Mrs Cockburn. I felt myself stupid, and I fear she thought me proud'.

17 JJR – JR, 28 Sept. 1851. RF L 4.

18 Writing to M.H. Spielmann in 1889 George Richmond said that the portrait was painted in 1842. It may have been begun at the end of 1842 but it was certainly not finished until 1843. The letter is inserted in Spielmann's own copy of his *John Ruskin*, now in the Pierpont Morgan Library.

19 RF MS 28.

Ruskin described the portrait in *Præterita*:[20] '... with amused interest in my youthful enthusiasm [for Turner], and real affection for my father, he painted a charming water-colour of me sitting at a picturesque desk in the open air, in a crimson waistcoat and white trousers, with a magnificent port-crayon in my hand, and Mont Blanc, conventionalised to Raphaelesque grace, in the distance...'

But Ruskin was not entirely pleased with the likeness. In *Friends of a Lifetime* S.C. Cockerell records that Ruskin had told him 'It is not a good picture or a good likeness – the nose is wrong', and to Dr John Brown at the end of December 1873 Ruskin wrote 'Who could tell from Richmond's amiable portrait of the Author of *Modern Painters* that he was capable of sweeping Regent Street with grape, if he saw need, and sleeping sound the night afterwards...'.[21]

In John James Ruskin's list of pictures in his home at Denmark Hill the portrait is listed under 'Ante Room, Study and Mrs R's Room'. Later, at Brantwood, the picture used to hang in the Dining Room where it was seen in the summer of 1928 by Haddon C. Adams. I believe it used to hang opposite to the door; thus the edge of its frame can be seen above the right hand sideboard in the photograph of the dining room in Figure 11 (page 24).

Three years later, at the dispersal sale of the contents of the house, the picture was lot 30 at Sotheby's on 20 May 1931. It was bought for £82 by Stevens and Brown, acting on behalf of Charles E. Goodspeed, the bookseller of Boston, Mass. Goodspeed was a Ruskin enthusiast and not all of his purchases at the Ruskin sales were destined for re-sale. George Goodspeed tells me that he recalls his father taking the portrait home and hanging it over the mantelpiece in his library, where, to the best of his recollection, it remained. Unhappily, Goodspeed's house was badly damaged by fire in February 1941 and the library was totally destroyed. It must be assumed that the Richmond portrait perished in the flames, together with other of Goodspeed's treasures, including a portrait by Ruskin of Rose La Touche. Among the manuscripts and books saved from the fire (though badly charred) was part of the rare *Præterita* manuscript, which Goodspeed subsequently gave to Yale University Library.

Figure 12

Writing to Spielmann in 1889 Richmond said 'The whole length [portrait] I have often wished to see engraved and I have no doubt that Mr Ruskin would grant permission, and I should be happy to touch the proofs for you without charge'. The portrait first seems to have been reproduced in 1891 when it was printed in the *Magazine of Art* by the half tone process.

The portrait was later engraved. There is a proof in the Whitehouse Collection. The engraved surface measures 18½" x 11⅞"; there is no indication as to the identity of the engraver.

Happily the portrait was also photographed. The photograph of it in the South London Gallery is reproduced on page 31, and the large engraving of it (Figure 12) is from the Whitehouse Collection print.

20 *Works* XXXV, p. 398.
21 National Library of Scotland, MS 9745.

16 John Ruskin, aet c.24, c.1843, by unidentified miniaturist

The present portrait was probably made at about the same time as Richmond's study of 'The Author of *Modern Painters*'. Indeed John Dixon Hunt suggests that it might be copied from the Richmond portrait. Although the two poses are *similar*, I believe the miniature to be an original portrait. It is not likely that it was copied from the original Richmond because the colours are not right. We know that when he sat to Richmond, Ruskin wore a red waistcoat, which is not the case in the miniature. If it *was* copied from Richmond, then it could not have been made before 1891 when it was first reproduced in Spielmann's first portraits article in the *Magazine of Art*.

At one time I had speculated that this may have been the miniature referred to as No. 45, the unlocated miniature of Ruskin by S.J. Stump which was offered to the Ruskin Centenary Exhibition. However, in the light of Collingwood's opinion that the 1919 miniature was not of Ruskin, and Richard Ormond's opinion, expressed to me some twenty years ago that the present miniature is not of good enough quality to be the work of Stump, that possibility can be eliminated.

16

17 John Ruskin, aet 26, 1845, with Auguste Gendron and [?] Eugène-Paul Dieudonné, by Johann-Ludwig-Rudolph Durheim (1811–1898) (Plate 6)

In 1845 Ruskin undertook his first continental journey without his parents. By 21 May he was in Pisa and writing to his father that he 'picked up two French artists in the Campo Santo, who, for Frenchmen, talk very like human beings.' They had 'been studying the old paintings of the right sort'.[22]

These two French artists were probably Eugène-Paul Dieudonné (b. 1825), a portrait painter, and Ernest-Augustin Gendron (1817–1881), a somewhat more prominent subject painter who exhibited in various salons from 1840 to 1877.

On 29 May Ruskin arrived in Florence where he was to stay until 7 July. Here he met another artist, Rudolph Durheim. Durheim was a native of Basle who had worked under Lugardon and Augnot Scheffer. Ruskin seems to have become friendly with Durheim and saw quite a lot of him during his stay in Florence. Gendron and Dieudonné had also arrived in Florence from Pisa, probably travelling with Ruskin.

On 3 July Ruskin wrote to his father[23] mentioning Durheim as 'a poor Swiss artist of very sweet character and great power'. Ruskin reported that he was going to drive out to the Certosa with Durheim that day, and that he had given Ruskin 'a sketch of a little blue-eyed Swiss cousin of his'. During his stay in Florence Ruskin spent most of his time in the galleries and churches studying paintings and writing notes on them in his diaries; his artist-friends spent their time copying Old Masters, and Ruskin was not always of the opinion that they were copying the best examples.

In his diary[24] Ruskin discusses three important oils by Ghirlandajo, all of them Adorations – two in the Uffizzi and the third at the Ospedale degli Innoscenti. 'The least important is that which Durheim was copying, which I think has no merit, except a hard, dry, severely right drawing and sometimes an approach to quite portrait-like dignity'.

22 Shapiro, *Ruskin in Italy. Letters to his Parents 1845*, p. 71.
23 Shapiro, *Ruskin in Italy. Letters to his Parents 1845*, p. 136.
24 RF MS 5B.

17

The friendship with Durheim and Dieudonné is recalled in *Præterita*.[25]

> I did make one friend in Florence, however, for love of Switzerland, Rudolph Durheim, a Bernese student, of solid bearish gifts and kindly strength. I took to him at first because of a clearly true drawing he had made of his little blue-eyed twelve-years-old simplicity of a goat-herd sister; but found him afterwards a most helpful and didactic friend. He objected especially to my losing time in sentiment or over-hot vaporisation, and would have had me draw something every afternoon, whether it suited my fancy or not. ... We separated, to our sorrow ... I went off to higher and vainer vaporisation at Venice; he went back to Berne, and under the patronage of its aristocracy, made his black-bread by dull portrait painting to the end of a lost life ... There was yet another young draughtsman in Florence, who lessoned me to purpose – a French youth; – his family name Dieudonné; I knew him by no other. He had trained himself to copy Angelico, in pencil tint, wrought with the point, as sure as the down on a butterfly's wing, and with perfect expression: typical engraving in grey, of inconceivable delicacy. I have never seen anything the least approaching it since, but did not then enough know its value. Dieudonné's prices were necessarily beyond those of the watercolour copyists, and he would not always work, even when the price was ready for him. He went back to France, and was effaced in the politeness of Paris, as Rudolph in the rudeness of Berne.

In the Berner Kunstmuseum in Berne is a small oil painting on paper laid down on a wooden panel. It is a triple portrait showing Ruskin between two other men. It was painted by Durheim and is inscribed on the reverse, probably by the artist.

1. oublie le nom	*John Ruskin Florence 1846*	*Auguste Gendron*

It seems probable that the unremembered person was the fourth member of the quartet, Dieudonné. The fact that the artist was unable to remember the name of one of his sitters suggests that the label was written many years after the portrait was painted. Durheim was probably also in error in dating the picture 1846. Ruskin was in Florence again in 1846 for three weeks but neither his diary nor that of his valet makes any mention of Durheim, Dieudonné or Gendron. I would therefore suggest that this portrait dates from the summer of 1845.

The painting was bought in 1898 by the Gottfried Keller Foundation and deposited in the Berne Museum, where there are a number of other examples of Durheim's work.

25 *Works* XXXV, pp. 361ff.

18 John Ruskin, c.1846, by an unknown silhouettist

In the 18th and 19th centuries there were a number of artists who took silhouette likenesses, either painting them, or cutting them out of black paper and pasting them onto white or coloured card. The present anonymous silhouette, which was probably made about 1846, falls into the latter category. It is cut out of black paper and pasted onto white card, the highlights being drawn onto the silhouette in bronze ink. There is no indication of the identity of the artist.

The likeness is particularly interesting because it is one of only two which show Ruskin wearing glasses – probably in this case the tinted glasses which earned him the nickname 'Giglamps' at Oxford. The silhouette evidently remained in the Ruskin collection until the Brantwood dispersal sale in 1931 when it was bought in the Lake District by Mrs Joan Hoare, who subsequently gave it to the Whitehouse Collection.

18

19–35 Portraits and sketches of John Ruskin, aet 34–35, 1853–54, by John Everett Millais (1829–1896) (Plates 7, 8 and 10)

27 Statue, after the Glenfinlas portrait, by K. Kitaji

28 'Ruskin (Millais)', after the Glenfinlas portrait, by Susan Herbert (Plate 9)

John Ruskin was married in 1848 to Euphemia Chalmers Gray. She was the daughter of Mr and Mrs George Gray of Perth, family friends of the Ruskins. John and Effie first met in 1840 when she was twelve and stayed in London with the Ruskins on her way to school. She stayed there again in the following year and during this visit she and John became friends. However she thought him a very serious person with learned interests, and she challenged him to write a fairy story – which he duly did. Ironically *The King of the Golden River* was to become perhaps one of Ruskin's best known and most re-printed books.

Ruskin and Effie next met at the end of 1843, the year in which George Richmond had painted the 24 years old 'Author of *Modern Painters*'. Effie was fifteen, the same age that Adèle Domecq (the daughter of John James Ruskin's business partner) had been when John had fallen in love with her in 1836. Effie featured frequently in Ruskin's diary during the visit and towards the end he wrote 'I am really very sorry she is going'. Three years later Effie was once more at Denmark Hill and during this visit John fell in love with her. They were married on 10 April 1848 at Bowerswell, the Grays' home at Perth, where earlier Ruskin's grandparents had lived and where his grandfather had committed suicide.

The story of John and Effie's married life, the visit to Normandy, the long stays in Venice while John was writing *Stones of Venice* and Effie was enjoying the social life of the city, of home life in London, and the eventual breakdown of the marriage, due partly to parental interference and partly to its non-consummation, has been admirably told by Mary Lutyens in her trilogy, *The Ruskins and the Grays*, *Effie in Venice*, and *Millais and the Ruskins*.

In August 1848, just a few months after John and Effie were married, Holman Hunt, John Everett Millais and Dante Gabriel Rossetti and one or two of their artist friends banded themselves together to form the Pre-Raphaelite Brotherhood. They wished to turn away from the artistic 'establishment' of the day, as exemplified by the Royal Academy, and to make a fresh return to nature.

19

20

But their revolutionary style of painting met with opposition from the establishment. If their paintings were hung at all, they were not well hung, and generally, their work was badly received by the critics. The Pre-Raphaelite exhibits in the 1851 Academy particularly were the subject of press ridicule. The Brethren were in need of a champion.

Several of their number knew Coventry Patmore, and one of them asked him to intercede on their behalf with Ruskin. Ruskin looked again at their paintings; he liked what he saw and he wrote two letters in their defence to *The Times*. It was inevitable, now, that the Ruskins and the Pre-Raphaelites should meet. As it happens, Effie and Millais had already met at a dance at Ewell Castle in 1846 when she was seventeen and Millais was a year younger. Probably during June 1851 they met again, when John and Effie visited Millais at his home in Gower Street. Soon they were all meeting occasionally, but it was not until the beginning of 1853, when Effie sat to Millais for the head of the woman in his 'Order of Release' that Millais became really friendly with the Ruskins – a friendship which was to have a far-reaching effect on the lives of all three of them.

The first sketch of Ruskin made by Millais seems to have been done in 1853 (No. 19). It shows John and Effie standing in a gondola which has just passed under the Bridge of Sighs. Millais himself did not go to Venice until 1865. Perhaps Effie had spoken to him of the city while she was sitting for the 'Order of Release' and these conversations prompted this imaginative sketch. Ruskin, in his usual wide-awake hat, stands with his arm around his wife's waist, pointing with his other hand to the bridge.

Miss Lutyens has pointed out[26] that this sketch is the only one by Millais which shows John and Effie in affectionate juxtaposition. It was not until the summer of 1853 that Millais learned the truth about the Ruskins' unhappy marital relationship and Miss Lutyens suggests that this drawing was almost certainly made *before* Millais was disillusioned about his friends' marriage.

At the end of June 1853 Ruskin and Effie, accompanied by Millais and his elder brother William, set out from London for a holiday in the Scottish Highlands. The journey north was broken for a week in Northumberland where the four stayed with Ruskin's friends, Sir Walter and Lady Trevelyan, at Wallington.

Millais spent much of the week sketching and one of the results of his endeavours was the first in

26 Mary Lutyens, 'Portraits of Effie', *Apollo* (March 1968), pp. 190-97.

the series of three portraits of Ruskin made between the middle of 1853 and the end of the following year (No. 20).

Writing to his father on the day that the party left Wallington,[27] Ruskin related the story of the first portrait.

> Millais ... made a sketch of me for Lady Trevelyan – like me, but not pleasing, neither I nor Lady Trevelyan liked it except as a drawing: but she was very proud of it nevertheless. Then he drew Sir Walter for her, most beautifully ... And then he drew Effie for her – and was so pleased with the drawing that he kept it for himself and did another for her – but he does not quite satisfy us yet with Effie...[28]

Describing the Wallington portrait, Thomas Woolner wrote[29]

> The likeness, so far as I can remember, was good, but the expression that of a hyena, or something between Carker and that hilarious animal. Enemies would declare that it did him an injustice. [On the subject of Ruskin's appearance] Rossetti told me that when a boy Ruskin had part of one of his lips bitten off by a dog. The mouth is the most expressive of all features, and tells the history of its owner's nature better than any other; but under the circumstances how would it be possible to read it accurately ... Of course the main force of his head is perception, this faculty being unusually developed; but, so far as I can remember, I do not think there is anything else out of the common in the shape of it. His expression is varied beyond all example in my experience.

This portrait remained in the Trevelyan family until it was sold in 1951 at Christie's when it was bought for the Whitehouse Collection.

The Ruskins evidently hired a carriage in Northumberland and it was in this that they set out from Wallington at 11.30 on Wednesday 29 June. Sir Walter Trevelyan accompanied them for the first nine miles across the moors in his dog cart. Miss Mackenzie[30] who had also been staying at Wallington went with them on the first stage of the journey, then probably returned to Wallington with Sir Walter. Ruskin resumes the story in his letter to his father[31]

21

> Sir Walter drove Effie and Everett Millais nine miles in his dog cart – before our travelling vehicle – William Millais and I therein – in a tremendous north west gale over the moors – Sir Walter drove through it all hatless – his hair driving back from his fine forehead as if it would be torn away. I kept inside the carriage – not liking such rough weather – we bid him goodbye within four miles of Otterburn, and drove on and lunched at a quiet and clean little roadside inn on the moors...

Ruskin omitted to mention (knowing what alarm the news would cause his parents) that the postillion was drunk. William had to ride on the box and take the reins while the postillion rode with the luggage on the top of the coach. On the following day William made the present sketch (No. 21) showing his brother Everett (he was called this to differentiate from *John* Ruskin) standing by the chaise containing Trevelyan, Effie and Miss Mackenzie. Ruskin, in top hat, hangs out of the coach window while William reins in the horses and the postillion stands at their head moaning 'Aw'm verrarr baad – aw canna ride – oh dearrr, oh dearrrr'. It is fortunate that this sketch was reproduced in J.G. Millais's biography of his father, for the original now appears to be lost.

The first night away from Wallington was spent at Jedburgh; by the next evening they had reached Edinburgh. After a couple of days in the capital they journeyed on by coach and train, via Stirling and Doune to Brig o'Turk where they intended

27 JR – JJR, 29 June 1853, partly quoted in Leon, p. 181.
28 Miss Lutyens ('Portraits of Effie', pp. 190-97) has suggested that this is the portrait now belonging to Miss Veronica McEwan.
29 T. Woolner – M.H. Spielmann, c.1891; *Works* XXXVIII, p. 208.
30 Miss Lutyens suggests in *Millais and the Ruskins* (London: John Murray, 1967), p. 52, that she was probably Louisa Stewart Mackenzie, later Lady Ashburton.
31 JR – JJR, 29 June 1853; *Millais and the Ruskins*, pp. 54-55.

spending Sunday at the inn. In the event, they stayed at Brig o'Turk for nearly four months.

Millais had been very impressed by Doune Castle and had decided to paint Effie there, framed by one of its ruined windows. He also planned a portrait of John standing by one of the rocky streams. Writing to Holman Hunt on the evening of their first day at Brig o'Turk, Millais told him that 'the Ruskins are *most perfect people*' and that Effie in particular was 'the most delightful unselfish kind-hearted creature I ever knew, it is impossible to help liking her'.

Having decided on a longer stay at Brig o'Turk, the party soon took rooms at the schoolmaster's cottage, a few yards from the inn. But there was insufficient accommodation for them all. From their letters we know that they had two bedrooms leading off their sitting room, which were apparently occupied by Effie and Millais. Frederick Crawley, Ruskin's valet, occupied an alcove of the sitting room. Ruskin seems to have slept on the couch in the sitting room, while William Millais, who only stayed for seven weeks, had a room in the inn. However a document in the Bodleian Library[32] prepared by Albert Gray and William Millais in 1898 suggested that Ruskin may also have had a room in the inn. But whether he in fact used it as a bedroom or a study is not clear.

The summer of 1853 was very wet but the friends spent as much time as they could outdoors, exploring the countryside and sketching. In addition, Ruskin was hard at work on the series of lectures on architecture and painting which he was to deliver in Edinburgh in November. Meanwhile, as Ruskin told his father on 6 July, plans for his portrait were going ahead, and

> Millais has fixed on his place – a lovely piece of worn rock, with foaming water and weeds, and moss, and a noble overhanging bank of dark crag – and I am to be standing looking quietly down the stream – just the sort of thing I used to do for hours together – he is very happy at the idea of doing it and I think you will be proud of the picture – and we shall have the two most wonderful torrents in the world, Turner's St Gothard – and Millais' Glenfinlas.

But there were delays before the portrait could be started. A canvas was ordered from Edinburgh, and when it eventually arrived it was found not to be white enough – so a fresh one was ordered from London. Meanwhile Millais learned more about

22

the figure and appearance of his would-be model as a result of a series of sketches that he made, recording their various activities at Glenfinlas.

William and Ruskin took to wading in the stream. Effie told her mother on 10 July

> John and William Millais take off their shoes and stockings and wade about the Torrent beds with Great Poles in their hands – they put Everett and me into fits of laughter, they are so like Tyrolese Tourists or American Scouts or Cochines and look so ridiculous, their legs so tremendously white and so frightened where they put their feet.

One sheet of Everett's sketches (No. 22) shows William and John at their wading. On the left of the same sheet is a sketch of Henry Acland who joined the party on 25 July, while at the top is Effie's dog Wisie, a little white Spitz which had been given to her in Venice by Count Thun.

23

32 Bodleian MS Eng. Lett. C.228, fol.67. See Mary Lutyens, 'Where did Ruskin sleep', *TLS*, 2 Jan. 1969.

On the same day that Effie wrote to her mother about John and William wading in the stream – Sunday 10 July – the party climbed Ben Ledi. Millais made another sketch (No. 23) chronicling the event. Ruskin and William can be seen on the left, walking ahead, while Effie and Everett are in the foreground with Wisie. The other figures are probably Scottish locals who went with them.

To while away the wet hours Ruskin and the Millais brothers became expert players of battledore and shuttlecock. Millais referred to Ruskin as the Herne Hill Gamecock and a sketch (No. 24) made soon after 23 July shows them at the game. William in the left foreground and Ruskin behind the table fight it out while Millais (we know it is he from the bandaged left thumb which he crushed on 23 July when building a bridge of stones across the stream for Effie) watches. Effie and the minister, Mr Monteath, look on from the doorway.

Henry Acland, who had given Ruskin his letter of introduction to Joseph Severn in 1840, joined the party at Glenfinlas on Monday 25 July. And at last everything was ready for the beginning of the portrait. The new canvas had arrived from London; the rain had stopped, and on Thursday 28 July Ruskin was able to tell his father 'you will be delighted to hear that my portrait is verily begun today and a most exquisite piece of leafage done already, close to the head – the finest thing I ever saw him do'. On the same day Millais made a preliminary sketch for the portrait (No. 25) which Acland must have begged.

25

Ruskin noted the timetable of sittings in his diary[33] (and apparently got it wrong).

> Millais' picture of Glenfinlas [No. 26] was begun on Wednesday; outlined at once, Henry Acland holding the canvas, and a piece laid in that afternoon. More done on Thursday – about an hour's work on Friday, – Saturday blank – Monday blank – Tuesday out at six in the morning till 9, and from 12 till 5 – Wednesday 11 to 6 – Thursday 11 to 6 – Friday 11 to 5 – Saturday 11 to 5. Next week three days 11 to 5, one nothing and two afternoons 4 to 7. Next week, Monday 4 to 7 – Tuesday nothing – Wednesday 1 to 8 - Thursday 1 to 5 – Friday 1 to 5 – Saturday 1 to 5. Next week Monday, Tuesday, Wednesday 12 to 6 – three days hardly anything. [The rain returned, and on 2 August] Out with Millais at 6, holding the umbrella over him as he worked and watching the stream, looking down at it due South, the sun of course on my left ...

24

As Millais worked on the background to the picture and Ruskin stood over him, watching, Millais talked of his childhood. Half a page of the diary is devoted to these memories.

33 RF MS 8, p. 69.

26

Alastair Grieve has identified and photographed the actual site of the portrait.[34] A comparison of his photograph (Figure 13) with the portrait shows how exactly Millais *did* work on the background. Dr Grieve has explained that the upper part of Glenfinlas was submerged behind a dam in 1965, but the burn flowing below, through its deep ravine where the portrait was painted, remains unchanged. The site, which is private, is very small, there being scarcely room for three people and their painting equipment. The burn flows due north-south and Ruskin is depicted standing on the east side looking diagonally up stream. While posing, Ruskin was observing the site, and it is also interesting to compare his study of the gneiss rocks beyond the stream (Figure 14)[35] with Dr Grieve's photograph.

Millais continued to record their activities. On Sunday 31 July they went to the little kirk on the banks of Loch Achray (No. 31). The day was wet and on the same day Millais recorded the group walking along the edge of the loch in 'Awey-ye goo' (No. 30). In 'Cruel Treatment of a Master to his pupil' (No. 29) Millais tickles Effie's face with a fern frond while Ruskin looks on.

Figure 13

Figure 14

34 A. Grieve, 'Ruskin and Millais at Glenfinlas', *Burlington* (April 1996). The photograph is reproduced here by courtesy of Dr Grieve.

35 Now in the Ashmolean Museum, Oxford. There is also a preliminary study of the stream and lower rocks in the Whitehouse Collection.

Acland left on the next day and a spell of dry warm weather followed. Work on the portrait continued slowly, and Ruskin wrote to his father on 4 August 'I think that the picture will be particularly beautiful because there is no sun in it; all dark rocks with plants hanging down over them and foaming water below – and Everett paints so brightly that he cannot possibly have too quiet a subject'. Another sketch made about now (No. 32) shows Millais working at the portrait while Effie sits nearby reading Dante. Presumably the top right hand quarter of the sketch which has been cut away, must have contained Ruskin.

By the middle of August Ruskin was telling his father that work was continuing very slowly, that Millais was having trouble with the rocky foreground, and that it seemed improbable that it would be finished before Ruskin had to go to Edinburgh in November. The planned companion picture of Effie by the arched window at Doune Castle was going to be further delayed; meanwhile Millais was making constant sketches of Effie ostensibly so that he could later fit her into the Castle background. In the event, the Doune Castle portrait of Effie was never made, but the Glenfinlas portrait of Ruskin was given its arched top to make it match the proposed companion piece. To John James's enquiry as to how much the Glenfinlas portrait was going to cost him, John said that the price would probably be between £200 and £300.

The weather deteriorated again and work continued through September and into October, with further expeditions, adventures and sketches, such as 'Scottish bog exercise' (No. 33) with Millais, Ruskin and Wisie extracting themselves from the mire, and 'Getting Mama up a Ben' (No. 34) in which Ruskin, Effie and a host of small boys assist a rotund lady up a steep slope.

Writing to F.J. Furnivall about this time Ruskin spoke of the portrait.

> Millais is painting a picture of a torrent among rocks, which will make a revolution in landscape painting if he can only get it finished. It is not nearly done yet, and the cold is coming fast ... I have stopped all this time to keep Millais company, to keep him up to the Pre-Raphaelite degree of finish – which I have done with a vengance, as he has taken three months to do half a background two feet over, and perhaps won't finish it now. But I have got maps of all the lichens on the rocks, and the *bubbles* painted in the foam ...

29

30

31

The Ruskins left Brig o'Turk on 26 October to go to Edinburgh. Millais was left behind to finish the portrait, but he, too, left almost immediately, joining the Ruskins in Edinburgh where he remained for two of John's lectures. Up to now, the figure of Ruskin had only been blocked in, work having been concentrated on the stream and background. Millais intended to return to Scotland in March to finish the background, eventually returning there between 24 May and 23 June to finish the waterfall.

By the end of the Scottish holiday Millais and Effie were in love. When sittings were resumed in Gower Street on 12, 17, 19 and 21 April Millais' feelings towards his subject were hardly the same as they had been in the previous summer. Writing to Mrs Gray, Effie's mother, on 3 March 1854 he said that he was only going on with the portrait for Effie's sake. 'If I had only myself to consult', he said, '... [I would] refuse to go on with the portrait, which is the most hateful task I ever had to perform'.

Later he told Mrs Gray that he hoped to finish the sittings with John on 21 April, but in fact they were continued after Ruskin returned from the continent in the autumn.

Eventually the portrait was finished and on 11 December 1854 Ruskin wrote to Millais

> We have just got the picture placed – in I think the very light it wants ... I am far more delighted with it now than when I saw it in your rooms. As for the wonderment of the painting ... there can of course be no question ... On the whole the thing is right and what can one say more – always excepting the yellow flower and the over-large spark in the right eye, which I continue to reprobate – as having the effect of making me slightly squint ... But my father and mother say the like-

32

33

34

ness is perfect – but that I look bored – pale – and a little too yellow. Certainly after standing looking at the rows of chimnies in Gower Street for three hours – on one leg – it is no wonder …

Work on the portrait outlasted the Ruskins' marriage. On 25 April 1854 Effie left her husband and returned to her parents' home at Perth. In July the marriage was annulled on the grounds that it had not been consummated – and on 3 July 1855 Effie and Millais were married.

According to John James Ruskin's account book, he paid Millais £350 for the portrait on 4 December 1854 and wrote to him on 20 December saying that although it was his custom to pay an artist and a friend more than the asking price, on this occasion 'I must beg you will allow me to consider all accounts between you and me settled by my late payment'. He also refused to allow the portrait to be exhibited, and in fact it was never shown in public until 1884.

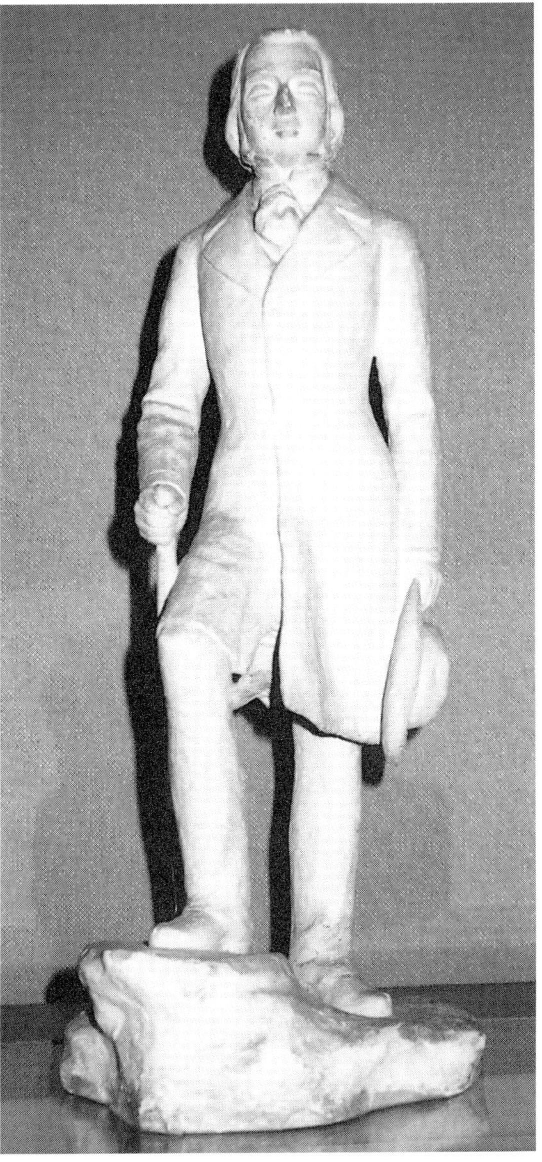

27

Ruskin's friends, Sir Walter and Lady Trevelyan, visited Denmark Hill probably on 22 January 1855 and saw the Glenfinlas portrait there. Neither of them cared for it as a likeness. Sir Walter thought that the portrait had a 'very unpleasing expression … tho' I do not like the subject of the background, a dark coloured rock with nearly invisible vegetation'. Lady Trevelyan admitted that the portrait was beautifully painted, but she considered the face 'detestable' while admitting that the 'figure is admirable'.[36]

The portrait remained in the Ruskin home at Denmark Hill where it is said to have been seen by a Mr Harrison on the day Effie and Millais were married. A couple of years later it was seen in Ruskin's bedroom. The story put about by Hall Caine of Ruskin's having to smuggle the portrait out of Denmark Hill to Rossetti's studio to protect it from his father's wrath is almost certainly apocryphal. It would be quite out of character for John James to destroy something which had cost him £350! When the Denmark Hill house was sold at the end of 1871, after both of his parents had died, Ruskin gave the portrait to Henry Acland, who hung it over the desk in his study. It remained in the Acland family for three generations until it was sold at Christie's on 16 July 1965 for a record 24,000 guineas.

No. 27 is a statue by K. Kitaji based on the Glenfinlas portrait. It was commissioned by Ryuzo Mikimoto, and it is in the Mikimoto Collection in Tokyo. For her book *Diary of a Victorian Cat*, Susan Herbert used the background of the Glenfinlas portrait in which to pose her frock-coated cat (No. 28) which stands there looking very like Ruskin. Her portrait is called 'Ruskin (Millais)'.

There is still one more portrait in the group made by Millais, to which reference has not yet been made. Effie's younger sister, Sophie Gray, returned to London with John and Effie at the end of 1853. We know from a letter written by Millais to Mrs Gray on 17 January 1854 that Sophie had been with John when he went to Gower Street for his sitting that morning. In addition to working on the Glenfinlas portrait on that occasion, Millais made a sketch of Sophie for Mrs Gray, and also made another sketch (No. 35) of Ruskin for his parents. Millais wrote

36 Virginia Surtees, *Reflections of a Friendship* (London: George Allen & Unwin, 1979), p. 97.

28

35

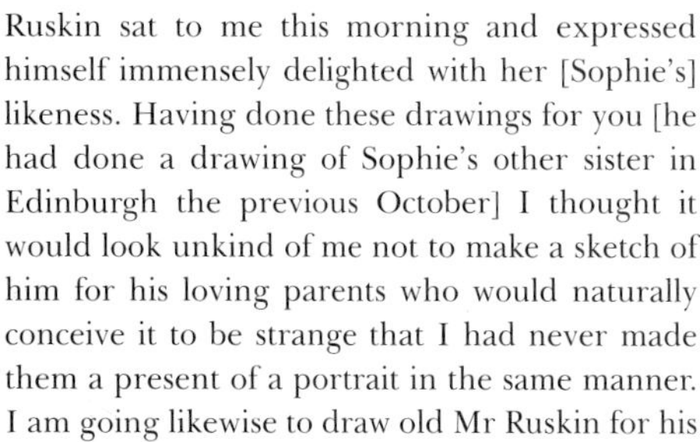
> Ruskin sat to me this morning and expressed himself immensely delighted with her [Sophie's] likeness. Having done these drawings for you [he had done a drawing of Sophie's other sister in Edinburgh the previous October] I thought it would look unkind of me not to make a sketch of him for his loving parents who would naturally conceive it to be strange that I had never made them a present of a portrait in the same manner. I am going likewise to draw old Mr Ruskin for his son who seems to be highly pleased at the notion of possessing a good likeness of his Father.

It seems unlikely that the portrait of John James was ever made. The present portrait of John remained in the Ruskin collection. Eventually it was inherited by the Severns and bought from Brantwood by F.J. Sharp. On his death it passed to Professor Viljoen, and eventually to the present owners, the Pierpont Morgan Library.

36 Sketch of Ruskin, 1856, by Edward Coley Burne-Jones (1833–1898).

When he was an undergraduate at Oxford, Burne-Jones became an ardent admirer of Ruskin's writings. In January 1856, Morris, Burne-Jones and others issued their *Oxford and Cambridge Magazine, conducted by Members of the two Universities*; Burne-Jones sent a copy to Ruskin with a request that he should become a contributor. Ruskin replied praising the magazine and promising to write for it. Burne-Jones was delighted and wrote to tell Cormell Price:

> I'm not Ted any longer, I'm not E.C.B. Jones now – I've dropped my personality – I'm a correspondent with RUSKIN, and my future title is 'The man who wrote to Ruskin and got an answer by return'. I can better draw my feelings than describe them, and better symbolise them than either.

Printing the letter in her biography of her husband[37], Georgiana Burne-Jones explained that beneath the letter 'is a drawing of himself prostrate on the ground before an aureoled and nimbused presence intended for Ruskin'. Unfortunately she did not reproduce the sketch, and the original is untraced.

37 Burne-Jones, *Memorials of Edward Burne-Jones*, vol. I, p. 127.

37–38 Photographs of John Ruskin, aet 37, 1856, by William Jeffrey

In the summer of 1853 there was a suggestion that the chapter 'On the Nature of Gothic architecture' from Ruskin's *Stones of Venice* – which William Morris later described as 'one of the very few necessary and inevitable utterances of the century' – should be re-printed as a pamphlet in its own right. But the plan was not fulfilled until October 1854 when it was re-printed by Furnivall and issued to all who attended the inauguration of the Working Men's College. The College, at first situated in Red Lion Square and later in Great Ormond Street, was begun under the leadership of the Rev. F.D. Maurice in order to bring to the working man the same kind of education available to the upper classes. Ruskin was persuaded to take the Art Class, which he did unaided from 2 November and thereafter on each Thursday evening for the rest of the term. Afterwards, such people as Rossetti, Ford Maddox Brown and Burne-Jones assisted from time to time. Ruskin taught drawing there from 1854 until 1858, returning for the spring term of 1860. He also acted as a member of the Council for a number of years.

A.J. Mumby recorded in his diary seeing Ruskin at the College on 8 November 1860 talking to Lushington about his ideas on social and political economy. He told him of things he would have written in *Unto this last* in the *Cornhill* 'only Thackeray wouldn't let him.' Ruskin described J.S. Mill as a 'a fine fellow but whose brain was full of confused fancies'. Mumby explained that while he was speaking Ruskin was rising up and down on his toes 'after his manner, with his hands in his tail pockets'. Finally Ruskin jaunted downstairs in the same springy fashion 'with the prim smile of Sir Oracle upon his dry lips'.

William Michael Rossetti, brother of Dante Gabriel, who was a careful and accurate recorder of fact and Diarist to the Pre-Raphaelite Brotherhood, attended Ruskin's early lectures at the Working Men's College, and has left his impression of Ruskin.[38]

> My own first sight of Ruskin was in November 1854, when he delivered some lectures, which I attended, upon matters of art. Ruskin was then nearly thirty six years of age, of fair stature, exceedingly thin (I have sometimes laid a light grasp on his coat-sleeve, and there seemed to be next to nothing inside it), narrow-shouldered, with a clear, bright complexion, very thick yellow hair, beetling eyebrows (which he inherited from his father), and side-whiskers. His nose was acute and prominent, his eyes blue and limpid, the general expression of his face singularly keen, with an ample allowance of self-confidence, but without that hard and unindulgent air which sometimes accompanies keenness. His mouth was unshapely, having (as I was afterwards informed) been damaged by the bite of a dog in early childhood. He had a sunny smile, however, which went far to atoning for any defect in the mouth. The cheek-bones were prominent, the facial angle receding somewhat below the tip of the nose. As my brother's report of Ruskin's personal appearance had never been eulogistic, I was agreeably impressed by what I saw of his looks, as well as by his voice and manner. There was a perceptibly Scottish tone in his speech, with a slight Northumbrian burr. As a public speaker he was at times most eloquent, and he never failed to be interesting and engaging; in fact, the extreme interest of his personality pervaded all that he said, and insured its acceptance from, at any rate, that point of view. I was by the end of 1854 a most ardent admirer of Ruskin's writings (unknown to me, as to almost all the P.R.B.s when the Brotherhood was first formed); and so I listened to his utterances as a lecturer with the liveliest

37

38 I am grateful to Miss Lutyens for drawing to my attention this extract from W.M. Rossetti, *Some Reminiscences* (London: Brown, Langham, 1906), vol. I, p. 177.

gratification and respect. At one of these lectures I became known to Ruskin, and was shortly invited to dine with himself and his parents in their house at Denmark Hill, Camberwell. The house was a well-looking detached edifice, white, with a pillared front, situate in its own spacious garden grounds.

I recollect Ruskin's father very well – a spare man, hardly up to middle height, of straightforward, observant aspect, and alert, frank address. He had a full crop of bristly grey hair and very bushy dark eyebrows. He was (as many of my readers will know) a sherry-merchant who, rising from small beginnings, had made an ample fortune; in one instance he brought to table some old Amontillado sherry which had been on board the 'Victory' when Nelson fell in the battle of Trafalgar. I drank the historical liquor with a due sense of satisfaction, but its flavour was almost gone. Mrs Ruskin, the mother, was a lady well advanced in years, of rather imposing presence; in her manner there was a certain reserved decorum mingled with essential kindliness. John Ruskin was at this time a strict Christian believer of the anti-Romanist order; no doubt his parents were the same, and I take it that any wilful intrusion of a contrary opinion would have been anything but welcome to them. There was something touching in the family relation between 'John' and his parents. He was necessarily regarded by them as a 'shining light' who had done and would continue to do very considerable things in the realm of thought; none the less he was their boy, living *en famille* as the subordinate member of the household. And his demeanour, so far as I ever witnessed it, was in full conformity with this estimate of the filial relation. I saw Ruskin pretty frequently between the years 1855 and 1860; chiefly at his own house, sometimes in my brother's studio or elsewhere. After this our meetings were fewer.

Did I like Ruskin? Most assuredly I did. His manner to me was gentle in the extreme, and almost profusely amiable, with more 'sentiment' in its tone than I had been used to in other circles; there was very little of that in the P.R.B. I did not find him dictatorial or pragmatic; but one element in our relative position was the tacit assumption on both sides that he knew a great deal about matters in which I also was interested, and that my cue was to profit by what he could and would impart to me. Founding upon this assumption, I held an intercourse with Ruskin both easy and alluring. There was no pretence on my part of unqualified acceptance of every word of wisdom that fell from his lips: I gave expression to my own opinions, with deference but also with candour.

Sir William B. Richmond, George's son, also remembered Ruskin from about now.

The first time that I remember seeing him was when I was about ten years old. Mr Ruskin used to come to my father's house to what we called 'high tea', ... How well I remember the gaunt delicate looking young man, not yet 40, with a profusion of reddish hair, shaggy eyebrows like a Scotch terrier, under them gleaming eyes which bore within them a strange light, the like of which I have never seen, except in his. A hooked nose denoting energy and will, nostrils arched and mobile, sensitive as those of a thoroughbred horse; and, be it said frankly, a singularly unattractive mouth ... He had a habit of sitting very low down in his chair, indeed reclining in it, with his head delved in the recesses of his chest.[39]

Charles Eliot Norton, who first met Ruskin at Denmark Hill in November 1855 and who eventually became one of his literary executors, also recorded his impressions.[40]

He was at this time thirty-six years old ... His abundant light-brown hair, his blue eyes, and his fresh complexion gave him a young look for his age; he was a little above middle height, his figure was slight, his movements were quick and alert, and his whole air and manner had a definite and attractive individuality. There was nothing in him of the common English reserve and stiffness, and no self-consciousness or sign of consideration for himself as a man of distinction, but rather, on the contrary, a seeming self-forgetfulness and an almost feminine sensitiveness and readiness of sympathy. His features were irregular, but the lack of beauty was made up for by the kindness of his look, and the expressiveness of his full and mobile lips.

Among the young men that Ruskin taught at the Working Men's College, some of whom also taught there themselves, were W.H. Hooper, the engraver, George Allen, a carpenter who went on to become a wood-engraver, mezzotint engraver, and later Ruskin's publisher, Arthur Burgess, another wood-engraver, John Bunney, an artist who spent much of his life painting in Venice, and

39 Sir W.B. Richmond, 'Ruskin as I knew him', *St George* V, p. 287.

40 C.E. Norton (ed.), *Letters of John Ruskin to Charles Eliot Norton* (Boston and New York: Houghton Mifflin, 1904), vol. I, pp. 4-5.

William Ward who helped Ruskin as a copyist and who remembered him as 'fair and somewhat slightly built, with deep penetrating eyes, and an inexpressible charm of manner'.[41]

William Jeffrey was also in Ruskin's class; he went on to teach at the Working Men's College himself and became an 'artistic photographer, and the College Photographic artist'. He photographed many of the people originally associated with the college and in 1856 took what are almost certainly the first two photographs of Ruskin.

In the first photograph (No. 37) Ruskin is seated with his elbow resting on a table and with the long watch-chain that he wore round his neck tangled round one of the buttons of his open frock-coat. A second, tidier, exposure was taken, with Ruskin facing the camera and with his jacket buttoned (No. 38). Ruskin gave a copy of the first photograph to George Allen who relates that Ruskin, 'on seeing the proof, was so disagreeably struck by the effect produced by the accidental twisting of his watch-chain round his coat button, and by the affected position of the hand, that he ordered the negative to be destroyed, although he was not dissatisfied with the likeness'.[42] The negative may have been destroyed, though Allen reproduced the photograph in 1900 in Attwell's *Thoughts from Ruskin*, and the print (now in my possession) from which the present reproduction is made, came from George Allen's collection.

A print of the second exposure, reproduced here, is still in the archives of the Working Men's College. Another, still at the Trevelyan home at Wallington and now owned by the National Trust, was given to Lady Trevelyan. On 1 January 1861 Ruskin wrote to her about it.[43]

38

> It was very naughty of you carrying off that frightful photograph with hanging lip. I won't scold Jeffrey however. I cannot think what it is that has made me so very ugly: I suppose that the kinds of instincts which enjoy colour and form are wholly sensual, and have the same effect on the features as mere love of eating or any other passion: – then I never have had any of my kindly feelings developed. (My best friends taking delight in Tormenting me – like some people I could name). – and so they – the pretty feelings – have all got crushed into a shapeless – wide comfortless and useless philanthropy which will not show in the face: – but the savagery which you rightly say Richmond has left out – though it is savagery against evil, is just as ugly as if it were savagery against good. The total want of wit and imagination lowers the forehead: there must however somewhere be evidence of some mathematical power: (for no one of my standing in my college knew his geometry as I did) but I don't know where it is; finally the irregular work of my life and its impulsive character have taken away what firmness there might have been in the mouth; and disappointment of all kinds – and dyspepsia – have destroyed any gleam of cheerfulness or colour that might have redeemed the shapelessness. After all – it is no wonder the photograph tells such a story...

41 W.C. Ward (ed.), *John Ruskin's Letters to William Ward* (Boston: Marshall Jones, 1922), p. 34.

42 See Henry Attwell (ed.), *Thoughts from Ruskin* (London: George Allen, 1900).

43 Bodleian MS Eng. Lett. C. 34.

39 John Ruskin, aet c.37, c.1856, perhaps by Henry Swan (1825–1889)

Henry Swan was another member of Ruskin's art class at the Working Men's College. Born in Devizes in 1825 he was apprenticed as an engraver and was to engrave the plates for Sir Isaac Pitman's book on shorthand. Photography attracted Swan's attention and in the late '50s and early '60s, probably the time when he was attending evening classes at the Working Men's College, he was concentrating on building up his photographic business in Regent Street. He perfected and patented in 1862 the 'casket portrait'. This was a type of miniature portrait; by using prisms the image appeared three dimensional and solid. Swan had wide interests. He invented systems of musical notation and phonetic spelling; he was a vegetarian, a Quaker and a Spiritualist. He was an early cyclist, and tried (and failed) to popularise the sport of boomerang throwing as an athletic exercise. Ruskin must have respected his artistic ability; he was an accomplished illuminator, and while he was living in London he made a number of copies from medieval manuscripts in the British Museum for Ruskin.[44] By 1856 he, in conjunction with R.P. Cuff, had engraved the plate of borders and initials from Ruskin's 14th century manuscript *Hours of Yoland of Navarre*, to form plate 9 of *Modern Painters* III. Ruskin described Swan as 'an honest though somewhat dreamy person' while George Allen succinctly described him as a 'crank'.[45]

By the 1870s Swan had moved to Sheffield in search of work as an engraver of silver and plate. He was already in correspondence with Ruskin about the latter's developing plans for the Guild of St George. In September 1875 Ruskin visited Sheffield in order to see Swan. At his home in Walkley, Swan had brought together a group of Sheffield working men who were interested in social reform. Robert Hewison has explained[46] how, following this meeting, Ruskin bought a small house in Walkley to form the Guild's museum. Swan was installed in the house as Curator, a post which he occupied successfully until his death in March 1889.

39

The authorship of the present portrait is uncertain. It is unsigned but its subject is indicated by the initials 'J.R.'. For this reason it was at one time thought to be by Ruskin. An old label on it records that it was once owned by Swan, who gave it to Charles Green. In turn, Green sold it in 1915 to a Mr Winder. He gave it to the Sheffield painter Charles Howarth, whose widow offered to sell it to the Graves Art Gallery in July 1980, assuming it to be the work of Ruskin. In view of its provenance, I suggest that it may well be the work of Swan. Indeed perhaps it was drawn by Swan at the Working Men's College art class while Ruskin stared intently at the work of one of the students.

44 Most of my information about Swan is taken from Janet Barnes, *Ruskin in Sheffield* (Sheffield: Sheffield Arts Department, 1985), p. 13.

45 See R. Hewison, *Art and Society. Ruskin in Sheffield 1876* (London: Routledge & Kegan Paul, 1979).

46 See Hewison, *Art and Society.*

40 Caricature of Ruskin leading a group of artists, c.1856, by William J. Hodgson (fl.1878–1903)

Ruskin's teaching at the Working Men's College was not restricted to the weekly art class. Sometimes there were expeditions, and perhaps on occasions the class (certainly individual members) visited Ruskin's home to see his pictures.

On 9 September 1855 Ruskin invited F.J. Furnivall to accompany them on one such expedition:

> ... I think you would like to come out with one of my sketching parties. I am only going to have two more, the next, D.V., on Saturday next. Cabs at Camberwell Green at half past three. Tea at the Greyhound Inn, Dulwich at seven. Come early or late as you find convenient, if you can come at all...[47]

I am grateful to Mr Alan Turvey for drawing the present caricature to my attention. It is doubly interesting because not only is it the earliest caricature of Ruskin that I know, it may well also record one of the Working Men's College excursions. The sketch is inscribed 'We all believe what our leader says. We account him infallible, every word that he says whether it be sense or nonsense has some deep and hidden meaning in it'. The paper has been folded twice, probably to enable it to fit into an envelope. A later owner has added 'Drawn by Willie Hodgson'. Hodgson became an illustrator and a black and white sporting artist. He worked for *Punch* in the 1890s.

40

41–43 Sketches and Portrait of John Ruskin, aet 38, 1857 by George Richmond

After the first meeting of Ruskin and Richmond in Rome in 1840, a close friendship sprang up which was to last for many years. Their paths were often to cross. In April 1857 for example, when Ruskin was called to give evidence before the Commission which was sitting to determine a site for the National Gallery, Richmond was among the commissioners sitting at the hearing. By this time he had already drawn John's portrait as 'The Author of *Modern Painters*' and had made a portrait of John James Ruskin[48] in 1847 as a wedding present for John.

The present portrait was commissioned by John James. We know from Richmond's diary and sitters' book, transcripts of which are in the National Portrait Gallery, that it was proposed on 4 February 1857 and accepted on the following day. There were seven sittings, beginning on 24 February. John James notes in his diary that he had been 'To See John's Portrait' on 18 March, and ten days later the portrait was finished. It must have been paid for immediately because John James's account book[49] records that he paid £42 for it in March, and also gave 'GR 1 doz wine'. The picture-framer's bill for £5 2s was, incidentally, not settled until 10 July. The portrait was duly hung in the Academy in the same year.

John James evidently was well pleased by the portraits of his son, and in 1858 he had it engraved by Francis Holl.[50] His diary for 8 May 1858 notes that he had seen 'John's proof at F. Holl'. On 5 June John James wrote to his son in Switzerland:

> Your picture done – and we are to have 12 proofs soon. Your autograph will go on it. The impressions cost about 31/6. It is a Capital Head only he has pulled your Lips more than you have done yourself. It is the only defect – making it full large as if you had a Cold but the Eyes and nose and Style of Dress Capital. – It is what Richmond says a portrait should be: The Truth Lovingly told.

47 T.J. Wise (ed.), *Letters from John Ruskin to Frederick J. Furnivall M.A., and other correspondents*, p. 58.

48 Now in the Whitehouse Collection.

49 RF MS 28.

50 The cost is in doubt. JJR's accounts (RF MS 29) record '1858 May Holl eng. Johns Portrait £40 £23'. It is possible that the first figure was for the plate and the second for the proofs of the engravings. There are prints of the engraving at Brantwood, Ruskin College, Oxford, and in the collection of General Goff Hamilton.

43

John had not been as enthusiastic as his father about having his portrait reproduced, and he added a footnote to his letter of 1 June, '*No* portrait is ever to go with any of my volumes, that I have anything to do with'.[51]

On 12 June John James noted in his diary 'Johns picture Eng[ravings] came home'. The original drawing must have been returned a little earlier because on 11 June JJR had told John that 'It occupies well the place of your large Rouen Architecture [drawing] – so you are in the centre of a Circle of Turner ... We have you all the Evening in Drawing Room'.[52]

The engraving was published on 15 June 1858 and was available at two guineas as a Colombier proof, or as an Imperial print at one guinea. It was published by Ruskin's publisher, Smith Elder & Co., and was advertised in the *Elements of Perspective*, *The Two Paths*, the *Oxford Museum* and *Academy Notes*, all published in 1859. Holl also engraved a smaller plate, and despite John's injunction it was printed for the first time as the frontispiece to the 1861 edition of Ruskin's *Selections*. It must however be added that the 'Advertisement' to *Selections* notes that 'The Publishers think it right to add that Mr Ruskin, though tacitly consenting to this publication, has taken no part in making the selections, and is in no way responsible for the appearance of the volume'. In fact the extracts were chosen by W. Smith Williams, the publisher's Reader.

It was John James Ruskin's custom to maintain a long list of the recipients of complimentary copies of his son's books[53] and in the same pages he recorded a dated list of the friends to whom India proofs of the portrait were presented.

18 June 1858	*gave*	*1*	*portrait to*	*MacDonald* [54]
19	-	*1*	-	*J.R. Richardson*[55]
		1	-	*R. Gray*[56]
22	-	*1*	-	*Dr Richardson*[57]
29	-	*1*	-	*Tweddales*[58]
30		*1*	-	*Lady Colquhoun*[59]
	-	*1*	-	*Dr Acland*[60]
		1	-	*Lady Trevelyan*[61]
		1	-	*Mrs Edwardes*[62]
		1	-	*John has*[63]
		1	-	*Mrs R[uskin]*
		1	-	*JJR[uskin]*
		12		

not proofs 4 servants

Towards the end of Ruskin's life, Mary Wakefield recorded[64] that this portrait by Richmond, together with Richmond's 1848 portrait of John James Ruskin both hung in Joan Severn's bedroom at

51 J. Hayman (ed.), *John Ruskin. Letters from the Continent 1858* (Toronto: University of Toronto Press, 1982), p. 26.

52 J. Hayman (ed.), *John Ruskin. Letters from the Continent 1858*, (1982) p. 47.

53 In his diary, RF MS 33.

54 William MacDonald with whom John had stayed at Crossmount in 1847 just before his marriage and who was perhaps John's closest friend at this time. MacDonald was the son of John James's old friend Mrs James Farquharson (born Rebecca Colquhoun) and had changed his name to Farquharson-MacDonald-MacDonald, on inheriting St Martin's Abbey, Perth, from his cousin in 1841. Elsewhere in his diary John James has recorded MacDonald's visit to Denmark Hill and that he 'gave him proof John and Box Cigars'.

55 John Ruskin Richardson, 1807–74, eldest son of JJR's sister, Janet Richardson.

56 Richard Gray, a friend of JJR's youth, who eventually lived near the Ruskins. John Ruskin described Mr and Mrs Gray as being among the friends who 'were most powerfully influential on my child life'.

57 Dr William Richardson, fifth son (and younger brother of J.R. Richardson) of JJR's sister.

58 JJR's mother had been born Catherine Tweddale. Her eldest brother had thirteen children (JJR's cousins). Which was the recipient of the portrait is uncertain, but in this case and in the case of Lady Colquhoun, JJR had it framed at a cost of 42s.

59 Lady Colquhoun was a frequent visitor to Denmark Hill and appears in other 'presentation' lists. She could have been related to William MacDonald's mother.

60 Dr Henry Acland, John's Oxford friend who had been at Glenfinlas when the Millais portrait was begun.

61 Lady Trevelyan of Wallington, Northumberland, who appears frequently in the story of the portraits.

62 Mrs Edwardes, formerly Emma Sidney, stepdaughter of Dr George Grant, who married (Sir) Herbert Edwardes, and to whose sister, Mrs Thomas Hayes, one of the 1841 cameos of JR had been given.

63 JJR had prints framed for his wife and son at a cost of 30s. each and for himself at 23s. He always seemed to keep his picture framer waiting. Payment of the account for framing the engravings is dated September 1858.

64 Mary Wakefield, 'Brantwood, Coniston, John Ruskin's Home', *Murray's Magazine*, November 1890, vol. 8, pp. 587-606.

41

42

Brantwood. At the dispersal sale at Sotheby's on 29 May 1931 this portrait by Richmond was lot 29 and was sold for £33 to Stevens and Brown, acting on behalf of Charles Goodspeed, for whom they also bought 'The Author of *Modern Painters*', and, like that picture, it is assumed to have perished in Goodspeed's fire.

The sketches for the portrait (Nos. 41 and 42) found their way into the collection of Henry Yates Thompson who also later owned several of Ruskin's finest medieval manuscripts. The sketches remained unknown to Ruskin scholarship until they were sold at Christie's in 1985.

44

44 Portrait head, aet 38, c.1857, by George Richmond (Plate 11)

This portrait was probably drawn about the same time as No. 43. It remained in the artist's possession during his lifetime and after his death in 1896 it was bought from his executors by the present owner, the National Portrait Gallery.

45 Miniature, c.1857, by Samuel John Stump (c.1783–1863)

Stump was a miniaturist and landscape painter who painted many portraits of stage personalities. I have been unable to trace any connection between him and the Ruskin family. The only reference to the present portrait which I know occurs in a letter written by S.J. Pegg of Leicester to J. Howard Whitehouse in 1919. At the time Whitehouse was arranging the Ruskin Centenary Exhibition to be held at the Royal Academy, and Pegg offered him

> ... a very interesting miniature of Ruskin when a young man. It was painted by the artist who painted Ruskin's mother (S.J. Stump). The portrait of Ruskin by Richmond in the National Gallery [No. 45] is very like my miniature.

Whitehouse appears to have been uncertain about the miniature and he sent it to Collingwood for his opinion.

> Thanks for the miniature received this morning. I have written to Mr Pegg asking for any information about it, and for leave to keep it a few days, to show to Mrs Severn. It might be a 'bogus' from an engraving, intended to represent Ruskin; but I don't think the hair at the back is quite his colour. A good many portraits have turned up, purporting to be of him, but only representing people of the period and in the costume he would or might have worn.

The consensus of opinion must have been against the miniature being of Ruskin and the offer must have been rejected for the miniature did not feature in the catalogues of the 1919 exhibitions in either Coniston or London. Neither the miniature of John, nor the portrait of his mother, have been traced. There is no reference to them in John James's accounts, nor in his lists of his picture collection.

46 Caricature, 'A Nightmare', May 1857, by Frederick Sandys (1829–1904)

Ruskin's championship of the Pre-Raphaelites in 1851 perhaps helped them to achieve prominence earlier than they would otherwise have done. But his name was by now securely linked to the Brotherhood. He had for years advocated honesty in painting and care in detail – qualities which he had found and admired in the Pre-Raphaelites. Thus he was disappointed when he found anything of a quality which was less than he expected.

When Ruskin visited the Royal Academy exhibition in 1857, in addition to Richmond's portrait of himself, he saw two pictures by Millais. One was entitled 'A Dream of the Past – Sir Isumbras at the ford'. This picture (Figure 15), which shows a knight in armour fording a river on his horse and carrying with him a girl and a small boy, was painted in Scotland. The horse gave Millais considerable trouble and was re-painted several times between 1856 and 1892. But the background, according to Effie Millais, was painted in a fortnight. What a change from the slow meticulously detailed work of the Glenfinlas portrait of three years earlier.

At the exhibition, 'Sir Isumbras' attracted almost universally adverse criticism in the press. Millais wrote to Effie, 'Ruskin, I hear, has a pamphlet in the press which takes a pitying tone at my failure'. One must stress here that any criticism on Ruskin's part was unaffected by his personal relationship with Millais as a result of his marriage with Effie. Millais wished to have nothing further to do with Ruskin, but Ruskin on the other hand could not understand this attitude and considered that the affair should make no difference to, at least, their professional relationship. Thus Millais both resented and took to heart Ruskin's criticism when he read it in Ruskin's annual pamphlet *Academy Notes*. 'Ruskin', Millais told Spielmann, 'said it was not a failure but a fiasco, so I kicked it over in a passion. The hole is there now'.

Certainly Ruskin was hard on the painting, and wrote 'The change in his manner from the years of "Ophelia" and "Mariana" to 1857, is not merely Fall – it is Catastrophe; not merely a loss of power, but a reversal of principle; his excellence has been effaced, 'as a man wipeth a dish – wiping it, and turning it upside down'. There may still be in him power of repentance but I cannot tell'. After such a beginning, Ruskin went on for several pages in detailed and adverse criticism, so Millais probably hardly noticed that towards the end Ruskin said that nevertheless his pictures were among the best in the Academy!

> As it stands, it can only be considered as a rough sketch of a great subject, injudiciously exposed to general criticism, and needing both modification

in its arrangement and devoted labour in its future realisation. I am sorrowfully doubtful, however, how far Mr Millais may yet be capable of such labour. For Mr Millais there is no hope but in return to quiet perfectness of work. I cannot bring myself to believe that powers were given to him only to be wasted, which are so great, even in their abberation, that no pictures in the Academy are so interesting as these, or can be for a moment compared with them for occasional excellence and marvellousness of execution.

46

Figure 15

One piece of criticism of the painting took the form of a parody on both the picture and the Pre-Raphaelite movement. This large print was by Frederick Sandys and it was published on 4 May 1857 by Ruskin's publisher, Smith Elder. (We do not know what John James thought of their publishing a lampoon of his son, but no doubt he made some very acid comments). The humorous verses attached to Sandys's skit were possibly written by Tom Taylor, the art critic, who had written the lines on Sir Isumbras for Millais which appeared in the Academy catalogue!

In the parody the knight's head has been replaced by a portrait of Millais himself, while the girl and the boy with a bundle of sticks on his back are transformed into the two other leading members of the PRB – Rossetti and Holman Hunt. Instead of sticks Hunt has a bundle of brushes on his back. The knight's sword is changed into a mawlstick and his dangling helmet into a paint pot bearing the initials PRB. The two nuns walking along the river-bank have become Michaelangelo, Titian and Raphael, who cry 'Orate pro nobis'. And the horse, which gave so much trouble, has become a braying ass, carrying the Pre-Raphaelites, with 'JR Oxon' branded on its flank.

The parody was a success and sold well. Writing on 10 June 1857 to Upperton, Walter Severn said:

> I think you will agree with me that it is one of the cleverest things of the kind ever produced … I know you admire Millais' picture very much … but the faults are so glaring that I must say he deserves this rap over the knuckles … I have seldom seen anything so well drawn, the background especially is so beautifully etched … I am told it is selling like wildfire.[65]

In his introduction to the catalogue of the 1973 Sandys exhibition held at the Brighton Art Gallery, Raymond Wilkinson notes that the caricature was printed from a zinc plate, probably by the anastatic process which was then popular. The process was a quick and cheap adaptation of the lithographic process, which would have appealed to the chronically hard-up Sandys.

65 The letter is quoted in *Ian Hodgkins's Catalogue* 79, Spring 1995, no. 376.

47 Portrait with Louisa Stewart-Mackenzie, aet 38, July 1857, by William Bell Scott (1811–1890) (Plate 12)

47

Ruskin was busy in the summer of 1857 preparing lectures. On 6 May he addressed the Society of Arts on Thomas Seddon, and in July he went to Manchester where an important Art Treasures exhibition was being held. He had been invited to lecture and he chose as his subject 'Art considered as Wealth'. There were two lectures, one on the 10th and the second on the 13th, published later in the year as *The Political Economy of Art*, a title which lasted for three editions, but when Ruskin prepared the lectures for inclusion in his Collected Works Series in 1880, he re-named them *A Joy for Ever, and its price on the market*.

From Manchester Ruskin was to join his parents in Edinburgh for a tour of the Scottish Highlands. On his way there he broke his journey at Wallington where he stayed with the Trevelyans from 15 to 21 July. At Wallington he saw the recently completed major alterations to the house, including the roofing over of the central courtyard to form a new central hall. Ruskin had contributed to the planning of these alterations by suggesting that the upper balustrade should be copied from one at Murano. The new central hall was decorated with scenes illustrating the history of Northumberland, by the minor artist, William Bell Scott. Scott was a master in the Government School of Design at Newcastle, and Ruskin had already met him at the Working Men's College where the two men had disagreed about methods of teaching art. Their feelings for each other were not improved when Lady Trevelyan told Scott to check his proposed plans for the decoration at Wallington with Ruskin. Ruskin found Scott at Wallington on his 1857 visit. Also staying there was Louisa Stewart-Mackenzie who was soon to marry Lord Ashburton. She was the friend of Effie who, it will be remembered, was staying at Wallington in 1853 when the Ruskins and the Millais brothers had called there *en route* for Glenfinlas.

During the visit of 1857 Ruskin gave some drawing lessons to Louisa Stewart-Mackenzie and Scott has recorded one of the lessons in the present portrait. The lower of the two inscriptions, 'Etching with a lithographic pen by way of giving a lesson in Drawing' is probably the contemporary one, and interestingly Ruskin is shown holding the pen between his thumb and index finger, whereas we have already seen that he did not normally hold it in this way. The second inscription, 'John Ruskin & Miss Stuart Mackenzie. Wallington – July 1864, W.B.S.' was probably a later addition, Scott mistaking the year.

The portrait was in the possession of Scott's friend Alice Boyd of Penkill Castle, and descended to Miss E.M. Courtney-Boyd. After her death it came into the possession of the National Trust and is now exhibited at Wallington.

48–50 Portraits, c.1857, by Thomas Richmond

When George Richmond painted Ruskin in 1843 as 'The Author of *Modern Painters*', Ruskin was beginning to become a prominent figure in the art world. This success sprang from the publication of the first volume of *Modern Painters* which began as a defence of J.M.W. Turner. The book, and the Ruskins' passion for collecting Turner's watercolours, led to a meeting between artist and patrons. What was probably a one-sided friendship sprang up – and when Turner died in 1851 Ruskin found himself one of the executors of Turner's will. Turner left some 19,000 sketches to the nation together with a substantial sum of money to establish a Turner Gallery, a scheme which Ruskin heartily applauded. But Turner's relations disputed the will, and Ruskin, wishing to have no part in the family squabble, renounced his executorship. Not until 1856 was the dispute settled. While he was in Scotland in 1857 Ruskin heard from Wornum saying that he could at last begin his planned work on the drawings of the Turner Bequest. He cut short his holiday and returned to begin the task in the basement of the National Gallery, of sorting, cataloguing and mounting selected examples of the drawings, a task which was to keep him busy well into the spring of 1858. He was helped in this work by two of his Working Men's College pupils, George Allen and William Ward. Allen told Cook and Wedderburn[66]

> I was at work altogether on the task for eight months. Mr Ruskin was very jealous of anyone but his own assistants touching the drawings, lest harm should befall them. After our day's work at the Gallery Mr Ruskin and I used to take the measurements of drawings to Denmark Hill, when I cut with my own hands about 800 thick passe-partout mounts – these were taken to the Gallery and the drawings inserted there.

It was about this time that the last in the series of portraits by the Richmond brothers were made. Cook and Wedderburn date as about 1857 a life sized head in oils by Tom Richmond, then (1912) in the possession of John Ruskin Richmond, the artist's son and Ruskin's god-son. There was also a smaller oil portrait of Ruskin's head in the possession of Richmond's daughter, Mrs G.H. Wollaston. Cook and Wedderburn also note a watercolour sketch for this latter. If they saw these portraits, they did not describe them and do not appear to have had them photographed.

At about this time Ruskin had meet Ellen Heaton, an enthusiastically artistic lady of Leeds. Tom Richmond had painted her portrait in 1849 and Virginia Surtees has suggested[67] that it was probably Richmond who introduced her to Ruskin, at her instigation. In the ensuing correspondence between Ruskin and Heaton there are a number of references to Richmond and to portraits. Writing on 20 December 1861 Ruskin said 'Mr Richmond is very kind in often going to see my father and mother. We will get the portrait finished'. Is it possible that Ellen Heaton had commissioned a portrait of Ruskin?

Of this group of portraits, the only description we have is by Mrs C. Shepherd, Richmond's granddaughter. Her father, G.H. Wollaston, was a geologist and a member of the staff at Clifton, Mrs Shepherd remembered[68] '... In a rather dark corner of the dining room was his [Ruskin's] portrait as a young man by my grandfather; a strange face with a loose mouth, fair hair and a loose tie'.[69]

In another draft for her talk[70] Mrs Shepherd said 'We had a portrait head and shoulders of Mr Ruskin as a young man which came to us about 1932 from my uncle.[71] None of us had any room to hang it and it wasn't a very good picture so it was put into a sale at Harrod's with my uncle's things. There was no bid for it – so we went to fetch it away. It had vanished without trace! So evidently someone *did* want a portrait of Mr Ruskin and got it'.

Evidently Tom Richmond's descendants were no more impressed by Ruskin's appearance than was Oscar Browning.

> The first time I ever saw Ruskin was on October 29, 1858, when he delivered his address to inaugurate the Cambridge School of Art. I remember his appearance in the old Guildhall, young and slim, and in no way remarkable.[72]

66 *Works* XIII, p. xxxvi.
67 See V. Surtees (ed.), *Sublime and Instructive* (London: Michael Joseph, 1972), pp. 146, 232, 235.
68 In a talk in the BBC series 'Listen awhile' on 24 October 1964.
69 This description probably refers to No. 50.
70 Sent to the author in 1967.
71 Presumably No. 48.
72 Oscar Browning, 'Personal Recollections of John Ruskin', *St George* VI, p. 136; a lecture given to the Ruskin Union on 12 Dec. 1902.

51 Caricature, c.1860, by James Smetham (1821–1889)

James Smetham, although a painter and etcher whose work was influenced by Linnell and Palmer, is now mainly known as the writer of a few articles and as the friend of Rossetti and Ruskin. Perhaps perversely however, his biographer W.H. Davies lists the adverse influences in his life as photography, Pre-Raphaelitism and Ruskinism.

Smetham read *Modern Painters* and met Ruskin in 1854 having attended one of his lectures, probably at the Working Men's College where he joined Ruskin's art class. On 5 February 1855 he was writing to a friend describing his visit to Denmark Hill.[73] He describes how he walked there through wintery weather and found 'a large house with a lodge, and a valet and a footman and coachman, and grand rooms glittering with pictures, chiefly Turner's.' John James Ruskin he considered 'a fine old gentleman, who has a lot of bushy grey hair and eyebrows sticking up all rough and knowing, with a comfortable way of coming up to you with his hands in his pockets, and making you comfortable ...' Smetham dined with the Ruskins and was shown the Turners and other treasures.

Smetham considered Ruskin one of the two most influential people he knew. He thought that the perfect critic, like the ideal artist, should be a good Christian. In Smetham's opinion the only living Englishman to fit the bill was Ruskin because he was endowed with 'what is called "the painter's eye". He can SEE. He knows how things LOOK in their subtlest changes of aspect ... He is thoroughly earnest, fearless, reverent, and simple'. Smetham admitted that although Ruskin had sometimes 'given vexation to enough artists ... he has done them material service, not only in the way of suggestions applicable to their own practice, but in the vastly enlarged interest in which his works have awakened in the mind of the reading public, and which have made the artist's life greatly more easy'.[74]

Smetham's caricature of Ruskin must have been drawn at about this time.

52 Head and shoulders image of Ruskin as a portrait in 'The Choice of Paris: An Idyll', 1860, by Florence Anne Claxton (fl.1859–1879)

Florence Anne Claxton was a figure painter and illustrator who in 1859 had signed the petition appealing to the Royal Academy to open its Schools to women. In the same year she had exhibited her 'Scenes of Life of an Old Maid' at the Society of Women Artists' exhibition. In the previous year she had shown her 'Scenes from the Life of the Female Artist' at the Society's second exhibition.

The present *tour de force*[75] ridicules Pre-Raphaelite principles through caricatures of Pre-Raphaelite pictures which had been exhibited in London during previous years. In its overall composition it imitates Holman Hunt's 'Converted British Family sheltering a Christian Missionary from the persecution of the Druids'. Many artists and their paintings are parodied in the painting. In the left background two gentlemen of the press, wearing dunces' hats, kneel before portraits of Millais, Barnum ('There's a sucker born every minute.') and Ruskin, identifiable from his blue tie and the rays of light which emanate from him. Prostrate before Ruskin is Sir Isumbras, while above, the three portraits of Van Dyck, Raphael and Reynolds have been turned to the wall.

53 Sketch of Ruskin aet 41, 1860, by Ann Mary Severn (1832–1866)

Titian's painting of 'Bacchus and Ariadne' was one of Ruskin's favourites in the National Gallery. There are frequent references to it in his writings, and he recommended it to his pupils. While visiting Wallington in 1857 he had written to Lady Waterford '... don't leave London without examining the head of Bacchus in Titian's picture in the National Gallery as a perfect example of breadth and finish'.[76] Later, in 1865, he was to tell his audience at the Royal Institute of British Architects, 'Two pictures which I would last part with out of our National Gallery, if there were question of parting with any, would be Titian's Bacchus and Correggio's Venus'.[77]

73 *Works* V, pp. xlvii ff.

74 J. Smetham, 'Modern Sacred Art in England', *The London Review* 1862, vol. 18, pp. 68-70.

75 See Sotheby's Catalogue 20 June 1989, lot 28, and W.E. Fredeman, 'Pre-Raphaelites in caricature: "The Choice of Paris: An Idyll" by Florence Claxton', *Burlington*, Dec. 1960, CII, pp. 523-29.

76 Surtees, *Sublime and Instructive*, p. 13.

77 *Works* XIX, p. 29.

Nat. Gally. 15. Sep. 60. J.R. works at Bacchus's nose —
M.S. dashes impudently at Titian's blue hills

53

The present sketch by Mary Severn shows Ruskin working alongside her in the National Gallery on 15 September 1860. 'J.R. works at Bacchus's nose', poring over his copy and clearly putting a great deal of detail into it, while 'M.S. dashes impudently at Titian's blue hills'.

Mary was probably the most talented of all of Joseph Severn's artistically talented family. She probably first met Ruskin about 1856 when she visited Denmark Hill with her fourteen or fifteen years old brother Arthur. Just before this sketch was made – all the Severns made dozens of sketches chronicling their activities – Mary had become engaged to Charles Newton. Newton had been at Christ Church with Ruskin and in 1854–5 he had discovered one of the Seven Wonders of the ancient world, the tomb of Mausolos at Halicarnassus. He brought some of the marbles to the British Museum and Mary Severn was introduced to him by a mutual friend as one who was competent to draw the discoveries. Later Newton was appointed British Consul in Rome. When he returned to London in June 1860 to become Keeper of Greek and Roman Antiquities in the British Museum, Joseph Severn was appointed to fill the vacant position in Rome. Charles Newton and Mary Severn were married on 3 May 1861, and it was while he was staying with his married sister that Arthur Severn was to meet Ruskin's cousin Joan Agnew and fall in love with her. Mary Newton died soon afterwards, in 1866, at the age of 34.

54 Sketch of the outside of his mouth, 1861, by John Ruskin

This drawing has been reproduced and referred to in an earlier part of this volume (page 8, Figure 2).

55 Portrait, aet 42, 1861, by Dante Gabriel Rossetti (1828–1882)

55

Ruskin first met Dante Gabriel Rossetti in 1853 as a result of being asked to give an opinion of one of Rossetti's paintings. Ruskin wrote to Rossetti, and a few days later he visited him at his studio. He was already familiar with Rossetti's work through his interest in and patronage of the Pre-Raphaelite Brotherhood.

After the first meeting a friendship quickly grew between the two men. Rossetti was a frequent guest at Denmark Hill. Ruskin was impressed by Rossetti's work; he told him 'I really do *covet* your drawings as much as I covet Turner's.' An arrangement was soon reached whereby Ruskin guaranteed to buy all Rossetti's drawings he liked, up to a certain figure each year. By this means, Ruskin had the first refusal of any drawings that he wanted and Rossetti was assured of a regular income at a stage in his career when this was particularly necessary. Ruskin soon came to a similar arrangement with Elizabeth Siddal, whom Rossetti was later to marry, to take all her work up to an annual value of £150. Although he knew that she was too ill to do much work in a year, by helping to support her, Ruskin knew that he was again helping Rossetti.

About 1859, it was arranged that Rossetti should paint a portrait of Ruskin for their mutual friend Charles Eliot Norton. Exactly when Norton commissioned the portrait is not clear, but Ruskin had difficulty in keeping Rossetti to the arrangement. Ruskin wrote from Schaffhausen to Norton on 31 July 1859[78]

> … It has not been my fault that the Rossetti portrait was not done. I told him, whenever he was ready, I would come. But when I go home now, I will see to it myself and have it done …

Having returned home, Ruskin wrote again to Norton[79]

> The first thing I did when I got home was to go to Rossetti to see about the portrait. I found him deep in work – but, which was worse, I found your commission was not for a little drawing like Browning's, but for a grand, finished, delicate oil – which R. spoke quite coolly of taking three or four weeks about, wanting I don't know how many sittings. I had to go into the country for a fortnight, and have been ill since I came back with cold and such like, and don't like the looks of myself – however I'm going to see R. about it again immediately …

But Rossetti was not to be bullied, and in May of the following year Ruskin was still writing about the portrait.[80]

> … I pressed Rossetti hard about the portrait, till I got so pale and haggard-looking over my book that I was ashamed to be drawn so. I think your chief object in getting it done would not have been answered. I hope to get into a natural state of colour (red-nosed, somewhat, by the way) among the Alps, and to send you the portrait for a New Year's gift and to behave better in all ways than I've done … P.S. I'm going to have the portrait done: tomorrow R. begins.

Time dragged on and at the beginning of 1862 Ruskin was able to report 'The portrait is in progress, and Rossetti seems pleased with it'.[81] However the oil portrait never seems to have been finished, although the present crayon drawing was probably one of the original sketches for it. It is of a predominantly red colour, in a style not unlike that which Rossetti

78 *Works* XXXVI, p. 311.
79 *Works* XXXVI, p. 329; 10 Dec. 1859.
80 *Works* XXXVI, p. 335; JR – C.E. Norton, 15 May 1860.
81 *Works* XXXVI, p. 405; JR – C.E. Norton, 19 Jan. 1862.

adopted for his portraits of the members of the Brotherhood. Ruskin is posed in an attitude frequently used by Rossetti. E.T. Cook described the portrait as 'an utter failure' and Ruskin himself called it 'the horriblest face I ever saw of a human being'.[82]

Clearly Rossetti had stamped his own impression of Ruskin on the portrait. In 1854 he had told George Price Boyce[83] that he thought Ruskin 'hideous'. Interestingly Ruskin seems to have been known to the Rossettis as 'Roughskin', a name to which Ruskin objected, and to which he referred in *Fors Clavigera*.[84]

Eventually the portrait passed into the hands of Crawford J. Pocock, a surgeon of Hove. Pocock was a friend of Ruskin and a collector of engravings and much else. His collection included one of the finest sets of Turner's *Liber Studiorum*, drawings by Ruskin, and the manuscript of his *Gold*[85] Pocock died on 26 March 1890[86] and the portrait was sold at Christie's in the following year. It was bought by Malcolm McClean and presented to the Ashmolean Museum.

56 Caricature sketch, c.1861, by Dante Gabriel Rossetti

Henry Treffrey Dunn, who became Rossetti's studio assistant in 1863–4, recorded that on his first day at Cheyne Walk he

> now had an opportunity of looking over and admiring a series of Rossetti's first ideas and sketches for many of his pictures, and studies of heads, which were contained in a large, thick book, lying on a little cabinet in a distant corner. It was a great and unexpected treat to see this collection, a most varied one, amongst which were many carefully finished likenesses, some in red chalk, and others in pencil and in pen and ink, including pencil sketches of John Ruskin (not bearded then)...[87]

The previous portrait, No. 55, may have been one of the sketches to which Dunn referred. The present unkind caricature may have been another – or it *may* have been made later. It is inscribed on the reverse by W.M. Rossetti, 'I consider this sketch is by my Brother. Am not sure as to the person represented, but inclined to think it is Ruskin. Face something like, and figure more especially'.

Because of their differing temperaments it was inevitable that the friendship between the two men should not last. In the period of his life following the death of his wife Rossetti quarrelled with all his friends. In *Some Reminiscences* W.M. Rossetti wrote 'Ruskin and my brother ceased to see one another in July 1865, though they resumed to a small extent after some interval'. As late as 1870 Ruskin wrote a 'perfectly amicable' letter to Rossetti, though in 1879 Rossetti was writing to Janey Morris that Ruskin had £800 a year from his books 'so it is to be feared he will not starve',[88] and six months later, 'I wish I had more news – for instance such tidings as that Ruskin was hanged, or something equally welcome...'[89]

56

82 *Works* XXXVI, p. 497; JR – C.E. Norton, 10 Oct. 1865.
83 V. Surtees (ed.), *Diaries of George Price Boyce* (Norwich: Real World, 1980), p. 12.
84 *Works* XXVII, p. 417.
85 Eventually sold by Mrs Pocock to T.J. Wise who printed it in an unauthorised edition. The manuscript is now in the Whitehouse Collection, RF MS 52/B.
86 See his obituary in the *Brighton Herald*, 29 March 1890.
87 H.T. Dunn, *Recollections*, quoted in Gale Pedrick, *Life with Rossetti* (London: Macdonald, 1964), p. 57.
88 J. Bryson (ed.), *Dante Gabriel Rossetti and Jane Morris, their Correspondence* (Oxford: Clarendon Press, 1976), p. 104: 25 July 1879.
89 Bryson, *Dante Gabriel Rossetti and Jane Morris, their Correspondence*, p. 127; 24 Dec. 1879.

57 Head only, c.1895, probably based on Ruskin's appearance about 1864–65, by Henry Treffrey Dunn (1838–1899)

57

Among his papers Dunn left a reminiscence[90] of a visit to Ruskin at Denmark Hill about 1868. Lots of white roses were needed in order that Rossetti could complete 'Lady Lilith'. C.A. Howell remembered that there was a profusion of the very roses in Ruskin's garden, and one afternoon Dunn, Howell and George Price Boyce went to Denmark Hill to get them. Dunn recalled how they saw lots of Turners and old engravings, how Ruskin criticised Howell for smoking in the garden, and how he criticised Boyce for painting cats on a wall in his picture of Blackfriars Bridge currently in the Old Water Colour Society's exhibition. At the end of the afternoon they departed laden with a large basket of freshly cut roses, and Rossetti was able to complete the top right hand corner of 'Lady Lilith'.

Dunn remained with Rossetti as his studio assistant and general factotum until the death of the latter in 1882. In the first few years that he was at Cheyne Walk Dunn must have seen Ruskin frequently. After Rossetti's death, Dunn gradually disappeared from the Rossetti circle and his health and habits degenerated. W.M. Rossetti lost track of him until his memoir of his brother was published in 1895. At this time Lena Ashwell wrote to tell Rossetti that some three years earlier she had come across Dunn in a second-hand shop in the King's Road, Chelsea, where he was painting tables and corner cupboards 'in the French style'.

Eventually Dunn found his way to The Pines at Putney where Theodore Watts-Dunton took pity on him. Watts-Dunton was already caring for Swinburne, and for the remainder of Dunn's life he

90 At one time with Mrs J.C. Troxell and partly quoted in V. Surtees, *Drawings and Paintings of Dante Gabriel Rossetti* (Oxford: Clarendon Press, 1971), vol. I, p. 117.

provided him with all his meals, gave him a studio at The Pines, and enough money to pay for a bedroom nearby.

While at The Pines Dunn seems to have painted more furniture. Swinburne's bed, two large surrounds for mirrors and a Jacobean cabinet are all painted by him. One of the panels of the Jacobean cabinet telling the story of St George and the Dragon contains a crowd of on-lookers in the left back-ground. Among them may be recognised Tennyson, Morris, Millais, Ruskin, Rossetti, Burne-Jones and Rossetti's mother and sister Christina.

Like the bed, the cabinet may have belonged to Swinburne. After his death in 1909 the furniture remained at The Pines. Watts-Dunton himself died in 1914; his wife continued to live there until 1938. After her death the contents of the house were dispersed. The cabinet sold for £2. It was bought by Lady Mander along with the bed and mirror, and all three are now at Wightwick Manor.

58 Self-portrait, aet 42, November 1861 (Plate 13)

59 Copy of No. 58 by W.H. Caffyn

60 Copy of No. 58 perhaps by W.G. Collingwood

Ruskin made a number of portraits of himself, of which this is the first. Although undoubtedly the first of the series, there has been much division of opinion as to its *actual* date.

It was first published in W.G. Collingwood's *Life and Work of John Ruskin* in 1893 where it was dated 1864. In the *Bookman* (March 1900), it was placed between 1864 and 1866, the black tie being said to indicate the recent death of his father which took place in 1864 – but the tie is not black.

In the catalogue of the Ruskin Exhibition in Manchester in 1904, compiled by Collingwood, it is dated 'about 1864'.

Cook and Wedderburn[91] suggest that the portrait's date is earlier, in fact 1861 – and they quote a letter to prove their case. By the time Collingwood compiled the catalogue for the 1919 Coniston Exhibition, he was converted to the new date. Derrick Leon, however, favoured 1864–5; Joan Evans placed it at 1861 when she reproduced it in her edition of the Ruskin diaries.

Although the opinion of Ruskin scholars seems to have come round to the date of 1861 for the portrait, there is still conflicting evidence. Cook and Wedderburn quote a letter from Ruskin to his father[92] written from Lucerne on 12 November 1861 and purporting to accompany the portrait, in which he says 'It is very sulky but has some qualities about it better than photograph.' (He was probably referring to portrait photographs in general rather than photographs of himself, but he could have been referring to the Jeffreys photographs, Nos. 37–38. Mrs Severn's account of the drawing,[93] however, was that it was made at the looking-glass in Ruskin's London bedroom, and given to her in the 'sixties. On her marriage it was hung at her house, 28 Herne Hill, where it remained until it was removed for reproduction by Collingwood.

Whatever was the date of the drawing, it seems to have been a good likeness. Ruskin himself seems to have been satisfied, and Collingwood, who knew him more intimately than the other biographers, has said 'The portrait is of unique value and interest; the original is a good likeness of a face whose most noteworthy expressions no artist or photographer has quite succeeded in catching...[94]

58

91 *Works* XVII, pp. cxiv-v, and *Works* XXXVIII, pp. 208 and 275.
92 *Works* XVII, pp. cxiv-v.
93 Ruskin exhibition, Manchester, 1904, Catalogue, p.115.
94 Collingwood, *Life and Work of John Ruskin*, vol. I, p. 9.

The portrait was bought at Brantwood *before* the sales from Miss Violet Severn by the late F.J. Sharp of Barrow-in-Furness. He died in 1957 and in the following year the portrait was bought by the Pierpont Morgan Library.

The chromolithograph reproduction of the portrait – with the signature added – was published in W.G. Collingwood's *Life and Work of John Ruskin* in 1893, and is an excellent reproduction.

The drawing by W.H. Caffyn (No. 59) was almost certainly copied from either the first edition of Collingwood, or the 1900 edition where it appears in black and white.

The copy of this self-portrait in the Coniston Museum, given by Mr & Mrs W.G. Collingwood, has always been thought to be one of the chromolithographic prints, with a little hand-touching in watercolour. However it has recently been examined by paper conservators and found to be entirely in watercolour, with no trace of lithography. In view of the provenance I suggest that Joan Severn was disinclined to allow the Ruskin original to go to the blockmaker's and so Collingwood made this copy for the blockmaker's use.

59

61–64 Photographs, aet 43, 1862, by Caldesi

61

62

Ruskin had taken an interest in photography since he first 'discovered' the daguerreotype as an undergraduate at Oxford. He built up a considerable collection of daguerreotypes, and later photographs, mainly of architectural subjects, which he used for study, and occasionally as the basis for some of his own drawings.

He himself was to be photographed frequently, particularly in later life. The first of the commercial photographic portraits to be made of him is the group of four studies made in 1862 by Caldesi, whose London studio at that time was at 13 Pall Mall East. This date was ascribed to one of the group when it was reproduced in *The Gentlewoman* on 27 January 1900, and Cook and Wedderburn saw no reason to dispute the date in *Works Catalogue*.

63

64

In the photograph reproduced in *The Gentlewoman* (No. 61) Ruskin stands by a high-backed chair with his right elbow resting on its padded top. His left arm is behind his back, drawing back his frock-coat. The photograph has actually been credited to Lombardi. The *carte-de-visite* print of No. 62 in the Whitehouse Collection is printed with the name and address 'L. Caldesi & Co. At P.D. Colnaghi, Scott & Co., 13 Pall Mall East, London'. It is clearly a different pose to No. 61, with Ruskin looking at the camera, and the excessive length of his coat sleeves being more apparent. Nos. 63 and 64 are two head and shoulders studies taken at the same time as Nos. 61 and 62. Prints of both in the Whitehouse Collection bear Caldesi's name. The confusion with the names is due to the fact that the firm of Lombardi took over the business and negatives of Caldesi about 1896.

65, 67, 69 Photographs of Ruskin standing with William Bell Scott and Dante Gabriel Rossetti, taken by William Downey in Rossetti's garden at Cheyne Walk, 29 June 1863, aet 44

70 Photograph of Ruskin sitting in Rossetti's chair, by William Downey, 29 June 1863

66 Copy of Ruskin and Rossetti, from No. 65, by Max Beerbohm

68 Cartoon of Ruskin and the Hinksey Diggers, the figure of Ruskin based on No. 67, by Douglas Percy Bliss.

71 Portrait of Ruskin, based on No. 70, by Thomas Scott

72 Portrait of Ruskin, based on No. 70, by Alfred Bryan

In the year following the group of photographs taken by Caldesi, Ruskin was photographed again. This time the photographer was William Downey of Newcastle-upon-Tyne. Professor Burd, in his article[95] on these Downey photographs, points out that they can be dated precisely, and that W.M. Rossetti's suggestion that they were taken in the autumn of 1863 is inaccurate. Since Downey's studio was in Newcastle, it is likely that he knew William Bell Scott who was head of the Government School of Design there. Downey also knew Rossetti, having photographed him in

95 V.A. Burd, 'Ruskin, Rossetti and William Bell Scott: a second arrangement', *Philological Quarterly*, XLVIII, No. 1, pp. 102-107.

65

December 1862. Professor Burd has suggested that perhaps it was at Scott's suggestion that Downey came to Cheyne Walk to photograph him with Rossetti, and he also suggests that he knew Ruskin planned to call on Rossetti on that same day.

Ruskin had spent 1863 on the continent until 1 June. On 15 June he had told W.M. Rossetti that he was going to 'hunt up Gabriel'; on 7 August Ruskin went north until 5 September. Meanwhile the Rossettis were abroad between 3 and 11 September and Ruskin went abroad again on 9 September, remaining there until mid-November. Thus the photographic session must have taken place between 15 June and 7 August. The diaries of Scott's friend Alice Boyd, now in the library of the University of British Columbia, show that Scott was only in London between 15 June and 8 July, thus narrowing the period still further. Entries in the diary record two visits to Rossetti – on 29 June and 6 July. The latter visit was a dinner engagement, but on 29 June Alice Boyd recorded that they went to Rossetti's in the morning and spent the day there. Although she does not mention that Ruskin was there at the same time, the evidence points to 29 June as being the most probable date for the photographs.

Downey assembled Ruskin, Rossetti, and Scott in the garden and Rossetti's painting chair[96] was brought out. 'I ... asked Mr Ruskin if he would sit down, and allow Mr Rossetti and Mr Bell-Scott to stand', recalled Downey in his *Reminiscences*[97], but 'To my dismay, Mr Ruskin flatly and sternly declined to avail himself of my invitation to sit. "Sit in the presence of Rossetti? Never!" he exclaimed. And I was compelled to take them as they are here' (No. 65).

The whole photograph has a somewhat untidy and unposed appearance. The chair has been hastily pushed aside and the truculent Scott rests his right hand on it. In the centre of the group, with his top hat on the ground behind him, Ruskin stands arm in arm with Rossetti, looking not unlike Walter Crane's memory of him.[98]

> ... still like that early remarkable full-length portrait by Millais, though perhaps nearer to Herkomer's fine watercolour head of him, before he grew a beard. I recall his tall thin figure with a

67

96 Frederic Shields's drawing of Rossetti sitting and working in this chair is reproduced in Rosalie G. Grylls: *Portrait of Rossetti* (London: Macdonald, 1964), pl. 18.

97 'A Grand Old Photographer, Some Reminiscences of Mr William Downey, Royal Photographer', *Pall Mall Budget*, 15 Jan. 1891, p. 21.

98 Walter Crane, aged 15, had first seen Ruskin in 1860. Crane was apprenticed to the wood engraver W.J. Linton and Ruskin had called to discuss a point with him. Crane recorded his memory in *An Artist's Reminiscences* (London: Methuen, 1907), p. 57.

69

70

> slight stoop, and his quiet, rather abstracted manner. He looked like an old-fashioned type of country gentleman with literary tastes, and wore the high velvet-collared coat one sees in his early portraits ...

Rossetti, gripping his soft hat in his left hand and with a handkerchief incompletely stuffed into an inside pocket, looks as if he is going to fall over. In the print held by the National Portrait Gallery archive the handkerchief has been touched out.

Clearly unhappy with the exposure, Downey moved the three men to a different position in the garden where they could have foliage instead of a brick wall as a background, and tried again (No. 67).[99] This time Scott rests his foot on the chair while Rossetti, now in the centre of the group, rests his hand round the finial on the chair back, while still gripping his hat. Ruskin, still linking arms with Rossetti and gripping his walking stick in the other hand, almost smiles at the camera. But at the crucial moment, Scott blinked, so his eyes appear closed!

Undaunted, Downey tried again (No. 69). Rossetti had changed his grip on the chair and turned his head a little more to the right. But Ruskin's expression shows that he was clearly tired of the whole business! And Scott moved his head.

Before the session ended, Downey took a fourth exposure (No. 70). This time it was a more formal study of Ruskin alone, seated in Rossetti's chair, apparently indoors.

That evening[100] Ruskin went to a party given by his friends Dr and Mrs Simon at 44 Great Cumberland Street. He was seen there by Mary Frances Bradford who had been a student at Winnington Hall, the girls' school in Cheshire in which Ruskin took an interest. She became a teacher and partner in Winnington. Writing to Margaret Bell, the headmistress of Winnington, she told her[101]

99 The print, reproduced by Burd, has been crudely tinted, perhaps by one of Arthur Severn's sons. It passed through the Sharp-Viljoen collections to the Pierpont Morgan Library. Fortunately an untinted print, reproduced here, is in the National Portrait Gallery. The print of No. 69 was given by Sir Sydney Cockerell to Mrs Virginia Surtees, by whose kind permission it is reproduced.

100 It is interesting to speculate where Ruskin changed from the clothes he wore in the afternoon for the photograph, into his evening dress. He would not have had time to make the journey from Cheyne Walk to Denmark Hill and back to Great Cumberland Street. Perhaps he changed at the Athenæum, although according to Arthur Severn, he was nervous of going there in case the servants might not recognise him. See J.S. Dearden (ed.), *The Professor*, p. 71.

101 Mary Frances Bradford – Margaret Bell, undated but datable because of the reference to the photograph. V.A. Burd (ed.), *The Winnington Letters* (London: George Allen & Unwin, 1969), pp. 406-407.

66

I saw Mr Ruskin last night ... he looked well, at least much better than I expected and so lonely ... He told me he was better, but still very unwell ... Mr Ruskin told me he had been photographed that afternoon in Rossetti's garden, Rossetti with him leaning on his arm, a truth telling position for Rossetti, and he knew it ... He promised to show the photograph to us, 'tho he said he would not show it generally – but I think he will relent and give it us ...

Friends of Ruskin and Rossetti were soon asking for prints of the photographs. Ellen Heaton asked through Rossetti's sister and in a letter postmarked 2 July 1863 Rossetti replied that

... they are not yet printed, and I do not know in the least whether he [Downey, or perhaps Ruskin] will allow them to be issued to any extent, but I think that I may undertake that you shall have one of each in any case, only it would be absolutely necessary to keep it strictly in your own possession, as I hear that a single copy getting out of the photographer's hands is legal warrant for anyone who can get hold of it to reproduce and publish it.[102]

When Ruskin finally saw the prints he was clearly displeased with them. On 17 September he wrote to Rossetti[103] from Chamouni:

That fellow whom you got me to sit to be photoed has published the photo. And it is all over London – you ought not to have induced me to sit to a man not to be depended upon – I am very angry with you – and I hope you will never have anything more to do with the vagabonds. – I had an interesting letter from Swinburne ...

yours,
J Ruskin

71

On the following day he told his father, 'I have written to Rossetti to scold him for letting that photo get abroad'[104] and in November he wrote to Miss Heaton 'I am glad to hear what you and my other friends say of the photograph. I don't think it like me – on the evil side it is as scandalous as both the Mr Richmonds are caricatures on the good side'. And in a bitter letter to Rossetti in 1865 Ruskin wrote '... the entirely blameable introduction you gave to a mere blackguard [Downey], to me, has been the cause of such a visible libel upon me going about England as I hold worse than all the scandals and lies ever uttered about me'.[105] W.M. Rossetti, who published this letter in *Rossetti Papers* suggests that it refers to the photograph of Ruskin seated alone and not to the groups. He considered No. 65 'second to none for genuine and agreeable likeness' of his brother, and he considered No. 70, Ruskin alone, 'a good though not an advantageous likeness'.

Ruskin was long to remember and regret the photographic session and the mutual disapproval which he and Bell Scott had for each other. Twelve years later he was writing to the *Pall Mall Gazette*

102 Surtees, *Sublime and Instructive*, pp. 252-53.
103 The original of this letter was in the F.J. Sharp collection; it is printed here from the transcript in the Barrow-in-Furness Public Library.

104 JR – JJR, Chamouni, 18 Sept. 1863; *Works* XXXVI, p. 454.
105 *Works* XXXVI, p. 491.

> Mr Scott is one of a rather numerous class of artists of whose works I have never taken any public notice, and who attribute my silence to my inherent stupidity of disposition. Mr Scott is also one of the more limited and peculiarly unfortunate class of artists who suppose themselves to have great native genius ... to my regret, he was once photographed in the same plate with Mr Rossetti and me...[106]

Despite Ruskin's disapproval of Downey's photographs a number of later artists liked them and put them to use.

Ruskin's head and shoulders were engraved from the photograph of the seated Ruskin (No. 70) for use as the unsigned frontispiece to Edmund J. Baillie's *John Ruskin* 1883, while an advertisement on the back cover of the publication announces 'A First-class Engraving of Mr Ruskin, drawn by Thomas Scott, printed on large plate paper, suitable for framing. Price 1s., post free'. I have never seen a print of this engraving; it may be a separate print on larger paper of the frontispiece, or an entirely separate portrait.

There is also an engraved portrait of Ruskin based on No. 70, by 'A.B.' who has been identified as the caricaturist Alfred Bryan. In addition to this depiction, he also drew several caricatures of Ruskin (see Nos. 141, 158–59, 169).

Max Beerbohm, who was to introduce Ruskin into several of his caricatures (see Nos. 300, 303, 307–08) was aware of the Downey photograph (No. 65) and there is a drawing of the figures of Ruskin and Rossetti on a sheet of studies (No. 66) in the Robert H. Taylor Collection at Princeton University Library.

More recently Douglas Bliss in his caricature of the Hinksey Diggers (No. 68 – see also Nos. 118–19) captioned 'The Gospel of Labour at the Home of Lost Causes: Professor Ruskin takes a class out to make roads' caricaturises the image of Ruskin from Nos. 67 or 69.

The Gospel of Labour at the Home of Lost Causes: Professor Ruskin takes a class out to make roads.

68

73 Bust, aet 45, February 1864, by Alexander Munro (1825–1871)

Alexander Munro came to London in 1848 and worked for some time carving the decoration of the new Houses of Parliament. Later he was to do some of the carving for the Oxford Museum in which Ruskin was interested. Munro was closely associated with many of the Pre-Raphaelites and seems to have been a particular friend of Rossetti. He took a modelling class at the Working Men's College and Ruskin thought highly of his work, describing him and Baron Marochetti as 'the two most noble sculptors of England'.

Who actually introduced Ruskin to Munro is unclear. Read and Barnes[107] quote a letter from Millais to Munro written from Brig o'Turk on 10 September 1853 in which Millais passes on a message from Ruskin 'that he will like you to model his wife's profile like mine, upon his return to Town', so, he adds, 'you will have hers and mine to exhibit at the R.A. next year, and a very pretty couple they will be'. However, the portrait of Effie was never made.

A couple of years later plans were afoot for Ruskin's face to be modelled by Munro, when Ruskin wrote to Rossetti: 'Don't bring Munro yet. I want to see him, but I can't see; and to speak to him, but I can't speak'.[108] As is evident from the following letter to Furnivall,[109] there had long been plans for Munro to make a bust of Ruskin.

> I shall be delighted to see Munro with French, and he can then tell me what he thinks can be done with this ugly head of mine, which I often look at very carefully, asking myself what I should think of it if it were on anybody else's shoulders

106 Letter to the editor of *The Pall Mall Gazette*, 11 Jan. 1875; *Works* XV, p. 491.
107 B. Read & J. Barnes (ed.), *Pre-Raphaelite Sculpture* (London: Lund Humphries, 1991), p. 61.
108 JR – D.G. Rossetti, 30 April 1855; *Works* XXXVI, p. 201.
109 JR – F.J. Furnivall, 17 July 1855; *Works* XXXVI, p. 218.

with much discomfiture and humiliation. If I could paint I could make something of the front face, but I cannot conceive how Munro could make anything fit to be seen, without gross fallacy, out of the side. He knows best, however, and, merely as a matter of curious difficulty, I should like to see him try ... Whatever of good or strength there is in me comes visibly, as far as I know myself, only sometimes into the grey of my eyes, which Millais ought to have got, but didn't and which Munro certainly cannot get. On the whole, I think (while I am very much delighted that Munro thinks he could make something of me) that nothing should be done, or shown, for a year or two yet. I will promise Munro that no one but he shall try it, when it is a proper time to try it, and shall be very grateful to him if he then will ...

But various events must have conspired to delay the making of the bust. Five years later Ruskin told Norton[110]

... Munro the sculptor, like all sculptors, lives in a nasty wood-house full of clay and water-tubs, so I can't go without catching cold ...

and six months later he told Elizabeth Barrett Browning[111]

'Photograph of me indeed' You shan't have anything of the kind. I can't conceive why I'm so ugly, but I *am* so ugly – the sun[112] says so. If I get a little strong again I'll let Munro or some other falsifying friend make me in clay, and put in a little good which that tiresome iron sun won't, though I know it's there ...

But eventually Munro did get a chance to go out to Denmark Hill to model Ruskin, in February 1864.

... I am kept from getting to town by the great kindness of Mr Munro – who comes out here to make a study of my unmanageable face – and I can't put more difficulties in his way than the thing itself does. I am sure he will be glad when he has done.[113]

At the time that Ruskin was sitting to Munro at Denmark Hill, the 79 years old John James Ruskin was seriously ill; he died on 3 March 1864. The sculpture of Ruskin now seems to have been overtaken by events and there is clear evidence that Munro was engaged in making the death-mask of John James. Munro also appears now to have been engaged in making preliminary sketches for a bust of John James, as well as his portrait of Ruskin.

However, the work seems to have again been delayed, and more than a year later, on 29 June 1865 Ruskin was writing to Munro[114] 'It has not been wholly by procrastination and mischance that I left you so long and so unkindly in doubt about this bust'. Ruskin said that it would remind him too forcibly of his father's death, 'its petty and useless sacrifice. I would have this bust executed, if it would be good for my mother to have it by her – but, as far as I can judge, it might reduce her to utter weakness of mind. I do not wish you to execute either this or mine'. He refers to his 'shivering pang of vexation' at the thought of a portrait. 'Forgive me this wrong'.

Ruskin continued 'I've sent my book to your wife – will *she* forgive me all this trouble I've given you ... I want the mask carefully packed so that it will not crumble away – then I will take charge of it – but I do not want to see it'.

Negotiations with Munro in connection with the portrait had dragged on for a long time, and in appreciation of the work that had been done and the trouble caused, Ruskin wrote a short note on 27 May 1869 from Verona to Mary Munro, enclosing a cheque for 120 guineas. This was followed on 18 June by a longer letter:

I sent the larger cheque because I know the trouble and deeply feeling care that Alic had given to that work were worth twice and thrice the labour given to ordinary busts. Do not think about it any more just now. If there is need, to relieve Alic's mind – anything may be sent to C.A. Howell Esq. North End. Putney – addressed to me but not to be sent to Denmark Hill. I do not want my mother to see it. She has too much already the habit of dwelling only on the past.

Cook and Wedderburn were unable to locate the sculpture of Ruskin. Mrs Macdonald is of the opinion that whatever may have been executed no longer exists. The death-mask of John James Ruskin which *does* seem to have been completed and ultimately sent to Ruskin appears to have disappeared without trace. Perhaps it did not survive the move from Denmark Hill in 1871.

110 JR – C.E. Norton, 4 Nov. 1860; *Letters of John Ruskin to Charles Eliot Norton*, vol. I, p. 102.
111 JR – E.B. Browning, 13 May 1861; *Works* XXXVI, p. 365.
112 i.e. photographs taken by the light of the sun.
113 JR – Julie Richmond, 17 Feb. 1864; *Works* XXXVI, p. 467.
114 Original in the possession of the sculptor's granddaughter, Mrs K. Macdonald, who interprets the word 'execute' as meaning 'to bring into its final form, i.e. cast or marble'. I am indebted to Mrs Macdonald for her help.

74–75 John Ruskin, aet 45, Spring 1864, by Samuel Laurence (1812–1884)

Ruskin's father, by this time 79 years old, was taken seriously ill at the end of February 1864. He had been unwell throughout January and was clearly in considerable pain throughout most of the following month. Perhaps he managed to conceal the severity of his illness from his wife and son until the end of the month, for in *Præterita* Ruskin refers to the suddenness of his death.

John James Ruskin continued to run his firm of Ruskin & Co. until the end of his life. On 27 February 1864, the day after the last entry in his diary[115] had ended in illegibility, he wrote two business letters in a clear firm hand. Both were on the subject of supplying sherry and the discounts which he could give. One was addressed to Gordon W. Clark, the other (quoted below) to Messrs J. Day Son & Watson.

Dear Sirs,

Sir Anthy Rothschild has sent to Billiter St desiring to have 2 Butts of Sherry from Mr Domecq. We extremely wish you could persuade this gentleman to take these wines through you, but we presume you do not want the order to go to another Shipper.

If we get Mr Domecq to send this wine, we cannot at the present enormous price of sherry secure you more than £10 per Butt Bonus. Would you kindly favour us with your sentiments on the subject.

We are
Dear Sir,
Respectfully
Yours very truly
Ruskin & Co.

Both letters[116] were subsequently enclosed in an envelope on which Ruskin wrote 'The last two letters my Father wrote. He sat up till past 12 waiting for me to come in, from London – (Working Men's College I think) – and read these to me. He was struck with his death-illness the following morning – 28th February'.

28 February was a Sunday and 1864 was a leap year. Four days later, on 3 March, John James Ruskin died.

The present portrait was drawn at the suggestion of the artist. The proposal was made just a couple of months before John James died. Ruskin wrote to Laurence on 13 January thanking him for the suggestion.

75

> It is kind and nice of you to propose doing the drawing so, but alas, my father and mother are both sharply ill just now ... How long do you like to have your sittings – I must think of some way of managing it when I get better. For me – short sittings are much best, for this reason. I can do about four hours work every morning, of various kinds, and life is short and if I don't do four hours today I can't do eight tomorrow, no, nor even five. But after my morning I could come to sit for an hour and rest and enjoy it, but if I gave you long sittings I should lose each *whole* day and you would have the face more stupid even than its wont...[117]

It is not clear whether the sittings began straight away, or did not take place until after John James's death.

Ruskin's friendship with Samuel Laurence has largely escaped the notice of his biographers. In *Academy Notes*, 1875, Ruskin refers to two beautiful drawings by Laurence of Sir Theodore Martin and John Hodgkin. But this is the only reference to the

115 RF MS 33.
116 RF L 30.

117 J.H. Whitehouse (ed.), *The Solitary Warrior* (London: George Allen & Unwin, 1929), pp. 55-56.

artist in the whole of Ruskin's works. There was, however, a firm friendship between the two men. The portrait does not appear to have been recorded until it was exhibited in the Ruskin Centenary exhibition in 1919.

I have been unable to see No. 74, but I believe it to be a preliminary study for the finished portrait, No. 75.

76 John Ruskin, aet 45, 12 December 1864, by T. Henderson

Ruskin's experiences with his drawing class at the Working Men's College, and the development of his thoughts during the early period of his life, when he is generally thought of as a writer on art, led him to wider views of the nature of the arts and the duties of philanthropic effort and social economy. He introduced some of his views on this into the fourth and fifth volumes of *Modern Painters* in 1856. His views on the place of labour in the social and economic system had already been concentrated into the 'Nature of Gothic' chapter of the *Stones of Venice* and reprinted as a manifesto at the opening of the Working Men's College in 1854.

In 1857 Ruskin had been invited to lecture in Manchester during the period of the Art Treasures exhibition. He had been studying political economy for some time but had not found the answers to the questions he had posed himself in any of the currently standard books. Ruskin wanted to know the best way of employing artists, of educating workmen, of regulating patronage. The acknowledged authorities had no answers, so Ruskin put his own answers into the two Manchester lectures, in which art was considered as wealth; the first lecture dealt with how to get it, and the second with how to use it. The lectures, which attracted considerable audiences were printed as *The Political Economy of Art*.

John James Ruskin had always viewed his son's pronouncements on social and political economy with a certain amount of trepidation, and occasionally letters to the press on the subject, which were always first submitted for parental approval, were not sent out of respect for his father's wishes. One wonders whether John James was actually opposed to some of his son's radical ideas or whether he merely considered the expression of them in association with the name Ruskin bad for business.

In 1860 Ruskin developed his views on economy in a series of articles called 'Unto this last'. They appeared in the newly established *Cornhill* magazine and Thackeray, the editor, terminated the series after the fourth chapter. A reviewer in the *Manchester Examiner* wrote 'If we do not crush him his wild words will touch the springs of action in some hearts and before we are aware, a moral floodgate may fly open and drown us all'. Thomas Carlyle was one of Ruskin's few supporters.

76

Two years later Ruskin published a series of essays on social and political economy under the title 'Munera Pulveris' in *Fraser's Magazine* and after the death of his father he felt free to extend this aspect of his work.

Towards the end of 1864 Ruskin was lecturing in Manchester again. On 6 December his first lecture, 'Of Kings' Treasuries', was delivered at the Rusholme Town Hall. Probably on 7 December Ruskin addressed the boys of Manchester Grammar School, and on 14 December his second lecture, 'Of Queens' Gardens', was given at the Town Hall in King Street.

During the period in which Ruskin was delivering his Manchester lectures he was staying at Winnington Hall, near Northwhich. He was probably there on 12 December, the date on which the present sketch was made (he certainly was on the day before), so the unknown T. Henderson may have actually seen and sketched him at Winnington on 12 December or he may have been in the audience at either the Rusholme Town Hall or the Grammar School and sketched the lecturer from memory.

77 Profiles, 29 June 1866, by Constance Hilliard

Ruskin first met Lady Trevelyan in June 1847, probably at the introduction of Henry Acland. Before she had married Sir Walter in 1835 she had been a Miss Pauline Jermyn. Her sister had married the Rev. J.C. Hilliard, and they had several children, one of whom – Laurence – was to become Ruskin's secretary in the 1870s. When Ruskin visited the Trevelyans at Wallington in August 1863 he found Pauline's eleven-year-old niece Constance Hilliard staying with her aunt and uncle. Five days after his arrival at Wallington Ruskin wrote to Lady Waterford[118] 'There is a nice enfant of eleven here just now – a little niece of Lady Trevelyan's, she asked us all formally to tea on the lawn on the day I came'. The Hilliards were to become close friends of Ruskin. Constance and her mother accompanied Ruskin and other friends on his continental tours of 1870 and 1872, and in 1866, on a trip to Switzerland, Ruskin was accompanied by the Trevelyans, Connie, and Ruskin's cousin Joan Agnew.

The party left London on 24 April 1866. Lady Trevelyan was really too unwell to travel, and at Neuchâtel on 13 May she died, just thirteen days before Constance's 14th birthday. The Rev. J.C. Hilliard rushed out to join the party; Lady Trevelyan was buried at Neuchâtel; Sir Walter returned to London, and the remainder of the party continued their tour.

They were in Lucerne between the 11th and 29th June. Ruskin 'worked hard' at his drawing of Lucerne in the morning of Friday 29th and in the afternoon they took the train to Berne where they arrived during a thunderstorm in the evening.

Constance Hilliard's diary of the 1866 tour is in the collection of Alan Cole, and it includes a series of slight profiles of faces which she almost certainly made on that train journey. One is faintly labelled in pencil 'Cuz', the name by which Joan Agnew referred to her cousin. Connie had also adopted the name for Ruskin and in her diary there are several references to 'Cussy'.

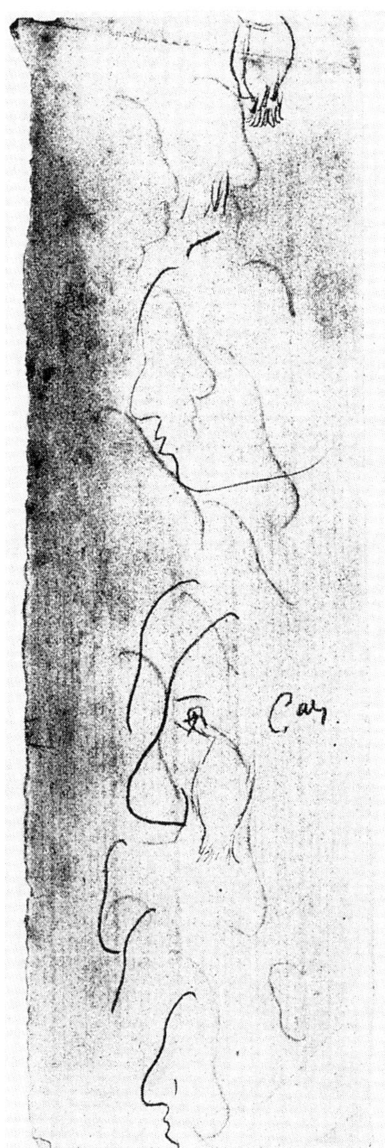

77

118 On 16 August 1863. Surtees, *Sublime and Instructive*, p. 51.

78 John Ruskin, 1866, by Edward Coley Burne-Jones (1833–98), never completed

After their initial meeting in 1856 (see No. 36) the Ruskin – Burne-Jones friendship developed quickly. In October 1856 Ruskin visited Burne-Jones and Morris at their rooms in Red Lion Square and on 12 December they were dining at Denmark Hill in company with the Trevelyans and Tom Richmond. In 1862 Ruskin took Edward and Georgiana Burne-Jones on a tour of Italy and Switzerland and in the following year they visited Winnington with him. There were plans for Burne-Jones to design for Ruskin a series of tapestries which the girls at Winnington would embroider, but the scheme was never finished because the designs were too complicated for the girls to work. Again in 1863–4 there was another abortive scheme for Burne-Jones to illustrate an edition of Ruskin's *Fraser's Magazine* articles on political economy.

Frustrated in his attempts to have Rossetti complete his portrait for Norton, in October 1856 Ruskin wrote to his American friend 'I have written today to Edward Jones, to ask if he'll do one [a portrait] for me and one for you. *He* can...'[119] The arrangement was confirmed in another letter to Norton[120] soon after the turn of the year.

> ... I got your letter yesterday evening, after posting one to you by the 5 o'clock post. I can only answer quickly today that I *have* written this morning to Edward Jones, begging him to have me to sit instantly ...

The sittings began immediately. On 3 February Ruskin promised Burne-Jones to 'come on Monday and then be steady I hope to every other day: – Proserpine permitting ... stay – it must be Monday, Tuesday and Thursday for I want to come on Thursday and drive you and Georgie back with me here to dinner – because it's my birthday'.[121]

Meanwhile Norton sent Ruskin a cheque for the portrait.

> The £50 have arrived safe. I don't tell Ned Jones the enormity of the sum, for it would make him nervous, and he would vow 'he couldn't do anything worth the fifth of it – and if you expected fifty pounds' worth out of him, it was no use his doing anything'. So I go and sit, and he makes various sketches; some one is pretty sure to come out fairly, and I'll pick up two or three besides and some bits of what he calls waste paper, of old designs – and so will make out your money's worth at last, I hope. All that you say of expression is very nice and right. But it's a wide world, and there's a great deal in it, and one's head is but a poor little room to study in after all. One can't see far into anything.[122]

On 27 March Ruskin reported that 'the portrait has been a little checked, but is going on well'.[123] He visited the Burne-Joneses regularly throughout the summer and presumably work continued on the picture.

> I have been in hopes every day of announcing completion of drawing for you, but Edward works at it and gets angry with himself, and then gives in; he is not well, and has gone into the country for a week or two. I have not drawn your cheque. I'll get him on if I can, as soon as he comes back ... Forgive this line – I have put it off too long – and you can't write to me while I'm swindling you out of your fifty pounds, without seeming to dun me for it...[124]

> I have not written to you because I *did* hope to have sent you some account of the portrait, but both Jones and I have been ill, – *I* very seriously, as far as any chronic illness can be serious, – being variously tormented, down in to the dust of death and near his gates, and no portrait seems finishable, for the present, so I have cancelled your cheque, sending you back the enclosed torn bit to assure you thereof; and if either he or I (for I suspect I can draw myself better than anybody can) can do anything worth your having, you shall have it for nothing.[125]

> I have just got your New Year's letter ... but I am vexed because you seem never to have got mine, giving account of Burne-Jones's breakdown with the portrait and enclosing a fragment of your fifty pound cheque to show that it was destroyed; and promising, if ever I can drawn again, to try and do you a sketch of myself'.[126]

119 JR – C.E. Norton, 10 Oct. 1865; *Works* XXXVI, p. 497.
120 JR – C.E.Norton, 11 Jan. 1866; *Works* XXXVI, p. 500.
121 JR – E. Burne-Jones, 3 Feb. 1866; Fitzwilliam Museum, (E.B-J. 11). Wrongly dated in *Works* XXXVIL, p. 500, as '?April' 1866. The 'Proserpine' referred to was Rose La Touche with whom Ruskin was in love. 'Did you see the gleam of sunshine yesterday afternoon? If only you had seen her in it, bareheaded, between *my* laurels and *my* primrose bank'.
122 JR – C.E. Norton, 28 Jan. 1866; *Works* XXXVI, p. 501.
123 JR – C.E. Norton, 27 Mar. 1866; *Works* XXXVI, p. 504.
124 JR – C.E. Norton, 18 Aug. 1866; *Works* XXXVI, p. 511.
125 JR – C.E. Norton, 28 Dec. 1866; *Works* XXXVI, p. 521.
126 JR – C.E. Norton, 23 Jan. 1867; *Works* XXXVI, p. 522.

The outcome of the scheme was referred to by Georgiana Burne-Jones in her biography of her husband.

> At this time he wished Edward to paint his portrait, and there were drawings made for it, but as these were not preserved I suppose they were unsatisfactory and the plan was never carried out. Truth to tell, portrait-painting was distasteful to Edward, who always said so on occasion, but special reasons overcame the feeling from time to time. He once wrote; 'I do not easily get portraiture, and the perpetual hunt to find in a face what I like, and leave out what mislikes me, is a bad school for it!'[127]

79 John Ruskin, c.1866, self-portrait

79

Disheartened by the failure of both Rossetti and Burne-Jones to produce a portrait of him for Norton, Ruskin may have immediately decided to keep his promise to 'do you a sketch of myself'. The main crop of self-portraits was not done for another nine or ten years, but the present sketch may represent a beginning. In it, Ruskin looks a little younger than he does in the more finished self-portraits and for this reason I date the present example as having been done about 1866. But there are striking similarities between this and the later portraits. Particularly, the shadows on the side of the face, across the temple, and from the nose across the corner of the mouth, are very similar to those in No. 117.

The portrait, 'a pen and ink drawing of John Ruskin', was included in the 18 May 1931 sale of Ruskin manuscripts at Sotheby's, as an uncatalogued lot 40A. The lot also included three photographs of Ruskin and 49 letters from John James Ruskin to Mrs Simon, the wife of their friend Dr John Simon. The inclusion of the portrait with these letters suggests that Ruskin eventually gave this sketch to the Simons. The lot was bought for £2 15s by J. Howard Whitehouse.

80 Sketch of the inside of his mouth, by John Ruskin, 19 January 1867

This sketch is referred to and reproduced in an earlier section of this book. See page 7, Figure 1.

127 Burne-Jones, *Memorials of Edward Burne-Jones*, vol. I, p. 299.

81 John Ruskin, aet 48, 1867, photograph, full face by Elliott and Fry

82 John Ruskin, photograph No. 81 reproduced on a Copeland plate in 1881

83 John Ruskin, painted on porcelain by Stephen Chesters after No. 81

84 John Ruskin, 1867, photograph, full face, by Elliott and Fry, identical pose to No. 81, but lips parted

85 John Ruskin, anonymous miniature, possibly after No. 84 (Plate 14)

86 John Ruskin, 1867, photograph, side face, by Elliott and Fry

87 John Ruskin, pencil sketch perhaps by Arthur Severn, after No. 86

88 John Ruskin, pencil copy by J.C. Barry Lindsay of no. 86

89 John Ruskin, miniature on ivory by J.C. Barry, after No. 86 (Plate 15)

90 John Ruskin, etching by S. Haydon, based on No. 86 but reversed

91 John Ruskin, relief in cream wax, perhaps by William Calder Marshall, 1882, based on No. 86

92 John Ruskin, watermark on 'Ruskin Linen' paper, based on No. 86

81

According to Cook and Wedderburn's *Works Catalogue*, Ruskin was photographed by Elliott and Fry of Baker Street in 1867 and again in 1882. However it is clear from the evidence of the photographs themselves that there were at least five, rather than two, sittings.

Works Catalogue (entry 21) says that No. 81 is reproduced as the frontispiece to *Works* XXVII where it is erroneously dated 1876. This dating error is corrected in *Works Catalogue*. However, in fact, Cook and Wedderburn reproduce their

82

83

No. 23 (my No. 86) in *Works* XXVII. Their No. 22 in fact refers to a second sitting which will be discussed later.

I see no reason to doubt Cook and Wedderburn's date of 1867 for the first sitting, and it appears that on this occasion three photographs were taken – No. 81, a full-face portrait, No. 84, an exactly similar pose except that the lips are slightly parted, and No. 86, a side-face portrait. Nos. 81 and 86 were widely circulated as *carte de visite* or larger prints and formed the basis for a number of other portraits or caricatures.

The better-known full-face photograph (No. 81) was reproduced in sepia in 1881 by Copeland as the centrepiece of a cream opaque china plate with a gold border (No. 82). This Ruskin plate was one of a series bearing portraits of Victorian notables and it was first distributed between March and November 1881.

The same photograph formed the basis of the portrait painted on porcelain by Stephen Chesters (No. 83) which is now in the possession of Mr David Harté, the great, great grandson of the artist. Stephen Chesters specialised in painting in enamel on porcelain. Between 1849 and 1857 he exhibited

84

85

86

88

87

90

91

twelve such works at the Academy, a thirteenth portrait being exhibited in 1885. Chesters lived for most of his life in the potteries, and painted for Spode.

No. 84, a full-face photograph with parted lips, almost certainly formed the basis for No. 85, a miniature painted on ivory and now in the possession of Dr Victoria Andros in America. The identical pose, parted lips, position of the eyes and clothing make it almost certain that the Andros miniature was painted from No. 84. However, the colouring is true to life and this suggests that it may have been painted by someone who knew – or at least had seen – Ruskin.

The side-face photograph, No. 86, is reproduced as little more than a pencil outline on a piece of paper in the Whitehouse Collection (No. 87), which almost certainly came from Brantwood and may perhaps have been the work of Arthur Severn.

An undated pencil copy (No. 88) of this photograph, also now in the Whitehouse Collection, was made by J.C. Barry Lindsay and was at one time in M.H. Spielmann's collection. A watercolour miniature on ivory (No. 89), also based on No. 86, turned up at a country sale in Cumbria a few years ago. An old inscription on the reverse of its frame describes it as Professor Ruskin LLD, DCL. This indicates that the miniature could not have been painted before November 1893 when Ruskin received his Honorary DCL. The old label describes the artist as J.C. Barry, (?) Preford Place, Larches St., Sparkbrooke. The coincidence of J.C. Barry and J.C. Barry Lindsay not being the same person is too great, but when

89

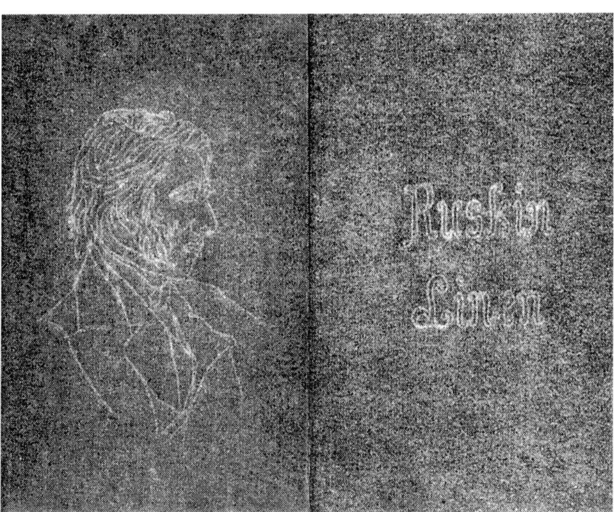

92

and why the Lindsay was dropped, or added, remains a mystery.

An oval etching, No. 90, after photograph No. 86, shows a reversed bust set on a laurel wreath. This was made and published by S. Haydon.

The side-face photograph also formed the basis for a relief, modelled in cream wax in 1882. When it was sold at Christie's in 1976 it was thought to be the work of William Mossman. However, when one realises that it is based on an 1867 photograph it immediately becomes obvious that it cannot be the work of Mossman who died in 1851! Rodney Engen has suggested to me that the relief could be the work of William Calder Marshall, who, amongst other work, was responsible for the figure of *Agriculture* on the Albert Memorial. This portrait of Ruskin was bought by a group of his friends in appreciation of the work of the late Lord Lloyd of Kilgerran and presented by them to Brantwood.

Finally, the image of Ruskin from No. 86 was used as an outline drawing in the watermark of notepaper called 'Ruskin Linen'. The late F.J. Sharp had a number of sheets of this paper and he gave one to me about 1947.

93 John Ruskin, 1867, photograph, full-face looking down, by Elliott and Fry (second sitting)

94 John, Ruskin, 1867, photograph, full-face looking ahead, by Elliott and Fry (second sitting)

93

94

No. 93 is listed by Cook and Wedderburn as having been taken in 1867. It is clear from the arrangement of the coat and waistcoat that it was taken at the same sitting as No. 94, but at a different sitting to Nos. 81, 84 and 86. Whether Nos. 93 and 94 were taken before or after Nos. 81, 84 and 86 is uncertain.

A note in the Whitehouse Collection by Ruskin's god-daughter, Constance Oldham, says that No. 93 was the best full-face photograph of Ruskin ever taken, 'giving a *little* of the tenderness and spirituality of the eyes – I had six copies of it made'. She had been less complimentary about No. 86 in the previous sitting, which she thought 'useless, except as giving profile'.

95 Caricature of Ruskin fondling two calves, 29 January 1868

Probably the first published press caricature of Ruskin appeared in *Judy* on 29 January 1868, following Ruskin's letter to the editor of the *Daily Telegraph* of 22 January 1868.

The *Telegraph* of the day before had carried an article about a girl called Matilda Griggs who had been stabbed and left for dead by her seducer. She had crawled into a field nearby and there lost consciousness. Two calves settled alongside her, keeping her warm and protecting her from the elements. Matilda recovered and entered into recognizances for £40 to prosecute her lover. But she had second thoughts, failed to prosecute, forfeited her recognizances and was imprisoned by the Chancellor of the Exchequer for debt. Taking pity on her plight, Ruskin sent a cheque for the Chancellor to the editor of the *Daily Telegraph*, who published his letter.

In due course the caricature entitled 'Nature and Art, respectfully dedicated to the Friends of Matilda Griggs' appeared in *Judy*, showing Ruskin fondling two calves.

The caricaturist, John Proctor (1836–98) was born in Edinburgh and moved to London in 1859 where he worked with the *Illustrated London News*. He was one of the best cartoonists for *Judy*. He also drew for *Funny Folk*, *Moonshine* and *Fun*.

NATURE AND ART.

[*Respectfully dedicated to the Friends of* MATILDA GRIGGS.

95

96 Caricature of Ruskin as a policeman, moving on an organ-grinder and his family, November 1868

Ruskin, of course, had strong ties with Edinburgh. His grandfather lived there; his father was born there. When his own career as a lecturer began in 1853 it was in Edinburgh, under the auspices of the Philosophical Institution, that he delivered his lectures on Architecture and Painting.

Chorus from Organ Grinder & Family (air Ka-foozle-um) "Oh. Oh. Politics. Politics. Politics.– Oh. Oh. Politics. the only thing we care for."
Police Constable Ruskin. "Move on there – you've nothing to do here."

96

In October 1868 there was a chance that Ruskin was to become a candidate in the election for Lord Rector of Glasgow University. However, in the event, Lord Stanley and Mr Lowe were nominated.

About a month later Ruskin was again a candidate in a Rectorial Election, this time at Edinburgh University. He had been seen as a fit successor to the previous Rector, Thomas Carlyle. The other candidates were Alfred Tennyson, Robert Lowe and James Moncreiff. The local man, James Moncreiff, was the most eminent of the Scottish Liberal MPs. Tennyson withdrew his candidature and Ruskin was proposed as his replacement, as the anti-Liberal figurehead. Ruskin's campaign was managed by supporters; he took no part in it himself.

A rash of broadsheets, handbills, caricatures and other ephemera was generated, including a parody, from *The Song of Lowe-awatha*, in praise of Robert Lowe. Ruskin had first appeared in a Hiawatha parody, 'Hiawatha'a Photography' in *The Train*.[128] Now, in 1868, 'Shortfellow' wrote:

Once there was proposed John Ruskin
He, the writer and the painter,
He, the pale-faced closet writer,
He, the writer so dogmatic
He, who vomits forth vast volumes,
of such vile and utter rubbish
On economy politic.

The present caricature was also issued in connection with the election campaign. Ruskin is shown as a police constable (Number A.1). He is moving on an organ-grinder and his wife who leads James Moncreiff by the hand. The organ-grinder's monkey wears a collar labelled 'Beales'.

James Moncreiff was the eventual winner of the election, the whole story of which has been told by T.J. Johnstone,[129] who points out that Ruskin did not have great success in Rectorial Elections, being defeated by Disraeli at Glasgow in 1871. At St Andrew's in the same year he was successful, but then, as a professor in another university, he had to be disqualified.

97–102 John Ruskin, aet 50, 1869, photographed by Elliott and Fry

103 Portrait based on No. 99, by Henry Matthew Brock R.A. (1875–1960)

In 1869 Ruskin was again photographed by Elliott and Fry. These six photographs are not listed by Cook and Wedderburn, but one of them – No. 97 – was reproduced in *The Bookman* in March 1900 where it is dated 'about 1869'. Since most of the material in that issue of *The Bookman* must have come from Ruskinian sources and since Ruskin's appearance in No. 97 is not at variance with the date, I am happy to accept 1869 as the date of this sitting. Nos. 97–102 were clearly all taken at the same time.

97

98

128 December 1857. See No. 122, below.

129 in *Ruskin for Rector. The Edinburgh Rectorial Election of 1868* (1980).

99

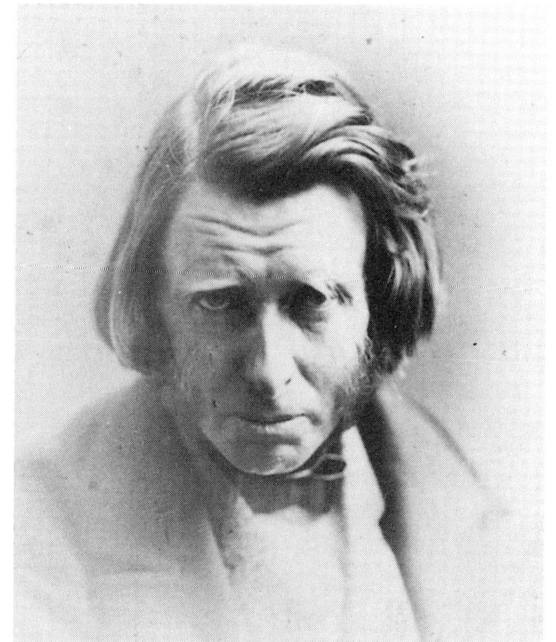

100

101

102

Ruskin was much in communication with Thomas Carlyle at this period, and prints of Nos. 98–102 must have been given to him. These prints are in volume 4 of the Carlyle Albums at Columbia University, where Carlyle has written Ruskin's name on Nos. 98 and 102.

Constance Oldham was of the opinion that No. 97 was 'the only likeness that gives some slight impression of the "Hebrew Prophet" aspect, and of the power of the (of course, *blue*) eyes – small head again'.

When H.M. Brock, illustrator, landscape painter, but mainly book illustrator, designed a dust jacket for the undated Blackie volume containing *Sesame and Lilies* and *Unto this Last*, he based his image of Ruskin on No. 99.

103

104 John Ruskin delivering his inaugural Slade Lecture, 8 February 1870, aet 51. Imaginative portrait by Alan Sorrell (1904–1974)

105 John Ruskin, working sketch for No. 104, by Alan Sorrell

When he died in 1868 Felix Slade bequeathed the sum of £35,000 for the endowment of Slade Professorships of Fine Art, at Oxford, Cambridge and London. It had long been Henry Acland's ambition to get Ruskin appointed 'Professor of Art' at Oxford, and with the Slade Bequest, he saw his opportunity. With Liddell and others, Acland put Ruskin's name forward and in the autumn of 1869 he was appointed Slade Professor of Fine Art at Oxford.

His appointment was a fitting one. He had been an established writer on art for over twenty years and was the most powerful and respected art critic in the country. He had also had considerable experience as a lecturer. Not only was the Establishment happy with the appointment; so too were the undergraduates to whom he seemed an Olympian figure. 'Imagine, then, our feelings', wrote Selwyn Image, 'when the news came that this Prophet of the Lord was actually to come among us in bodily presence'.

Ruskin began to prepare his first series of lectures on New Year's Day 1870 but after the first week he met with a month's interruption and was not able to finish working on his inaugural lecture, which was scheduled for 8 February, until a few days before its delivery. The date of the lecture happened to be Ruskin's fifty-first birthday, and lecturing to the Ruskin Union in 1903[130] Selwyn Image described the events of the day.

> The lecture was appointed for two or three in the afternoon in the lecture room of the University Museum ... My rooms were in New College Lane, and more than an hour before the time I hurried off. As I turned the corner a continuous stream of people, graduates, undergraduates, dons, ladies, townsfolk, met me, hurrying to the lecture room ... The lecture room reached and in a corner of it I found the last spot of standing ground. ... A gowned figure almost immediately rose behind the lecturer's desk, and said 'Ladies and gentlemen, it is very flattering to Mr Ruskin that such crowds of you are flocked to hear him. This large room is clearly too small to hold you. We must adjourn to the Sheldonian Theatre'. ... One was thankful to get a place anywhere high up in the gallery of that spacious building. It was packed quickly from floor to ceiling with a crowd the most motley and expectant ever on such an occasion – one would imagine – gathered there.

130 On 25 June 1903. The lecture was printed under the title 'Some personal recollections of John Ruskin' in *St George* VI, pp. 287-301. Although Image was recalling events of nearly thirty years earlier, his account of the lecture is confirmed by contemporary reports.

104

... Ruskin, in a long, old-fashioned silk gown and master's hood, passed up into the pulpit, and bowing to the vice-chancellor and proctors, began in a low, thin voice, to all appearances entirely calm and collected, that superb first lecture. He spoke low and very deliberately ... To those of you who never heard him, or never heard him at least in such days, it is perhaps impossible to convey any adequate impression of what a lecturer he was. In bodily presence small, slight to fragility, at times almost as it were crumpled in appearance – with a voice neither powerful, nor in itself musical, with even a slight impediment in his utterance – how he held his audience, how he imposed himself on them, how he charmed them! ... This slight, almost insignificant man towered over his audience. He had the fire and force of a prophet. His eyes flashed upon you. Always beginning in a low voice, slowly and quietly, he grew more and more full of sparkle and vigour as he proceeded. But he never lost command of himself, or became the plaything of his eloquence. Towards the end of his lecture he generally grew more quiet. Those perorations, those incomparable perorations, were delivered very gravely, with the most exquisite sense of cadence, of rhythmic modulation.

During the course of the lecture Ruskin told his audience,

There is a destiny now possible to us – the highest ever set before a nation to be accepted or refused. We are still undegenerate in race; a race mingled of the best northern blood. We are not yet dissolute in temper, but still have the firmness to govern and the grace to obey ... Will you, youths of England, make your country again a royal throne of kings; a sceptred isle, for all the world a source of light, a centre of peace; mistress of Learning and of the Arts; – faithful guardian of great memories in the midst of irreverent and ephemeral visions; – faithful servant of time-tried principles, under temptation from fond experiments and licentious desires; and amidst the cruel and clamorous jealousies of the nations, worshipped in her strange valour, of goodwill towards men? ... This is what England must either do, or perish; she must found colonies as fast and as far as she is able, formed of her most

> energetic and worthiest men; – seizing every piece of fruitful waste ground she can set her foot on...[131]

One young man who was to be profoundly influenced by Ruskin's words was Cecil Rhodes. Although he may have attended other Ruskin lectures at Oxford, it is improbable that he was at the Inaugural Lecture. It seems more likely that he was inspired by the lecture when he read reports of it in the *Pall Mall Gazette* (9 February), or *The Athenæum* (12 February), or he may have read the lecture itself in *Lectures on Art*, issued in July 1870.

Alan Sorrell, the artist of the present picture, shows Rhodes seated below the rostrum, leaning on the rail, although he does not appear to have gone to Oxford as an undergraduate until October 1873. His career there was spasmodic and he did not graduate until December 1881.

Cecil Rhodes's birthplace at Bishop's Stortford was opened as a museum to commemorate the centenary of his birth. An adjacent building was added to form the memorial museum. One room was designed to represent the period of Rhodes's life at Oxford and a series of six drawings to illustrate it (of which the present is one) were commissioned from Alan Sorrell by the architect Geoffrey Jellicoe in 1953. The pencil sketch of Ruskin (No. 105), which Mr Alan Turvey has suggested could be based on the Boehm bust (No. 149), and a copy (No. 194) of the D.S. MacColl drawing of 1883 (No. 193) are included in the series of sketchbooks used by Sorrell, which are now in the possession of Mrs Sorrell.

105

106 John Ruskin, c.1870–1875, an anonymous sketch

This anonymous little sketch of Ruskin was bought in 1956 by the Pierpont Morgan Library from an English dealer. It has not been possible to trace its previous history. It was suggested to the present owners that it was a self-portrait. The style is, however, not typical of any of Ruskin's work and the word 'Ruskin' below the drawing is certainly not in his hand, although it is not unlike it. The point which clinches the argument is the fact that the image is not reversed, as it would be in a self-portrait.

The sketch shows, in a rather exaggerated fashion, the slight stoop which Ruskin had in middle age. This exaggerated stoop, bordering on a humped back, is also evident in the *Vanity Fair* cartoon (No. 109) of 1872. Ruskin jokingly referred to his stoop in a letter to Joan Severn in January 1870, '... I'm humpbacked. All humpbacked people

106

131 *Works* XX, pp. 41-42. Ruskin repeated this passage, which he described as 'the most pregnant and essential' of all his teachings, in the first of his series of 'Pleasures of England' lectures at Oxford in 1884.

are remarkable people – intellectually. Though I'm humpbacked, I'm not Richard III…'[132]

I would tentatively date this sketch between 1870 and 1875. This dating is based on a comparison with other portraits and photographs, particularly the photograph taken in 1875 by the Rev. C.L. Dodgson (No. 122).

The drawing was made on the reverse of some old notes of a medical nature, and then cut into a rough oval. The notes appear to have no connection with Ruskin and afford no clue as to the identity of the artist of the sketch.

107 John Ruskin, aet 53, 1872, sketch by Adriano Cecioni (1838–1886)

108 John Ruskin, sketch by Adriano Cecioni

109 John Ruskin, full-length caricature by Adriano Cecioni (Plate 16)

The career of the Italian sculptor, painter and caricaturist Adriano Cecioni was fostered by his association between 1863 and 1867 with the Neapolitan realists. His success at the Paris Exhibition of 1870 brought him to London. He was soon producing (in all, twenty six) regular cartoons of well-known figures for *Vanity Fair*, which had been begun a couple of years earlier by Thomas Gibson Bowles. Bowles owned and edited the magazine until he sold it to Arthur Evans in 1889. Cecioni's experience as a *Vanity Fair* caricaturist led him on to the comic sculptures for which he earned a reputation on his return to Italy.

The two sketches (Nos. 107 and 108) were probably made from life. Although I can find no reference to artist and subject actually meeting, Cecioni would have had ample opportunity to see Ruskin, perhaps at one of his lectures.

Charles Fortescue-Brickdale, who as an undergraduate in the 1870s attended Ruskin's Oxford lectures, described[133] him as

> … then clean shaven, except for well-clipped yellowish whiskers, showing a sensitive and expressive mouth; fresh complexioned, nose rather prominent, with clear eye and a good deal of straight brown hair worn rather long and brushed well back from the forehead. The cut of his double-breasted frock coat was that of a well-dressed man of the late forties – high collared and

107

108

132 *Works* XXXVII, p. 4.

133 letter to *The Times*, 9 May 1932.

rather full at the opening, which generally displayed a broad neckcloth (he would never have called it a 'tie') of a bright blue colour, carefully adjusted into a neat bow. Altogether rather an exquisite. The *Vanity Fair* drawing, though, of course, a good deal exaggerated, gives a vivid and true idea of his general appearance at the date when his Slade professorship began.

The full-length caricature (No. 109) appeared in *Vanity Fair* on 17 February 1872, with the title 'Men of the Day, No. 40 – The Realisation of the Ideal'. The title was taken from the text on the reverse of the caricature, by 'Jehu Junior'.[134]

There is perhaps no harder fate in store for a man than to be irredeemably at variance with the spirit of the country and the times in which he lives; and it is Mr Ruskin's great misfortune to be an incurable poet and artist in a materialistic and money grubbing generation. He is so entirely out of harmony with all of modern life that surrounds him that he is by many regarded as an anachronism rather than as a man, and that his views are looked upon rather as vain protests than as serious opinions by those who have not bowed the knee to the modern Baal. He (Ruskin) will be greatly remembered as one preaching in the wilderness the abandonment of the grosser things of life and the realisation of the Ideal.

Another note in that issue of *Vanity Fair* says:

The English people have become meanly practical, and he [Ruskin] is grandly unpractical; they have become essentially commonplace, and he is gloriously poetical; they believe in nothing more than cash, he believes in nothing less.

Ruskin was not flattered by the caricature and four years later, discussing the Ruskin Drawing School casts, he wrote in *Flors Clavigera*[135]

Well, I hope I *am* handsomer than the [Elgin] Theseus; it's very pleasant to think so, but it did not strike me before. May I flatter myself it is really your candid opinion? Will you just look at the 'Realisation of the (your?) Ideal' in the number of *Vanity Fair* for February 17th, 1872, and confirm me on this point?

It appears from Ruskin's letter of 24 December 1874 to Joan Severn that *Vanity Fair* was also not satisfied with Cecioini's caricature. He wrote to her

109

They say, the Liddells, that both the Dean and I are to be in *Vanity Fair* soon – they weren't satisfied with mine and sent their best man down to study the Dean in chapel, and me lecturing! ...

But the second caricature (No. 121) was never published, and the sketch has not been located.

134 Almost certainly T.G. Bowles.

135 Letters 66, June 1876. *Works* XXVIII, p. 620.

110 John Ruskin, caricature by Edward Linley Sambourne (1844–1910) in 'Vision of Burlington House, Sixth of May', 1872

Ruskin was a regular visitor to the Royal Academy Summer Exhibitions and from 1855 to 1859, and again in 1875 he published his very popular *Academy Notes* in which he criticised selected pictures in the exhibition. As it happens, one of the exhibitions which he missed was that of 1872.

This period of Ruskin's life saw a number of dramatic changes in his domestic arrangements. Following the death of his father in 1864, a young distant cousin, Joan Agnew, had come to live at Denmark Hill as a companion to the elderly Mrs Ruskin. Ruskin became fond of Joan, almost looking on her as a daughter. In April 1871 she was married to Arthur Severn, the son of Joseph whom Ruskin had first met in Rome in 1840. Later in the same year, in June, Ruskin was seriously ill for several weeks while staying at Matlock in Derbyshire. The Severns went there to nurse him. At the height of his illness he is reported to have said to Dr Acland that he would feel better if only he could lie down in Coniston Water. Soon after his recovery and return to Denmark Hill, he had a letter from William James Linton who had emigrated to America, saying that he wished to sell his house, Brantwood, on the eastern shore of Coniston Lake. Ruskin immediately paid Linton's asking price of £1,500 and Brantwood became his home for the rest of his life. Today the house and estate are maintained as a national memorial to him. He first visited Brantwood in September 1871 and arranged for improvements and alterations to be made.

Margaret Ruskin died at Denmark Hill on 5 December 1871 and Ruskin decided to sell his old home, spending his last day there on 28 March in the following year, before moving to his rooms in Oxford. As a London base the Severns offered a room in the house at Herne Hill which Ruskin had given them as a wedding present, and where he himself had lived before the family had bought the Denmark Hill house. Meanwhile Brantwood was not going to be ready for some time and on 13 April Ruskin took Joan and Arthur Severn, Mrs Hilliard (the sister of Lady Trevelyan) and her daughter Connie, and Albert Goodwin on a continental tour which was to last for several months. On 6 May, the day on which the Academy exhibition opened, they were in Lucca.

Edward Linley Sambourne who followed in Tenniel's footsteps at *Punch* had a talent for the grotesque and produced impeccably drawn cartoons. During his career with *Punch*, which began in 1867, Sambourne featured Ruskin in

VISION OF BURLINGTON HOUSE, SIXTH OF MAY.

110

several of his cartoons, of which 'The Vision of Burlington House' is the first.

The exhibition rooms at Burlington House are encompassed by the outline of a crown. The populace of London throng into the crown while the artists sit on its top. One drinks champagne while another dangles a fishing rod baited with a £1,000 canvas over the heads of the crowd. In the cellars below, the servants of the Academy catch the shilling admission fees and shovel them into £100 sacks. Mr Punch asks the 'Official Catalogue', 'You call yourself a catalogue?', while the agonised Ruskin flees from the crowd, at once covering his ears and tearing his hair.

111 John Ruskin, caricatured as an Angel of Light, by Frederick Waddy, 1872

Waddy's cartoon first appeared in *One a Week* for 25 May 1872. It was re-printed in *Cartoon Men of the Day* in 1873. Ruskin, as the Angel of Light, is seen hovering over the dismal buildings of London, labelled 'The World of Light'. Above him shines the bright star of High Art, while he drops his books as flowers of wisdom – *Ethics of the Dust*, *Stones of Venice*, *Seven Lamps of Architecture* and *Modern Painters* – on the city beneath.

Very little is known about Frederick Waddy. He seems to have exhibited once at the Royal Academy, in 1878. Other than that, a number of his caricatures of notable men of the day appeared in *Illustrated London News* and elsewhere. He also engraved ornamental initials for a number of journals.

Waddy's caricature of Ruskin was re-drawn by Michael Hadley in 1973 as the cover design for my *John Ruskin* in the Lifelines series. In that version, Ruskin is shown flying above the Oxford Museum.

ART CRITICISM.

111

112 John Ruskin, aet 53, photographed with the Severns, Hilliards and Albert Goodwin, June–July 1872

The Ruskin menage left Lucca and by 8 May 1872 they were in Florence. From there they went to Rome for a week's stay. Ruskin, who did not really like the city, had only been there once before. But the real purpose of this visit was to allow Arthur Severn to introduce his wife to his father, Joseph, who was still English Consul and living near the Trevi Fountain. By 22 June the party arrived in Venice, where they stayed at Danieli's until 14 July.

While they were in Venice they saw a great deal of John Wharlton Bunney, an English artist who had lived there for a couple of years. Bunney, nine years younger than Ruskin, had been in his drawing class at the Working Men's College when Ruskin had first noticed his work. In 1859 he had given up his job with Ruskin's publishers, Smith Elder & Co., to become a drawing master. After working with Ruskin in Switzerland and Italy, Bunney finally left England in 1863 to settle in Florence, and later, in 1870, in Venice where he remained until his death in 1882. He executed many commissions for Ruskin. One of his last works was a large oil painting, 5' x 7', of the west front of St Mark's, painted for the Guild of St George, which took six hundred mornings to complete.

For many years the only original print of this photograph which I knew was that owned by the late Michael Bunney, grandson of Ruskin's Venetian friend. It is inscribed on the reverse by J.W. Bunney's son, G.C. Bunney: 'John Ruskin / Lady ? / Lady ? / Lady ? / Arthur Severn (standing) / Albert Goodwin'. The combination of people making up the group and the presence of the print in the Bunney Collection makes it almost certain that the photograph was taken in Venice in 1872. Perhaps it was taken either by Perini or Vinetti, both photographers whom Bunney employed occasionally to photograph his own paintings, or architectural details for Ruskin. A second print subsequently turned up in the Raven Collection. Presumably that print had originally been given to Kate Smith, Ruskin's housekeeper, by Ruskin himself.

Ruskin sits, in a singularly uncomfortable looking pose on the left of the group, looking much as he did in the 1867 Elliott and Fry photograph (No. 86). Bunney had recorded in his diary

112

that Ruskin looked better than he ever remembered him looking. Next to Ruskin stands Mrs Hilliard, wife of the Rev. J.C. Hilliard of Cowley near Uxbridge and one of Ruskin's inner circle of friends. The twenty-six years old Joan Severn is seated in the centre with her thirty years old husband resting his hand on her chair back. Constance Hilliard is seated at Arthur's feet and wears on a ribbon round her neck the Florentine cross which Ruskin had given her. The twenty-seven years old artist Albert Goodwin sits on the right.

Bunney's views on the party are interesting.[136] He did not 'see any prospect of getting work out of' Ruskin. Mrs Hilliard 'didn't seem to care very much' for his drawings. 'Art isn't her forte, I expect'. Severn, he considered, 'doesn't look a very clever follow' while Goodwin 'seems to have great appreciation [of Bunney's pictures] and he chose nearly always that which I consider very fairly done. He is evidently a man of great talent ... a friend of Arthur Hughes. He has almost the same slothful manner that Burgess [another of Ruskin's protégés] had, an affectation which no doubt young Englishmen cultivate, nowadays, slouchy in his dress and I noticed that one of his shoes was only half laced up, the lace having been broken short and he too idle to put in another'.

113 John Ruskin, portrait by Charles Herbert Moore (1840–1930)

C.H. Moore was an American painter who specialised in the study of medieval architecture. He was the author of studies in Renaissance art, but particularly medieval architecture. Moore was the first Curator of the Fogg Art Museum and in 1896 he became Professor of Art at Harvard.

Charles Moore was influenced by Ruskin's work, and seems to have been introduced to him by Charles Eliot Norton. In February 1873 Ruskin told Norton that 'I will take every pains to assist Mr Moore'; the promise was repeated in December of the same year.[137]

Ruskin and Moore were in Venice at the same time in 1876–77 and they saw a certain amount of each other. They worked together on their copies of Carpaccio's St Ursula. Ruskin told Joan Severn that his time had been devoted '... most pleasantly always – to Mr Moore, who is as fond of Carpaccio as I'.[138] Ruskin was to meet up again with Moore at Simplon on his return journey to London; in June they spent three days there together.

Perhaps Moore had obtained a print of the 1872 photograph (No. 112) from Bunney in Venice, or perhaps he had got it through Norton. Whichever was the case, it is certain that he based the present watercolour on the photograph. However, some of his own observation of Ruskin also went into the portrait. For example, it is not possible to see the *texture* of the waistcoat in the photograph, and an observer unacquainted with Ruskin would not have known that the line which follows the edge of his jacket lapel in the photograph was, in fact, the watch chain which Ruskin wore round his neck.

113

Moore gave the portrait to Norton – indeed Norton *could* have commissioned it – and it passed through his family, appropriately, to the Fogg Art Museum.

136 These are taken from his diary and were first quoted by kind permission of the owner, Mr Michael Bunney, in J.S. Dearden, 'The Ruskin circle in Italy in 1872', *Connoisseur*, April 1972, pp. 240-45.

137 J.L. Bradley & I. Ousby (ed.), *The Correspondence of John Ruskin and Charles Eliot Norton* (Cambridge: Cambridge University Press, 1987), pp. 281, 300.

138 JR – Joan Severn, 29 Sept. 1876; RF L41.

114 John Ruskin, aet 54, self-portrait, January 1873 (Plate 17)

It seems likely that this portrait was painted at the beginning of 1873 for Charles Eliot Norton, but never sent to him. Norton was in London in the winter of 1872 and it is possible that when Ruskin saw him, he promised (yet again) to make the portrait. Ruskin may have been referring to this promise when he wrote to Norton on 27 December 1872, 'I will do S[usan (Norton's Wife)] her drawing and yours, at Brantwood'.[139]

The promised drawing was begun on 28 January. 'Begun portrait of self for Norton'. On the following day Ruskin 'worked hard at letters and portrait'.[140] The portrait, which is now know as 'the portrait with the blue neckcloth' is probably the finest of Ruskin's self-portraits. But it was apparently never sent to Norton for at the beginning of the next year Ruskin was still promising to send him one. The 1873 self-portrait stayed at Brantwood. Perhaps Ruskin gave it to Joan Severn whose second child was born a few days after it was drawn. (It is inscribed by Joan 'Di Pa by himself'.) It was eventually acquired from Miss Violet Severn by the late F.J. Sharp, and sold after his death by Mrs M. Holmes to the present owners, the Pierpont Morgan Library, in 1959.

114

115 John Ruskin, aet 54, autumn 1873, photographed by Frank Meadow Sutcliffe (1853–1941)

1873 was a year in which his Oxford work kept Ruskin very busy. In the spring he delivered his three *Love's Meinie* lectures on the Robin, the Chough and the Swallow, repeating two of them at Eton. June to October was spent mainly at Brantwood, returning to Oxford in the autumn to deliver the ten lectures on Tuscan art which Ruskin called *Val d'Arno*. In addition to preparing and delivering these lectures, he was preparing those of the previous year for publication, and revising and seeing through the press new editions of both *Modern Painters* and *Stones of Venice*.

Frank Sutcliffe was a professional portrait photographer of Whitby who is most famous for the fine pictures he took in and around his home town. As a youth he had photographed two fine old Scots pines at Rievaulx. Years later he described[141] how Ruskin saw a print of this photograph 'on the table at the house of a lady who lived ... a little way down the lane [from Brantwood – perhaps Susan Beever at The Thwaite]' and wrote to ask if he would like to come to Coniston to take some views of Brantwood.

Sutcliffe describes how he arrived at Coniston 'one fine autumn evening ... in 1872'[142] and on the following morning he went to Brantwood taking with him all his photographic paraphernalia in a cart. He seems to have spent two days there and

139 *Letters of John Ruskin to Charles Eliot Norton* vol. II, p. 55.
140 *Diary*, 29-30 January 1873.
141 F.M. Sutcliffe, 'Photographer to John Ruskin', *Photographic Journal*, June 1931, p. 255.
142 In fact it must have been 1873.

115

during that time took photographs of the house with the morning sun on it and another view of the house from the Coniston gate, groups by the harbour, the lodge, many exposures of Lily Severn, some ferns growing on a rock a little way down the lake, and several other things.

After lunch on the first day of the visit Ruskin asked Sutcliffe what he would like to photograph next.

> 'Yourself, sir' came the answer, replied to by a smile in the blue eyes. So after John Ruskin had been put into a new grey frock-coat by his man, the camera was set up opposite a honeysuckle covered hole in a wall which had once held three or four bee hives, and John Ruskin sat down and the camera got to work. After that, John Ruskin said he would find a much more pleasing subject than himself who would suit the surroundings better than he, and he brought a charming young lady with a striped gown, who was asked to tuck herself into a hole in the wall and pretend to read the book she had under her arm ...'

Sutcliffe does not reveal the identity of the 'young lady in the striped gown'. It is unlikely that it was Joan Severn as he does refer to *her* on several occasions (as Ruskin's niece). There were several visitors to Brantwood in the early autumn. Dawtry Drewitt and his wife Dora were there from the third week of August until at least 15 September; Connie Hilliard arrived on 1 September and stayed until Ruskin returned to Oxford on 18 October; and Alfred Hunt, his wife and children were frequent visitors. Connie was there for the longest period, so she must be the best candidate for the lady in the striped dress.

Unfortunately many of the plates which Sutcliffe exposed at Brantwood were spoiled. His photographs were taken by the wet plate process and Sutcliffe describes how his 'dark tent' had been set up in one end of a potting shed. After the plates had been developed they were leaned on a shelf to dry, face upwards, and during the photographer's absence a gardener decided to sweep out the shed, thus damaging many of the plates. Happily the negative of Ruskin survived and is still at The Sutcliffe Gallery in Whitby.

In his article written nearly sixty years after the visit, Sutcliffe dated his journey to Coniston as 1872. Another article[143] written in 1900 does not mention the year, but does refer to taking a photograph of the 'new lodge'. The building of the lodge at Brantwood did not begin until the end of 1872, thus ruling out that year to Sutcliffe's visit. It was finished by the following spring, and in autumn 1873 could be described as 'new'. Ruskin was not at Brantwood in the autumn of 1874 and by the next year the lodge was no longer new. Thus Frank Sutcliffe's visit to Brantwood must have been in the autumn of 1873. In later years he advertised himself as 'Photographer to John Ruskin'.

116 John Ruskin, aet 55, self-portrait, head and shoulders, Spring 1874

117 John Ruskin, aet 55, self-portrait, head only, Spring 1874 (Plate 18)

At last Charles Norton was to have his portrait of Ruskin! He had waited nearly fifteen years since it was originally promised in 1859. Rossetti hadn't produced it; Burne-Jones hadn't finished his, and Ruskin never sent the self-portrait *he* had promised. But on 15 February 1874, he wrote to Norton from Oxford, saying 'I shall make you a little drawing of myself positively before I go abroad'. In the end, Ruskin made two portraits – a pencil drawing (No. 116) and a watercolour (No. 117). By 23 February he was back at Brantwood and with the exception of a few days in London at the end of March, he remained at Coniston until he went abroad on 1 April. Thus it seems likely that the portraits were made at Brantwood.

On 9 April he wrote again to Norton, from Pisa.

> I have told Burgess to send you the two beginnings of myself I made for you. All that is good in me depends on terrible subtleties, which I find will require my very best care and power of completion – all that comes at first is the worst. Continually I see accidental looks, which, if I could set down, you would like ... only I let these failures be sent to show I have been trying.

Ruskin had been particularly depressed in the spring. He was very worried about Rose La Touche and his love for her was causing him much grief. His appearance was beginning to be aged by this worry and sadness, and it shows in these two portraits.

116

143 F.M. Sutcliffe, 'A day's sunshine at Brantwood', *The Amateur Photographer*, 9 Feb. 1900, pp. 107-108.

Norton, who inscribed Ruskin's name on the front of the pencil drawing (No. 116) probably did not realise how much his friend had aged since he had seen him in the previous year, and he wrote on the reverse of the drawing 'Not a good likeness'.

After Norton's death the two portraits were sold in 1919. No. 116 was bought by J. Howard Whitehouse who exhibited it at the Ruskin Centenary Exhibition in the summer. It is now in the collection at Brantwood. No. 117 was bought by Charles Goodspeed, who presented it in 1920 to Wellesley College Library (his two daughters were educated at Wellesley), thus probably saving it from the fire which later destroyed the two portraits by George Richmond.

117

118 John Ruskin, caricature, 'Ruskin and Realism', April 1874

119 John Ruskin, caricatured as 'President of the Amateur Landscape Gardening Society', by INO, 1874

The present two cartoons relate to a practical scheme of work which Ruskin set his Oxford undergraduate friends. Eleven years earlier, in the fifth of his *Fraser's Magazine*[144] articles on political economy, his Oxford scheme had been foreshadowed when he wrote

> ... a large portion [of agricultural labour] should be done by the upper classes; – bodily health, and sufficient contrast and repose for the mental functions, being unattainable without it ...

At Oxford, a favourite walk of Ruskin's was to Ferry (or North) Hinksey where the carts on the track across the damp fields cut them into ruts. In March 1874 he told Henry Acland[145] that he wanted to show his Oxford Drawing class what a country road should be by draining the fields to get the ruts out of the track and sowing the banks with wild flowers. But he wrote 'my chief object is to let my pupils feel the pleasure of *useful* muscular work'. Before their work, Ruskin entertained his 'diggers' to breakfast at Corpus. The digging was

144 'Government', *Fraser's Magazine*, April 1863; *Works* XVII, p. 235.

145 JR – Henry Acland, 28 March 1874; *Works* XX, p. xli.

162 FUN. [April 18, 1874.

RUSKIN AND REALISM.

"How much better, oh, Oxonians, is this then the vain pursuits of rowing and cricket!"

Thus also may your sing-songing——

And your bird-slaughter become useful to man!

The sons of labour, having nothing else to do, will go in for being amateur-gentlemen. And we shall all live happily ever after!

118

superintended by Ruskin's gardener, David Downs, and the greatest part of the heavy work was done while Ruskin was abroad, though he did join parties of diggers in the autumn. Among the undergraduates who helped with the scheme were Alexander Wedderburn (later to be a K.C. and his editor and executor), W.G. Collingwood (later his secretary, editor and first biographer), F.G. Stokes, A.E. Street, Arnold Toynbee, W.H. Mallock, Oscar Wilde, H.D. Rawnsley, J.R. Anderson, Stewart Wortley and Leonard Montefiore.

Hardwick Rawnsley, later to take a great interest in Ruskin and as a result of his teaching to become one of the three founders of the National Trust, described in an article[146] how Ruskin joined the diggers.

'I can see him', wrote Rawnsley, 'in blue frock coat and blue cloth cap, with ear flaps pulled about his ears, sitting cheerily by the roadside breaking stones not only with a will but with knowledge, and cracking jokes the while'.

Both the scheme and the diggers came in for a certain amount of ridicule in the press, though being abroad when the scheme began Ruskin missed the brunt of it. It became a popular pastime (not only confined to undergraduates) to go out to Hinksey to watch and jeer. A drawing of the undergraduates at work published in the *Graphic* of 27 June 1874 shows a couple of families and at least one clerical gentleman among the spectators.

GREAT GUNS OF OXFORD. PRESIDENT OF THE "AMATEUR LANDSCAPE GARDENING SOCIETY."

119

The cartoon which appeared in the 18 April 1874 issue of *Fun* (No. 118) shows the slim Ruskin wearing labourer's boots and the nimbus of 'High Art' – and wielding a pick, while two virtuous undergraduates dig and a figure in the background looks on. In the other three quarters of the cartoon undergraduates indulge in less worthy activities.

The drawing by INO (No. 119) appeared in the window of Shrimpton's shop in Broad Street and photographs of it were on sale. The identity of the artist, INO, has long remained a mystery. The original drawing found its way into the collection at Ruskin College.

Writing soon after the opening of Ruskin Hall, as it was then called, on 22 February 1899, J.A. Dale and L.T. Dodd[147] explained that the College did not bind itself to follow the tenets of any leader but that its activity had for its motive that same enthusiasm which had inspired all Ruskin's life and teaching founded on the Dignity of Labour and the Necessity of Faithful Living. 'It is with absolute faith in the rightness and ultimate triumph of these principles that the founders of Ruskin Hall are beginning their mission'.

The Ruskin College exhibit in the Franco-British Exhibition of 1908 included the original caricature. The writer of the catalogue note clearly knew the identity of INO and gave us the best clue we have. He said that INO was an undergraduate in 1874 and a Royal Academician in 1908. In fact none of the R.A. undergraduates of the period fit the bill, the most likely being Briton Riviere, who took his M.A. in 1873.

146 *Atlantic Monthly*, April 1900, pp. 572-76.

147 J.A. Dale & L.T. Dodd, 'Ruskin Hall, Oxford', *St George* II, p. 95.

120 John Ruskin, aet 55, self-portrait as St Francis, June–July 1874 (Plate 19)

Ruskin wrote to his father from Florence on 30 June 1845 to tell him that by 'speaking Italian' he had seen a *portrait* of St Francis by Cimabue in S. Croce, which had made an impression on him.[148] However, this painting is not now considered to be the work of Cimabue.

Thirty years later, in 1874 in Assisi, Ruskin had scaffolding erected in the lower church and busily engaged in examining and copying Giotto's Allegories of Marriage with St Poverty, to the exclusion of all else. But on 19 June by chance he 'discovered Cimabue in the lower church, altering my thoughts of all early Italian art'.[149] He hoped to begin copying details of the fresco, which showed the Madonna and Child with four angels and St Francis, starting his copy of the Madonna on 24 June. He later reproduced the drawing as the frontispiece to *The Bible of Amiens*. By now he had written to tell Norton[150] that he had been 'altogether amazed at the power of Cimabue, before wholly unknown to me ... the Cimabue is a discovery to me – wholly unexpected ...', and a couple of days later, 'Giotto is a mere domestic gossip – compared to Cimabue'. Later in the year at Oxford, Ruskin lectured on Cimabue, and gaps in his manuscript probably indicate that he showed his audience the copies he had made in the summer.

In addition to the Madonna, he had also copied St Francis, with whom at Assisi that summer he had felt a particularly affinity.

It is now several years since the late Dr Helen Viljoen sent me colour transparencies of the original Cimabue (Figure 16) and Ruskin's copy, and drew my attention to the copy's likeness to Ruskin himself. I must admit that as a copy it is not a very good likeness of Cimabue's St Francis; and it *does* bear a certain resemblance to Ruskin. I am sceptical about the *intention* to make a self-portrait as St Francis, but feel that I cannot justify its omission from these pages.

Making the original drawing available for Dr Viljoen's New York exhibition in 1965, the owner, Professor Ross, wrote in the catalogue:

Figure 16

120

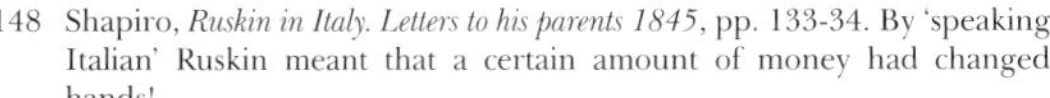

148 Shapiro, *Ruskin in Italy. Letters to his parents 1845*, pp. 133-34. By 'speaking Italian' Ruskin meant that a certain amount of money had changed hands!

149 *Diary*, p. 796.

150 Bradley and Ousby, *The Correspondence of John Ruskin and Charles Eliot Norton*, pp. 316-17, 318.

Compared with Herkomer's portrait of Ruskin [No. 153], or C.L. Dodgsons's photograph [No. 122], both of about the same time, clearly the drawing is far from a realistic self-portrait, but Ruskin's own face stares out beneath the monk's tonsure. The face is emaciated and the expression is weary, sad, and with a look of bitterness that does not appear in the original. This portrait is meant to give a glimpse of the soul within, without the inappropriate disguise of the blue tie and velvet collar of his daily dress.

Ruskin gave the drawing to Norton when he was staying at Brantwood at the end of June 1883 and it was eventually inherited by his daughters. In turn they gave it to Professor Sydney Ross. About 1978 Ross gave it to the present owner, R. Dyke Benjamin; thus throughout its history the drawing has never been *sold*.

121 John Ruskin lecturing

See Nos. 107–109.

122 John Ruskin sitting in an arm chair, photographed by Charles Lutwidge Dodgson (1832–98) 6 March 1875, aet 56

123 John Ruskin sitting at a table, photographed by C.L.Dodgson 3 June 1875

124 John Ruskin, portrait by Charles Herbert Moore (1840–1930) based on No. 123, c.1877

122

At the time that these photographs were taken, Rose La Touche, with whom Ruskin had been in love for the past ten years, was dying.

Rose was born on 3 January 1848, the youngest child of John and Maria La Touche of Harristown in County Kildare. Ten years later she met Ruskin, whom her mother hoped would teach her children drawing. The friendship between Rose and Ruskin eventually deepened into love, but Rose who was almost fanatically religious was deeply upset by Ruskin's religious scepticism. 'How could one love you if you were a pagan' she wrote to him.

Rose began to have serious and unexplained illnesses but by 1865 she had temporarily recovered and on her 17th birthday Ruskin asked her to marry him. She told him to ask her again in a year's time – but in any case she would answer when she was twenty-one. Not until now had the senior La Touches realised the situation between Ruskin and their daughter. They determined that the pair should forget each other and forbade them to meet for a few years.

There were occasional meetings but the strain was telling on both of them and it may well have been a cause of Ruskin's illness at Matlock in 1871. In the hope of a reconciliation, Ruskin had prematurely terminated his 1872 continental tour and rushed back to London to see Rose.

With the turn of 1874 Rose's physical and mental condition deteriorated rapidly. While she was still able she wrote several letters to Ruskin which gave him much pleasure, and on one occasion he was able to visit her. By December the last traces of sanity had left her, and by January 1875 Ruskin knew that she was dying. He was able to visit her on 25 February and calm her during her illness. This was probably the last time he saw her. She was taken home to Ireland where she died on 25 or 26 May 1875. Ruskin wrote to Carlyle '... the story of my wild Rose is ended, and the hawthorn blossoms this year would fall – over her'.

Ruskin was in Oxford occasionally in the early part of 1875 and it appears that the first of these two photographs (No. 122) was taken there on 6 March.[151] The photograph was evidently taken in Dodgson's study at Christ Church because Ruskin is sitting in Dodgson's own chair, the chair in which he photographed several of his subjects – his uncle Skeffington Lutwidge, Alice Liddell, F.D. Maurice, and his own self-portrait. Several friends asked Dodgson for prints and he wrote seeking Ruskin's permission. Ruskin replied 'Buy No. 5 of *Fors Clavigera* for 1871[152] which will give you your answer'. But Dodgson wrote that he couldn't afford the price, and finally Ruskin gave his permission. Copies were printed by H.P. Robinson of Tunbridge Wells.

Cook and Wedderburn describe it as one of the best photographs of Ruskin. Joan Severn sent a print to the family solicitors, and inscribed it on the reverse 'I enclose you what *I* consider *the* best photograph done of the Professor – (by Dodgson, author of *Alice in Wonderland*) ... He himself hates all portraits of himself'.[153]

Ruskin was photographed a second time by Dodgson who wrote in his diary[154] '3 June 1875. With some difficulty I persuaded Ruskin to come and be photographed, and to stay luncheon with us'. Ruskin's own diary entry for the following day confirms the event, 'Yesterday at lunch with Mr Dodgson'. The photograph reproduced here as No. 123 occurs in my own collection as a Stereoscopic Company print and in the Whitehouse Collection as a glass lantern slide in a 'Portraits' series issued by 'G.W.W.' G.W.W. was the Scottish

123

124

151 A print of the photograph in the possession of Mr D.J. Behrans of Mere is inscribed on the reverse in Dodgson's hand: '2309/Mrs Macmillan/ from the Artist/taken Mar. 6 1875'. Professor Morton Cohen confirms that the writing is Dodgson's and in his style of inscribing photographs. The number 2309 is Dodgson's negative number; he kept a register of negatives, but it has not survived. There is no entry in Dodgson's diary for this date, but he was certainly in Oxford. The Mrs (Emma) Macmillan to whom the photograph was given was the wife of Alexander Macmillan, the publisher. She was a friend of both Ruskin and Dodgson. The present owner is Mrs Macmillan's great nephew.

152 Where Ruskin had written: 'You think it a great triumph to make the sun draw brown landscapes for you. That was also a discovery, and some day may be useful. But the sun had drawn landscapes before you, not in brown, but in green, and blue, and all imaginable colours, here in England. Not one of you ever looked at them then'.

153 The photograph is in the possession of Smiles & Co., successors to Ruskin's solicitors.

154 R.L. Green (ed.), *Diaries of Lewis Carroll* (London: Cassell, 1953), vol. II, p. 340.

photographer George Washington Wilson, said at one time to have had the largest photographic publishing business in the world. The company did not start producing lantern slides until after Wilson had died and most of the photographs reproduced were bought from commercial studios. As far as I know there is no evidence to indicate that Wilson ever photographed Ruskin.

The opinion of Dodgson authorities are divided as to whether or not No. 123 is by him. But there is no evidence to show that Ruskin was photographed by anyone other than Dodgson between 1873 and 1879. Because of the similarity between Nos. 122 and 123 and because there is direct evidence that Dodgson photographed Ruskin on two occasions, I suggest that No. 123 is his second exposure, taken on 3 June 1875.

Rose La Touche had died between the first and second photographs (in fact nine or ten days before the second) and the strain can be clearly seen in Ruskin's face. There is a strange pouchiness about the cheeks which is absent from other portraits and photographs, with the exception of course of one of the two portraits by C.H. Moore which is based on No. 123. For the association between Ruskin and Moore, see above, No. 113.

The photographer, the Rev. Charles L. Dodgson, was a lecturer in Mathematics at Oxford from 1855 to 1881. He and Ruskin had a number of mutual friends and interests. For example on 23 November 1874 Dodgson noted[155] that Ruskin came to his rooms at Christ Church 'at my request to talk about the pictures Holiday is doing for the "Boojum"'.[156]

Of course another mutual friend was Alice Liddell, daughter of the Dean of Christ Church, for whom Dodgson, in the guise of Lewis Carroll had written *Alice in Wonderland* in 1865. Dodgson published a number of other humorous works. His parody on *The Song of Hiawatha*, entitled *Hiawatha's Photography* first appeared in *The Train* in December 1857. In the parody, the various members of a family in turn make suggestions about how they should pose for their photographs, one of them basing his idea on Ruskin.

> Next the Son, the Stunning-Cantab.;
> He suggested curves of beauty,
> Curves pervading all his figure,
> Which the eye might follow onward,
> Till they centred on the breast-pin.
> He had learnt it all from Ruskin
> (Author of 'The Stones of Venice',
> 'Seven Lamps of Architecture',
> 'Modern Painters', and some others);
> And perhaps he had not fully
> Understood his author's meaning;
> But, whatever was the reason,
> All was fruitless, as the picture
> Ended in an utter failure.

I must mention here my thanks to Mr Tim Hilton who has drawn my attention to the similarity between Ruskin's profile and that of the man dressed in white paper in one of Tenniel's illustrations for Carroll's *Through the Looking Glass*.

Figure 17

155 M. Cohen, *Lewis Carroll. A Biography* (London: Macmillan, 1995), p. 406.
156 *The Hunting of the Snark*.

125 John Ruskin, plaster medallion by Charles Ashmore, c.1875

Spielmann[157] records another portrait done at this period. 'In 1875 or thereabouts, a clever modeller, by name Mr Charles Ashmore, of Aston, a suburb near Birmingham, produced a plaster medallion that is an excellent likeness of Ruskin's features; but it fails to import any vivacity to the face or to give any of the expression of intellectuality such as is never absent from it. This work probably took a photograph for its basis'. Between 1849 and 1886 Ashmore exhibited regularly at the Birmingham Society of artists; between 1850 and 1870 he showed at the Academy and British Institution.

I have never seen a reproduction of a portrait actually described as being by Ashmore. However, there is in the Whitehouse Collection an unascribed photograph of what appears to be a plaster relief portrait of Ruskin. I reproduce it here in the belief that it *may* be the medallion by Charles Ashmore.

125

126 John Ruskin, caricatured in Lady of the Lake Loquitur, by E.L. Sambourne, February 1876.

In 1875 there was a suggestion that the London and North Western Railway should extend its line from Windermere to Ambleside and Rydal. Ruskin gave his support to the campaign opposing the extension – which in the event did not take place. Sambourne's cartoon which appeared in *Punch* on 5 February 1876 sprang from this protest. Ruskin as the Knight of High Art, fights a train to save the Lady of the Lake.

126

157 *Spielmann* II, p. 122.

127 John Ruskin, caricatured in Playing with Edged Tools, by T.C., March 1876

FUN.—March 29, 1876.

PLAYING WITH EDGED TOOLS.

AN UNDESERVED SNUB FOR SHEFFIELD.

MR. FUN CANNOT HELP THINKING THERE IS MUCH MORE GOOD IN ONE DAY'S HONEST LABOUR THAN IN YEARS OF SUPERFINE, OFTEN SUPERFICIAL, CRITICISM.

127

Perhaps the Sheffield Society of Artists knew in February 1876 that in the following April Ruskin would be in their city to attend a meeting at the museum which he had established for the Guild of St George. They asked him to address them, and received an acid reply.

> I lose a frightful quantity of time because people won't read what I ask them to read, nor believe anything of what I tell them, and yet ask me to talk whenever they think they can make a shilling or two at the door by me. I have written fifty times, if once, that you can't have art where you have smoke; you may have it in hell, perhaps, for the Devil is too clever not to consume his own smoke, if he wants to. But you will never have it in Sheffield. You may learn something about nature, shrivelled, and stones, and iron; and what little you can see of that sort, I am going to try and show you. But pictures, never.[158]

The outcome was the cartoon in *Fun* on 29 March in which 'Saint Rusty' wearing the halo of 'Super-Fine Art' turns his back on smoky Sheffield. The cartoon is sub-titled 'An undeserved snub for Sheffield. Mr Fun cannot help thinking there is much more good in one day's honest labour than in years of superfine, often superficial, criticism'.

128 John Ruskin at Brantwood, by Arthur Severn, ?June 1876, aet 57 (Plate 20)

128

Describing a typical evening in the Brantwood drawing room Collingwood wrote[159] that Ruskin would pull 'the four candlesticks close to him at the drawing room table' and read aloud from his favourite novel *Redgauntlet* (or whatever else was currently favourite), while 'we sketched furtively in corners, Laurence Hilliard and I, and the ladies plied their needles'.

Laurence Hilliard, brother to Connie of the 1872 photograph (No. 84) became Ruskin's principal secretary at Brantwood in January 1876. The figure sketching behind the table looks very like him. Perhaps the lady sitting next to him is Sara Anderson, secretary to Ruskin, Kipling and others – a sort of super-secretary, Cockerell called her. Joan Severn would be the figure with her head

158 The original place of publication is unidentified. The letter was re-repinted in *Arrows of the Chase* (*Works* XXXIV, p. 521)

159 Collingwood, *Ruskin Relics*, p. 15.

bent over her sewing and her back to the artist. Ruskin sits reading on the right. Out of the picture is the artist himself, Arthur Severn. In June 1876 they were all at Brantwood, and I think this is when the present watercolour was made.

The drawing room at Brantwood then was only about two-thirds its present size, the Severns lengthening it after Ruskin's death. In the corner behind Sara and Lollie can be seen the suggestion of the bookcase which stood there. The line of the lake and Coniston Old Man can be seen through the window.

When Spielmann was preparing his articles on the portraits Severn wrote to tell him[160]

> I have two by myself, but not very good – one is interesting – of Ruskin reading in the evening Sir Walter Scott, with 6 tall candles. But it is only a small watercolour and done more to show the contrast of black cold mountains outside windows (blinds are up) with warm light inside – this one, I hope to use some day – if every I write something about Ruskin.

Severn did eventually write something about Ruskin. His *Memoir* was largely finished by about 1911, but it was not published until 1967 when I edited it as *The Professor*. The present watercolour would have formed an ideal illustration for *The Professor* but unfortunately it could not be traced. It later transpired that it had been bought from Brantwood in the 1920s by the late Haddon C. Adams, and it came to Bembridge with his bequest in 1971.

129 John Ruskin on his way to the wood, sketched by Laurence Jermyn Hilliard (1855–1887), ?23 June 1876, aet 57

130 John Ruskin pausing to look at the view, sketched by L.J. Hilliard, ?23 June 1876

129

130

160 Arthur Severn – M.H. Spielmann, 16 ?July 1889, in the author's collection.

When he was at Brantwood Ruskin habitually spent part of each day working on his estate. He was particularly fond of woodchopping and on occasions had to be stopped from chopping down trees so that his (frequently) young lady companions could more readily reach the nuts. There are many references to wood chopping in his diary, one such being on 23 June 1876. '...Diddie (Sara Anderson) and Lolly (Hilliard) cutting trees with me in the wood by the great rose bush'.

The present pair of sketches, captioned by Wedderburn 'Ruskin at his wood chopping at Brantwood at which he wore a very frock coat' may well have been made at this time. Their artist, Laurence Hilliard, was for ever sketching and drawing caricatures. He continued as Ruskin's secretary from 1876 until 1883 when ill-health caused him to leave Brantwood. But he remained in Coniston and was beginning to make a name for himself as an artist when he died in 1887 at the age of 32.

131 John Ruskin, etching by 'Pilotell', Georges Labadie (1844–1918), 1876, aet 57

Ruskin was a frequent visitor to the National Gallery. On one occasion that he was there in 1876, standing looking at Turner's 'Apollo killing the Python' he was seen and sketched by Georges Labadie. 'Very rapidly' Pilotell told Spielmann[161] the sketch was made, 'about 30 minutes'. The artist then re-drew his portrait in dry point onto copper (without, incidentally, reversing it) and it was included in a series of portraits of notabilities which he was producing for Mr Noséda.

Pilotell made a name for himself as a caricaturist in France at the end of the Second Empire. He also set up a short-lived newspaper, worked at the Prefecture of Police, and was Director of Fine Arts. With the return of order after the Commune, Pilotell sought refuge in London where he exhibited etchings at the Royal Academy in 1875.

131

161 G. Labadie – M.H. Spielmann, 11 July 1889; Pierpont Morgan Library.

132 John Ruskin, aet 58, portrait by Charles Fairfax Murray (1849–1919), or a self-portrait, April 1877 (Plate 21)

In February 1876 Ruskin had again been re-elected Slade Professor. But the state of his health was such that he felt incapable of lecturing and he was given a year's leave of absence. On 24 August he left London to travel to Venice where he arrived on 14 September and remained there until 23 May 1877. At first he lodged at the Grand Hotel, later moving to the Calcina on the Zattere.

While in Venice much of his time was taken up in writing various numbers of *Fors Clavigera*, *St Mark's Rest*, *Guide to the Principal Pictures in the Academy of Fine Arts at Venice*, *Laws of Fésole*, *Proserpina* and other books. He also devoted a lot of time to copying paintings, in particular Carpaccio's 'Dream of St Ursula'. St Ursula had become associated, in his mind, with the dead Rose La Touche and he studied this painting and worked on his copies for over twelve weeks.

At this time Ruskin renewed his friendship with J.W. Bunney. He also met C.H. Moore from Harvard. Two young Venetians became his friends – Giacomo Boni, who was trying to preserve the Ducal Palace sculptures, and Angelo Alessandri, an artist who was copying many Venetian paintings for him. In fact Ruskin was surrounded by friends and pupils and his time in Venice was very fully occupied.

Another young artist who was working for Ruskin at this time was Charles Fairfax Murray. Murray was often ridiculed by his contemporaries, because of his bow legs, the smallness of his stature, and because of the number of his children. Rossetti frequently referred to him as 'little Murray' and A.C. Benson said that 'his legs had a great outward curvature – the word bandy-legged only faintly expressing the pronounced nature of this strange deformity' which is said to have come from sitting cross-legged when he was a tailor's apprentice. Nevertheless he was a very competent artist. In 1865–66 he was a studio assistant to Burne-Jones and drew Burne-Jones's designs onto glass for Morris & Co.

Ruskin seems to have commissioned him to make copies of some Italian Old Masters by 1873, but the bulk of his work for Ruskin was done in 1877. Murray was in Siena in February 1877 when he heard from a traveller that Ruskin was in Venice. Having confirmed this by an exchange of letters[162] with Bunney, he went to Venice, perhaps in the hope of obtaining commissions from Ruskin. He was not disappointed, and was able not only to copy paintings for him, but also to make other studies. 'Can you join me on St Mark's place tomorrow at half-past nine with your drawing materials?' wrote Ruskin.[163] 'I am going up into the gallery behind the organ at St Mark's to study a mosaic. A sketch of it will be the most important work you or I have yet done in Venice'. Murray's stay in Venice resulted in his executing many commissions for the Guild of St George.

132

Murray was not only by far the most successful of the group of artists commissioned by Ruskin to work for the Guild, he was also a shrewd and clever collector and dealer. For example when a 13th century manuscript Psalter, which he had bought about 1883, sold at Sotheby's in 1997 it was described by the auctioneers as being 'by any standards an extraordinary artefact ... and probably the most important and certainly the most famous German gothic manuscript in private hands'. It

162 C.F. Murray – J.W. Bunney, 22 Feb. 1877; in Bunney Collection.

163 JR – C.F. Murray 20 May 1877; T.J. Wise (ed.), *Letters on Art and Literature by John Ruskin* (London: private publication, 1894), pp. 51-52.

was during the 1877 visit to Venice that Murray found, for Ruskin and the Guild, Verrocchio's Madonna and Child.[164] Later, in 1880, he found for Ruskin in Florence the faience Madonna and Child by Luca della Robbia[165] which was to hang above Ruskin's study mantelpiece for many years. In later years Murray's splendid collection of Old Master drawings was sold to J. Pierpont Morgan, and his unrivalled collection of Pre-Raphaelite drawings was bought by the Birmingham City Art Gallery. He had a passion for fruit tarts and babies, but in Rossetti's opinion was 'a meritorious though cocky little cove'. He certainly was a successful *marchande amateur*, as *The Times* obituary described him.

While Ruskin and Murray were in Venice, Murray painted Ruskin's portrait. To this event there appears to be but one reference in Ruskin's diary on 25 April, 'Y[esterday] ... Murray began my portrait'. Murray, however, was more meticulous in recording the sittings in his diary. On 24 April he noted 'Commenced portrait of Mr Ruskin in water colours'. Further sittings are recorded on 25, 26, 28, 29, 30 April and 3 May. There was no sitting on 27 April, as Ruskin explained in a letter to Murray: 'I was certain I had forgotten something – it was that I must go to see a friend Padre Issaverdens, who has been ill, this afternoon at the Armenians so that I can't sit today: but tomorrow at 4 am wholly at your command...'[166]

The last reference in Murray's diary is on Sunday 20 May when he 're-touched portrait of Mr Ruskin'.

The present watercolour which was bought by Paul Oppé in 1921, just a couple of years after Murray's death, is possibly the Venetian portrait in question. There is evidence to point to it being the Murray portrait, but there is also evidence against it. I do have certain reservations against saying categorically that this is the long-lost Murray portrait.

In favour of it being by Murray are the facts that we know that Murray began a portrait of Ruskin, we know that the present portrait was at one time in Murray's possession; and we know that it was bought by Paul Oppé with other watercolours by Murray, and it has always been believed to be by Murray by Paul Oppé, and by his son.

But it will be noticed that the portrait bears a striking similarity to the 1873 self-portrait (No. 114) and a convincing argument can be put forward for it, in fact, being an unrecorded self-portrait.

To begin with, Ruskin usually posed himself rather carefully when he was being painted, and the present very foresquare pose seems to be rather out of character – but it is not inconsistent with an artist sitting in front of a mirror painting himself. One can argue however, that the background *is* inconsistent with its being a self-portrait. It seems improbable that Ruskin would paint a self-portrait out of doors. The business with the mirror would make it too inconvenient. And it would be entirely against Ruskin's artistic philosophy to paint in a background that in fact was not there. The suggestion of a background that there *is* in the painting does not really look very Venetian.

There are certain features which point *directly* to this being a self-portrait. One immediately notices that the hair is parted on the wrong side – that is, the side on which it would appear in a self-portrait (i.e. mirror image), whereas it would appear to be on the other side in a drawing by another artist. But there *is* evidence of Ruskin parting his hair on the opposite side to usual in at least two instances – in the portraits by Thomas Richmond (No. 14) and Samuel Laurence (No. 75). Perhaps the most strikingly similar feature between this and the self-portrait of 1873 (No. 114) are the rather V-shaped lines on the forehead, which do not seem to have been noticed by other artists.

The eyes are another interesting feature. People's eyes are not symmetrical, and Ruskin's were no exception. Observe that in the present portrait the eye on the left is much rounder than that on the right. This is also the case in the 1873 and in the two 1874 self-portraits. The waistcoat, on the other hand, though it cannot be seen too distinctly, appears to be crossed over as it would be seen by another artist.

Thus the evidence for the present portrait being by Murray and for being a self-portrait is clearly conflicting. The fact that it was at one time in Murray's collection means little in this context: he was a well-known picture collector; what would be more natural than that Ruskin should give him the portrait?

And what of the inscription on the reverse, which is not in Murray's hand – 'John Ruskin; s.m. circa 1875 aet at 56?' The approximation of the date merely suggests that the inscription was written several years after the picture was drawn. But could the s.m. stand for *sua manu* – 'John Ruskin, by his hand'?

164 I am indebted to Paul Tucker for drawing my attention to Murray's 1877 diary in the Fandation Custodia, Paris, wherein he records that on 24 May he paid Manfrini 2350 francs 'for Verrocchio and carried it away'. It is now in the National Gallery of Scotland.

165 Now in the National Gallery in Washington.

166 Morgan Library, MA 2150.

133 John Ruskin, bust by the Countess Isabel Curtis-Chomeley in Birmani, 1877, aet 58

Another of the people with whom Ruskin struck up an acquaintance in Venice was the Countess Isabel Curtis-Chomeley in Birmani. There are various references in his letters and diary to his dining with the Countess, and her address – Palazzo Mula, S.Pio, Venice – is noted at the beginning of his Venetian diary. In *St Mark's Rest* Ruskin refers to a translation of a Venetian legend by the Countess, but Cook and Wedderburn note that it doesn't appear among her few printed works. In addition to her literary talents, Ruskin told Joan Severn on 16 February 1877 '...the Contessa Bowwow is a sculptress – inspired and so on'.

Ruskin's letters to Joan written during this Venetian visit are not as informative as usual. Among the things that he omitted to tell her was that the Countess Bowwow was in fact sculpting a bust of him. The late Michael Bunney drew my attention to entries in his grandfather's diary after Ruskin had left Venice. In May Ruskin wrote to Bunney

> The bundle in shelf of cabinet ... is the Contessa Birmani's cast of me – I don't think Joannie will like it and I won't [illegible] myself about – could not tell Countess this – so don't you. But pack the thing in another box like the box I've left – carefully and send to Arthur Severn, Herne Hill, S.E. London, my constant address.

It is evident from Bunney's diary that the Countess also made a cast of her bust of Ruskin and in October he noted that he had sent away 'Mr Ruskin's [packing] case with two busts and photographs sent by the Contessa Birmani'.

Whether either the original bust or its cast were ever moved from Herne Hill to Brantwood is uncertain. Neither appears in any of the dispersal sale catalogues and they remain untraced.

134A Portrait of John Ruskin with Mr & Mrs J.W. Bunney, in a painting of St Mark's and the Piazza, Venice, by John Wharlton Bunney (1828–82), 'No. 180', 1877–78

134B Portrait of John Ruskin with Mr & Mrs J.W. Bunney in a painting of St Mark's and the Piazza, Venice, by John Wharlton Bunney, 'No. 189', 1877–79

Ruskin seems to have been introduced to the Bentincks by his Venetian friend Rawdon Brown, and there are occasional references to them. In his diary he recorded 'Bentincks at lunch' on 15 September 1869. On 7 December in the next year, writing from Oxford after one of his *Aratra Pentelici* lectures, probably 'The School of Athens', he told Joan Agnew 'ugly woman – Mrs Bentinck –

134

pounced out of a barouche on me (Mr Brown's friend) – had to be civil – & take her in to lecture'. Meanwhile in January 1871 Rawdon Brown was writing to Ruskin 'I am glad you were pleased with the Bentincks ... *they* most certainly appreciated the flattering except[ion] made by you when accepting their hospitality'.

'The Bentincks' were probably Mrs Bentinck and her daughter, Jessica Anne Christina Cavendish-Bentinck. I am indebted to Miss Sarah Bunney for telling me that it is evident from the diary of her great-grandfather, J.W.Bunney, that he too knew Miss Bentinck, from at least 1871 and possibly earlier. They were perhaps also introduced by Rawdon Brown.

In 1874 Jessica Bentinck married Sir Tatton Sykes, Bt., of Sledmere in Yorkshire. Later in the year they were in Venice and Bunney recorded in his diary,

> 7 November 1874. Went out this morning with Lizzie [his wife] & children to find shawl [?] for baby. We took a boat to Piazzetta when who should come across but Miss J.C. Bentinck as was but who is now married. She and her husband called this afternoon to see my things. They expressed themselves pleased asked various prices among them the Broglio drawing which I asked 100£ for. They promised to come again.

Two days later Bunney noted:

> This morning we went to buy some necessities in way of clothes. While out Sir T and Lady Sykes came. They came again in the afternoon and have decided to like the drawing of under the Broglio and have ordered a companion sketch which is to be the front of St Mark with the Piazza & I have offered to do it for £100 with which they are content. Lady S paid me for the Broglio in paper 2750 lira. I am to frame it nicely & let it go to Zen's the antiquity dealer here for him to send home with things for her father.

A month later Bunney made his preliminary sketch for the Piazza picture, and five weeks later he was working on it again in the Piazza; he was working again on the following day, but had to give

134 (detail)

up because of thick fog! There are further diary references throughout the spring of 1875 to work on the picture, and on 24 May,

> My boatman did not come so I sat down to write the letter to Miss Ewart & while about it who should come bursting in but Lady Tatton Sykes – she looked very well. They have been through Syria and Palestine ... She was very pleased with the S Marco drawing ...

On 3 August Bunney began the Sykes painting and by 18 September he had devoted 27 sessions to it.

On this same day Bunney noted that he had been 'Drawing out Ellis S Marco'. Lt Col. Arthur Ellis was Equerry to the Prince of Wales and had first met Bunney in April 1872 when he was in Venice with the Prince and Princess of Wales and Prince Metternich. Bunney called, by appointment, on the royal party at Danieli's, taking with him some of his sketches and photographs of drawings. Presumably Ellis commissioned his painting of the Piazza as a result of this visit.

Work must have continued throughout the year – and the next – on both paintings. By October 1875 Bunney had devoted 36 sessions to the Sykes painting. The frame for it was delivered on 7 December; by 2 February 1876 there had been 63 sessions devoted to the Sykes Piazza and on 12 February 'Today a delightful letter from Lady Sykes enclosing a cheque for 100 guineas to pay for the San Marco picture', but still it wasn't finished and work continued. By September 1876 Ruskin was in Venice, and he called on Bunney.

> I showed him first Lady Sykes picture of the Piazza, and he expressed himself much pleased and grateful. He found but little fault and praised immensely the work as a whole and the truly artistic putting in of the figures.

Ruskin's reaction indicates to me that the work was still not finally complete.

Meanwhile work was continuing on the Ellis painting, which Bunney described in his diary on 15 February 1878.

> Felt thankful and light-hearted today for the Ellis picture is finished, one feels as if a new career was opening up when a big job like this is brought to a conclusion – it's fairly successful, I think. I have introduced a group of figures standing talking together consisting of Mr Ruskin, Lizzie [Mrs Bunney] and myself all of which are successful, Lizzie and Mr R very much so, and she comes so pretty and picturesque ... In the picture there are sixty figures sufficiently large to have to be painted carefully and many others in groups more or less made out with no end of pigeons. The largest figures are $3^1/_4$ inches high and I have got together all the modern inhabitants of Venice who congregate on the Piazza. The time is just before sunset as the shadow having covered the Piazza begins to creep up the façade of the church while the upper part is flooded with the sunset light, an extremely difficult effect to do with a difficult subject to begin with.
>
> I have worked continuously upon it for the last 2 months and this is only the finishing of the parts that were all laid in before and have been drying for some months. I partly have used linseed oil boiled with a very little [?]de Harleem no turpentine in any part and all the shadow parts and sky I painted over with water colour light or Venetian red upon the ordinary ground of the canvas.

Three days later Bunney noted that he had signed the Ellis picture and 'Made it No. 180'. A later diary entry, for 14 July, refers to payment for the painting. Bunney noted that he had written to his friend and London agent W. J. Malleson '...asking him to get one of his clerks to call on Ellis and try to get the money for the picture', and a letter from Malleson's clerk on 19 August 1878 confirms that payment had been received.

Since Ruskin did not react, in 1876, to his portrait appearing among the figures in the Sykes painting, I assume that the Ruskin–Bunney group was a last minute addition!

In dating the Ellis painting 1877–78, Bunney must have forgotten when he actually began it. This must also have been the case with the Sykes picture which he dated 1877–79. Miss Bunney pointed out that the numbering of the pictures causes confusion because Bunney tended to number them when he dispatched them. Thus although the Sykes picture was *begun* first, it is No. 189, while the Ellis painting, which must have been *delivered* first, was numbered 180.

135 John Ruskin, portrait sketch by Edward William Andrews, ?1877

136 John Ruskin, portrait by Edward William Andrews

Arriving back in England on 16 June 1877 Ruskin was soon re-acquainting himself with the London art world. He attended the opening of the Grosvenor Gallery on 23 June where he saw and disapproved of pictures by Whistler. Later, when he visited the Royal Academy exhibition, he would have seen a portrait of himself by E.W. Andrews.

Telling Spielmann of the origins of this portrait the artist said that

> Mr Ruskin was engaged for some days in making studies from one of Turner's works – if I recollect rightly, the 'Apollo slaying the Python' – in one of the large rooms at the National Gallery, where I was at work near him, and it was during this time that I made my small studies of Mr Ruskin, from which the larger work was produced. Thus the portrait was taken from sittings, although Mr Ruskin was an unconscious sitter .[167]

It seems quite possible that Andrew's sketches were in fact made in 1876 the year in which Pilotell also drew Ruskin at work on the 'Apollo' in the National Gallery.

137 John Ruskin, full length portrait by Arthur Severn, c.1877

Writing to Spielmann in 1889[168] Severn said that he had two portraits of Ruskin by himself. One (No. 128) has already been discussed. The other, Spielmann described as an 'interesting little picture, painted full length'.[169] He dates it as having been painted about 1877. This portrait is untraced.

138 John Ruskin, caricature, A Modern Art Professor, by Reginald Blomfield, 1877

Ruskin continued to occupy the chair of Fine Art at Oxford and in November and December 1877 his lectures there consisted of readings from *Modern Painters*.

Describing Ruskin's lecture on the *Nature and Authority of Miracle* at the Metaphysical Society a couple of years earlier, R.H. Hutton referred to Ruskin's

> deep-toned, musical voice which dwelt with slow emphasis on the most important words of each sentence, and which gave a singular force to the irony which the speaker's expression of belief was freely mingled.[170]

But A. Shadwell was not equally impressed by Ruskin's lectures.

> I also attended Ruskin's lectures at Oxford in the seventies. He talked incessantly about himself, especially in the second course, and the chief impression left on my mind was that he carried egoism to the point of insanity.[171]

138

167 *Magazine of Art*, March 1891, p. xxii.
168 Dearden, *The Professor*, p. 9.
169 Spielmann, *John Ruskin*, p. 175.
170 Cook, *Life of John Ruskin*, vol. II, p. 209.
171 Letter to the editor, *The Times*, 29 February 1932.

Mr Shadwell's opinion is illustrated by the present caricature by Reginald Blomfield, a Stapledon Scholar at Exeter College. Blomfield, who became an architect and Royal Academician, wrote[172]

> ... Ruskin was a beautiful draughtsman in his own way, and I sometimes wish he had painted more and written less on architecture. I attended some of Ruskin's lectures, but I heard so much about Ruskin and so little about anybody else that I gave it up. The atmosphere of rapt adoration with which Ruskin and all that he said was received by the young ladies of Oxford was altogether too much for me, and I relieved my feelings by making a pen-and-ink drawing of Ruskin blowing two trumpets, his own above, Turner below. This I sold to Mr Shrimpton, the publisher of *Oxford Caricatures*, and with the proceeds bought a much-coveted engraving.

It seems unlikely that the caricature was ever published by Shrimpton, for copies of a printed version have never come to light.

139 John Ruskin, bust by Benjamin Creswick (1854–1946), modelled from photographs, 1877

140 John Ruskin, bust by Benjamin Creswick, modelled from life, September 1877

Benjamin Creswick was a grinder living in Sheffield. He seems to have been a frequent visitor to the Guild of St George Museum at Walkley, and became friendly with the curator, Henry Swan. Creswick was interested in sculpture and Swan lent him some photographs of Ruskin, from which he modelled a bust. This bust was exhibited at the Sheffield Society of Artists (No. 222) in June 1877 together with four other busts by Creswick of local worthies. Copies of all five busts were offered at three guineas.

Swan and his wife visited Brantwood on 22 August – 'a quite frightful fit of depression brought on by my curator and his wife coming when they shouldn't'.[173] It appears that Swan showed Creswick's bust to Ruskin and Ruskin offered to give the young sculptor sittings. Creswick was duly invited to Brantwood and Ruskin noted in his diary that he was there on 14–15 September.[174] After the first sitting of an hour Ruskin asked how many more the sculpture would require, to which Creswick replied 'Five'. 'After what I have seen of your work', replied Ruskin, 'I will give you as many as you want'. While it was still in progress, Ruskin described the bust as 'unsurpassed in modern sculpture except by Thorwaldsen'.

140

This second bust was exhibited at the Sheffield Society of Artists (No. 127) in 1878 and casts were available at one guinea. What exactly happened to the original second bust during its first year is unknown, until October 1879 when it was presented to Prince Leopold. In a report of the prince's visit to the Guild Museum at Walkley we read:

> Prince Leopold mentioned that he had yesterday received from Coniston a most charming present. This referred to a request that he would accept a bust of Mr Ruskin, by Creswick, a young Sheffield artisan of much promise, who has the advantage of Professor Ruskin's teaching and help. While Mr Ruskin was modestly disclaiming any

172 R. Blomfield, *Memoirs of an Architect* (London: Macmillan, 1932), p. 27.
173 H.G. Viljoen (ed.), *The Brantwood Diary of John Ruskin* (New Haven: Yale University Press, 1971), p. 42.
174 Viljoen, *The Brantwood Diary of John Ruskin* , pp. 48-49.

connection with the present, Mr Swan explained that it had been made without Mr Ruskin's knowledge.[175]

The bust was subsequently returned to Brantwood, perhaps after the death of Prince Leopold in 1884. It was bought at the Brantwood dispersal sale in 1931 for J. Howard Whitehouse.

A number of casts were made. The original, which is modelled in plaster, is hollow, and its back is quite different to the solid backs of the plaster casts. The backs of the casts are engraved with 'B. Creswick Sculpt.' and 'AD 1877'.

The casts seem to have been sufficiently popular to need a second casting in 1887. There is a copy bearing this date, and cast in terracotta, in the collection of Mr Peter Wardle. In the case of this cast the plinth appears to be slightly shorter.

For several years Ruskin seems to have supported Creswick and his family. Later, he was to work in London, sculpting the head of Carlyle on the tablet in Cheyne Walk, the frieze on the front of the Oxford Street shop of the hatters Henry Heath, and the terracotta frieze on the front of Cutlers' Hall in Sheffield.

141 John Ruskin, aet 59, caricature by Alfred Bryan (1852–1899) March 1878

This fine caricature of Ruskin appeared in *The Hornet* on 20 March 1878 as No. CIX in the series 'Men and Women of the Day'.

Ruskin was seriously ill for several weeks at Brantwood in the early spring of the year, and the text which accompanies the caricature begins

> Everybody interested in art matters regrets the serious illness of Mr Ruskin. This world now and again contains men who excite interest in themselves as well as their work. They have their detractors, but they also have their admirers ...

The text continues by surveying Ruskin's career, and concludes

> Mr Ruskin's views of Art were not received with general applause. His theories have been controverted with virulent asperity by professional art-critics, and the illustrations by himself to some of his works excited the laughter of men who consider themselves his opponents. There can be no doubt much of this ridicule was deserved. No sooner had he become fashionable than he became eccentric. His eccentricities have now become second nature. He has no hesitation in offering an opinion on any matter that may be suggested to him, and he propounds his views with the air of a man who at any moment can put himself in privileged communication with Providence. Mr Ruskin is in his 60th year.

The artist, Alfred Bryan, began his career as a political and theatre-page caricaturist in *Judy* in the early 1870s. Soon he was also contributing to *The Hornet* and other journals. His gift for portraiture

141

175 *Sheffield and Rotherham Independent*, 23 October 1879, reprinted in *Igdrasil* III, 16 March 1892, p.261.

made him one of the outstanding cartoonists of the time. He was greatly admired by Max Beerbohm, who especially liked his work in *Moonshine*.

The likeness in the present drawing is probably based on photographs, though it is evident from later drawings that Bryan had seen Ruskin and was also caricaturing him from life. (See also Nos. 158–59, 169).

142 Cartoon, An Appeal to Law, by Edward Linley Sambourne (1844–1910), December 1878

143 Caricature of John Ruskin as a blackbird, 28 December 1878

AN APPEAL TO THE LAW.

Naughty Critic, to use bad Language! Silly Painter, to go to Law about it!

142

When Ruskin visited the exhibition at the Grosvenor Gallery in June 1877 he saw a group of five paintings by J. A. Mc N. Whistler. Ruskin was appalled at what he considered a lack of honest workmanship in the paintings – and he said so in forceful terms in Letter 79 of *Fors Clavigera* which he was currently writing. His libellous observations on Whistler led to the immediate disappearance of the artist's market. The well-known libel action followed in November 1878. Ruskin was found guilty, though his opinions of Whistler's art were upheld by the court who fined him one farthing damages. However, the findings of the court – or rather the fact that the statement of his opinions had taken him to court, coupled with his failing health, caused Ruskin to resign from the Slade professorship early in the following year. Sambourne summed up the whole affair in his cartoon in *Punch*, 'Naughty Critic, to use bad language! Silly Painter, to go to Law about it!'

In the second, anonymous, caricature which appeared in *Funny Folk* on 28 December 1878 Whistler is shown in his garden hanging his canvases out to dry. He had said, in giving evidence, that he put his paintings 'in the open air so that they may dry well'. His 'Nocturne in Black and Gold' stands on the ground waiting to be pegged out, while Ruskin, shown as a blackbird, hovers above. Whistler gave names such as 'Arrangement in Brown', 'Harmony in Amber' and 'Symphony in White' to his paintings, and the verse accompanying the caricature reads:

BLACK & GOLD
WHISTLER IN THE GARDEN
HANGING OUT HIS SYMPHONEES,
DOWN CAME A CRITIC,
WITH A FARTHING DAMAGEES.

143

Whistler in the garden
Hanging out his Symphon*ees*,
Down came a critic
With a Farthing Damag*ees*.

144 Caricature by 'G. Pipeshank' depicting Ruskin as Carlyle's squire, 1878

In 1878 the Liverpool tobacco firm of Cope published an advertising pamphlet entitled *The Plenipotent Key to Cope's Correct Card of the Peerless Pilgrimage to Saint Nicotine of the Holy Herb.* The folding frontispiece by 'G. Pipeshank' is a take-off of the Canterbury Pilgrims and shows many famous Victorians journeying to the Shrine of St Nicotinus. Ruskin (a dedicated anti-smoker) is shown as a squire riding in the procession alongside Thomas Carlyle. The pre-amble to the accompanying poem refers on page 12 to 'Ruskin, the ever youthful squire, so "wonderly deliver"'.

Singing he was, or floyting alle the day,
He was as freshe as in the moneth of May[176]

Ruskin is also treated to twenty three lines of the poem itself.

176 G. Chaucer, *The Canterbury Tales*, prologue.

144

Him [Carlyle] followeth his loyal Squire; and he
Hath wrought brave things in Venice of the Sea,
And many another spot; by lakes and fountains,
And wreathed with clouds and snows on Alpine
 mountains,
In many a wild wood green and windy gorge;
He rideth ramping like a new St George,
His style embroidered 'as it were a mede
Al ful of fresshe floures white and red:'[177]
Beneath his horse a scurvy wretch[178] is sprawling,
With vast jaws open for a monstrous bawling;
A lank and long-eared mar-joy, mainly bent
On shuffling through the sloughs of discontent;
Incapable of pleasure even in pelf,
He'd have all others wretched as himself;
A blatant bawler, bilious and bad-blooded,
With heart, mind, soul and sense all muddle-
 muddied;
An Anti sour 'gainst all things sweet and good,
Who'd make earth ante-hell an if he could,
Whose head is wooden and himself stark wood;
A puny infidel to our sweet Saint:
There let the horses kick him till he faint;
Why should he come a-lying by the way
In hopes to disarrange our fair array?

144 (detail)

177 Chaucer, *The Canterbury Tales*, prologue.
178 In the cartoon the 'scurvy wretch' is labelled 'Cant'.

145 John Ruskin, aet 60, photographed with a group on the ice off Brantwood, by J. Lund of Coniston, January–February 1879

145

145 (detail)

Every once in a while there comes a winter which is more severe than usual. That of 1878–9 was such a winter; reports said that it was the severest in the Lake District for twenty-seven years. The frost started on 1 December, and with the exception of four days, it continued to freeze for more than two months. The lowest temperature reached was 4°F and just before Christmas, for four days it never rose higher that 18°F. The north end of Coniston Lake was completely frozen over on Christmas Day when about three hundred people enjoyed themselves, skating and listening to the Rifle Volunteer Band, which played on the ice.

But the ice also brought tragedy. Jane Anne Kitchen, a domestic servant employed at The Thwaite by Ruskin's friend Susan Beever, took a short cut from Coniston to The Thwaite across the ice on 16 January; she fell through and was drowned.

The ice nearer Brantwood was safer and the *Ulverston Mirror*'s correspondent reported that

> the ice on Coniston Lake has not been so strong for 27 years. ... Mr Ruskin's mansion, Brantwood, is close upon the shore of Coniston Lake, which is now frozen over, and the great critic may be seen daily enjoying himself upon the ice, and not infrequently having (as boys say) a 'cold pie'.[179]

Still a boy at heart, despite his sixty years, Ruskin notes in his diary[180] 'Yesterday in bright sunshine sliding on the lake – might have crossed; – several boys did from the Tyson pier'. On the following day he 'crossed the lake on its marble surface, with Joanie and the children, in bright sunshine, this morning at eleven...' The next day he found the 'lake a sheet of marble and hills in folded lace – veils of snow – lake a sheet, I say – except one great pool that will not close, though the rest has borne these four days'. A week later he was still enjoying himself 'over the lake sliding to call on Susie [Beever]; back down the middle of it to promontary of hall; and so straight across back'.

The *Ulverston Mirror* published on Ruskin's birthday recorded some of the merrymaking on the lake.

> The north end of Coniston Lake presented a lively appearance on Saturday last. A large number of skaters arrived by train from Millom and other places, and various games were played on the ice. A respectable sized potato pie, brought from the 'Crown', was quickly disposed of and evidently enjoyed on the lake shore. Snow fell to a depth of several inches on Saturday and again on Wednesday, putting a complete stop to any further skating enjoyment. We are pleased to add that no accident occurred of a serious nature.

On 8 February Ruskin told his diary that he had 'the most cheerful birthday I've had for years ... Coniston band came and made the evening merry'.

Ruskin was in fact spending the winter quietly. During the previous March and April he had been seriously ill at Brantwood with an attack of 'brain fever'. Now he was avoiding all intellectually demanding work so that his health would continue to recover.

The exact date of the present photograph taken on the frozen lake some yards out from Brantwood

179 *Ulverston Mirror*, 25 Jan. 1879.

180 Viljoen, *The Brantwood Diary*, p. 150; 21 Jan. 1879.

harbour is uncertain. However it was probably taken at the end of January or beginning of February. The figure on the right is Ruskin's valet, Peter Baxter, who joined the Brantwood staff in 1876. Ruskin stands leaning on his alpenstock and holding the hand of the 3½ years old Agnew Severn. Seated too are Arthur and Lily (4½ and 6 years respectively). The young ladies are perhaps the children's nurse and Connie Hilliard. The man on the left may have been David Gould of Ambleside, an assistant who was working at Brantwood colouring engravings. I think the lady standing to the left is Mrs Talbot. I have seen her described as looking a little like Queen Victoria, and as she records in her account[181] of her association with Ruskin, 'It was in January 1879 that I first went to Brantwood'. She was an early and important benefactor of the Guild and she seems to have been at Brantwood for a little while. She records how 'on one day a "devoted admirer" called. Such a queer man, a member of the Guild I think he must have been'. Ruskin's diary records that on 15 January Mr Salt and Mr Riley came. They were both involved with the Guild's farm at Sheffield. Perhaps it was one of these that Mrs Talbot remembered. Indeed perhaps the photograph was taken on 16 January when Salt came to Brantwood on his own. Perhaps *he* is the figure on the left.

The only print of this photograph which I know came to the Whitehouse Collection from the Adams Bequest. The name of the photographer printed on it is J. Lund of Coniston. Lund appears to have been a man of many parts – photographer, clock repairer, and for a while, manager of the Coniston Co-operative Stores.

146 John Ruskin, wood engraving by Heinrich S. Uhlrich, 1879 aet 60

146

The present portrait, a fine wood engraving, was published as a supplement to *The Graphic* of 5 July 1879. Ruskin approved of the portrait and wrote to Uhlrich that he considered it 'out and out the best portrait of me yet done'. A number of copies were later printed with Ruskin's comment facsimilied at the foot. The artist was later to engrave a number of plates for the *Library Edition*.

181 Fanny Talbot, *A Visit to Brantwood* (Bembridge: The Ruskin Association, 1980).

147 John Ruskin, full-length statue modelled in clay, by Sir Joseph Edgar Boehm (1834–1890), 1879, aet 60

148 John Ruskin, bust modelled in clay, by J.E. Boehm, 1879

149 John Ruskin, head and shoulders in marble, by J.E. Boehm, 1879 (Plate 22)

150 Caricature of Sir J.E. Boehm contemplating his bust of Ruskin, by 'Spy', January 1881

151 'Bust of John Ruskin in the Ruskin School of Drawing', by Douglas Pittuck

Sir Joseph Edgar Boehm was born in Vienna of Hungarian parentage. He came to London and first exhibited at the Royal Academy in 1862, soon attracting considerable popularity as a portrait sculptor. Among his better-known works are the sarcophagus of Dean Stanley in Westminster Abbey, and the statues of the Duke of Wellington at Hyde Park Corner and Thomas Carlyle in Chelsea.

Ruskin was impressed by his work, and writing to tell Norton about the Carlyle statue in 1875, he said[182] 'Boehm is a jewel, not a Jew. A perfect type of intense blue-eyed Harz-bred German. I *hope* he will like me, and ask to do me, – that will be ever so much better than if I ask him, or you either. But if he doesn't, I will ...'

About a week later Ruskin told Joan Severn[183]

> Carlyle took me to Boehm's – who *is such* a duck – The very ideal of noblest intense Germanism – with the grey gleaming eye, and inexhaustible will – rationalism – imagination – and bodily vigour. – And he's done the only horse I ever cared for – such a love – rearing, and hitting out straight with his right forepaw – hoof I mean.

On Ruskin's retirement in 1879 from University life a number of his Oxford friends commissioned Boehm to sculpt the former Slade Professor. It seems possible that he was told of the scheme by Henry Acland, to whom Ruskin wrote in November 1879[184] 'Your letter is very touching to me ... For the bust, I shall be only too glad to sit to Boehm anywhere and any time he likes, and will stay in town as long as necessary ... Curiously I gave equal *carte-blanche* to Herkomer[185] yesterday ...'

Sittings to Boehm and Herkomer started almost immediately, as Ruskin described in his letter of 1 December to Sara Anderson[186] 'I've been quite a prisoner to Mr Herkomer ... and before that, I had to go over to Kensington every day to Boehm, who is doing a yet more like thing in clay, – but I think my eyes are a loss in that'.

148

On 27 May 1880 an appeal was launched to commission the statue for Oxford.

> Many friends of Mr Ruskin have expressed a desire that a statue of the author of *Modern Painters* should be placed in the School of Drawing, Oxford, which owes its existence to his generosity and bears his name. A bust of Mr Ruskin has been executed by Mr Boehm, A.R.A., in Terra-cotta, of which one copy is now being

182 *Letters of John Ruskin to Charles Eliot Norton* II, pp. 117-18; 15 July 1875.
183 JR – Joan Severn, 26 June 1875; RF L 40.
184 *Works* XXXVII, p. 301.
185 See below, Nos. pp. 152-53.
186 *Works* XXXVII, p. 303.

> exhibited at the Royal Academy and another may be seen in the Turner Room at the University Galleries. Mr Boehm has also made a full-length sketch of Mr Ruskin in clay. It is proposed to raise by subscription a sum sufficient to procure a life-sized statue modelled upon this sketch. The cost of executing this would be in Terra-cotta, £700; in Bronze, £1000; in Marble, £1200.

The subscription list which followed was headed by Prince Leopold and the Marquis of Salisbury. The appeal was also printed in *The Times* on 26 May.

But evidently all of Ruskin's friends did not agree with the choice of Boehm as the sculptor, nor indeed did they know that Ruskin had already sat to him. On 21 August 1880 Mary Wakefield wrote to him[187]

> I have been asked by a lady who is very much interested in Mr Warrington Wood the sculptor to try and influence you in his favour with regard to your own bust, is it, or statue? And I think I cannot do better than forward to you a portion of her letter ...
>
> [letter enclosed] – 'I hear that Mr Ruskin is thinking of employing a Hungarian sculptor for the statue for the Art School. I wish instead he would think of the English sculptor Mr Warrington Wood, his reputation is sufficiently shown by the fact that he is elected a Professor of the Academy of St Luke at Rome – He is such a true artist in every way, a great admirer of Mr Ruskin: & such a good noble man that I do wish you could tell Mr Ruskin about him...'

In answer to this plea, Ruskin wrote[188]

> Paris 5th Sept. 80
> (I'm simply vaporised by the heat and my brain's in a cloud)
>
> I heartily wish I could be of any service to your friend's friend – but I have nothing whatever to do with any manner of self-exhibition – Dr Acland asked me to sit to Boehm, and I did, to please Acland and because I wanted to talk to Boehm – since the sittings were ended I neither care – no – nor ask – what anybody has done or means to do. Portraits of anybody are the last things I ever think of and my own would be the last of those ...

149

Despite Mary Wakefield's intervention, plans for the Boehm commission went ahead, although it is evident that insufficient funds were raised for the life-sized full length statue, and the clay model for that was probably destroyed. In due course a marble bust was placed in the Drawing School. The column on which it stands is inscribed:

Hanc
Johannis Ruskin
Hujusce scholæ fundatoris
effigiem
Amici P.P.
MDCCCLXXXI

187 RF L 24.

188 JR – Mary Wakefield, Paris, 5 Sept. 1880. Forgetting that he had already replied, he wrote again on the same day: 'I wish I could help your friend's friend. – but I have nothing whatever to do with any busts or portraits of myself. I sat to Boehm because I wanted to talk to him – and to Mr Creswick at Sheffield to please the Sheffielders – once the sitting's over – I never look at or think of the things more – and I know nothing of what is doing or to be done at Oxford'.

150

When Boehm discussed Ruskin's sittings with M.H. Spielmann about 1890, he told him 'I never saw any face on which the character and the inside of the man was so clearly written. He can never have *tried* to dissimulate'.[189]

When 'Spy'[190] caricatured Boehm in *Vanity Fair* in January 1881, he depicted him working on his bust of Ruskin. It is evident that Ruskin saw the caricature because in his letter of 3 February 1881 to Jessie Leete he asked

> Have you seen *Vanity Fair* with Boehm at work on my ideal Bust?[191]

Douglas Pittuck (b.1911) of New College, Oxford, attended classes at the Ruskin Drawing School over a period of nine years between April 1930 and January 1939, winning several prizes during the time. In 1932 he won the Albert Rutherston Life Drawing Prize and in 1935 the Albert Rutherston Short Poses Prize. Pittuck made this undated study (No. 151) of the Ruskin bust in the Drawing School (No. 149) and in 1948 he gave it to Albert Rutherston who was the Ruskin Drawing Master from 1929 until 1949. It is now in the Ashmolean Museum.

151

Meanwhile, a terracotta cast, probably the one which had been exhibited in the University Galleries, belonged to Sir Henry Acland and was eventually presented to the Ashmolean Museum. The second terracotta cast is reported to be in a private collection.

Several casts were made from the marble bust. One was given to the National Portrait Gallery by the Earl of Carlisle, a second, with a dark finish, is in the Geelong Art Gallery in Australia, and a third was bought from Boehm's trustees for the Guild of St George and is now in the Ruskin Gallery at Sheffield.

On 8 March 1916 Joan Severn wrote to Gill Parker, Curator of the Guild's collection, asking for a photograph of the Sheffield bust '... because there is some idea of having a plaster Boehm bust in the Ruskin Museum at Coniston'. Nothing seems to have come of this scheme.

189 *Magazine of Art*, Feb. 1891, p. 122.
190 Sir Leslie Ward (1851–1922).
191 JR – Jessie Leete, 3 February 1881, Wilson Library, University of North Carolina.

152 John Ruskin, portrait sketch for No. 153, by Sir Hubert von Herkomer, R.A. (1849–1914), 1879

153 John Ruskin, aet 60, portrait by Sir Hubert von Herkomer, 1879 (Plate 23)

154 John Ruskin, portrait after No. 153, by Herbert Johnson Harvey (1884–1928)

On Ruskin's retirement from the Slade Professorship Hubert Herkomer, whom he knew and whose pictures he had criticised in *Academy Notes*, was nominated his successor. Ruskin was delighted with the choice and wrote to tell Dean Liddell so, and that he would be able to work with Herkomer. However, Herkomer had to withdraw his candidature because of ill-health, and another of Ruskin's friends, Sir William Richmond, was appointed.

Perhaps Herkomer's proposed appointment served to strengthen the friendship between the two men for in due course he asked Ruskin's permission to paint his portrait. In November 1879 Ruskin told Acland '... I gave *carte blanche* to Herkomer yesterday, who wishes to make an etching [of me]. I really hope ... there may be a little more kindly and useful truth known of me than from photographs'.[192]

The sittings began immediately in Ruskin's study at Herne Hill. On 1 December he wrote to Sara Anderson, 'I've been quite a prisoner to Mr Herkomer, who has, however, made a beautiful drawing of me, the first that has ever given what good may be gleaned out of the clods of my face ...'[193]

Writing later about the sittings in an American paper, Herkomer said:

> ... He seemed most anxious not to look at the painting until I quite finished it; whilst sitting he was theorising about the methods of painting. I used in those days to paint abnormally large watercolours, and always covered the paper first with a wash of some ochre or grey, then sketched the subject with charcoal. I would then commence with a hog-hair brush, working up the ground colour with some fresh tones, and out of a kind of chaos produce a head. Ruskin queried even the possibility of this, and would hardly believe that my final outlines and delicate bits of drawing were put in last ...[194]

Later he told Ernest Chesneau[195], 'Herkomer's portrait is full of character, but not *like* in the ordinary sense'. E.T. Cook in his *Life of Ruskin* was not of the same opinion; 'Herkomer's portrait is too soft and lacks force of character', while Spielmann said that it 'placed before us the philanthropist, quiet, kindly and self-possessed', with 'all the cheery gentleness and old-world sweetness of disposition that distinguished him'.

153

Herkomer had taken to mezzotinting about the time that he painted Ruskin. He was to inaugurate an important revival of the art. His own engraving of the Ruskin portrait was published by The Fine Art Society on 21 July 1880 in a limited edition. The proof in the Whitehouse Collection is numbered '9'.

The presence of what appears to be a sketch for the portrait (No. 152) has been reported to me by Mr Simon Reynolds as belonging to an elderly gentleman in Bombay.

No. 154 is a copy of the portrait by the Birmingham artist, H.J. Harvey, son of the better-known landscape painter, J.R. Harvey.

192 Partly quoted above.
193 Partly quoted above.
194 *Works* XXXVIII, p. 210.
195 28 Dec. 1882; *Works* XXXVII, p. 427.

Plate 1. John Ruskin, aet $3\frac{1}{2}$, 1822, by James Northcote [1]

Photo courtesy of Sotheby's

Plate 2. John Ruskin, aet c.12, an imaginative portrait by Arthur Severn [7]

Ruskin Foundation (Ruskin Library, University of Lancaster)

Plate 3. John Ruskin, aet 17, 1836. Miniature portrait by Alfred Edward Chalon [8]

Private collection

Plate 4. John Ruskin, aet 21, 1840–41, by Constantin Roesler Franz [10]

Ruskin Foundation (Ruskin Library, University of Lancaster)

Plate 5. John Ruskin, aet 22, c.1841, by Thomas Richmond [14]

Ruskin Foundation (Ruskin Library, University of Lancaster)

Plate 6. John Ruskin, aet 26, 1845, with Auguste Gendron and [?] Eugène-Paul Dieudonné, by Johann-Ludwig-Rudolph Durheim [17] *Gottfried Keller-Stiftung, Kunstmuseum Bern*

Plate 7. Portrait of John Ruskin, aet 34–35, 1853–54, by John Everett Millais [20]

Ruskin Foundation (Ruskin Library, University of Lancaster)

Plate 9. 'Ruskin (Millais)', after the Glenfinlas portrait, by Susan Herbert [28]

Courtesy of Thames & Hudson Ltd

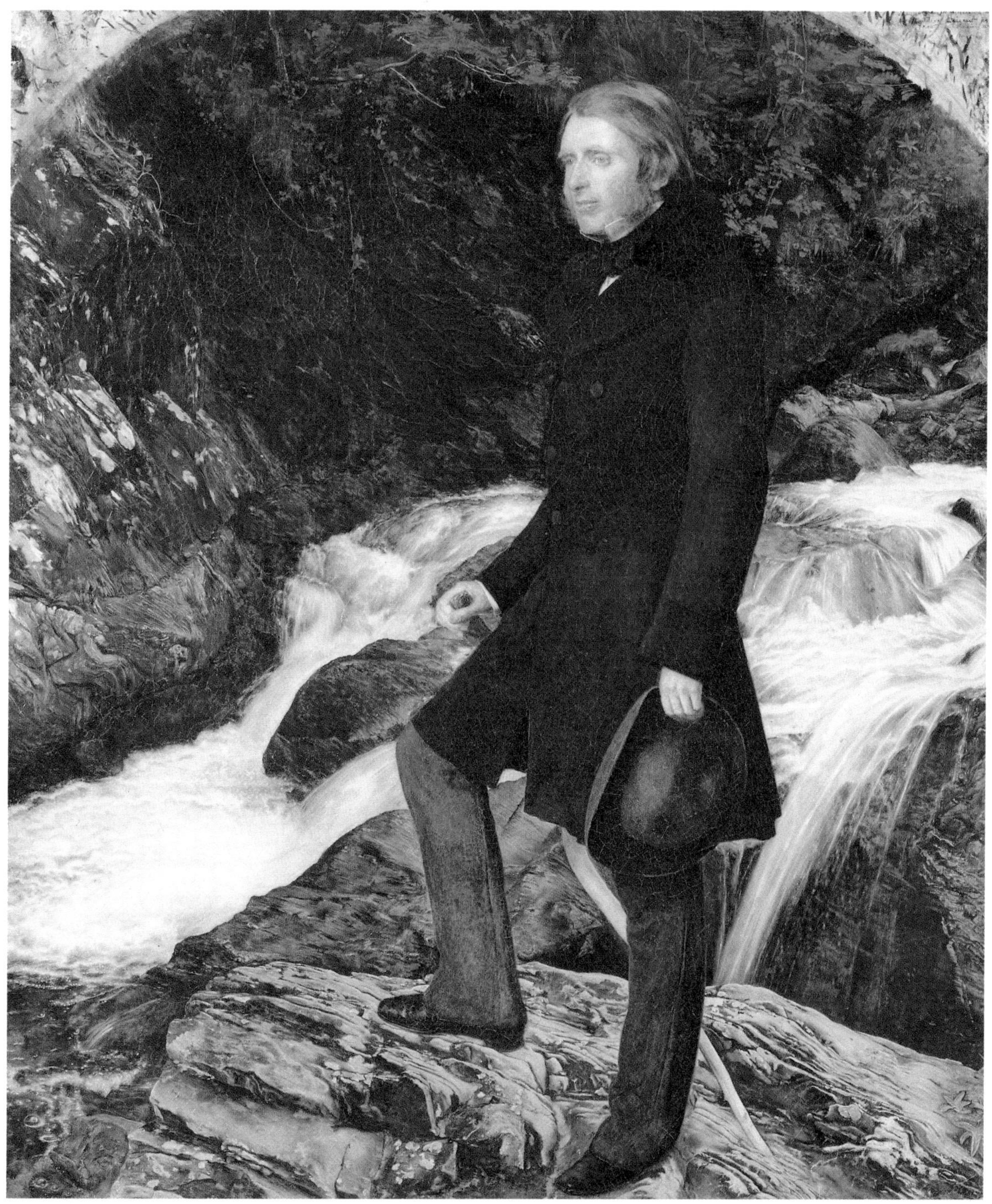

Plate 8. Portrait of John Ruskin, aet 34–35, 1853–54, by John Everett Millais [26]

Private collection

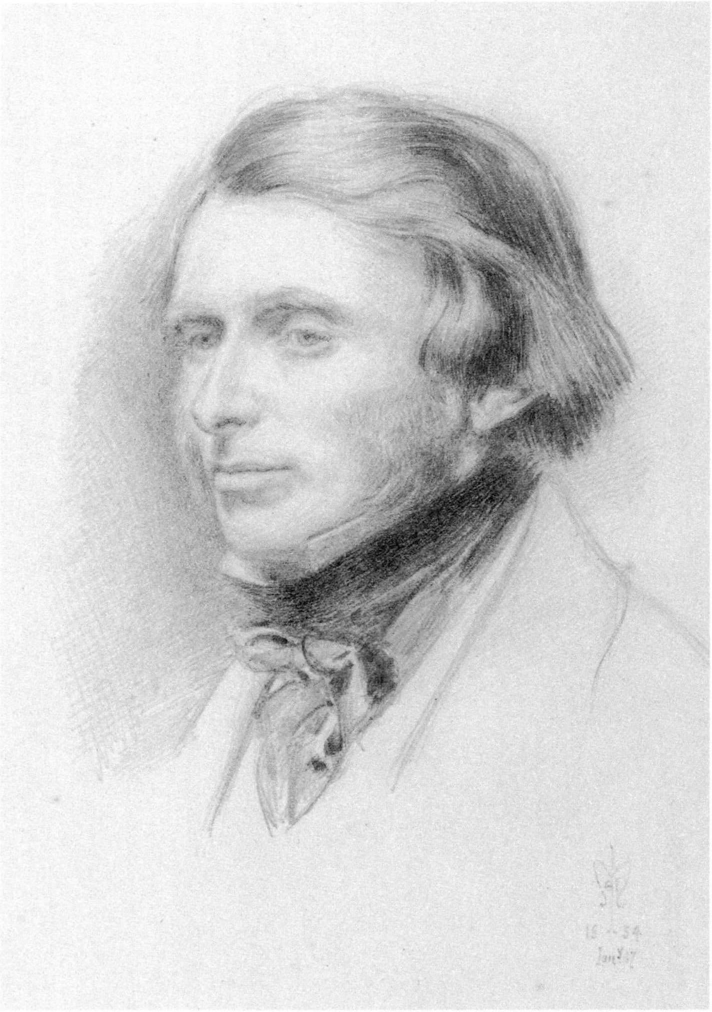

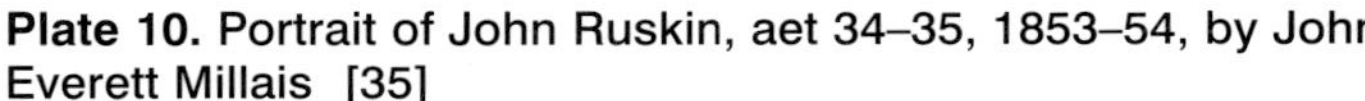

Plate 10. Portrait of John Ruskin, aet 34–35, 1853–54, by John Everett Millais [35]

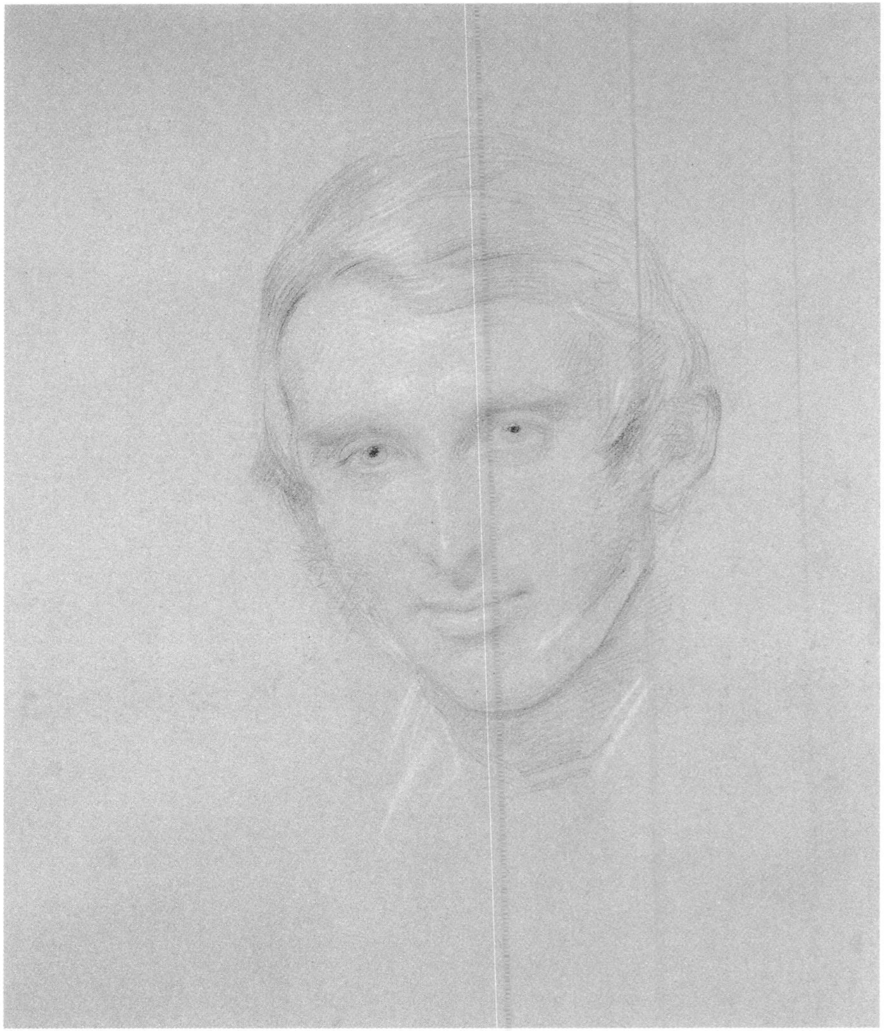

Plate 11. Portrait head, aet 38, c.1857, by George Richmond [44]

By courtesy of the National Portrait Gallery, London

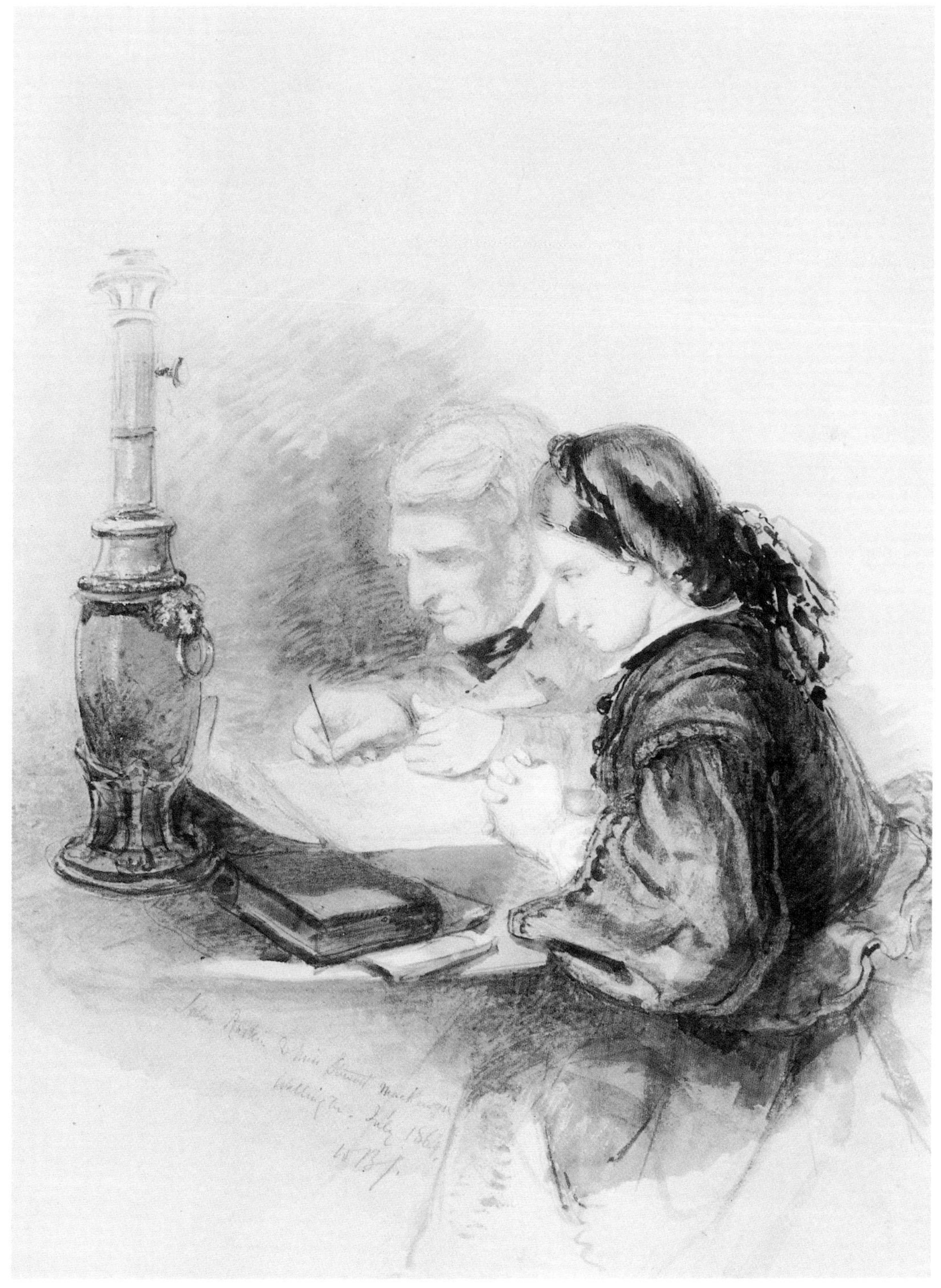

Plate 12. Portrait with Louisa Stewart-Mackenzie, aet 38, July 1857, by William Bell Scott [47]

National Trust Photographic Library

Plate 13. Self-portrait, aet 42, November 1861 [58]

Plate 14. John Ruskin, aet 48, 1867, anonymous miniature [85]

Courtesy of Victoria Andros

Plate 15. John Ruskin, miniature on ivory by J.C. Barry [89]

Ruskin Foundation (Ruskin Library, University of Lancaster)

Plate 16. John Ruskin, full-length caricature by Adriano Cecioni [109]

South London Gallery

Plate 17. John Ruskin, aet 54, self-portrait, January 1873 [114]

Plate 18. John Ruskin, aet 55, self-portrait, head only, Spring 1874 [117]

Reproduction courtesy of Wellesley College Library, Special Collections. Gift of Charles Eliot Goodspeed.

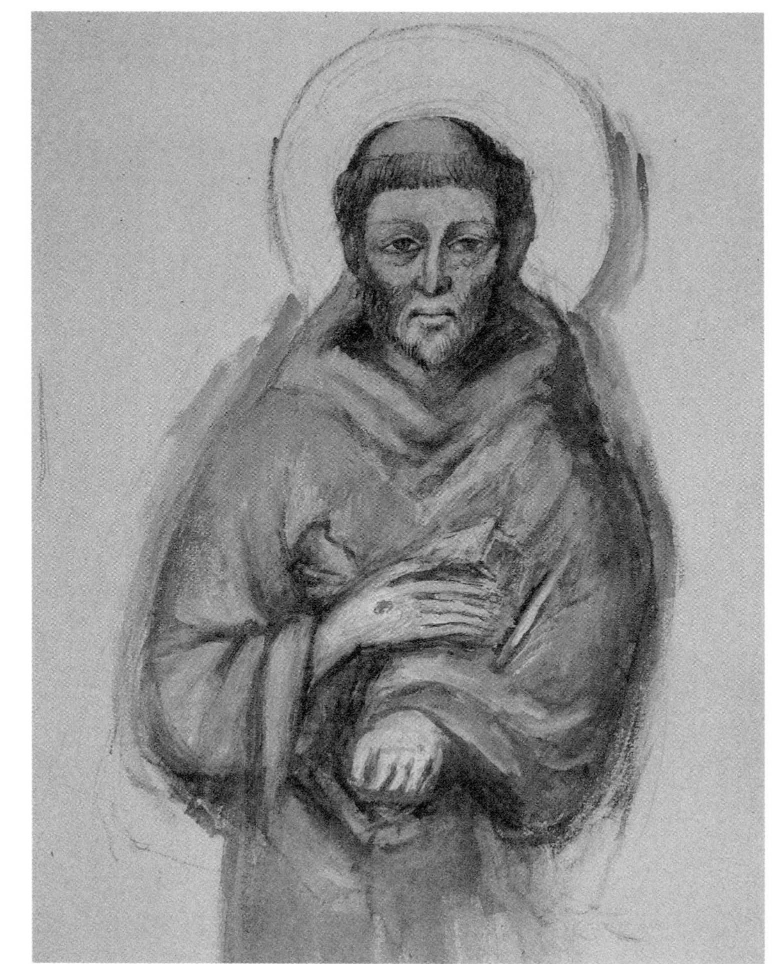

Plate 19. John Ruskin, aet 55, self-portrait as St Francis, June–July 1874 [120]

Courtesy of R. Dyke Benjamin

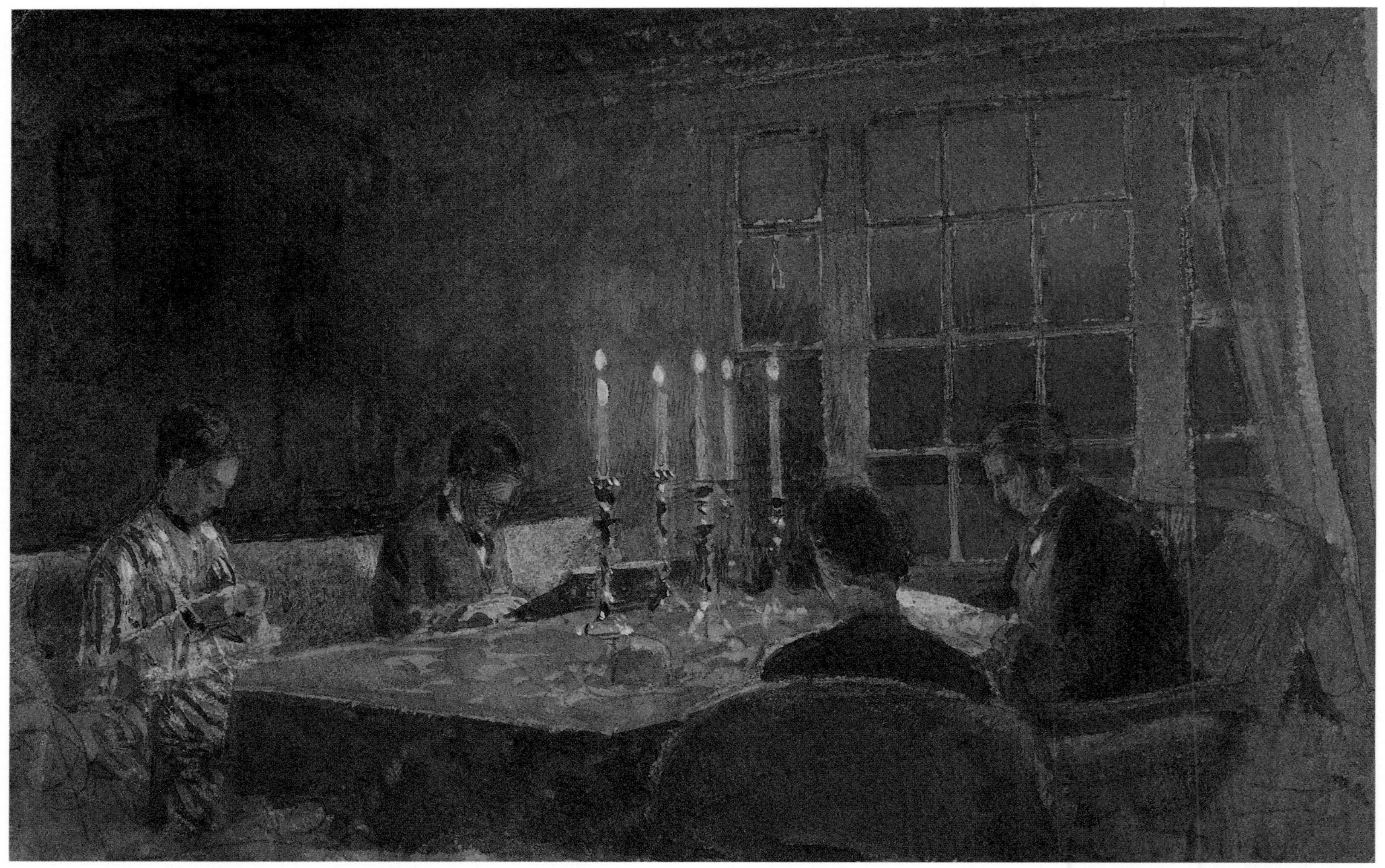

Plate 20. John Ruskin at Brantwood, by Arthur Severn, ?June 1876, aet 57 [128]

Ruskin Foundation (Ruskin Library, University of Lancaster)

Plate 21. John Ruskin, aet 58, portrait by Charles Fairfax Murray, or a self-portrait, April 1877 [132]

Plate 22. John Ruskin, head and shoulders in marble, by J.E. Boehm, 1879 [149]

Ruskin School of Drawing and Fine Art, Oxford

Plate 23. John Ruskin, aet 60, portrait by Sir Hubert von Herkomer, 1879 [153]

By courtesy of the National Portrait Gallery, London

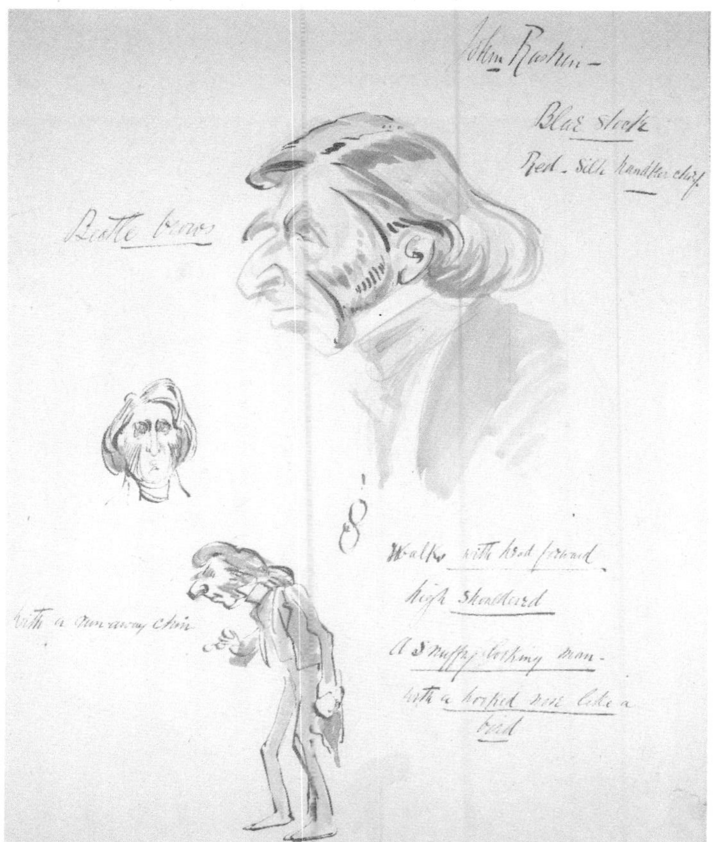

Plate 24. A sheet of caricature sketches, by Alfred Bryan, c.1880 [158]

Courtesy of Dr W.A. Stewart

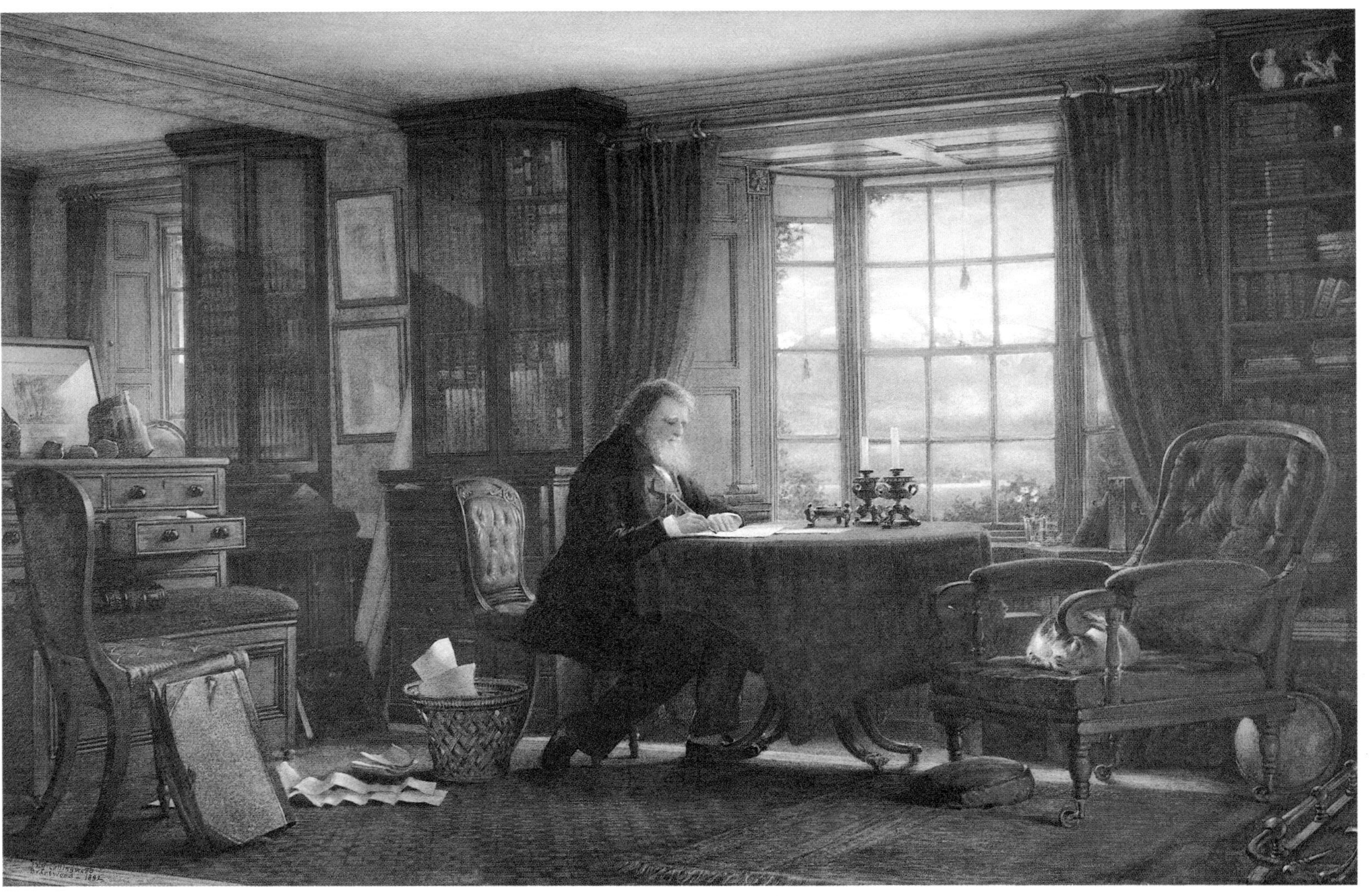

Plate 25. Portrait with Laurence Hilliard posing as Ruskin in his study at Brantwood, by William Gershom Collingwood, February 1882. [166]

Courtesy of the Ruskin Museum, Coniston

Plate 26. John Ruskin, by Valentine Cameron Princep, 1882, aet 63 [170]

Plate 27. John Ruskin, portrait by Isabella Jay, c.1882 [174]

Plate 28. John Ruskin, portrait bust based on No. 171, by Roland Morris, 1882–87 [175]

Collection: Stephen Wildman

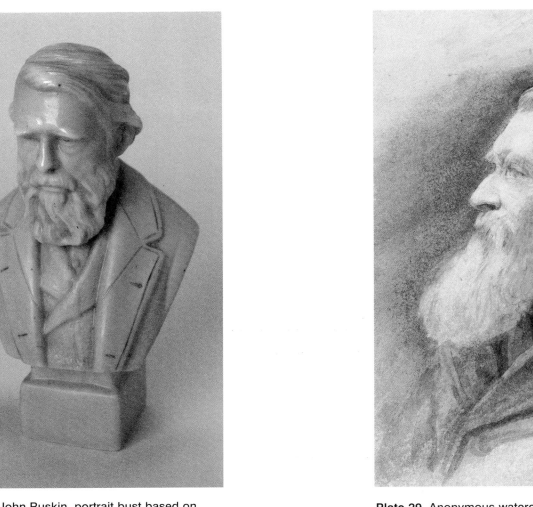

Plate 29. Anonymous watercolour based on No. 213 [214]

Ruskin Foundation (Ruskin Library, University of Lancaster)

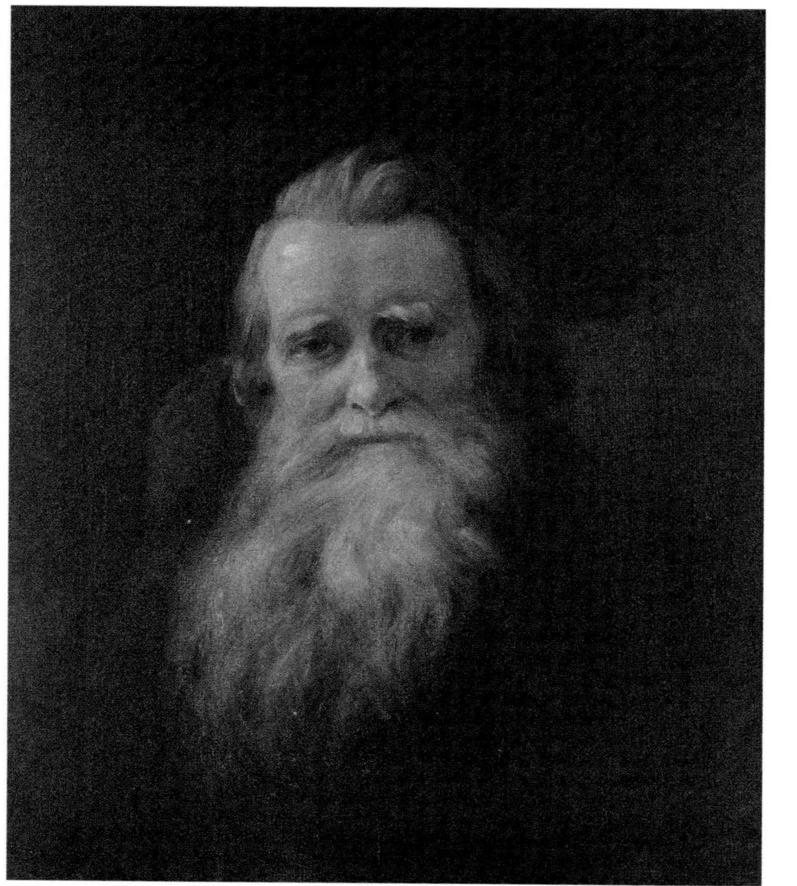

Plate 30. Oil sketch by W.G. Collingwood, 1897, aet 78 [272]

Plate 31. Portrait by W.G. Collingwood, 29 January 1897 [273]

Plate 32. Portrait by W.G. Collingwood, 19 February 1897 [275]

Ruskin Foundation (Ruskin Library, University of Lancaster)

Plate 33. Portrait by Arthur Severn, watercolour, 1897–1900, aet 78 [276]

Ruskin Foundation (Ruskin Library, University of Lancaster)

Plate 34. Portrait, based on No. 276, by Arthur Severn, oil, 1898–99 [277]

Courtesy of The Ruskin Museum, Coniston

Plate 35. Photographed in the study, by John McClelland [279]

Ruskin Foundation (Ruskin Library, University of Lancaster)

Plate 36. Ruskin, head and shoulders, holding a copy of *Stones of Venice*. Illustration by Geoffrey Appleton for Michelle Lovric's *Carpaccio's Cat* [325/1]

Courtesy of Geoffrey Appleton

Plate 37. Ruskin with Carpaccio's 'Two Venetian Ladies with their Pets' and 'The Languid Knight' from the St Ursula cycle. Illustration by Geoffrey Appleton for Michelle Lovric's *Carpaccio's Cat* [325/16]

Courtesy of Geoffrey Appleton

155 Cartoon, 'The Morris-Dance round St Mark's', by Edward Linley Sambourne (1845–1910), 10 January 1880

156 Cartoon, 'A Caution to snakes', 24 March 1880

157 Cartoon, 'A Concert by the Powers', 23 October 1880

158 A sheet of caricature sketches, by Alfred Bryan, c.1880 (Plate 24)

159 Caricature, 'Mr Ruskin. The Complete Letter-writer in spite of himself', by Alfred Bryan, 1880

160 Cartoon, 'Punch's Fancy Portraits, No. 12 – Mr Ruskin', by E.L. Sambourne, 18 December 1880

Throughout 1880 Ruskin was to provide cartoonists with material. Sambourne was particularly active.

Both Ruskin and William Morris were against the restoration of old buildings and in 1879–80 Morris had frequently been speaking on behalf of his Society for the Protection of Ancient Buildings against the re-building of the west front of St Mark's, Venice. In Sambourne's first *Punch* cartoon Ruskin joins the 'Morris-dancers' around St Mark's.

In March Ruskin lectured on snakes at the London Institute, giving his 'spiritual version of the development of the species' as opposed to Huxley's version of their origin, thus leading to the cartoon in the *London Figaro*.

In October he appeared in *Moonshine* in a cartoon called 'A Concert by the Powers'. Below the heading is the quotation from Ruskin's letter in the *Glasgow Herald* of 12 October 1880 in connection with his appointment as Lord Rector of Glasgow University – 'Had you ever read ten words of mine with understanding, you would have known that I care no more either for Mr Disraeli or Mr Gladstone than for two old bagpipes...' In the cartoon Gladstone and Disraeli are shown as bagpipes while Ruskin stands between them blowing a trumpet.

The sheet of sketches by Alfred Bryan is important. It is unsigned, but Ruskin's caricatured likeness to, for example, No. 159 which is signed with Bryan's initials, is unmistakable. It is clear that these caricatures are actually drawn from the life, because they are accompanied by noted observations which Bryan could only have made from seeing his subject. He has noted around the three drawings:

Beetle brows
with a run-away chin

John Ruskin
Blue stock
Red silk handkerchief
Walks with head forward
high shouldered
A snuffy looking man
with a hooked nose like a bird

156

2 PUNCH, OR THE LONDON CHARIVARI. [JANUARY 10, 1880.

THE MORRIS-DANCE ROUND ST. MARK'S.

A MORRIS! a Morris! Æsthetics, Artistics,
  Slade scholars, Professors, High-Art *dilettante*,
Up with your polemics, if not with your fistics,
  In defence of San Marco against the *birbante*,
The Brigands, the Vandals, the Goths, the Bœotians,
  Who come forth to destroy on pretence to restore.
And whose sinister interests or Philistine notions
  May soon flay San Marco from finial to floor!

They may tell you their aim 's but to fix his foundations,
  To stay what is sinking, make good what is gone:
Gammon! That 's but to mask their accurst operations;
  You judge what they *will* do, by what they have done.
Or if your sharp eye on these jobbers and Vandals
  Have put spokes in their wheels, their profane hands have stayed,
The virtue 's not theirs, but your vigilant candles',
  The light they have thrown, and the noise you have made!

It will be noted that Ruskin is wearing a tail-coat in the lowest sketch, indicating that Bryan had seen him in an evening – presumably when he was lecturing; perhaps he was present at the London Institute lecture on snakes.

The similarity between 'The Complete letter-writer' and Bryan's previous sheet of sketches is easily seen. The present caricature is re-printed from an undated cutting and I have been unable to find the publication which carried it.

The 'Complete letterwriter' could refer to one of several events in 1880. It may be in response to Ruskin's letter to the *Glasgow Herald* (see No. 157). In the postscript to the letter quoted above, Ruskin added: 'You had better, however, ask the Conservatives for a copy of my *entire* letters to them'.

Alternatively in the June and July 1880 issues of the *Contemporary Review* Alexander Wedderburn published two long articles containing a selection of Ruskin's public letters, and in December of the year, the two volumes of *Arrows of the Chase*, Wedderburn's collection of Ruskin's letters to the press, was published.

Ruskin was well-known for the asperity of some of his public pronouncements. For example when asked for his opinion on the style of the proposed Bradford Wool Exchange, he said 'If ... I had answered "I won't come, I don't care about the Exchange of Bradford" you would have been justly offended with me ... In a word, then, I do not care about this Exchange, – because you don't, and because *you* know perfectly well I cannot make you'.

Punch, of 23 October 1880, included an article:

The complete Letter-writer
containing specimens of letters suitable
for all possible or impossible occasions
by John Ruskin Esq

I quote from two of Ruskin's imaginary letters printed therein:

> To the President of a Conservative Club, on being asked to stand as a Parliamentary Candidate for a Borough.
>
> My Dear Sir, who the deuce are you? ... I beg to assure you that you have as much right to ask me to stand as a Candidate as you have to make the same request of the Prince of Darkness himself ...
>
> On being invited to accept the Freedom of a City
>
> My Dear Mr Mayor, Confound your impertinence! Beelzebub – who, by the way, was quite a gentleman – is modest and unassuming compared with your entirely dastardly impudence ...

A CONCERT BY THE POWERS!

"Had you ever read ten words of mine with understanding, you would have known that I care no more either for Mr. Disraeli or Mr. Gladstone than for two old bagpipes, with the drones going by steam; but that I hate all Liberalism as I do Beelzebub; and that, with Carlyle, I stand—we two alone now in England—for God and the Queen."—*Mr. Ruskin.*

157

MR. RUSKIN.
The complete letter-writer in spite of himself.

159

The last in this group of cartoons is also by Sambourne. He was the son of a prosperous city merchant who was apprenticed at sixteen to a Greenwich marine engineer. He later met the editor of *Punch* and his first drawings were accepted in 1867. Within four years he had joined

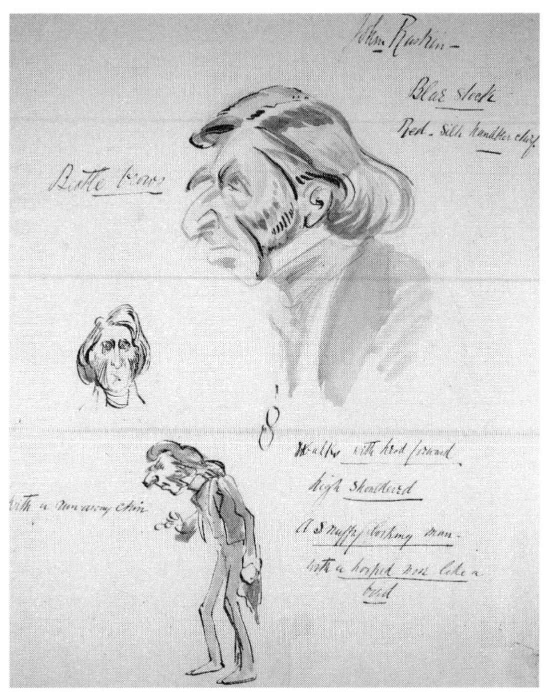

158

the editorial board and he eventually succeeded Tenniel as the journal's leading artist.

In 'Punch's Fancy Portraits – No. 12' Sambourne shows Ruskin prostrate before an altar labelled 'Sacred to the Memory of J.M.W. Turner', admiring his own reflection in a pool. Interestingly, and I don't know why, this caricature appeared in *Punch* of 18 December 1880 above *two* different captions. In one version, the caption 'Mr Narcissus Ruskin' is followed by the extract from Shakespeare's Sonnet 84:

> Who is it that say most? Which can say more
> Than this rich praise, that You alone are *you*!

The second version, merely captioned 'Mr Ruskin', is followed by the quotation from the *Merchant of Venice* Act I, scene I

> I am Sir Oracle,
> And when I ope my lips let no dog bark[196]

PUNCH, OR THE LONDON CHARIVARI.

PUNCH'S FANCY PORTRAITS.—No. 12.

MR. NARCISSUS RUSKIN.

"WHO IS IT THAT SAYS MOST? WHICH CAN SAY MORE,
THAN THIS RICH PRAISE,—THAT YOU ALONE ARE *YOU!*"

160

PUNCH, OR THE LONDON CHARIVARI.

PUNCH'S FANCY PORTRAITS.—No. 12.

MR. RUSKIN.

"I AM SIR ORACLE,
AND WHEN I OPE MY LIPS LET NO DOG BARK!"

160 (alternative caption)

196 I am indebted to Professor Michael Wheeler for identifying the two quotations for me. The version with the 'Mr Narcissus Ruskin' caption is found in his set of *Punch*.

161 John Ruskin, self-portrait silhouette climbing hillside with a party, ?15 September 1881, aet 62

Ruskin returned to Brantwood from the continent at the end of 1880 and on the following 20 February was taken ill again with a 'month of terrible delirium'. It was during this illness and immediately afterwards that his beard was allowed to grow – because he was too unwell to be shaved. The outline of the neatly trimmed beard may be seen in the present silhouette, which is the first portrait of the new hirsute Ruskin.

The sketch was perhaps made on 15 September 1881 at Brantwood when Ruskin had recorded in his diary that he had 'a happy day with Diddie [Anderson] and Alic [Wedderburn], Rosalind and Peggy. Happy walk on moor before one o'clock and garden afterwards begun'. The expedition appears to be setting out to clear part of the wood behind Brantwood. It will be noticed that Ruskin is carrying a bill hook; another figure carries a pick and two bill hooks and he is followed by a third figure also with a bill hook.

Such expeditions on the Brantwood estate were commonplace, as Collingwood explained.[197]

> After luncheon, if letters are done, all hands are piped to the moor. With billhooks and choppers the party winds up the wood paths, 'the Professor' first, walking slowly, and pointing out to you his pet bits of rock-cleavage, or ivied trunk, or nest of wild-strawberry plants. You see, perhaps, the ice-house – tunnelled at vast expense into the rock and filled at more expense with the best ice ... and so you come out on the moor. ... Not to tire a new-comer, he takes you away after a while to a fine heathery promontory, where you sit before a most glorious view of lake and mountains.

Rosalind and Peggy were two of the talented children of R.T. Webling. Ruskin had first met Peggy and her sister Ethel when he had been to tea with the newly-married Marcus Huish in 1879. Peggy, who was eight at the time, remembered this first meeting.

> The scene is like a half-forgotten picture to me – Ruskin sitting in a low, deep chair pushed back

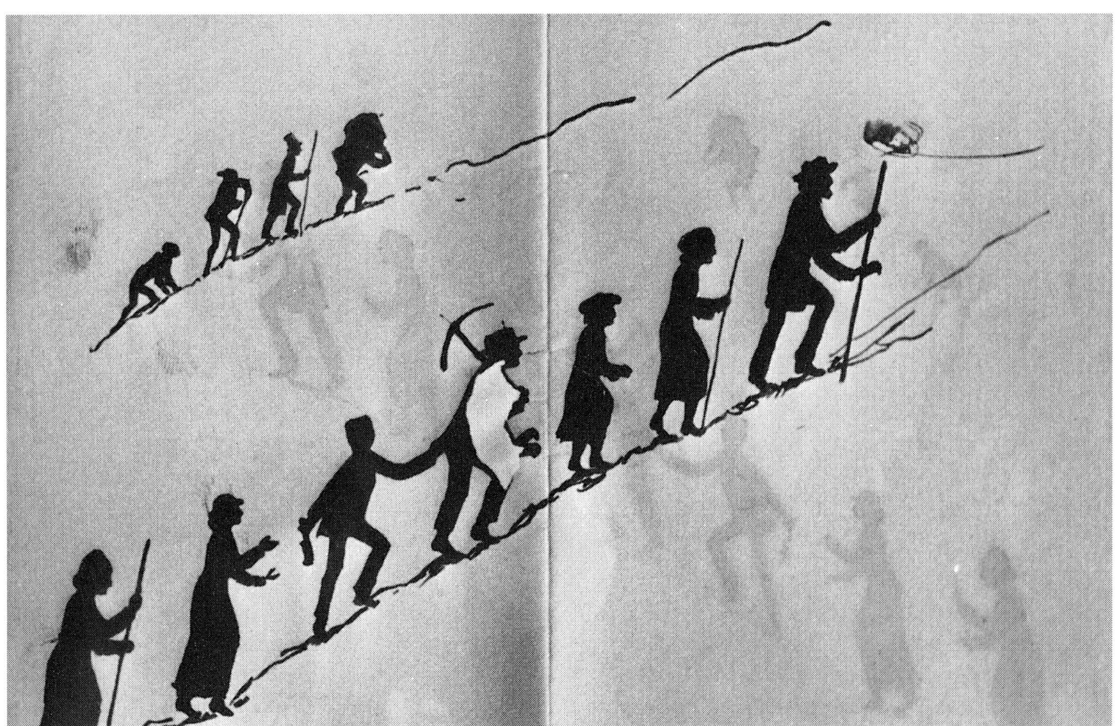

161

197 Collingwood, *Life and Work of John Ruskin*, vol. II, p. 199.

from the fire, with his long thin legs stretched out and his long, thin hands clasped together, his head sunk a little on his chest, his quick, smiling glance passing from face to face ...[198]

Later in the year Ruskin attended one of the recitations which the Webling sisters gave at the Steinway Hall. Peggy and Rosalind seem to have spent a month at Brantwood in 1880 and in the following year they were there again, from early August till mid-September, returning for a few days in October with their mother and sister Josephine.

In her autobiography[199] Peggy remembered their first arrival at Brantwood.

> The Professor was at the door when we arrived. I can see him now! He was wearing a suit of his favourite grey, with a wide blue silk stock, and a long, thin watch chain round his neck. Both hands were outstretched. He was bareheaded, heedless of the raindrops shaking from the boughs, as he came forward in eager welcome ... The Professor used to take Rosalind for long moor-land walks by stream and crag. I can see them now as they start out, the tall, wiry figure of Fidelity [their familiar name for Ruskin] in his grey clothes, soft grey hat and blue stock, stick in hand ...

The sketch, on a sheet of Brantwood note-paper, was folded (causing off-setting) and probably sent by Ruskin to one of the other sisters who was at home in London. It is among a group of letters to the sisters presented to Brantwood by Major Ruskin Watts, Josephine's son.

161 (detail)

162 Drawing of the façade of The Fine Art Society, Ruskin standing outside, by T. Raffles Davison, 1881

163 Drawing of John Ruskin, by T. Raffles Davison

John Ruskin had a long association with The Fine Art Society in Bond Street.[200] From the beginning, in 1876, its managing director was Marcus B. Huish, and the Ruskin-Huish correspondence started in 1875 before the Society opened its doors.

One of The Fine Art Society's first exhibitions in 1876 was of copies of Turner watercolours by William Ward from Ruskin's collection. Two years later Ruskin arranged his major Turner exhibition for them. Its catalogue, *Notes by Mr Ruskin on his Collection of Drawings by the late J.M.W. Turner R.A.* (1878), went through thirteen editions, and when the collection was re-shown in 1900 there were two further editions.

In 1879 Ruskin arranged a further exhibition for them, of drawings by Samuel Prout and W.H. Hunt. Meanwhile Ruskin had published his famous libel of Whistler and his paintings. Following the hearing, Ruskin's friends and admirers subscribed to a fund managed by The Fine Art Society to pay his legal costs. Whistler, who won the case, had temporarily lost his market and was

198 Peggy Webling, *A Sketch of John Ruskin* (London: published by the author, 1914), p. 13.

199 Peggy Webling, *Peggy: The Story of One Score Years and Ten* (London: Hutchinson, n.d.), p. 51.

200 Detailed in J.S. Dearden, *John Ruskin and the Alps* (Lancaster: The Fine Art Society, 1991), pp. 26-35.

bankrupt. The Fine Art Society commissioned *him* to go to Venice (out of reach of his creditors) to make a series of etchings, subsequently buying his plates for £700.

In 1881 The Fine Art Society commissioned the architect E.W. Godwin, whose work Ruskin had praised, to design a new frontage for their premises. This was duly built and the 16 December 1881 issue of the *British Architect* carried the present drawing of the re-designed building, by the editor, T. Raffles Davison. Tongue in cheek, Davison showed Ruskin and Whistler deep in conversation on the pavement outside.

The catalogue of the 1904 Ruskin Exhibition held in Manchester includes as No. 368 a sepia drawing of Ruskin by Raffles Davison. This remains untraced, and its relationship to The Fine Art Society façade drawing is unknown. At the time of the Manchester exhibition the drawing was owned by the Ruskin collector W.E.A. Axon who in 1879 had published his *Bibliographical Biography* of Ruskin in the *Papers of the Manchester Literary Club*.

162

164 John Ruskin, bust by G. Atkinson, ?December 1881, aet 62

165 John Ruskin, bust by G. Atkinson, cast by Jabez Thompson

Another visitor to Brantwood at the end of 1881[201] was G. Atkinson a sculptor who was a stranger to Ruskin. Atkinson wished to sculpt a bust; Ruskin found him lodgings, and provided him with a workshop and a place at his table. Work on the bust was slow. As Collingwood explains,[202] 'One reason, perhaps, for Mr Atkinson's difficulty was that Ruskin had just grown a beard and the well-known face was no longer there to mould.'

The original bust itself may not have survived; certainly I have been unable to trace it. However, we are fortunate that it has survived in another form.

201 Writing about his Christmas to Peggy Webling on 26 December (original at Consiton Museum) Ruskin told her 'there was no one here (except Mr Collingwood and Mr Atkinson)'.

202 Collingwood, *Ruskin Relics*, p. 136.

165

In 1967 Mr John Challinor gave a bust of Ruskin to the Whitehouse Collection. At that time I was unable to identify the sculptor. Cast in terra-cotta and coated in aluminium paint, the bust is stamped on the reverse

RUSKIN
JABEZ THOMPSON
NORTHWICH

The firm of Jabez Thompson, tile, brick and terra-cotta manufacturers, flourished in Northwich until about 1914. The firm made good-quality bricks and probably supplied bricks for the I.C.I. works which grew up around Winnington Hall in 1873. As a side-line the firm also produced moulded terra-cotta figures for garden ornaments and other purposes. The present bust had been given to Mr Challinor about 1952 by a builder. It had been in his store for a number of years, having come from a building demolished by his father.

It was possible to identify the bust as having been cast from Mr Atkinson's original when a second copy was found at St Anne's College, Oxford. This copy is stamped on the reverse

JOHN RUSKIN
MODELLED AT BRANTWOOD 1881
BY G. ATKINSON
PUBLISHED BY JABEZ THOMPSON
NORTHWICH
REGISTERED [DEVICE].

Below the device is a number 36.

The bust at one time belonged to Miss J.K. Macdonald, daughter of Alexander Macdonald, the first Master of the Ruskin Drawing School. It was in her house in Woodstock Road when she bequeathed it, in the 1930s, to the Society of Oxford Home Students, as St Anne's College then was.

Subsequently cast No. 12 was bought for Brantwood from Thorntons of Oxford, in whose premises it had been for many years. No. 23 is also now in the Whitehouse Collection, and No. 22 was bought in 1996 by Abbot Hall Art Gallery, Kendal.

The sculptor, 'G. Atkinson', may be identified as the sculptor Arthur G. Atkinson, who is recorded as having exhibited at the Royal Academy between 1879–91.

Tony Flood has made a new mould from one of the versions at Brantwood and a number of new casts have been made for sale there.

166 Portrait with Laurence Hilliard posing as Ruskin in his study at Brantwood, by William Gershom Collingwood (1854–1932), February 1882. (Plate 25)

167 Portrait, copied from No. 166, by W.G. Collingwood, 1893

W.G. Collingwood, son of the landscape painter William Collingwood, met Ruskin at Oxford in 1872. In the following year he first visited Brantwood. Two years later he was staying at Brantwood with Alexander Wedderburn, translating *Xenophon* for Ruskin, and helping with the construction of the harbour. Collingwood was back at Brantwood in 1881–82 as an assistant. After his marriage in 1883 he settled near Coniston, later moving to Lanehead, about a mile from Brantwood, and devoted himself to Ruskin as secretary, biographer and editor.

The present is the first in a series of portraits of Ruskin by Collingwood. It had unusual origins and is perhaps one of the most interesting portraits that there is of Ruskin. Not only does it show the man himself, it is also a detailed portrait of his study. When the picture was reproduced by W. Holmes of Ulverston, Collingwood wrote the following account to accompany it.

Mr Ruskin was in the habit of doing most of his literary work before breakfast, and in the winter half of the year would often begin before dawn, writing by candle-light. In the picture, the sunrise has just caught the snowy top of Coniston Old Man, seen through the window; while the lake and tall chimneys of Coniston Hall below are still in shade. Inside the room, the candles on the table have been put out, but the fire shines on the arm-chair in which the old tortoiseshell cat is taking her ease. Mr Ruskin (who gave special sittings for the portrait) wears a blue coat and grey trousers, blue stock and creased wristbands, with a long gold chain; the costume familiar to his audiences at Oxford and elsewhere. He writes with a cork pen-holder, the paper flat on the table, and the rough notes of his subject laid out before him. Slips of proof and sheets of paged revise are laying on the floor, and the spent copy is in the waste-paper basket. The accessories are all accurately represented as they were at the time. On the left of the picture a Turner drawing of Florence from Fiesole stands on the chest of drawers, behind a row of selected minerals illustrating his theory of Agates. The open drawer

166

167

holds the St George's Guild business papers (in connection with which he was then at work). Below it, on the velvet cushioned top of the case for framed Dürers, is a favourite MS bible of the fourteenth century which he used to read as a beginning to his day's work; and against the chair is a portfolio of drawings for the St George's Museum. The cabinet behind it is that which held Liber Studiorum prints; beside it is a roll of lecture diagrams; above are two sketches by Prout, to the left of which is the 'Geology' bookcase, the celestial globe, the mineral cabinet hardly seen behind the Turner Florence. The bookcase in the middle of the picture holds 'Botany'. In the window are some of his own books in the Ruskin purple calf bindings: grass of Parnassus in a tumbler of water, and a box of early daguerreo-types of Venice. In the shelves on the right are a vase and archaic figurine of a horseman from Cyprus, cases of coins, books, and a terrestrial globe on the floor. In the fender, much foreshortened, is the once famous Ruskin Shovel, designed by himself and made by the Coniston Blacksmith.

The end of 1881 and beginning of 1882 was a time of depression for Ruskin. Apart from one short visit to Seascale he had not been away from Brantwood since his illness in the Spring of '81. He decided that his health and spirits would be improved by a trip to London. At the beginning of February he went to Herne Hill, and at first the change did him good.

Meanwhile at Brantwood Collingwood and Laurence Hilliard were planning a surprise for Ruskin.

> ... I'm working vigorously. I'm doing a drawing 21" x 30" of the Brantwood study seen from the fireplace – showing the bow window and the Professor's table where he writes and Coniston Old Man out of the window in the sunrise – and the Old Man at his table. And if the watercolour is successful I'll do an oil from it for the Academy.
>
> Hilliard who is such an actor is going to sit for the Professor – and I'll do the face out of my head – I think I can. Also the favourite cat is in the arm chair. I think that will be a good picture.
>
> Mr Ruskin is coming on the 25th and I want to get it done before he comes.[203]

203 W. G. Collingwood to his fiancée, Miss Isaac, 17 February 1882; transcript kindly made available by Miss Janet Gnosspelius.

Three days later Collingwood wrote to his fiancée 'I'm dreadfully busy with my picture – trying to get it done before Mr Ruskin comes back so I have very little time for anything more than to send my love ...'

But Collingwood's plans were disrupted. In London Ruskin caught a cold which prevented him from sleeping. This ended in another severe mental breakdown. It was some time before he recovered, and then he did not return to Coniston, but on 10 August he left with Collingwood and Baxter for a continental trip which did not end until 2 December. Ruskin was not back at Brantwood till 4 January 1883.

If indeed Ruskin *did* sit for the portrait, it could not have been until after the beginning of January 1883, and there are no references to sitting in his relatively full diary for this immediate period. In the context of the events of 1882, Collingwood's observation that Ruskin 'gave special sittings for the portrait' is interesting. Did he, indeed, sit for the portrait after he returned to Brantwood, or is Collingwood's '*special* sittings' a veiled way of indicating that the portrait was actually painted from observations and memory? I think the latter is probably the case.

No. 167 is a reduced copy of the portrait, signed and dated 1893 by Collingwood. It appeared for sale at Christie's in 1988 and was first exhibited in the following year. Collingwood's purpose in making the copy is uncertain. However, I would suggest that, like No. 60 above, it was probably copied so that the *copy*, rather than the much larger original, could go to the blockmaker for reproduction. Perhaps Collingwood was planning to use it as an illustration for his biography of Ruskin which appeared in that year. In the event, it does not appear to have been reproduced until 1902, but it seems likely that Holmes's reproduction of that year was made from No. 167, rather than the larger original.

168 John Ruskin, portrait by Ethel Webling, ?February-March 1883, aet 63

When Ruskin was in London in 1882, probably before his breakdown in February, or possibly afterwards during his convalescence, he visited the Weblings at their home, 5 Alpha Road, Regent's Park. Peggy Webling remembered one of the first visits, and how the sisters entertained him. Josephine read him fairy stories she had written, Rosalind talked to him, and Ethel, the artist of the family, made the present silver-point drawing of him.

168

MAY 6, 1882.]
MOONSHINE.
205
POOR GEORGE ELLIOT
WITH A GREAT HISTORIAN
RUSKIN
O POLITICS I HATE 'EM.
AH WELL HE AINT SICH A BAD UN ARTER ALL
O MY DEAR. YOU GO UP AN' ASK MISTER RUSKIN. HE'S VERY KIND TO SICH AS US
HE DISLIKES POLITICS — BUT HE IS VERY GOOD HEARTED
HE LIKES A COUNTRY WALK
I WONDER WHAT HE WILL SAY ABOUT ME
AT AN EXHIBITION
HE TURNETH ROUND ON A FASHIONABLE ARTIST.
HE HAS NOT TOLD US WHAT HE THINKS OF OSCAR.
HE TOLERATES CLAUDE LORAINE
BUT
J. M. W. TURNER
HE LIKES HOLMAN HUNT
HUMPH! DON'T THINK I shall SHAVE THIS MORNING
WHAT HAPPENED LATELY
THE RESULT
HE WORSHIPS TURNER
HE KEEPS LATE HOURS
DAYS WITH CELEBRITIES. (46).
MR. RUSKIN.

169 Caricature, 'Days with celebrities – Mr Ruskin', by Alfred Bryan, May 1882

In the caricature which appeared in *Moonshine* on 6 May 1882, Ruskin is shown dipping his quill into an inkwell of gall. In the surrounding sketches which illustrate his activities and interests, he worships Turner, stabs Whistler with his pen, and talks to Holman Hunt. Two old ladies say '... he's very kind to such as us'; an artist at an exhibition wonders 'what he will say about me', and the caricaturist points out that 'He has not told us what he thinks of Oscar [Wilde]'. This was the first caricature to be published after Ruskin had grown his beard, and this is illustrated in two of the lower sketches, 'Humph, I don't think I shall shave this morning' and 'The Result'.

170 John Ruskin, by Valentine Cameron Princep (1838–1904) 1882, aet 63 (Plate 26)

Val Princep was the son of Henry Thoby Princep, an Indian civil servant. The Princeps lived at Little Holland House in Kensington. Their 'At Homes' were a feature of London's artistic life and Val was a member of the Pre-Raphaelite circle. The Princeps helped Burne-Jones at the beginning of his career and G.F. Watts lived with them for some time. Julia Margaret Cameron, the portrait photographer who had told Ruskin that he was unworthy of photographs, was Mrs Princep's sister.

Ruskin was an occasional visitor to Little Holland House and he may have first met Val there. In 1857 he would have seen more of him when Rossetti, Burne-Jones, Morris, Princep and others were painting their murals in the Oxford Union Debating Hall.

Princep's little portrait of Ruskin, to judge by the length of the beard and contemporary photographs, was probably made about the same time as the Webling silver-point drawing – in the spring of 1882.

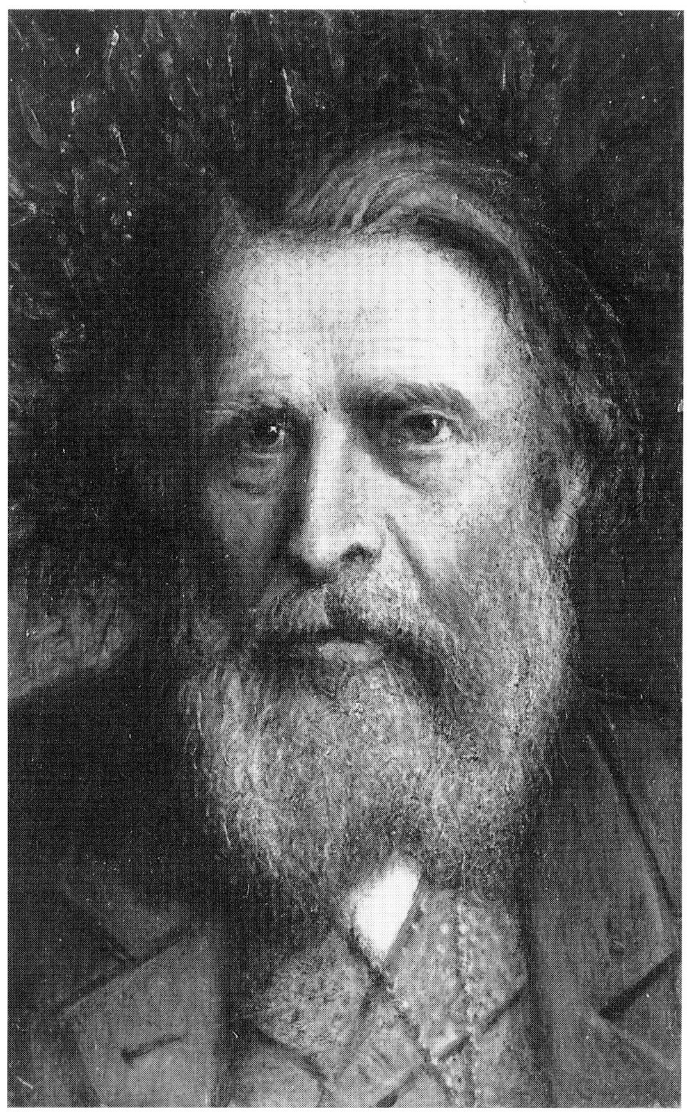

170

171 John Ruskin, photographed full face by Elliott & Fry, 1882 (First sitting)

172 John Ruskin, portrait based on No. 171, by Phoebe Anna Traquair (1852–1936), 1885–86

173 John Ruskin, portrait based on No. 171, by M. Ethel Jameson

174 John Ruskin, portrait based on No. 171, by Isabella Jay (d. 1919), c.1882 (Plate 27)

175 John Ruskin, portrait bust based on No. 171, by Roland Morris, 1882–87 (Plate 28)

176 John Ruskin, portrait bust based on No. 175, by K. Kitaji, c.1931

177 John Ruskin, portrait based on No. 171, by Herbert Cole

Probably in the early part of 1882 Ruskin was photographed again by Elliott and Fry. From now until the end of his life Ruskin was to be a frequent photographer's subject. In fact there are three Elliott and Fry photographs dating from 1882. Two of them (Nos. 188, 190) were taken on 9 August, the day before he left for the continent. In the third, the present photograph, he is wearing different clothes and so this must represent a different sitting earlier in the year. This is one of the best known photographs of Ruskin and at least three other portraits are copied directly from it.

171

No. 172 is a portrait of Ruskin based on the photograph, by Phoebe Traquair. She was a Scottish artist who was influenced by Ruskin's writings. The decoration of the Royal Hospital for Sick Children's Mortuary Chapel in Lauriston Lane, Edinburgh, marked her debut as a professional artist. The murals were painted in 1885 and early 1886 (and restored in 1896–8). The right hand side of the panel on the south wall depicting the Three Maidens (Divine Powers) is bordered by a series of lunettes containing portraits of critics, writers and artists admired by Traquair. These include Blake, Burne-Jones, Watts, Rossetti, William Bell Scott, Noel Paton and Dr John Brown. Ruskin appears between Carlyle (below) and Tennyson (above).

Ethel Jameson's portrait of Ruskin (No. 173), also based on the Elliott & Fry photograph, was

173

172

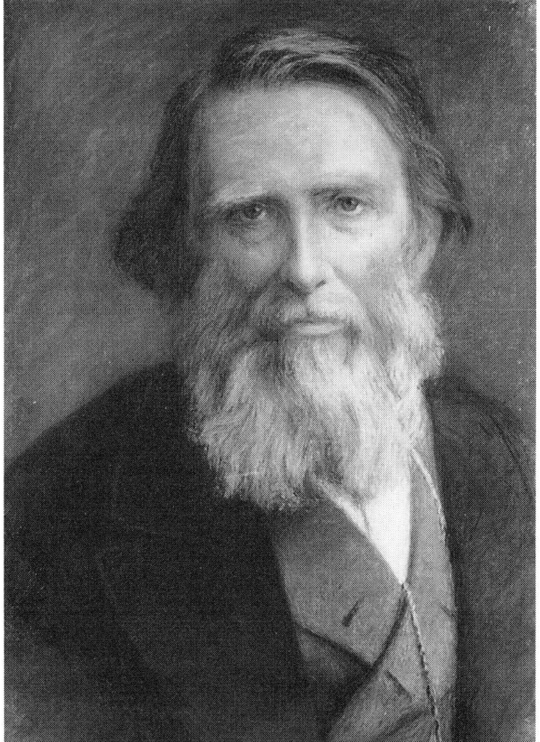

174

drawn by her to illustrate her book, *A Bibliographical Contribution to the Study of John Ruskin* (1901).

No. 174 is an undated copy in pastel by Isabella Jay who was a copyist specialising in the work of Turner. She was patronised by Ruskin who wrote on 4 January 1868

> Miss Isabella Jay's copies of Turner's pictures are the most accurate and beautiful I have yet seen, in many respects attaining fully to the expression of the master's most subtle qualities: and I think that such copies are much more valuable and instructive possessions than the original drawings of second-rate artists.

Writing to her again on 21 November 1870 he said

> ... I hope you will persevere in this work: many women are now supporting themselves by frivolous and useless art: I trust you may have the happiness of obtaining livelihood in a more honourable way by aiding in true educational efforts, and placing within the reach of the general public some means of gaining better knowledge of the noblest art.

175

175 (small version)

176

The portrait was one of the nineteen pictures which the artist bequeathed to J. Howard Whitehouse in 1919.

No. 175, a bust in Parian ware, was also based on the Elliott and Fry photograph. The manufacturers, Robinson and Leadbetter (established in 1850) produced busts of many Victorian celebrities. Their work is outstanding for its quality and photographic likeness to the subject. All examples were made in Parian ware (a kind of white porcelain), a substance which the firm continued to use well into the 20th century, long after it had been abandoned by other manufacturers. Robinson and Leadbetter employed a celebrated young modeller, Roland Morris, who was almost certainly responsible for modelling Ruskin from the Elliott and Fry photograph. Much of the firm's work is unmarked; however the Ruskin bust is impressed with their stamp 'R & L' enclosed in an oval, on the back of the right shoulder. The firm added 'Ltd' to its stamp in 1887 so we must assume the present bust to have been made between 1882 and 1887.

The firm of Robinson and Leadbetter and W.H. Goss were connected in some way and do not seem to have duplicated each other's subjects. No Goss bust of Ruskin is known, and the fact that there is one by Robinson and Leadbetter probably indicates that Goss never used him as a subject.

No. 176 is another bust based on the early 1882 Elliott and Fry photograph. Naturally it is very similar to the Robinson and Leadbetter bust, though it is a little taller. It was modelled by the Japanese sculptor K. Kitaji for the well-known Japanese Ruskinophile, Ryuzo Mikimoto. There is a photograph dated 1 October 1931 of the bust in the Mikimoto collection and this *may* represent the date of the bust. The Kitaji bust is cast in bronze and there also seems to have been a plaster cast of it in the Mikimoto collection at one time.

No. 177, a small portrait by Herbert Cole, is in the collection of J.J. Challen of Beaverton, Oregon. It was commissioned by J.M. Dent for Ruskin's *Unto this Last* in one of their series of books, and it remained in Dent's archives until it was bought by Ian Hodgkins to appear in one of his 1990 catalogues.

A small stained glass panel in the Royal Oak at Keswick, an hotel where Ruskin occasionally stayed, may also be based on this photograph.

177

178 John Ruskin, photograph looking left, by Herbert R. Barraud, April 1882

179 John Ruskin, photograph, full face, by H.R. Barraud

180 John Ruskin, portrait by T.H. Stephenson, based on No. 179

181 John Ruskin, portrait by Joseph Stimpson, based on No. 179

182 John Ruskin, anonymous portrait based on No. 179

183 John Ruskin, anonymous portrait based on No. 179

184 John Ruskin, bust in Carlton China, based on No. 179

185 John Ruskin, photograph, full face, eyes looking right, by H.R. Barraud

186 John Ruskin, portrait by Henry H. Sands, based on No. 185

187 John Ruskin, photograph, full face turned slightly to the right, by H.R. Barraud

In April 1882 Herbert R. Barraud visited Herne Hill and took four photographs of Ruskin in Arthur Severn's studio. The following letter[204] which Ruskin wrote to him was facsimilied and used by Barraud as a testimonial.

Dear Mr Barraud,
We are all much more than pleased with these results of your extreme skill and care; – they are the first photographs ever done of me that express what good or character there is in me for my own work; and as pure photography, they seem to me to go as far as the art can at this day – (– and I do not believe it can ever do much better.)

The portrait of Baby[205] is also a rare success, both in your choice of action, and the precision of

204 Dated 30 April [1882].

205 One of the Severn children.

178

179

180

effect; it is extremely and singularly beautiful – Mr Severn very good – and my Lucerne drawing better than itself – only my favourite Ruth[206] has failed – however, – it was as well, seeing the hitherto difficulty of getting an enduring likeness of me for those friends who care for me that you gave your time to that immediate business.

I admit – for once – as you have managed to use it – the good of Studio light! – But some day – you must please do one of me in open light – for the sake of fair play to the Day and – to your own skill, which I am sure can conquer more difficulties than you have tried –

And so believe me always gratefully
and faithfully Yours
J Ruskin

One of the photographs – No. 179 – was copied, perhaps in the 1920s, by T.H. Stephenson, a painter who lived in Coniston. Stephenson may never have seen Ruskin, and probably based his likeness exclusively on the photograph. The paint-

206 Ruth Mercier, who had nursed Ruskin through his illness.

181

183

184

ing was probably commissioned by Edward Woolgar, one-time Coniston station-master and a keen Ruskin collector.

The same photograph also formed the basis for a portrait by Joseph Stimpson and two further anonymous portraits. No. 183, which originally appeared in the *Sheffield Weekly Telegraph* was probably copied by an artist employed by that journal.

Photograph No. 179 was also used in modelling a bust made by the Carlton China factory. Like No. 175, the bust is made in Parian ware, though the workmanship is of a much inferior standard. The Edwardian era was the heyday of crested china. The Carlton series of busts began with royalty and generals, and continued through figures well-known in the arts. The bust of Ruskin

182

185

186

187

was certainly made after 1901 and before 1914, probably about 1910–11. The imaginary Coniston coat of arms on the porcelain plinth seems to be based on the arms of a well-known Furness family, the Flemings (a branch of which at one time owned Coniston Hall), and on arms similar to those of Furness Abbey, another landowner of the Coniston district.

Photograph No. 185 formed the basis of another, slight but significant, portrait – No. 186. This small oil was painted by the minor Birmingham artist Henry H. Sands. We know from an old label on the reverse that it was painted for Howard S. Pearson; on his death it was given by his daughter to 'K.H. Sept. 1923'.

Pearson had a predominating influence on the cultural life of Birmingham at the turn of the century. He was a lecturer and writer who also taught evening classes at the Birmingham Institute and Mason's College. I had always assumed that it was probably Pearson who first introduced J. Howard Whitehouse to the writings of Ruskin when he attended evening classes. Since Pearson commissioned this portrait, it appears that he was particularly devoted to Ruskin's work, thus making it almost certain that he was initially responsible for creating Whitehouse's interest. I was especially pleased that it was possible to add this portrait to the Whitehouse Collection in 1994.

In reproducing Photograph No. 187 in his life of Ruskin, W.G. Collingwood described it as 'the photograph which Mr Ruskin has considered the best likeness of himself'.[207]

207 Collingwood, *The Life and Work of John Ruskin*, vol. I, p. x; vol. II, p. 215.

188 John Ruskin, photograph, full face, by Elliott & Fry, 9 August 1882

189 John Ruskin, portrait based on No. 188, by Harrison Ruskin Fowler, after February 1919

190 John Ruskin, photograph looking half right, by Elliott & Fry

188

190

These two photographs, the second sitting to Elliott & Fry in 1882, were taken on 9 August, the day before Ruskin and Collingwood embarked on their continental tour that was to take them to Rheims, Geneva, Turin, Lucca, Florence and Paris, and would keep them from England until 1 December.

The portrait by Harrison Fowler, based on No. 188, is in beaten copper; he subsequently made a pencil drawing of the relief for reproduction in *Ruskin's Guild of St George* (1931) the book written by his sister-in-law, Edith Hope Scott. The relief was probably made after February 1919 because the reproduction of No. 188 in *The Bookman* of that month was probably his only access to the image.

Fowler appears to have made a speciality of beaten copper portraits. Peter Wardle tells me that he remembers the relief of Ruskin, together with a companion portrait of Thomas Carlyle, hanging in the dining room of the Fowlers' home in Liverpool. He also has beaten copper relief portraits by Harrison Fowler of his great grandparents, Eleanor and David Scott.

Harrison Ruskin Fowler was born in Liverpool. Like his father, J.E. Fowler, he was a member of the Liverpool Ruskin Society and part of the Ruskin community of that city. He was enrolled as a Companion of the Guild of St George by George Baker, the second Master, 1900–10. An artist and craftsman he became head of the Londonderry School of Art before, in 1912, in common with others in that community, taking up small-holding farming in the Wyre Forest, near Bewdley. After the First World War Fowler returned to Liverpool. In the 1920s he served for several years as Secretary of the Guild.[208]

208 See Wardle and Quayle, *Ruskin and Bewdley* (St. Albans: Brentham Press for the Guild of St. George, 1989), pp. 38-41 and passim.

191 Sketch portrait of John Ruskin, aet 63, by William Gershom Collingwood, 18 August 1882

192 Sketch portrait of John Ruskin, aet 63, with W.G. Collingwood and Frank Randal, by Charles Randal (1851–1928), 19–20 August 1882

191

On 10 August 1882, the day following his photographic session with Elliott & Fry (Nos. 188–90) Ruskin left Herne Hill station at 10.10[209] and travelled by rail with W.G. Collingwood and his valet Peter Baxter, 'by Chatham and Dover line through Kent, looking entirely lovely with perpetual corn and copse', to Dover where they embarked for Calais, crossing 'in breezy light scud of shower and sunshine'.[210]

They travelled by Laon and Rheims to Troyes where they arrived on 16 or 17 August. Ruskin wrote enthusiastically in his diary of the delicate geranium and vine carving on the cathedral's north porch and Collingwood[211] noted that Ruskin was sketching hard at St Urbain and the cathedral.

Before they left Troyes on the 18th, Collingwood made the present sketch, which he must have given to Ruskin. A number of years later Ruskin gave it to C.E. Norton, inscribing it then (and mis-dating it) 'J.R. in contemplation of a mediaeval town, (Troyes) Drawn by G. Collingwood. 18th Aug. 1884'.

They were at Avallon on 19 August and stayed there until the 30th. On 24 August Ruskin dated the preface to the new edition of *Sesame and Lilies* from there. The town was new to Ruskin and because of its name, which he always spelled 'Avalon', he associated it with King Arthur – so it *must* be interesting. Ruskin had arranged to meet Frank Randal, who was working on a group of drawings for St George's Guild, at Avallon. He had also arranged to meet another artist-architect friend here, Charles Maundrell.

Two letters to Joan Severn chronicle some of the activities in Avallon.[212] Writing of the porches of the Romanesque church, he told her,

> Sunday 20 August 1882 ... neither Collie nor I can find words of wonder enough at them – 12th century of grandest style. The week I stay here is to be spent on them – with the help of Randal & Maundrell – who are both here by my direction. Maundrell is a young architect whom I met at Amiens ...
>
> Tuesday 22 August ... my beard's come out of curl – I cut the end of it off because it tickled me – and the remainder is a great source of worry & anxiety ...

The sketch No. 192 shows Ruskin with his untidily trimmed beard, hand in hand with Collingwood (left) and Frank Randal. It must have been made on 19 or 20 August, It is captioned 'Modern Artists' with an added note, 'N.B. The third artist will arrive in a few minutes by the train in the background'. The third artist must have been Charles Maundrell.

Confusingly the sketch occurs at the head of a letter from Frank Randal's brother Charles to his sister Fanny, both of whom were in England. The

209 Evans & Whitehouse (ed.), *Diaries of John Ruskin* (Oxford: Clarendon Press, 1956-59), vol. III, p. 1014.

210 Evans & Whitehouse, *Diaries of John Ruskin*, vol. III, p. 1014.

211 Collingwood has written a detailed account of the whole tour in ch. iv., 'Ruskin's Old Road' in his *Ruskin Relics*, pp. 47-62.

212 JR – Joan Severn, RF L 44.

AVOLLON
Charles Randal Del et Invt
Sept 7. 1882
"MODERN ARTISTS"
N.B. the third artist will arrive in a few minutes by the train in the background.

192

sketch is inscribed and dated 'Charles Randal Del et Invt. Sept 7. 1882' and the letter, which includes no reference whatsoever to the sketch, was written on the following day.

One must assume that Frank had written to his brother recounting the activities in Avallon – including the beard-trimming and the arrival of Maundrell – and Charles had then drawn the sketch incorporating all the facts. It is interesting to note that Ruskin is wearing a top hat in both this sketch and in Collingwood's, whereas I would have expected him to wear a 'wideawake' when on tour. The figure on the right is unmistakably Frank Randal; perhaps Charles Randal did not know Collingwood and thus almost totally covered his face with his large hat!

193 John Ruskin lecturing at Oxford, aet 64, by Dugald Sutherland McColl (1859–1948), 9 March 1883

194 John Ruskin lecturing, copy of No. 193 by Alan Sorrell

Ruskin returned refreshed from the continent in December and he considered his health sufficiently improved to allow him once more to take up the Slade Professorship. William Richmond having obligingly resigned, Ruskin was re-appointed at the beginning of January 1883. Richmond must have seen Ruskin about now, and wrote to his father, George Richmond:[213]

> ... the fact is that his face *is simply beautiful!* There is the same calm brow, but that puckering of cynical lines about the nose has gone. The whole face answers now in perfect concord, and a concord of wonderful beauty – strange, very sad, introspective, but saintlike in idealism for search of some thing outside the ordinary ken of humanity ... There is a sense of strife, inward and outward, revealed, and a dreamland yet unexplored, not burning, but smouldering with the strong sense of a fine fire existing. The presence of a life of work, with all the emblems of immortality, are lighted by the lamp of true and humanitarian impulse. There is the reflex of a spiritual world, fanciful, Utopian, cosmotic (if the realists like so to call the idealists) upon a face that once was repulsive to me and now is angelic. How I would like to paint him!

193

Ruskin delivered the first lecture of his new term of office on 9 March. His subject was 'Realistic Schools of Painting' and dealt with the work of Rossetti and Holman Hunt. The popularity of Ruskin's earlier Oxford lectures had now been forgotten and the *St James's Budget* reported on 16 March 1883[214]

> 'Mr Ruskin's first lecture at Oxford attracted so large an audience, that half an hour before the time of its delivery, a greater number of persons were collected about the doors than the lecture room could hold. Immediately after the doors were opened, the room was so densely packed that some undergraduates found it convenient to climb into the windows and on to the cupboards...'

Thus was set the scene for the first lecture, attended by the artist of the present portrait, who takes up the story himself.[215]

> I was present as an undergraduate at Ruskin's lectures in 1883–4 ... The written passages were fragmentary and eked out by impromptus, while the lecturer paced the platform. But four of the *Pleasures of England* series were published by Ruskin, and two more delivered; for the remaining two quieter subjects were substituted. The facts are fully and exactly given in volume 33[216] ... along with the lectures and supplementary reports by E.T. Cook, who was present throughout ...
>
> It may amuse some of you readers to see a sketch I made of the lecturer from the awkward perch of a window-sill at the crowded first lecture on March 9, 1883. It is a poor affair save in one respect, likeness.

Writing in *John o'London's Weekly*[217] McColl described Ruskin as a lecturer in the 1883–84 period.

213 Stirling, *The Richmond Papers* (London: Heinemann, 1926), p. 293.
214 Reprinted in *Igdrasil* III, p. 267.
215 Letter to the Editor of *The Times*, 5 March 1932.
216 *Works* XXXIII, pp. lxvii-lxix.
217 *John o'London's Weekly*, 9 April 1932.

> … he stood before his great audience to deliver those early lectures, clad in long blue frock coat, with thick blue silk neck-tie. As his voice thrilled and he became excited, first one of the long tails of his coat was tucked up under his arm and then the other, until they stood out like the wings of an Assyrian cherub …

These lectures were lively affairs. One authority who was in attendance has recorded that on occasions Ruskin 'suddenly began to dance and recite, with the strangest flappings of his M.A. gown, and the oddest look on his excited face'.[218] To Quiller-Couch, on the other hand, 'Ruskin [was] to me a bent figure in gown and velvet cap, moving Oxford with eyes that under bushy brows, seemed to look inward on torture, rarely outward, but then always with unsuppressible love'.[219]

To Ruskin, this first lecture seemed to be successful. He wrote on the same day to tell Joan

> I think the lecture went off nicely. The vice Chancellor (Jowett) made a very pretty speech of welcome afterwards. The undergraduates cheered no end – and Baxter said the people going away who couldn't get in were like a church coming out. I was obliged to promise to give the lecture again tomorrow…[220]

194

No. 194 is a copy of McColl's drawing made by Alan Sorrell, possibly at the time in 1953 when he was working on the mural for the Rhodes Memorial Museum.

195 John Ruskin, medallion by Clement Emptmeyer, 1883

This untraced medallion, exhibited at the Academy in 1883 is described by Spielmann[221] as unauthentic and unofficial, from which we may assume that it was based on an earlier portrait or photograph.

It was in 1883 that Norton next saw Ruskin. He paid a brief visit to Brantwood in the late summer, and writing in the *Atlantic Monthly*[222] he described the change he found in Ruskin since he had last seen him ten years earlier.

> I had left him in 1873 a man in vigorous middle life, young for his years, erect in figure, alert in action, full of vitality, with smooth face and untired eyes; I found him (in 1883) an old man, with looks even older than his years, with bent form, with the beard of a patriach, with habitual expression of weariness, with the general air and gait of age. But there were all the old affection and tenderness; the worn look readily gave way to the old animation, the delightful smile quickly kindled into full warmth and at moments the unconquerable youthfulness of temperament reasserted itself with entire control of manner and expression. He had become more positive, more absolute in manner, more irritable, but the essential sweetness prevailed, and there were hours when the old gaiety of mood took possession of him with its irresistable charm.

218 G.W. Kitchin, *Ruskin in Oxford and other studies* (London: John Murray, 1903), p. 41.
219 A. Quiller-Couch, *The Victorian Age, Studies in Literature 2*, a lecture delivered at Cambridge.
220 JR – Joan Severn, 9 Mar. 1883; RF L 45.
221 Spielmann, *John Ruskin*, p. 180, where it is dated 1888. In fact the medallion was exhibited in 1883 and there is a manuscript correction to this effect by Spielmann in his own copy of the book in the Pierpont Morgan Library.
222 *Atlantic Monthly*, Sept. 1904, p. 383.

196 John Ruskin, aet 65, portrait by Kate Greenaway (1846–1901), February 1884

At the beginning of 1880 Ruskin wrote to Kate Greenaway to express his admiration for her drawings for *Under the window* which he had seen at The Fine Art Society. This was the beginning of a new friendship which filled a large part of Ruskin's later life. They were to exchange literally thousands of letters, many of hers being illustrated with her charming sketches of children. It was also her practice to send Ruskin drawings of children each year as Christmas and birthday cards. Although the friendship began in 1880, the two did not in fact meet until late December 1882. Kate stayed at Brantwood between 11 April and 7 May in the following year; this was the first of many visits.

Kate Greenaway designed a cover for one of the chapters of *Christ's Folk of the Apennine* which Ruskin was publishing in 1887, though it was never used. Ruskin *did* use some of her drawings in *Fors Clavigera* and *Dame Wiggins of Lee*, though he declined her offer to illustrate *Præterita*. She designed a dress for Ruskin's May Queen festival. The fourth lecture of Ruskin's *Art of England* series at Oxford in 1884 was devoted to the work of Mrs Allingham and Kate Greenaway.

At the beginning of 1884 she seems to have asked Ruskin to sit to her. 'I wonder how you can bear to think of drawing me – and how you mean to do it!' he wrote to her. 'Sitting always tires me a good deal, but perhaps John [her brother] will let me lie down in his room for a quarter of an hour before tea'.[233] To friends at Brantwood he wrote in the same month 'Out to Holloway – sat for my portrait to K.G.'.

Unfortunately the sittings did not continue and the portrait was never finished, as Kate Greenaway told Spielmann years later: 'I *have never* Painted any Portrait of Mr Ruskin. It never Progressed beyond a few lines – I Can't imagine How any idea that I did one has come into existence'.[234]

197 John Ruskin, aet 65, by an unidentified artist, 11 February 1884

197

Ruskin had been interested by the sky, clouds and weather all his life. As early as 1835 he had taken on tour with him a 'cyanometer', using it daily to measure and record the depth of blue of the sky. Throughout his life one finds observations in his diaries and in the 1880s he was becoming obsessed by 'plague wind' and storm clouds. He was of course observing atmospheric pollution and realised that the unnaturally dark clouds, which he saw now but which he hadn't seen in his youth, were caused by 'smoke mixed with damp'.

On 4 and 11 February 1884, dates spanning his 65th birthday, he delivered two lectures on 'The Storm-Cloud of the Nineteenth Century' at the London Institution.[225] When Ruskin's lectures were illustrated, this was usually done by an assistant presenting large diagrams usually drawn and painted on paper mounted onto canvas. However, on this occasion Arthur Severn and Collingwood had enlarged some of Ruskin's drawings, and these were projected onto a screen using lime-light.

223 JR – Kate Greenaway, 11 Feb. 1884; Spielmann & Layard' *Kate Greenaway* (London: A&C Black, 1905), p. 135.

224 Kate Greenaway – M.H. Spielmann, 27 July 1893; sold at Sotheby's, 16 December 1964, lot 571, to John Rylands Library.

225 The London Institution in Finsbury Circus is not to be confused with the Royal Institution in Albemarle Street. Ruskin had lectured at the London Institution three times before, and a further two planned lectures had to be cancelled in 1878 due to his illness. He had also delivered a number of lectures at the Royal Institution.

The present portrait was made by a member of the audience at the second Storm-Cloud lecture on 11 February, although he had mis-dated the sketch 1883. He was one of the few portraitists to capture Ruskin wearing spectacles.

The drawing is signed with a monogram made up of the letters C, J and K. It cannot be the work of Charles Keene, as it was at one time thought. Not only is the drawing not good enough, the initials are also wrong![226]

198 John Ruskin, head, and study of eyes, aet 65, by Theodore Blake Wirgman (1848–1925), February 1884

199 John Ruskin, aet 65, portrait by Theodore Blake Wirgman, February 1884

Drawn in the same month as the Kate Greenaway sittings, the Wirgman portrait is probably one of the least known of the published portraits.

The portrait was made at Wirgman's suggestion. The request was made to Ruskin through a mutual friend, Mrs Walter Severn, Arthur's sister-in-law. Replying to the request, Ruskin wrote

> I'll sit – since you have asked me, but I always refuse in general, however I'll have this portrait different from any that have been yet – only I always fall asleep in a quarter of an hour, so everything in the way of expression must be got – tell the artist – in ten minutes.[227]

In due course the sitting was arranged and took place in Ruskin's study at Herne Hill. After Ruskin had given the lease of the house, his old home, to the Severns as a wedding present, his old nursery was kept as a study for his use when he was in London,

199

226 Two artists working at the right time, with the right initials, are James Kellaway Colling and C.J. Keats.

227 Quoted in T.B. Wirgman – M.H. Spielmann, 24 April 1893, in the author's collection.

198

and this portrait is interesting in recording the room's appearance. Of the sitting, Wirgman wrote

> ... when I asked what his wish was with regard to the view I should take of his face, he without answering rushed out of the room and returned with a bedroom looking-glass, saying 'Get behind me, and you will see reflected the particular view I wish you to take'. After sitting for two hours with no pause in the conversation, which was most interesting and charming, he promised me another sitting if I should wish it.[228]

The second sitting was arranged eventually and took place at Burne-Jones's studio.

> When the drawing was finished, the professor said 'Yes, I see, you have got the hair from the eyebrow across the eye – it is quite right, but I usually pull it out when I go into society...'

The hair did not quite satisfy Ruskin and he touched it up with a few strokes of a chalk pencil, easily noticeable in the original.[229]

No. 198 comprises preliminary studies for the finished portrait.

200–207 John Ruskin, head and shoulders, aet 65, various versions of bust modelled by Conrad Dressler, June 1884

The spring of 1884 was a busy time for artists portraying Ruskin! Having sat to Kate Greenaway and Wirgman, Ruskin went to Coniston in March, returning to London at the end of April to visit Prince Leopold's widow at Esher, and to attend some exhibitions. On 7 May he returned to Brantwood once more to continue the literary work which he had on hand, before the arrival of a succession of visitors at the end of the month. The first visitors were Ernest Chesneau and his son, followed immediately at the end of May by Conrad Dressler, who apparently stayed for a week. On 6 June Ruskin wrote in his diary, 'Very sorry to part with Dressler'.

In a long letter to Spielmann,[230] Dressler described how he first met Ruskin, and how he went to Brantwood to sculpt the bust.

> It was in the summer of 1883 that I first made the acquaintance of Professor Ruskin. He came to Chelsea to see the memorial of Mr Osborne Gordon which I was then modelling for Christ Church, Oxford.
>
> He remained looking at things and chatting for an hour or two, and as he left, he invited me to his country house. I was only able to go in the following spring.
>
> I took materials with me and commenced his bust in May 1884. The Severns had not yet arrived at Brantwood, but there were other visitors, Monsieur Ernest Chesneau, the French critic and his son.
>
> It would be impossible to describe the charm of Mr Ruskin's hospitality. I soon felt quite at home under his roof. His friendliness went so far as to drop all convention. He asked to call me by my christian name and treated me more like a son than even a friend. As the Frenchmen had their breakfast taken up to them in their bedrooms he invited me to come and have mine with him in his library and this I continued to do until the end of my visit. What delightful conver-

228 T.B. Wirgman – M.H. Spielmann, 24 April 1893.
229 T.B. Wirgman – M.H. Spielmann, 27 April 1893.
230 C. Dressler – M.H. Spielmann, 18 June 1890; Pierpont Morgan Library, PML 54632.

201

I cannot tell how many sittings we had. They took place in the coach house, a very convenient place for my purpose, and I had as many as I wanted. Some were long and some were short as the humour served. I had with the help of the old butler made a little platform for the Professor to sit upon. From this position he could watch me at my work for a couple of hours sometimes, talking most of the time, telling me of the great works which he knew in Italy and of the spirit which animated them, often deploring the change in the spirit of modern times. He would also criticise my work and tell me to seek for more harmony and suavity; the treatment of the hair appeared to him very rough at first. After four or five sittings he was however so pleased with the result of my labours that he said he was sure I would only spoil it now. When I told him however that if I did spoil it I should bring it right again in the end he bade me go on in my own way.

Meanwhile the two visitors had left. Mr Ruskin gave orders for my traps to be moved into the turret room which adjoins his own bedroom, a mark of favour which touched me greatly. He brought some magnificent woodcuts of Dürer and Holbein which I had admired downstairs and with his own hands hung them about my room.

Then the Severns arrived and I [illegible] the pleasant family life at Brantwood. In the day time

202

sations we had there. What treasures he showed me. I had here the first opportunities of studying his noble face, so often lit up by enthusiasm as youthful as any I could have. His interest in my plans and aspirations were as deep as if my concern had been his own.

Upon some points I found him difficult; to follow his scorn of many qualities in art which I had been taught to admire and value as main stays and guiding lines was sometimes distressing to me. I speak of [illegible] and other scientific aids. He looked on these as inventions of the devil. He told me that he used to think a very great artist might use them without detriment to his art, but that Michaelangelo had convinced him that the greatest and noblest natures must succumb to the vanities which these sciences bred in them.

After all these years I am better able to see his meaning; at that time I begged his leave to let me hold on to methods, which at all events led to a safe result while there was so much danger in seeking only abstract qualities which had no firm footing upon scientific facts. He laughed and told me to go on my own way.

we went boating, picnicing on the island, seeing native sports &c. In the evening, when the lamps were lit we sat and looked at collections of gems, or listened to music, or the Professor read aloud. For my benefit he read portions of Pope's *Illiad*, the beauties of which he pointed out to us.

My deepest recollection of Professor Ruskin is as he stood, one evening, after dinner (the conversation I remember had been about his life and his work and had been more animated and touching than usual) at the open window overlooking the lake. The sun had gone down and he wistfully looked towards the Old Man behind which the sky was still aglow – as it so long remains in that northen latitude. One could see that he was mentally reviewing his life's work. His head was held up although his body was slightly stooping. His right hand was behind his back. The left was holding onto the open casement for support. In his gaze there was a mystery which I had never seen so strongly marked before. I was even then deeply impressed and I determined to endeavour to reproduce what I had seen. I am only too conscious that I have fallen short of my ideal.

Shortly afterwards I left the Professor loaded with fresh marks of kindness in the shape of books and coins which he gave me. But the most valuable present I brought away with me was one that I was not aware of at the time and which I have realised since and am still realising. It is that of his sweet influence towards what is good, brave, tender and lovely in this world.

204

The original bust, No. 200, was probably modelled in clay or plaster, and it is at present unlocated. At least three plaster casts were made from it. Dressler gave one of them to Ruskin. This remained in the Severn collection in their London home until 1931 when it was bought at Sotheby's by H.H. Silbert. He intended giving it to Ruskin College, Oxford, but finally in 1932 decided to present it to the library of Hendon, the London borough where he had lived for the previous fourteen years. This (No. 201) has subsequently been lost by the library.

Another of the plaster casts was acquired by Whitelands College (No. 202), an establishment in which Ruskin had taken an interest since he was instrumental in establishing a May Day Festival there in 1881.

A third was presented by Thomas Thornton to the Ruskin Memorial Hall at Bournville, later the Bournville School of Arts and Crafts, and now the Department of Foundation and Community Studies, Birmingham Institute of Art and Design, a part of the University of Central England.

The scheme for the Ruskin Memorial at Bournville was almost certainly first suggested by J. Howard Whitehouse. As a young man Whitehouse was employed for a number of years by Cadbury Bros at Bournville and he had been the originator of a number of social schemes, including the Bournville Youths Club and the Youth Club Magazine, which grew into the Bournville Works Magazine. He was also a founder of the successful Ruskin Society of Birmingham.

The Ruskin Memorial, 'to take the form of a library, art gallery and museum which would place at the disposal of those living in the country some of those educational influences which must now be sought for in the most part in the large town', was first considered by the Council of the Ruskin Society in March 1902. The Bournville Village Trust donated the land and members of the Cadbury family were among the subscribers. The foundation stone was laid in October 1902.

In addition to the three plaster casts, two terracotta casts were also made. One of these, No. 204,

205

207

was exhibited in 1888 at the New Gallery. In 1902 it was presented to the National Gallery where it stood in the Turner Room. The donor was again Thomas Thornton, a cloth manufacturer at one time resident at Toynbee Hall. He had subscribed to the Guild of St George, and was a collector. After his death his widow presented some Ruskin letters and books to the British Museum. The bust was transferred to the Tate Gallery in 1912.

The second terracotta version is an interesting variant. This, No. 205, is a head only, set onto a square terracotta plinth. It was sold in London in 1982, but is presently untraced.

There is a second variant to the original 1884 bust. Mr John Hutchinson has a slightly smaller bust (No. 206) in which the overall conformation of the shoulders is a little different. This is modelled in terracotta-coloured plaster and is set onto a round plinth. It is dated 1888. It is said to have been given by Ruskin, or the Severns, to the Rathbone family of Liverpool, with whom they were friendly.

It was perhaps from this bust (No. 206) that in about 1900 Dressler cast a number of bronzes (No. 207). Dressler gave one of the casts to M.H. Spielmann. Another was acquired by Arthur Jones of Bath who gave it to the National Portrait Gallery in 1924.

Ruskin was, as might be expected, not entirely satisfied with Dressler's bust. When in 1888 Spielmann was printing an article in his *Magazine of Art* by Edward Bradbury on 'A visit to Ruskin's Museum', he asked Ruskin's permission to illustrate the article with a reproduction of this bust. 'Oh *please*, no bust! Dressler's better than Boehm's – but looks more frantic than I've ever been. My likeness has nothing to do with the Museum'.[231]

231 JR – M.H. Spielmann, 8 May 1888; *Works* XXXVII, p. 604.

208 John Ruskin, portrait head by W.G. Collingwood, c. August 1884

Cook and Wedderburn date the present portrait as 'circa 1879' and it certainly shows Ruskin's appearance at that time, before he grew his beard. But as it was made as a design for the seal of the Liverpool Ruskin Society, it cannot in fact have been drawn until at least 1883 when the society was founded. The society had as its objects 'the circulation and study of the writings of John Ruskin and the furtherance of social work on the lines of his teaching'. The Liverpool society was just one of several similar societies founded about now.

208

The portrait was engraved by Hugh Allen, a son of Ruskin's publisher. A slip attached to a proof (in the author's collection and formerly in the Allen collection) describes it as an 'India proof from portrait of Ruskin, engraved on steel by Hugh Allen about 1885 which displeased Ruskin'. Ruskin was probably displeased by the portrait because of the way that Collingwood had drawn the mouth, mis-shapen from the dog-bite of Ruskin's youth.

Two letters in the Bodleian Library, dated by Wedderburn as 'August 1884' underline this displeasure. To George Allen, Ruskin wrote[232]

> I was never more painfully surprised than by your having executed that portrait of me for the Ruskin Society without submitting it to me. Let the plate be immediately destroyed, and all recoverable impressions of it, and never again let me hear of either book or plate issuing from Sunnyside[233] without my leave.

This was followed by another letter to Allen from Sara Anderson.

> Mr Ruskin doesn't write himself – he is too tired – but he bids me say that of all things on this earth his portrait is the last on which you should have let your son try his young hand.[234]

The engraving is reproduced here in the size of the original.

209 Fancy portrait by T.G. captioned 'The Pleasures of England', December 1884

Ruskin's Oxford lectures in the autumn of 1884 were entitled 'The Pleasures of England'. The present fancy portrait which appeared in *Fun* in December of that year is based on an earlier photograph (No. 86) and has, as part of its caption, the sentence 'One of the greatest of these pleasures is that of listening to Mr Ruskin'. However, T.G.'s view was not universally held. *The World* of 19 November 1884 carried an article called 'Ruskinomania, an Academic Farce', which gave a rather different opinion.

> Every Saturday and Monday there is enacted in the Theatre of the Museum at Oxford a farce, out of which the humorous elements have long since departed. It is on those days that the Slade Professor of Fine Arts in the University delivers the lectures which he has so fancifully christened 'The Pleasures of England'. There can be no question that the entertainment is still popular, though this may perhaps be explained by the paucity of dramatic exhibition in Oxford. But the central figure has passed out of the region of solemn tragedy; he has even left the melodramatic sphere behind him, and has descended to the level of those more or less dreary afterpieces by which the spirits of the audience are supposed to be cheered before they leave the precincts of the theatre. There are many tragic figures still left in Oxford, men on whose grey hairs seems to rest the crown of a noble and majestic past; there are some even among the professors who are not devoid of a certain power in comedy; but Mr Ruskin shares with the Dean of Chichester the enviable notoriety of being one of the few legitimate pantaloons left to the academic stage …

232 Bodleian MS Eng. letts. c. 47, fol. 133.
233 Allen's home at Orpington, whence were published Ruskin's books.
234 Bodleian MS Eng letters. c.47, fol.139. Hugh Allen was 23 at the time.

"THE PLEASURES OF ENGLAND."

Notes at the Ruskin Lectures.—One of the greatest of these pleasures is that of listening to Mr. Ruskin, and so say all of us.

209

Professor Ruskin, lecturing to a motley crowd of aesthetic youths, sentimental young ladies, *soi-disant* lovers of art, and veritable lovers of amusement, may be said fairly to have eclipsed a past history, which has not been undistinguished by similar farcical feats. [A description of the lecture follows] ... Then, with hands thrust into the pockets of his coat-tails, Professor Ruskin worked himself for his grand *coup de theatre*. [He produced the pictures of the Protestant pig and the Salvation Army preacher.] ... But the lecturer should have ended with this admirable theatrical surprise, for the audience were in no mood to listen to a reading out of Scott. The curtain should have descended on the pig and the concertina, the Slade Professor of Fine Art standing in comic pose between the two highest flights of his genius ... It is time that the truth should be told about these weekly lectures of Professor Ruskin ... His should be a sacred figure in the annals of nineteenth-century literature; some kindly and benevolent veto should be placed on these ignoble antics ... For very shame let his admirers interpose. Professor Ruskin's lectures may have become a nuisance in the University, a nuisance to the more serious teachers in the Museum, and a nuisance to all those who care for the dignified dullness of the professoriate.[235]

235 On Ruskin's own copy of the cutting, in the Whitehouse Collection, he has heavily scored the margins of the final passage.

210–12 Photographs by Barraud, three-quarter length, leaning against a tree, May–June 1885

213 Photograph by Barraud, head and shoulders looking left

214 Anonymous watercolour copy of No. 213 (Plate 29)

215 Photograph by Barraud, head and shoulders, head turned slightly left

216–17 Photographs by Barraud, seated at a table

218 Engravings by W. Burton, based on No. 217

219–20 Photographs by Barraud, seated at a table

210

211

Pleased with the outcome of the photographic session with Barraud at Herne Hill in 1882, Ruskin promised that he would pose again in his studio. He was in London or its environs from 7 May until 13 June in 1885 and the present group of photographs – the outcome of the promise – must have been made now. When they were reproduced in *The Bookman* (March 1900) they were variously dated 1885, 1886 and 1888; however they all appear to date from the one sitting of 1885.

They fall naturally into three groups – three exposures of Ruskin in frivolous mood standing against a sylvan background, two head and shoulders studies, one of which No. 213 was subsequently copied as a watercolour portrait now in the Whitehouse Collection and four exposures seated at a table. No. 217 was subsequently engraved by W. Burton to illustrate Collingwood's *John Ruskin, a biographical outline*. When No. 219 was reproduced in *The Bookman* art work to the chair and table legs changed the appearance of these items, but this photograph is clearly from the same group.

212

213

214

215

216

217

Writing to Susan Beever, Ruskin told her

> ... They've been doing photographs of me again, and I'm an orang-outang as usual, and am in dispair. I thought with my beard I was beginning to be just the least bit nice to look at. I would give half my books for a new profile.[236]

218

236 *Works* XXXVII, p. 536.

219

220

221 Photograph, full length, leaning against a wall at Brantwood, by T.A. & J. Green of Grasmere, 1885 aet 66

After he returned to Brantwood in June 1885 Ruskin again was photographed in a sylvan setting. But on this occasion his beard had been trimmed so that it was nicer to look at, and the setting was natural, not artificial. Ruskin in fact posed against the wall of the north drive at Brantwood. The photographers were the Green Brothers of Grasmere. J.W. Graham who visited Ruskin at Brantwood in July 1884 has described his appearance at this time.

> We are probably familiar from portraits with the refined delicacy of his features, accompanied with a certain shagginess of eyebrow and beard, but the sweetness of his blue eyes and the peculiarly kindly smile were a glad surprise. ... His utterance was sufficiently slow to be perfectly accurate, distinct, and impressive. His lips indeed seemed to make an effort to give every word full force. He is rather short than tall, and has now a very pronounced stoop. He seems to wear a good deal of clothing, and some of the ladies noticed that he had a large and conspicuous Oxford blue tie, and an ornamental waistcoat...[237]

The Greens' negatives were eventually taken over by Abrahams, another well-known Lakeland photographer, and reproductions of this image are sometimes found acknowledged to them.

237 J.W. Graham, 'John Ruskin at Home', *Proceedings of Warrington Literary and Philosophical Society* (1897).

221

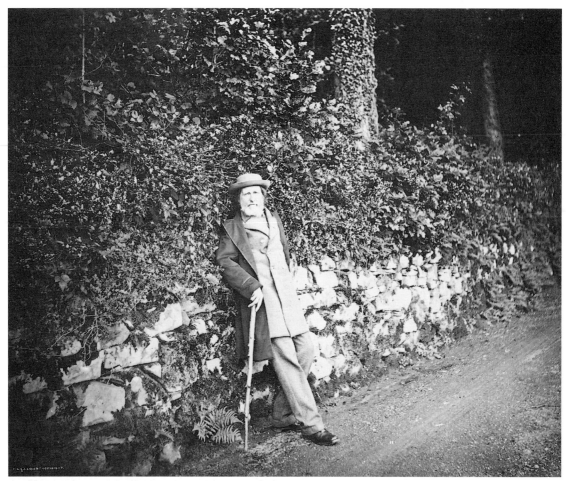

222 Caricature, Ruskin with a number of shrimps, 1886

This caricature, from an unidentified source, was published in response to Ruskin's letter to the *Pall Mall Gazette*[238]

> My shelves are loaded with books on natural history, but I could find nothing about shrimps except that they swim in water, or live upon the sand in shoals, and are taken in multitudes for the Table.

Mr. Ruskin has been complaining that he can find no books about the shrimp, as he was "under the impression of having seen jumping shrimps on a sandy shore express great satisfaction in their life." Mr. Ruskin's ignorance of this marine delicacy is shocking. As the shrimps he saw on the shore have turned out to be sandhoppers, we are sadly afraid that his only acquaintance with shrimps is confined to their condition at "9d. per head."

222

238 Of 15 February 1886, reprinted in *Works* XXXIV, pp. 587-88.

223 Caricature, Ruskin as the 'Gauche-hen', by ?L.T., June 1887

In this caricature from *Punch* of June 1887 Ruskin is shown as the 'Gauche-hen'. The coins shown are the 1887 Jubilee issue. They were designed by J.E. Boehm, and due to their extreme unpopularity, the issue only lasted for five years. Only the 4s., 2s. 6d, and 2s. coins had this obverse. I can find no reference to Ruskin's connection with this issue of coinage.

The caption to the caricature reads:

> The New 'Hatch'
> Mr P. 'Ah! They're an awfully ugly lot! I *did* think the old gauche-hen – (ahem!) – would ha' done better than that!'

223

224 Portrait, aet 68, in a group at the Royal Academy on 30 December 1887, by Henry Jamyn Brookes

In 1887 Ruskin's active life was drawing to a close. He was writing against time to finish *Præterita*, his last important book. Mrs La Touche and Margaret Ferrier Young visited him at Brantwood in the summer and Miss Young noticed 'his beetling brows, and rather long greyish hair, with his sky-blue stock, made him look quite different from other people'.[239] Later in the summer he was taken seriously ill. On his recovery he went to convalesce for the rest of the year and early part of 1888 at Folkestone and Sandgate, making occasional visits to London.

On one of these visits he was seen by E.T. Cook.[240]

> Spielmann came to tell me yesterday afternoon that Ruskin was staying at Morley's Hotel, having come up from Folkestone to see the doctors for rupture. So this morning I went ... He was dressed in his usual style – blue frock coat over brown homespun, double-breasted waistcoat, with the untidy cuffs (of *Hortus*), and slippers ...

224 (detail)

239 Margaret Ferrier Young, 'Some personal recollections of John Ruskin', article in unidentified magazine.

240 J.S. Mill, *Life of Sir Edward Cook* (London: Constable, 1921), quoting Cook's diary of 28 Oct. 1887. In a letter of 1882 included in *Hortus Inclusus*, Ruskin had told Susan Beever how his starched cuffs kept getting the better of him. *Hortus* was published on 29 Sept. 1887 so Cook could only just have finished reading it; thus the cuffs were fresh in his mind.

> He... looks physically weaker than when I saw him last, and far more melancholy. Very bright in conversation, but in momentary pauses a weary look is in his eyes'.

Another visit to London was made to attend the private view of the Royal Academy's 'Old Masters' exhibition, probably on Friday 30 December 1887. (The exhibition was opened to the public on Monday 2 January). The scene at the private view was sketched by H. Jamyn Brookes, who painted this large picture with its fifty eight portraits, in 1889. The group includes many artists and patrons of the arts – Baron Ferdinand de Rothschild, Millais, George Richmond, W.P. Frith, Lawrence Alma-Tadema, Edward Poynter, Sir Frederic Leighton, Edgar Boehm, G.F. Watts.

Ruskin, second from the right in the detail and partly obscured by John, Fifth Earl Spencer (who four years later sold his great Althorp Library to form the nucleus of the John Rylands Library) is in conversation with his old friend Holman Hunt. Standing behind and between Ruskin and Hunt are Mrs Street and Henry Tankworth Wells.

On leaving the Academy Ruskin met Watts and they discussed the path of the isolated dreamer which had been followed by Burne-Jones and by Watts himself, a path of which Ruskin disapproved. 'Paint that as it is', he shouted to Watts, pointing to a heap of refuse at the foot of a lamp-post, 'that is the truth'.

Brooks's painting was deposited on loan with the National Portrait Gallery in 1909 and was presented to the Gallery ten years later, by the artist.

225 Miniature, aet 69, by Ethel Webling, 1888

225

Perhaps on one of his visits from Sandgate, Ruskin visited the Weblings. The present miniature by Ethel Webling seems to date from about now. Ethel specialised in portrait miniatures and her portrait of Ruskin was exhibited at the Royal Academy in 1888. It was given to her nephew, Josephine's son, who was the next owner and namesake of the subject.

226 Caricature, John Ruskin sees a cyclist, by 'Kuklos', c.1888

227 Caricature, 'Mr Ruskin' in ' 'The New Gallery' of Portraiture', by F.C.G., 21 April 1888

Tit-Bits of 31 March 1888[241], in its column 'Tit-Bits of General Information', reprinted the following unascribed quotation:

> Ruskin on 'Cycling – 'I not only object, but am quite prepared to spend all my best 'bad language' in reprobation of the bi-, tri-, and 4- 5- 6 or 7 cycles, and every other contrivance and invention for superseding human feet on God's ground. To walk, to run, to leap, and to dance are the virtues of the human body, and neither to stride on stilts, wriggle on wheels, or dangle on ropes, and nothing in the training of the human mind with the body will ever supersede the appointed God's way of slow walking and hard working'.

The present pair of caricatures by 'Kuklos' from an unidentified source clearly relate to the same quotation.

It is interesting to remember that two people close to Ruskin – Henry Swan and George Allen, were both keen cyclists!

Impressed by the long-faced, head in hand, caricature of Robert Louis Stevenson which appeared in the April 1888 issue of *Century*, F.C.G. drew caricatures in a similar vein of Henry Irving,

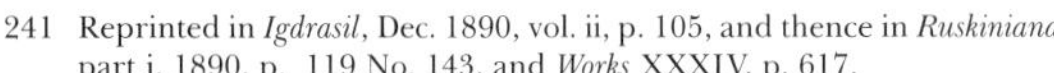

226

227

241 Reprinted in *Igdrasil*, Dec. 1890, vol. ii, p. 105, and thence in *Ruskiniana* part i, 1890, p. 119 No. 143, and *Works* XXXIV, p. 617.

Lord Tennyson, W.H. Smith and Ruskin, which duly appeared in the 21 April 1888 issue of the *Pall Mall Gazette*.

Mrs Allan Harker described Ruskin's appearance in 1888 in an article in *The Outlook*.[242]

> He looked an old man even then, in '88, as he stood in his favourite place on the hearth-rug in the Brantwood drawing-room. His face, fair-complexioned and refined, framed by long straight brown hair and beard, both hair and beard browner than grey, though there was much of grey in both. His eyes were the youngest eyes I have ever seen in adult face, blue and clear like a child's, with the child's large direct gaze. A slender stooping figure, but full of forcible quick gesture ...

Interestingly, at the time of the publication of F.C.G.'s caricature, Ruskin had come up to town from Kent for a few days. On Thursday 19 April he met Kathleen Olander, by arrangement, at the National Gallery. On the day the caricature was published – Saturday 21 April – Kathleen Olander remebered[243] that he attended the Private View of the Old Watercolour Society's Annual Exhibition at the Grosvenor Gallery. Sixty five years later she still had a newspaper cutting reporting the Private View.

> ... The next most interesting object, and perhaps the most welcome, was the figure of Mr Ruskin, who, in his familiar fawn-coloured wide-awake[244] and bright blue cravat, wandered with stately step from room to room, the victim of universal recognition.

228 Portrait by Edward Robert Hughes (1851–1914), 24 April 1888, aet 69

Ruskin's active life had little over a year to run when E.R. Hughes sketched him on one of his last visits to the South Kensington Museum in April 1888. Writing to Joan Severn on the same day Ruskin told her

> I am really out of heart today after looking at the pulpit of Pisa and all the things I used to love so at Kensington – and finding them all dead to me.[245]

E.R. Hughes studied under his uncle, Arthur Hughes, and Holman Hunt. He was a friend of Juliet Morse and had, with her, made a copy of Ruskin's portrait of Rose La Touche. In 1902 he gave the present portrait to her, telling her 'I send you the little sketch of J.R. done in '88 in the S.K. Museum. It seemed to me very like him when I did it'.[246]

This is probably the last portrait of the active Ruskin. Age and over-work and worry were taking their toll, although 1888 was quite an active year for him. June, July and August were spent in northern France with Arthur Severn, Sydney Cockerell and Detmar Blow. In Abbeville, much to his amusement, Ruskin was arrested for sketching the fortifications. He travelled on to Switzerland. In Sallenches he was seen by H.W. Nevinson, who noted in his diary[247] that

> He looked much older than in Oxford ten years ago; has grown a beard, tawny where it is not grey, longish but worn into an irregular peak by the inclination of the head to the right, the left shoulder being now noticeably higher than the other, giving the whole figure a stooping, and even sloughing appearance. The eyes are set deep under shaggy light brown eyebrows, and are greyish – keen, looking quietly into your face, without hesitation or self-consciousness. They are surrounded by multitudes of tiny wrinkles; otherwise, there is not, at first sight, much humour in the face. The nose is hooked, though not quite so much as in the photographs, which otherwise are exactly like him. His hands, as one might suppose, are long, thin, delicate, with loose, soft skin in wrinkles of age – just a thought too soft, perhaps. He wore a longish black coat, large, loose grey waistcoat, and grey trousers ...

In Venice by 10 October, Ruskin and his friends stayed at the Albergo Europa. Ruskin struck visitors as very frail and somewhat vague. While in the city he called on the archaeologist and politician, Sir Austen Layard, who described the visit in a letter to Sir William Gregory[248]

242 *The Outlook*, 11 Feb. 1899.
243 R. Unwin (ed.), *The Gulf of Years* (London: George Allen & Unwin, 1953), pp. 40-41.
244 Ruskin was becoming erratic in his dress habits – a wide-awake in London, but a top hat in Troyes and Avallon!
245 JR – Joan Severn, RF L 56.
246 E.R. Hughes – Juliet Morse, 21 Dec. 1902; RF L 65.
247 Diary of H.W. Nevinson, 12 Sept 1888, quoted by him in 'Some Memories of Ruskin', p. 154
248 Sir Austen Layard – Sir William Gregory, 13 October 1888. British Library, Add.MSS.3890. I am indebted to Dr Jaynie Anderson for drawing my attention to this letter.

Ruskin is here and in a very gentle humour but in very low spirits. He speaks in his usual exaggerated way of the National Gallery and declares that it is beyond all comparison the finest and most important collection in Europe. He came to see my pictures two days ago and expressed himself as much delighted with them. The Cima he pronounced the finest he had ever seen, and the Carpaccio, Luini and Gentile Bellini's entirely lovely. He is very much aged and bent and has been half devoured by mosquitoes – the condition of his face giving you the impression that he is suffering from an attack of the measles. He is a strange creature! Instead, as I expected, of denouncing Venice and all its works, he says that the penny steamers are in no way objectionable, that the restorations of St Mark's have been lovingly and carefully done, that the new capitals of the columns supporting the ducal Palace are so admirably executed that you could not tell them from the old etc. etc. On the other hand he declares that no one will ever see the Lake of Geneva again on account of the smoky haze generated by the steamers which obscures the sky and turns the water from blue to brown, and that the only country worth living in is France, that the Frenchmen are the best people in the world, and that he will settle at Beauvais to study French Gothic architecture which surpasses all other. Dolly Tennant is here with him, and conducts him about, and he is accompanied by two young men whom he calls pupils to be instructed in the Ruskinian mysteries'.

228

229 Portrait in stained glass, c.1889

In the 1880s Ruskin had taken an interest in Whitelands Training College in Chelsea. He had established there a May Queens Festival, and had become friendly with Miss Martin, one of the members of staff. When she became principal of the Cork High School for Girls, Ruskin took an equal interest in that establishment, beginning there a Rose Queens Festival (in honour of Rose La Touche).

A portrait, almost certainly based on photographs, was commissioned by Robert Day, F.S.A., a member of the College Council. This was executed in painted glass from the 'recently established' glass works in Youghal and was apparently one of the earliest examples of painted glass made there. A report of the 1889 May Day celebrations[249] noted 'It may be of interest to notice here that a picture of The Master hangs in the window of the first hall'. Although I have corresponded with several people who later remember the portrait hanging in the staircase window, it has defied all attempts to trace it.

249 W. Marwick (ed.), *Ruskin Reading Club Journal* (Orpington: George Allen *et al*, 1889), June 1889 edition, p. 171.

230 Imaginative portrait of Ruskin standing in the Brantwood study, 1890

230

In the summer of 1889 Ruskin's active life ceased as ill-health confined him for most of his remaining eleven years to Brantwood. The present imaginative portrait is probably based on one of the 1885 Barraud photographs, and Alexander Macdonald's painting of the study where Ruskin was to spend much of his remaining years.

231 Caricature in 'Ariel's Album', 1891

Like No. 230 this caricature, drawn to illustrate a biographical sketch in 'Ariel's Album', was based on an earlier photograph.

231

232 Photographed in 'Jumping Jenny' with Joan Severn, Arthur Severn standing in his boat beyond, probably by Lund of Coniston, Summer 1891

233 Photographed in 'Jumping Jenny' with Joan Severn, Arthur Severn sitting in his boat beyond, probably by Lund of Coniston, Summer 1891

234 Photographed in 'Jumping Jenny' with Arthur Severn in his boat centre, probably by Lund of Coniston, Summer 1891

232

233

During the last seven years of Ruskin's life there are at least thirty-nine photographs of him, either taken singly or in groups. In the present series of photographs, Ruskin is seen holding the oars of his own rowing boat, the 'Jumping Jenny'. He is accompanied in his boat by Joan Severn, while Arthur Severn is in attendance in *his* boat. Severn's yacht, 'Lily of Brantwood', is moored beyond.

The 'Jumping Jenny' was Ruskin's personal boat, designed to his specifications by Laurence Hilliard and built in the boat-house across the lake at Coniston Hall in 1879. She is still preserved at Brantwood. She was named after Nanty Ewart's brig in Ruskin's favourite *Redgauntlet*.

At one time I though that this series of photographs was taken by John McClelland (for details of whom see No. 237 ff.). But there is evidence that this is probably not the case. Inside the lid of McClelland's wooden negative box now belonging to the National Portrait Gallery is pasted a list of the fifty negatives once contained in the box. No. 8 on the list is 'Professor Ruskin & Mrs Severn in Boat on the Lake Aug '93 16369'. The entry occupies the entire line and written at the right hand end of the next line below the negative number 16369 is 'Percy Lund & Co'. This has every appearance of being a continuation of the line above, because it does not immediately follow the listing for negative No. 9 – which has a shorter entry – but comes at the extreme end of the line. This leads me to think that the photographs of Ruskin in the 'Jumping Jenny' were originally taken by Lund and that McClelland's negative No. 16369 was copied by him from Lund's original, in August 1893. Lund had already photographed the group on the ice in 1879 (No. 145).

It is possible to date these photographs, and the next, No. 235, by a letter of 22 March 1892 from Joan to Mrs Alexander in which she tells her

> ... We are having lovely summer weather and your Figlio is wonderful. The photo of him with me (No. 235) was done by an amateur and has never been mounted. The other is his boat with me, and old Arthur in one beyond, and his sailing boat at her mooring from our Harbour makes a nice little group...[250]

Despite the summer weather in March, the leaves were on the trees when these photographs were taken, so they must have been taken in the previous summer.

234

250 L.G. Swett (ed.), *John Ruskin's Letters to Francesca* (Boston: Lothrop, Lee and Shephard, 1931), pp. 202-203.

235 Photographed with Joan Severn, by Captain Walker, Spring 1892, aet 73

This is the photograph with Joan 'done by an amateur' referred to above. The head and shoulders were re-drawn for inclusion in Collingwood's *Life of Ruskin*,[251] and Cook and Wedderburn[252] identify the photographer as Captain Walker.[253] The photograph appears to have been taken by the Brantwood arch at the foot of the steps leading up to the hillside behind the house.

236 Caricature of Ruskin standing on Whistler's head, by Philip William May (1864–1903), January 1892

Ruskin, it seemed, was still getting in Whistler's hair more than a decade after the libel action. In 1892, the year in which Whistler's book, *The Gentle Art of making Enemies* went into its second edition, Whistler was appointed an officer of the Legion d'Honneur. He was in Paris when this caricature was published in *Pick-me-up* on 9 January 1892.

Phil May originally worked as a scene painter in Leeds. At sixteen he went to London and soon obtained work for *Society*, *Penny Illustrated*, *St Stephen's Review* and *Pictorial World*. Later he worked for the *Graphic* and other publications.

235

236

251 Collingwood, *Life and Work of John Ruskin*, vol. II, p. 244.
252 *Works Catalogue*, No. 57.
253 Captain Walker is otherwise apparently unmemorable in Ruskin circles!

237 Photograph standing by a leafy wall at Brantwood, wearing hat, by John McClelland, Summer 1892

238 Photograph standing by a leafy wall at Brantwood, holding hat, with Joan Severn, by John McClelland, Summer 1892

It is a pity that more is not known about John McClelland, who was a competent photographer. We know from the 1881 Census Returns that he lived at Deva House, Mount Pleasant Road, New Brighton. He originated from Scotland and was then thirty-three years old. He was employed as a bank clerk. McClelland's wife Ann, aged thirty, was a native of Liverpool. They had twin daughters, Marguerite and Winifred, aged one. The McClellands employed a housemaid and a nursery maid, so presumably his bank clerk's salary was supplemented by fees from photographic work and perhaps lecturing. McClelland disappears from local directories after 1900.

The fact that he visited Brantwood from Liverpool on at least five occasions between 1892 and 1898 indicated some connection with the Ruskin circle. I suggest that he was either the elder brother, or possibly cousin, of Marion McClelland. 'Clennie' had joined the Severn household as governess to their children in 1882, at the age of nineteen, and probably stayed with them either at Herne Hill or Brantwood for at least ten years. She was the favourite niece of Miss Tolmie who seems to have lived at Coniston with Harriette Rigbye and the original introduction probably came through the Rigbye-Tolmie-Severn-Ruskin friendship.[254]

A large collection of John McClelland's lantern slides of his own photographs is in the Williamson Art Gallery at Birkenhead, and a substantial collection of his negatives is in the National Portrait Gallery. These help in the positive identification of unascribed photographs of Ruskin. Some dated prints and negatives, and differing dress in photographs, makes it possible to identify the various photographic sessions at Brantwood and place the various photographs into their correct groups.

237

This first photographic session seems to have taken place in the summer of 1892 when only two portraits of Ruskin were taken, although others of the house and grounds may date from now. Both Nos. 237 and 238 are little-known; the former is a pleasant photograph but I doubt if either Ruskin or Joan Severn would have been happy with No. 238!

254 For further details see Ethel Bassin, *The Old Songs of Skye* (London: Routledge & Kegan Paul, 1977), pp. 72ff., 155ff.

238

239 Photograph by Sarah Angelina Acland (1849–1930), 1 August 1893, aet 74

240 Portrait by B.C. Leeming, 1901, based on No. 239

241 Photograph, with Sir Henry Acland, by S.A. Acland

242 Photograph with Sir Henry Acland and Joan Severn, by S.A. Acland

Sir Henry Acland was Ruskin's senior by four years. They had first met at Oxford more than fifty years before. In the summer of 1893 Acland, who had been created a baronet three years earlier, stayed at Brantwood with his daughter Angie. Angie was a talented photographer and during her visit, on 1 August, took these three photographs outside the front door. It was not uncommon now for Ruskin not to recognise his friends. Writing to Linton, Mumby recounts hearing tell that when Acland went to Brantwood, 'Ruskin stared at him, unconsciously, then suddenly embraced him, saying 'I know you – but I don't know who you are!'[255] While Acland was at Brantwood, Ruskin was told that their book, *The Oxford Museum*, was to be reprinted. He gave Acland a message, which was incorporated into the preface of the new edition.

> Say to my friends in the Oxford Museum from me, May God bless the reverent and earnest study of Nature and of Man, to His Glory, to the better teaching of the Future, to the benefit of our Country, and to the good of all Mankind.[256]

No. 240, a stark indian ink pen and wash portrait based on No. 239 was probably made for line block reproduction, but I have been unable to trace its publication.

255 A.J. Mumby – W.J. Linton, 17 Mar. 1894; original at Yale.

256 *Works* XVI, p. 240.

239

240

241

242

About this time Ruskin's portrait was almost painted by G.F. Watts, but at the last minute it had to be cancelled.

> He [Watts] had a great wish to see Mr Ruskin again, and I a great hope that he might be able to paint him. The inappropriateness of this omission from the number of the men of mark represented by Signor's hand was so obvious. He told me that in former years he did not make the attempt, as he knew the very presence of the critic would make failure a certainty. Now in these later days the critical faculty was allowed repose. He had heard from Mrs Severn and from Sir Henry Acland of the deep quiet of that once active mind – 'speaking little and in short sentences', Sir Henry had said. But Signor was not well on the morning when we were to start for Coniston; the journey was put off, and another opportunity did not occur.[257]

243–247 Group of photographs, by John McClelland, August 1893

243

244

This second group of photographs taken at Brantwood by McClelland is more successful than those taken a year before. Ruskin looks fitter and more alert. The curved fitted wooden seat on which he is sitting (with and without Joan Severn) is against the curved wall near the top of the zigzag path climbing up the hillside from the kitchen garden, which Ruskin had laid out in 1873.

The study photograph shows him sitting in his armchair by the fireplace. Above it may be seen the della Robbia faience plaque found for Ruskin in Florence in 1880 by Charles Fairfax Murray. Below it on the mantelpiece is the carved wooden Swiss figure bought by Ruskin's mother, perhaps on one of their early tours. On shelves fitted around the della Robbia plaque are antiquities which came from General Cesnola's archaeological work in Cyprus which Ruskin financed in 1874–75.

257 M.S. Watts, *George Frederick Watts* (London: Macmillan, 1912), vol. II, p. 237. Cook and Wedderburn in *Works* XXXVI, p. lvii, date the proposed visit as 1898, but in view of the reference to Acland, 1893 seems a more likely year.

245

246

247

248 Caricature by John Wallace depicting Ruskin as St George, 1893

249 Fancy portrait by John Wallace of Ruskin standing in a gondola, 1893

250 Fancy portrait by John Wallace of Ruskin seated before Brantwood, 1893

248

249

250

It will be remembered that in 1878 Ruskin had featured in Cope's lampoon of the Canterbury Pilgrims. In 1893 Ruskin again featured in one of their advertising publications. 'Cope's Smoke Room Booklets No. 13' was entitled *John Ruskin on himself and things in general*. Apart from its advertising leaves, the pamphlet comprised a six page biographical note on Ruskin followed by fifty-one pages of extracts from his writings, all printed without permission.

The illustrations were by John Wallace. Ruskin is featured on the cover as St George, while on the frontispiece he stands in a gondola, book and pen in hand, with Venice in the background; on the title page he sits on a garden seat in front of Brantwood.

Ruskin and his advisors did not object to these caricatures and fancy portraits, and apparently they did not object to Ruskin's name being used to advertise tobacco (although he heartily disliked smoking). But they did object to the piratical use of his writings, and issued a writ against Copes. On 22 November Copes stopped issuing copies of the pamphlet and sought the return of any unsold copies that they might be destroyed. They reserved the right to use the cover, title, frontispiece and bibliography (pp. 58–59), but the booklet does not seem to have been re-issued in any other form.

251 Sheet of sketches showing Ruskin's head and shoulders, and his hand, by John Gutzon Mothe Borglum (1867–1941), c.1893

252 Sketch, head only, by Gutzon Borglum, c.1893

253 Sketch, full length, standing, by Gutzon Borglum, c.1893

254 Statue of Ruskin seated in his armchair, by Gutzon Borglum, 1903–1904

255 Bust, head and shoulders only, based on No. 254 by Kotaro Takamura (1883–1956), 1906–1907

256 Model of Ruskin's left hand, by Gutzon Borglum, 1903–1904

251

252

When Ruskin was at Sandgate in 1887 he engaged the organist H.S. Roberts of Folkestone to visit him and play Bach, Corelli and Rossini to him. Ruskin and Roberts were soon on friendly terms. Roberts, it appears, knew the American artist Gutzon Borglum, who studied in Paris and London between 1893 and 1901. In Leeds about 1893 the two men met. Roberts was on his way to Brantwood and he invited Borglum to accompany him. While Ruskin and Roberts talked, Borglum studied Ruskin and made several sketches of him. He found that Ruskin 'had drawn into himself. He knew his worth. He had full confidence in his own strength, but he was sad. The most marvellous, magnificent, unappreciated genius the world has ever known'.[258] Deeply impressed, Borglum told his wife Lisa, 'As soon as I have time, I will make a statue of Ruskin'.[259]

258 J.W. McSpadden, *Famous Sculptors of America* (1927).

259 A. Willadene Price, *Gutzon Borglum, Artist and Patriot* (Chicago: Rand McNally, 1962), pp. 48, 61, 63.

253

Borglum, who up to this time was known as a painter, found time to model his statue of Ruskin for the 1904 World Fair held in St Louis. At the same Fair he exhibited one of his first statues, 'Mares of Diomedes' for which he was awarded a gold medal.

The Ruskin statue, which stands 15" high, was cast by the Gorham Corporation of New York. Their records, which are incomplete, show three separate code numbers relating to the figure, which suggests that three models were probably cast, though there must have been others. When David Peel & Co. had one of the statues in 1965, they told me that it was no. 3 of a set of four. *Exactly* how many were cast is difficult to determine. The Metropolitan Museum has had one since 1906, and the Detroit Institute of Art since 1919. The cast acquired by the Rhode Island School of Design in 1929 and sold in New York in 1949 *may* be the one bought about 1955 by Mr Warren Howell. Additionally David Peel & Co. had their cast in 1965 and in 1931 J.H. Whitehouse was offered one by his agents, B.F. Stevens and Brown. Another cast, once in the collection of Kerrison Preston, was sold at Sotheby's in 1968.

Pleased by the success of the hands in the statue, Borglum subsequently made a separate model of the left hand. Several bronze-casts were made (see Figure 6, page 11) which he gave to his friends as paper-weights. Perhaps Borglum cast these himself for the Gorham Corporation have no record of this work.[260]

Writing about contemporary American sculptors in 1907 Selwyn Brinton[261] singled out Borglum, and chose to reproduce and refer to his Ruskin statue.

> Among the younger sculptors now working at New York perhaps none is of more interest and promise than Mr Gutzon Borglum; in his work I

254

260 Information from the artist's son, Lincoln Borglum. Mr Borglum had been unable to discover how many had been cast. He was able to borrow one, from which he made a mould, and cast a plaster model for my own collection.

261 Selwyn Brinton, 'American Sculptors of To-day', *Studio* Feb. 1907, pp. 34-42.

> feel more of M. Rodin's influence than in that of any other American sculptor. He worked here for many years ... Absolutely different in conception is his *Ruskin* – a figure monumental in its repose. This fine portrait study was taken in the last year of the great critic's life at Windermere [sic], and met M. Rodin's full approval. There is real characterisation in Mr Borglum's portrait work ...

One of America's leading sculptors, Borglum is probably best known as the carver of the colossal sculpture of presidents Washington, Jefferson, Lincoln and T. Roosevelt on Mount Rushmore in the Black Hills of South Dakota, and the Confederate Memorial on Stone Mountain, Georgia. Among his other notable works are a large head of Lincoln (Capitol, Washington) and figures of the Apostles for the Cathedral of St John the Divine, New York.

In the early years of this century a young Japanese sculptor, Kotaro Takamura, visited America. In New York between February 1906 and June 1907 he became Gutzon Borglum's assistant and later he recorded

> Among my Master's sculptural works 'Ruskin' is supremely famous, besides the aforesaid 'Mares'. This is a statue of aged Ruskin's whole body done according to his own memory got while he met the latter in person: though only some 38cm high as a whole, it's an excellent sculpture, rare in that field in America: it does have more inner substance than the one among the world-famous cleverly wrought statuettes by Troubetzkoi. This is Ruskin reposing on an armchair, wrapped in a blanket, with his hand over a book: my Master specifically loved this hand of the statue, which he was often witnessed caressing when alone.[262]

While he was in New York, Takamura sculpted a small head and shoulders of Ruskin (No. 255), taking his likeness from Borglum's statue. Some casts were probably made at the time in New York. Others were made subsequently. Exactly how many were made is difficult to determine.

I am indebted to Taichi Kitagawa and Professor Masami Kimura[263] for drawing my attention to references to various casts.

In 1910 Naoya Shiga, novelist and a founder and editor of *Shirakaba* recorded visiting the Masamune exhibition in Tokyo and writing 'I wanted to have the little Ruskin bust'.[264]

254

255

The Rokando store's records for 29 April 1911 show 'a Ruskin figure' being sold for ¥6 to Mr Tokoku Kono.

A memorandum by Toyochika Takamura of 15 January 1916 records the casting of another bust, apparently by the lost-wax process.

Saisui Sakai remembered being presented with a cast on his retirement, in December 1915, as editor of the *Bijutsu-Shimpo* [*Fine Art News*].[265]

262 Kotaro Takamura, 'Mr Gutzon Borglum, American Sculptor', *Shin-cho (New Tide)*, June 1917, p. 207.
263 In extended correspondence.
264 *Shirakaba* I, 3, June 1910.
265 K. Anazawa *et al.* (ed.), *Kotaro Takamura's Whole Sculptural Works* (Tokyo: Rikuyosha, 1973), p. 171.

There is a cast of the Takamura sculpture in the Mikimoto collection in Tokyo. The late Mr Y. Mikimoto told me that he remembered his father saying that he had bought it in Italy. Subsequently he seems to have obtained at least one more cast which his daughter, Mrs Homma, gave to me when she visited England. There are photographs with the Mikimoto family which suggest that there could also have been a larger version of the bust.

On leaving New York, Kotaro Takamura travelled to London and Paris, and perhaps to Italy. He became one of those responsible for introducing the western style of sculpture into Japan.

257 Photograph, seated in Brantwood study, by C.P. McCarthy, May 1894, aet 75

In the last decade of his life, Ruskin at Brantwood became something of a peep show. He was visited by many friends and strangers alike, who wished to write about him or photograph him. Among the many photographers, amateur and professional, who constantly recorded his appearance at this time, was C.P. McCarthy. He visited Brantwood in May 1894 and photographed Ruskin sitting in his favourite study arm chair, between the bow window and fireplace.

257

Life at Brantwood may by now have been a little quieter with both young Arthur and Agnew Severn at Oxford. (Arthur managed to stay for four years without passing a single exam.) But there were frequent visits from other members of the Severn family. Ruskin still wrote the occasional short letter. Just before she died in 1893 he wrote to Susan Beever; in March of the present year he wrote to his old friend Lady Simon, and in June to Joan Severn, while the following year saw another note to Joan and one to Sir John Simon.

Meanwhile new books – both authorised and unauthorised – continued to appear. Two volumes of selections from his writings which were published in this year were Mary Wakefield's *Ruskin on Music* and W. Jolly's *Ruskin on Education*. George Allen also published *Verona and other lectures*, edited by W.G. Collingwood, and *Letters Addressed to a College Friend*, while Thomas J. Wise issued the unauthorised *Letters to Ernest Chesneau* and *Letters on Art and Literature*.

258 Photographed in the Brantwood grounds with W. Holman Hunt by Frederick Hollyer, September 1894, aet 75

259 Photographed with Joan Severn, by Frederick Hollyer

260 Photographed alone, by Frederick Hollyer

261 Photographed in the study, looking left, by Frederick Hollyer, 'Datur hora quieti'

262 Portrait based on No. 261, by Garschagen, 1902

263 Photographed in the study, full face, by Frederick Hollyer

258

A visitor to Brantwood in September 1894 was Elbert Hubbard, who wrote

> Mr Ruskin has the faculty of making his interviewer do most of the talking. He is a rare listener, and leans forward, putting a hand behind his right ear to get each word you say ... Although his form is bowed his regularity of life has borne fruit in the rich russet of his complexion, the mild, clear eye ... His hair is thick and nearly white; the beard is now worn quite long and gives a patriarchal appearance to the fine face.[266]

In the same month, Pre-Raphaelite W. Holman Hunt visited Brantwood in company with the photographer Frederick Hollyer. Hollyer was one

266 Elbert Hubbard, *Little Journeys to the Homes of Good Men and Great – John Ruskin* (New York: G.P. Putman's Sons, 1895).

259

of the great photographers of his day, and he did a great deal of work for contemporary painters, either providing them with working photographs of their subject, or photographs of the finished paintings.

Unfortunately there is little information about the present group of photographs, other than a rather ambiguous statement by Canon Rawnsley[267] who refers to No. 261 as 'that admirable portrait which Holman Hunt arranged for Hollyer to take'. Was Rawnsley saying that Hollyer simply visited Brantwood at Hunt's suggestion, or is he saying that Hunt actually arranged the poses, as would an artist?

Which ever was the case, Ruskin was a passive subject. Nos. 258–60 were taken in the grounds. In No. 258 Ruskin stares in a mystified way at Hunt, perhaps wondering who he was, just as he had done with Acland in the previous year. In No. 259 Hunt has given way to Joan Severn – but Ruskin has barely moved. For No. 260 Ruskin did move his head and re-clasp his hands.

A print of No 259 in the Whitehouse Collection is dated September 1894, thus pin-pointing the visit. Although the well-known portrait by Hollyer of Ruskin gazing out of the study window, No. 261, had been dated 1896, it seems likely that this, and the lesser known No. 263, were also taken during the 1894 visit.

No. 261 is a fine photograph, and if we accept Rawnsley's statement at its face value, then it is the pose which Hunt would have chosen had he painted Ruskin's portrait. A portrait by Hunt was in fact proposed five years later. The National Address of Congratulation to Ruskin on the occasion of his eightieth birthday in 1899 included the words

260

> It will be a great happiness to us if you will consent to your portrait being painted by your life-long friend, William Holman Hunt, and accept the same as the national property of the St George's Guild, in token of our affectionate devotion.

However, as J. Howard Whitehouse, who presented the Address to Ruskin, wrote[268]

> Collingwood further advised us in reading the Address to the Master to omit the reference to the

261

267 H.D. Rawnsley, *Ruskin and the English Lakes* (Glasgow: James MacLehose & Sons, 1901), pp. 194-95.
268 Diary of J.H. Whitehouse, Coniston, 7 Feb. 1899.

262

painting of his portrait by Holman Hunt. Ruskin liked his works, but not his portraits and would not care to have his portrait painted by him. Collingwood added that if anyone painted it, it should be G.F. Watts. Under the circumstances we decided to omit the request.[269]

263

No. 262 is an oil copy of No. 261 by the Dutch painter Garschagen done in 1902. It has descended to the present owner through his father's family.

264 Photograph taken on the ice, by [?] P. Baxter, 14 February 1895, aet 76

265 Photograph taken on the ice, by John McClelland, 14 February 1895

266 Photograph taken on the ice, by John McClelland

267 Photograph of Ruskin alone, by John McClelland

268 Photograph of Ruskin and Baxter with 'Bramble' (who moved)

269 Photograph of Ruskin and Baxter with 'Bramble' (who didn't move)

270 Photograph of Ruskin sitting in basket chair, with stick

271 Photograph of Ruskin sitting in basket chair, without stick

The winter of 1895 was severe. The *Barrow News* of 5 February reported that three days earlier there had been 34 degrees (!) of frost in the Lake District. Coniston lake was completely frozen over and during that weekend several people walked across from Brantwood to Coniston Hall, a distance of about half a mile. The Coniston correspondent of the *News* reported in the next issue that

> A snow storm visited us with a vengeance on Wednesday night [6 February]. By eight o'clock in the morning, the snow was six inches thick,

269 Printing the words of the Address in *Works* XXXIV, p. 734, Cook and Wedderburn gave the 'official' reasons that 'the state of Ruskin's health made this [the Hunt portrait] impractical'.

264

and a strong wind blowing, it was found useless to employ the snow-plough to clear the roads, as the drifts were so changeable. At five o'clock the down-fall had not abated, and travelling was most difficult...

By the end of the day there was over a foot of snow at Brantwood and then it froze hard again, so two days later, when Ruskin celebrated his 76th birthday, Brantwood must have defied all the attempts of its occupants to keep warm.

265

The big frost of 1895 presented an excellent excuse for photography and there is in the Whitehouse Collection a series of six photographs taken at this time. They form an interesting group because not only do they all show Ruskin, but most of them also include at least one other member of the Brantwood household.

Perhaps the most interesting photographs of the series are the groups taken on the ice several yards out from the harbour at Brantwood (Nos. 264–66). There are three slightly different versions of this group.

A 1971 acquisition by the Whitehouse Collection is photograph No. 265 and we are fortunate that this print is inscribed by Joan Severn with the date on which it was taken and a list of those in the group. We know from her notes that it froze after the snow-fall on 6 February and that on 8 March the lake was still 'mostly ice'. The photograph itself was taken on 14 February (Valentine's Day, as Joan has noted), when the lake was 'completely frozen over'.

The figures in the group (Nos. 265–6) are, from left to right, George Usher, Dawson Herdson, John Ruskin, Joe Wilkinson, Joan Severn, Mr Clarke, Lily Severn, Charlie Baxter, Jimmie Baxter, Peter Baxter and John Wilson.

266

George Usher was the Coniston builder, and in the preceding twenty four years, since Ruskin bought the house, he had been responsible for most, if not all, of the extensions which had transformed Brantwood from a cottage into a rambling country house. Exactly what brought him to Brantwood on Valentine's Day 1895 remains a mystery.

Seated next to Usher is Dawson Herdson, who had been head gardener at Brantwood since Ruskin bought the property in 1871. At the time of the photograph he was 59. Herdson was more than just head gardener. In the words of his obituary in the *Westmoreland Gazette*, he was

> ... a most valuable servant, whether in door or out. Whenever a difficulty arose, the cry was 'Send for Herdson', and his advice, given after some deliberation, was always acted on, for his knowledge of the district was remarkable, as was also his memory ...

He helped to nurse Ruskin through his illnesses of 1878 and 1881. On his last working day (probably in 1899), he and Joan Severn put the completing touches to the Harbour Walk, the azalea-lined path leading from Brantwood to the harbour,

267

268

269

which they had created together, and which is still one of the beauties of Brantwood.

Standing behind Ruskin is Joe Wilkinson. Born on 14 April 1859 he entered Ruskin's service as post boy soon after Ruskin came to Coniston. It was his duty to row with the post to the head of the lake and meet the Hawkshead mail coach. After a short break he returned to Brantwood to become an under-gardener, eventually succeeding Herdson as head gardener. In 1918 he went to live in the Brantwood lodge, dying there on 28 October 1952.

The voluminous Joan Severn stands talking to Ruskin. At the time of the photograph she was two weeks short of her 49th birthday. Lily, her eldest daughter, standing next to Joan, had celebrated her 22nd birthday three days earlier. Her father's favourite child, she died of typhoid on 14 June 1920.

The man with the alpenstock standing in the background between Joan and Lily is Samuel Clarke of neighbouring Atkinson Ground. Joan merely lists him as 'Clarke'. With Usher, Wilkinson and others, he was to be a bearer at Ruskin's funeral in 1900. On his tricycle is Peter Baxter, an Irishman who would have been fifty at the time. He came to Brantwood as Ruskin's valet in 1876. The Baxters lived at the lodge, and he died there on 13 December 1918 aged 73. He had six children of which the two youngest, Charlie (left, aged 14) and Jimmie (right, aged 9) stand next to him on the ice.

John Wilson, the youth on the right of the group, was 21 at the time of the photograph. He started at Brantwood as stable boy and eventually became the coachman.

A comparison between Nos. 264, 265 and 266 shows that the four figures on the left, Ruskin, Wilkinson, Usher and Herdson, have hardly moved during the time that Joan was organising the group. Clearly No. 266 is the formally posed group. Charlie and Jimmie Baxter stand to attention, their father rides to attention, and Wilkinson has only one hand protectively on the back of the Master's chair. But during the taking of the two preliminary photographs there were some interesting comings and goings.

In No. 264 there is an additional figure standing in the centre of the group at the back – and Baxter is missing. By the time that No. 265 was taken, Baxter has appeared and the mysterious standing man has gone – not to return for the formal group. I suggest that he was the official photographer who had been called in, and who stood discreetly in the background while Joan arranged the group. Baxter, who is absent in No. 264, presumably took that photograph. We know that two of Ruskin's earlier valets, George Hobbs and Frederick Crawley, had been photographers, and there is no reason to assume that Baxter was not also expected to be adept in the art.

While the photographer was at Brantwood he took at least five other exposures, Nos. 267–71. No. 267 shows Ruskin standing alone, in the same clothes worn on the ice – light coloured felt hat, double-breasted overcoat with velvet collar and sealskin gauntlets. Fortunately this photograph was reproduced in *The Bookman* of March 1900, where the caption both dates it and names the photographer as Mr J. McClelland of Liscard. By chance there are also negatives of two of the series in the National Portrait Gallery's collection of McClelland's negatives, thus confirming that he was at Brantwood for his third photographic session.

In the next two photographs of the 1895 sequence Ruskin appears with Baxter and his dog. In 1893 Collingwood tells us that the reigning canine favourite at Brantwood was Bramble, and from the somewhat aged appearance of the beast we assume that no change has taken place in the intervening couple of years. Baxter seems to have

271

been *too* intent on controlling Bramble because at the crucial moment he (or she) turned to see what all the fuss was about. This presumably accounts for the second exposure, with the re-seated Bramble, and all three posers remaining motionless. These photographs, and presumably also No. 267 (from which the background has been touched out) seem to have been taken on the drive near the front door.

But Ruskin was not to get indoors from the cold yet! His basket chair had been carried up from the ice and positioned on the terrace outside his study window. Deprived of his hat, and in ten or more degrees of frost, Ruskin was positioned for another exposure. But having taken it, someone thought that he would have looked better *without* his walking stick. That being removed, the *final* exposure was taken!

The whole sequence of photographs form an interesting record of a day towards the end of Ruskin's life.

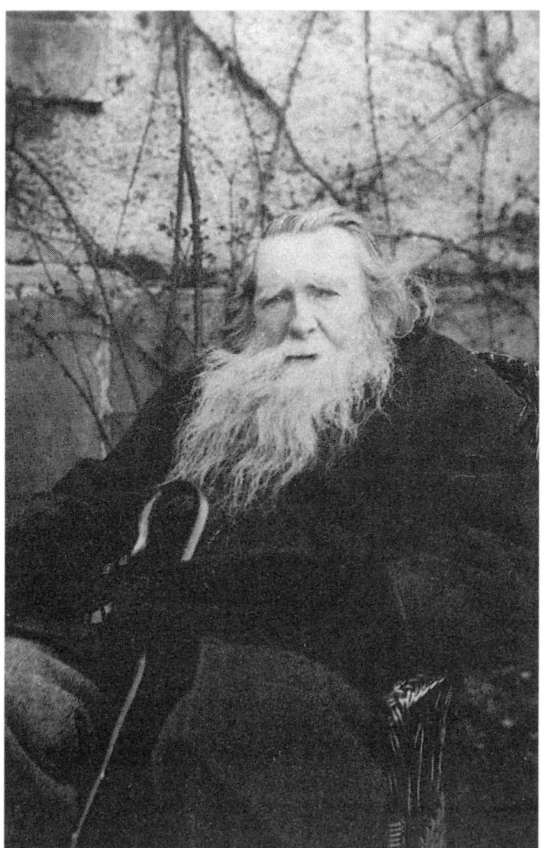

270

272 Oil sketch by W.G. Collingwood, 1897, aet 78 (Plate 30)

273 Portrait by W.G. Collingwood, 29 January 1897 (Plate 31)

274 Portrait based on No. 273, by Bryan Thorpe

275 Portrait by W.G. Collingwood, 19 February 1897 (Plate 32)

272

273

J.W. Graham, who met Ruskin again in 1896, described his appearance then.[270]

> He has now the appearance of an ancient seer; his beard is long and flowing, and the grey overhanging eyebrows, and uncut locks make up the typical picture of an aged Elijah. His stoop has naturally grown upon him; with the slowest of feeble steps he paces a little on fine days on the road, accompanied by a manservant and a large dog; but if you catch the bright eye, and hear the deep musical voice, as it speaks with admiration of the sunset, you recognise still the *ardens ingenium* and the rich nature of days gone by.

At the beginning of 1897 W.G. Collingwood made his preliminary oil sketch for this series of portraits. For some twenty five years Collingwood had been one of Ruskin's most faithful friends and helpers. Since Ruskin's working life ceased in 1889, Collingwood had written many of his business letters for him. He had written the first authoritative biography in 1893, and had edited and seen through the press various of Ruskin's books – *Poems* (1891), *The Poetry of Architecture* (1893), *Verona and other lectures* (1894), *Studies in Both Arts* (1895) and *Lectures on Landscape* (1897). Naturally Collingwood shows in his series of portraits the elderly teacher, and prophet of the nineteenth century.

From the head and shoulders oil sketch, Collingwood painted two three-quarter length finished portraits of Ruskin sitting in his favourite armchair near the table where he used to work in winter months past. Behind him is a section of his bookshelves and on the table along side him, a vase of roses (unseasonably!), two books and his spectacles; additionally in one of the portraits, his cork penholder rests on sheets of blank notepaper. The two portraits are both dated at Brantwood on 29 January and 19 February respectively.

270 J.W. Graham, 'John Ruskin at Home', *Proceedings of Warrington Literary and Philosophical Society* (1897).

274

Collingwood's neighbours, the Holts of Tent Lodge, visiting Lanehead on 8 April 1897

> saw two of the portraits that Mr Collingwood has done of Mr Ruskin lately. The finished one[271] has been sent up to the Academy, but the ones we saw, especially the first sketch, we thought beautiful'.

The sketch, No. 272, remained in the Collingwood family, on the walls of the drawing room at Lanehead, where I first saw it. In 1966 it was sold at Sotheby's and went to America. It was

275

bought by the late Warren Howell, a keen Ruskin collector and a descendant of Ruskin's Richardson relations. Following his death it went to the Pierpont Morgan Library.

No. 273 was on loan to the Coniston Museum by 1919, and probably Collingwood eventually gave it to the museum, where it remains. No. 275 was either given to or bought by Ruskin. It remained at Brantwood until the 1931 sale when it was bought by Mrs C.D. Cooper. She presented it to the Whitehouse Collection.

No. 274 is one of the most recent Ruskin portraits. It is based on No. 273 and was designed and executed in cross-stitch by Bryan Thorpe. It was made for his relation, Alan Turvey, who, like myself has long had an interest in Ruskin portraits, and to whom I am indebted for assistance.

271 This must have been No. 273, which in fact was exhibited at the Royal Society of British Artists Exhibition.

276 Portrait by Arthur Severn, watercolour, 1897–1900, aet 78 (Plate 33)

277 Portrait, based on No. 276, by Arthur Severn, oil, 1898–99 (Plate 34)

276

277

It is evident from a number of remarks in his *Memoir of Ruskin*[272] that Severn considered Ruskin a silly old man, and something of a trial. Thus it is not surprising that his 1897 portrait, No. 276, shows Ruskin as a rather frail and pathetic old man, wearing knitted mittens and with a brightly checked rug covering his lap. The late Mrs B.C. Gnosspelius, Collingwood's daughter, told me that she recollected her father and Severn painting their very different portraits of Ruskin at the same time.

The watercolour sketch was begun in 1897. From it in the next two years, Severn made his finished oil painting, No. 277, which is now in the Coniston Museum. Immediately after Ruskin's death in 1900, Severn finished the watercolour sketch for Robert E. Cunliffe of Ambleside who had assembled an important collection of Ruskin's drawings. No. 276 was subsequently bought by J.H. Whitehouse.

272 See Dearden, *The Professor*, passim.

278 Photographed in the study, hands visible, by John McClelland, 17 July 1897, aet 78

279 Photographed in the study, hands invisible, by John McClelland (Plate 35)

278

279

Cook and Wedderburn infer that these are the last photographs of Ruskin which were taken, but we know from the dating of some of McClelland's negatives that he was at Brantwood again in the following year, as detailed below.

In taking No. 278 McClelland posed Ruskin in his usual arm chair, the strong light from the nearby window falling on the side of his face. He subsequently wrote

> knowing his decided objection to anything unnatural, no artificial means of lighting the darker side of the face was adopted, so that although the result hardly does full justice to the face or to the magnificent blue eyes of the Master, it is a true picture of him in his later years as he sat in his study.[273]

Walter Crane saw Ruskin about a month after McClelland had taken his photographs.

> Mrs Severn, who watched most assiduously over Ruskin, allowed me to see him. The first time was in the garden. It was rather a shock. Ruskin looked the shadow of his former self – the real living man with all his energy and force had gone, and only the shadow remained. He was carefully dressed and scrupulously neat, having gloves on, which, seeing a visitor approach, he began to pull off rather absently, when Mrs Severn said, 'Never mind the gloves', and I took his hand, but, alas! He had nothing but monosyllables, and soon went away on the arm of his constant attendant. Another time, Mrs Severn brought me into his room, a library, where Ruskin sat in his arm chair. He had a benign expression, and looked venerable and prophetic, with a long flowing beard, but he seemed disinclined to talk.[274]

Hall Cain saw him

> ... in the last year but one before Ruskin's death. I had the pleasure to meet him in the flesh in his house at Coniston. He had then been for years silent, and so far as active interest in the affairs of life went, he had long been dead. I found him very old and bent and feeble, a smaller, frailer man than I looked for; well in health both of body and mind, but with faculties that were dying down very slowly and gently and almost imper-

273 *Bookman*, March 1900, p. 194. McClelland is quoted as having said this in the caption there, to No. 278.

274 Crane, *An Artist's Reminiscences*, p. 446. The visit was on 10 August 1897.

ceptibly – as the lamp dies down when the oil fails in it.

His head was not so full as I expected to find it, and it hardly seemed to me in form or size either grand or massive; his eyes were slow and peaceful, having lost their former fire; and his face, from which the quiet life of later years had smoothed away the lines of strong thought and torturing experience, was too much hidden by a full grey beard. He spoke very little, and always in a soft and gentle voice ...[275]

Photographs taken in July 1898 by John McClelland

Sitting A	**280**	**In wheel chair, 25 July**
	281	**In wheel chair, Joan seated, 25 July**
	282	**In wheel chair, Joan standing, 25 July**
Sitting B	**283**	**On garden bench, with Bramble**
	284	**On garden bench, with Joan**
Sitting C	**285**	**Standing, with sunshade and Joan**
Sitting D	**286**	**Relaxing in study arm chair**
	287	**Sitting in study arm chair, three quarter length**
	288	**Sitting in study arm chair, Joan behind**

We know from the negatives listed in McClelland's negative box in the National Portrait Gallery that he was back at Brantwood again in 1898. In the list, he specifically dates Nos. 280–82 as having been taken on 25 July 1898. To judge by the relative clothing worn by Ruskin and Joan Severn in Nos. 280–88, I suggest that these nine photographs were taken at four separate sittings in July 1898. Perhaps on that occasion McClelland stayed at Brantwood for several days. Whether the *un*dated photographs in this group were taken before or after Nos. 280–82 I do not know. For purposes of this catalogue, I group the photographs into Sittings A–D.

In Sitting A, Nos. 280–82, Ruskin wears a light tweed coat and is sitting in his wheelchair by the Brantwood front door. In Nos. 281–82 Joan Severn holds his light coloured hat, and wears rings on two fingers of each hand.

Nos. 283–84 I categorise as Sitting B. Ruskin, wearing the same clothes, is sitting with Bramble on a wooden bench in the grounds. In No. 284 Bramble has gone and Joan, wearing different clothes, and rings on only *one* finger of her right hand, has joined Ruskin on the bench.

Sitting C only comprises one photograph, No. 285. Again Ruskin is wearing the same clothes and holds the sunshade which leans again his wheel chair in Nos. 280 and 282. Joan wears a third outfit.

280

275 Hall Caine, *Recollections of Rossetti* (London: Elliot Stock, 1882), p. 87.

Ruskin and Joan now go back into the study for Sitting D, in which they *both* wear different clothes. In Nos. 286–88 Ruskin appears to be wearing the same coat that he wore in Nos. 278–79 in the previous July. But I do not think that these *were* taken in 1897 because Ruskin does not look *quite* the same – and the arrangement on the table is different. Thus I include them in the 1898 sessions. The lower book on the table in No. 288 appears to be Collingwood's *Thorstein of the Mere* (1895).

281

283

282

284

285

286

287

288

289 Portrait by C. Hertschel, 1899

Ruskin's 80th birthday on 8 February 1899 resulted in considerable press coverage. The present drawing, based on some earlier likeness, was made to illustrate an article in the *Daily Chronicle* by H.W. Nevinson.

On his birthday J.H. Whitehouse, secretary of the Ruskin Society of Birmingham, and William Wardle, secretary of the Liverpool Society, went to Brantwood to deliver the National Address of Congratulation. The young Whitehouse was much impressed by meeting his idol and that evening at the Dove Hotel in Coniston he wrote up his diary.[276]

289

> We were then conducted to Mr Ruskin's presence. He was dressed and sitting in an arm chair before a little table. As we entered he attempted to rise, but was evidently too feeble to do so. We shook hands, and I told him I was glad to hear he was so well. I then explained that we brought him a national address, and I read it to him. As I was doing so I occasionally heard him give a low exclamation – half sob it seemed to be. When I had finished he tried to reply but could only utter a few broken words. He was evidently deeply moved and quite overcome with emotion ... What most impressed me when I saw the Master were his wonderful eyes. They are blue and very clear and bright. When, during the reading of the address, I looked up at him, I found them fixed upon me as though he were searching me through and through. No one who meets his eyes can doubt that his mind is perfectly clear.

290 Portrait by Isaac Broome, based on a photograph, 1899

The last two decades of the 19th century saw the establishment in America of several communities dedicated to implementing Ruskin's teaching in *Fors Clavigera*, and putting into practice there what Ruskin had hoped to do through the Guild of St George in England. Ruskin, Tennessee, and the Ruskin Commonwealth there was founded in 1894 by the Indiana newspaperman, Charles Wayland. By the late '90s there were some 250 habitants living in 70 whitewashed wooden houses grouped around the printing works where *The Coming Nation* was produced. However, ultimately there was internal strife; the Ruskin Commonwealth collapsed, and the inhabitants dispersed – some going on to found Ruskin, Georgia. Ruskin, Tennessee soon became a ghost town.

One of the leading inhabitants of Ruskin, Tennessee, was Isaac Broome. One of his contributions to the community in its last days was described in *The Coming Nation*[277] as 'a beautiful life-size portrait in oil of John Ruskin, from his latest photograph. It is a magnificent picture of a noble man'. I know nothing of its ultimate fate.

276 In the Whitehouse Collection. Whitehouse was in error in writing that he stayed at the 'Dove' Hotel; in fact he stayed at the Crown, whose landlord was Mr Dove.

277 *The Coming Nation, Colony Notes*, 2 September 1899. I am indebted to Dr A.A. Miller of Ruskin, Florida, for drawing this to my attention.

291 Portrait by W. Small of Ruskin lying in state, 24 January 1900

291

John Ruskin just outlived the century of his birth. He lived for just twenty days into the twentieth century. Though much had passed him by in the last eleven years, he must have seen changes – even at Brantwood. He may just have seen a very occasional motor car passing the house.

Hardly a house in Coniston was free from influenza in January 1900. Though every precaution was taken at Brantwood, it was evident on the evening of 18 January that the efforts had been in vain. On the following day he appeared to be a little better, but about 10.30 on Saturday 20th his health collapsed and he became unconscious. By the end of the afternoon he was dead. The news was quick to travel. In Birmingham that evening, Whitehouse wrote in his diary 'The Master is dead. Know ye not that there is a Prince and a Great Man fallen this day in Israel'. Collingwood wrote 'How marble-calm and dear the face when I lifted the covering'.[278]

A grave was offered in Westminster Abbey, but he had said, 'If I die here, bury me at Coniston' and his wishes were respected. It was suggested that a cast should be made of his face and hand. But again his wishes were respected and this was not done. On the evening of the 22nd his coffin was brought downstairs to the study. The face was left exposed, framed by a laurel wreath sent by G.F. Watts from a tree in his own garden only cut before for Tennyson, Leighton and Burne-Jones. There were many other wreaths, including one from the village tailor, with its card, 'There was a man sent from God, and his name was John'.

The nation's press carried reports from Coniston. The *Graphic* sent its artist Arthur Cox to make a series of sketches of Brantwood and the funeral. It reported that

> The remains of Mr Ruskin were removed from Brantwood on the morning[279] before the funeral and arrived at Coniston Church shortly after twelve to lie in state there until two o'clock the next day, an hour before the time fixed for the funeral. The coffin having been placed at the foot of the chancel steps, a short service was held, conducted by the Rev. C. Chapman, the vicar. The Hymn 'Peace, perfect peace', was sung with much feeling, and was followed by silent prayer and the Lord's Prayer. The service concluded with the Dead March in 'Saul'. The coffin contained a glass panel, through which the face could be plainly seen. The features appeared little changed, and bore a serene and peaceful expression. During the afternoon a large number of people passed by the coffin.[280]

One of Cox's sketches was of Ruskin's face wreathed by Watts' laurels as the coffin lay in the church. This was re-drawn and reproduced in the *Graphic*.

A Memorial Service was held in Westminster Abbey at 1pm on the Thursday, the funeral following in Coniston at 3 o'clock.

At the memorial service in the abbey, the hymn 'Now the labourer's task is o'er' was sung. The anthem, for soloist and choir, was 'He giveth his beloved sleep'. The words were taken from Elizabeth Barrett Browning's poem 'The Sleep' and set to music by the abbey organist Sir J. Frederick Bridge in 1889 for the funeral of Robert Browning.

For the funeral at Coniston, Canon Rawnsley had written a 'Hymn in Loving Memory of John Ruskin': 'The prophets cease from out the land, The counsellors are gone ...' Mary Wakefield sang 'Evening and Morning' by Rev. Gregory Smith, set to music by Sir Herbert Oakley. The Introit, played on the harmonium, was 'But the Lord is mindful of his own', from Mendelssohn's 'St. Paul'. The funeral service was conducted by the Rev. Charles Chapman. The vicar of Hawkshead, the Rev. E. W. Oak, read the opening words of the service and the lesson was read by Canon Richmond representing the Bishop of Carlisle. Canon Rawnsley also took part in the service, which was followed by the Funeral Tea, held across the road from the church, at the Crown Hotel.

278 Collingwood, *The Life of John Ruskin*, p. 404.
279 Wednesday 24 January.
280 *The Graphic*, 3 Feb. 1900.

292 Portrait medallion by A.C. Lucchesi on the Friar's Crag Memorial, 1900

293 Portrait medallion probably cast from the original model for No. 292, by A.C. Lucchesi

John Ruskin first saw Derwentwater when he was five years old on a tour in the Lake District with his parents. He always remembered the view of it from Friar's Crag and described the visit in *Modern Painters*:

> The first thing which I remember, as an event in life, was being taken by my nurse to the brow of Friar's Crag on Derwentwater; the intense joy, mingled with awe, that I had in looking through the hollows in the mossy roots, over the crag into the dark lake, has ever associated itself more or less with all twining roots of trees ever since.

Canon Rawnsley was responsible for raising subscriptions for the erection of a memorial to Ruskin on Friar's Crag. He described[281] the monument as 'a simple monolithic block of Borrowdale stone, rough and unhewn as it came from the quarry. It is of the type of the standing stones of Galloway, which are the earliest Christian monuments of the Celtic people now extant. This form has been chosen as linking us here with that land across the Solway, whence Ruskin's fore-fathers came. Upon one side is incised a simple Chi-Rho, enclosed in a circle after the fashion of those early crosses'. Beneath the cross is a quotation from Ruskin's *Deucalion*. 'On the other side of the monolith, facing the lake and the scene which Ruskin once described to a friend of mine as 'one of the three most beautiful scenes in Europe', we have a medallion in bronze, the careful work of Signor Lucchesi, representing Ruskin not as an old man and invalid of later days, but as he was in his prime, at the time I knew him best, at Oxford, in the early seventies'. Above the portrait is incised 'John Ruskin'; below it appear the dates 'MDCCCXIX–MDCCCC', and the inscription 'The first thing that I remember as an event in life was being taken by my nurse to the Brow of Friar's Crag, Derwentwater'. The lettering was designed and drawn by W.G. Collingwood and cut by the nephew of Mr Bromley, the stone cutter who selected the block.

The memorial was unveiled by Mrs Severn on a wild day, 6 October 1900. It was erected with the permission of the Lord of the Manor, and was vested in the National Trust, so becoming the Trust's first property in the Lake District. In 1922 Friar's Crag itself was bought by subscription and presented to the Trust as the Rawnsley Memorial.[282]

292

The profile portrait of Ruskin is closely based on the photograph by Elliott and Fry of 1867 (No. 86) though it shows the left side of his face. The profile is circled by a 'Crown of Wild Olive' with Ruskin's motto, 'To-day' at the top.

Bronzed plaster casts were made. One was lent to the 1900 Ruskin exhibition at Coniston and subsequently given to the Museum there by Canon Rawnsley. This cast was also exhibited in the 1919 Centenary Exhibition. Another, formerly owned by Rawnsley, came from Allan Bank to Brantwood after the death of his widow. A third used to hang in the vestibule outside the Senior Common Room at Corpus Christi College, Oxford, of which Ruskin was a Fellow.

281 In his speech at the unveiling ceremony. This and Joan Severn's speech are printed in Rawnsley, *Ruskin and the English Lakes*, pp. 209-18.

282 The National Trust had been founded in 1895 by Octavia Hill, Canon Rawnsley and Sir Robert Hunter, as a direct result of Ruskin's teaching.

Lucchesi also made a number of small bronze replicas (No. 293) of the medallion. These were probably cast from his original model for the memorial. There is the following correspondence in the Coniston Museum Archive between Andrea Lucchesi and the Curator, Herbert Bowness, relating to these.

> *7 September 1901* Canon Rawnsley tells me you have kindly offered to exhibit and take orders for my little bronze medallion of John Ruskin. Will you please let me know if I am to send you a sample.
>
> *12 September 1901* I am sending by same post a copy of my medallion of John Ruskin for exhibition in your museum.
>
> *1 July 1903* Will you kindly send on to me the little Ruskin medallions that you have of mine as I am in want of them.
>
> *16 July 1903* I must apologise for not writing before as the medallion arrived safely some days ago & I thank you very much for sending it to me. I am now sending it back to you to favour me by placing it in the Ruskin Museum & letting it remain there permanently. Should anyone wish to buy one they might write to me as I have sold several lately at two guineas each & that must be the price in future.
>
> *27 July 1903* Will you kindly let me know on enclosed card if you received the medallion safely.

292 (detail)

Bowness had received the medallion safely. It is still in the Coniston Museum. There does not appear to be any record of how many he actually sold. One certainly was sold to Canon Rawnsley, and this copy subsequently came from Allan Bank into the Whitehouse Collection.

294 Portrait medallion by Farmer & Brindley in St Paul's Church, Herne Hill, 1901

It was appropriate that there should be a memorial to Ruskin in south London, where he lived for many years. Accordingly a memorial was placed in St Paul's Church, Herne Hill, and was unveiled at a service in the evening of 8 February 1901. Among those present at the ceremony were the Bishop of Southwark, the Manor and Councillors of Camberwell, Alexander Wedderburn (one of Ruskin's literary trustees), and many others. Speaking after he had unveiled the memorial,[283] Holman Hunt, the last surviving member of the Pre-Raphaelite Brotherhood, spoke of himself as one left alone after a great conflict of certain definite principles. Ruskin, Hunt said, had ever tried to spread the spirit of reverence. He had endeared himself by his private character, a man not only to be admired but loved. The effect of *Modern Painters* was electrical; materialistic movements in art were transitory. Ruskin showed that art must have soul and mind. A memorial address was given by Professor A.C. Beeching.[284]

The monument was designed in the Venetian Byzantine style by W. Brindley and the work was carried out by the firm of Farmer and Brindley.

283 Hunt placed a posy of red, white and violet flowers bound with a broad white ribbon on the memorial, where it remained, 'though faded, for quite a long time'..

284 Beeching's address is printed in *St George* IV, pp. 275-80.

Arthur Severn gave some hints for the portrait medallion and Sir William Richmond also saw the drawings and made some useful suggestions.

The official history of the church describes the monument, which incorporates most of the important marbles used in St Mark's in Venice.

> It contains a portrait medallion of Ruskin sculptured in the Greek statuary of Pentelicus, on either side of which are panels in rose Giallo Antico, the whole under a canopy of white alabaster supported by columns of Verde Antico from Thessaly, with carved capitals copied for those in the apse of the Duomo of Murano. Between these columns is an inscription panel of Rosso Antico, of Laconia, with letters in white enamel,[285] and under this is a frieze of antique Cipollino marble, and the whole being carried by a corbel carved with a Greek acanthus bossed in the centre to contain a circular plaque of Egyptian red porphyry, the same material as the grand columns on either side of the central portal of St Mark's. The Cipollino marble is that used there for 'incrustation' of the walls and great piers of St Mark's, the quarries of which are at Carystos, in Greece.

The whole goes together to make what surely must be the most inappropriate Ruskin memorial imaginable.

294

295 Portrait medallion in Westminster Abbey, by Edward Onslow Ford (1852–1901), 1901

296 Portrait medallion based on No. 295, by Alan Turvey, 1996

In February 1900 a notice appeared in the national press saying that Mrs Severn had suggested to the Dean Of Westminster that a 'mural tablet in Westminster Abbey, would be a fitting and grateful tribute to Ruskin'.

On 10 April an announcement appeared in the *Daily News* to the effect that the Dean had given his 'hearty consent' to the proposed memorial. A committee was formed consisting of the Earl of Carlisle, Sir Edward Poynter P.R.A., C.E. Norton, the Dean of Christ Church, E.T. Cook, Lionel Cust (Director the National Portrait Gallery), Dr Dawtry Drewitt, Frederic Harrison, J.T. Micklethwaite (the abbey architect), Edmund Oldfield, Arthur Severn,[286] Mrs A. Murray Smith and Alexander Wedderburn.

Various proposals were made for a site in the abbey. Writing on 28 April to E.T. Cook, the secretary of the committee, Frederic Harrison[287] said

> I will attend the meeting re Ruskin on the 4th. I have been inspecting sites in the abbey and feel great difficulty. The queer corner by the Argyll Mausoleum is intolerable. There would be room

285 The long inscription, recording Ruskin's life and his connection with the parish, may be found in *Works* XXV, p. xlix

286 Arthur Severn has left some amusing anecdotes of the meetings which were held in Lionel Cust's room at the National Portrait Gallery which particularly relate to the discussion about whether or not Ruskin should be depicted with a beard. See Dearden, *The Professor*, pp. 135-36.

287 For years Harrison had been urging that an extension to the abbey should be built to house memorials, which as a Positivist he believed to be important reminders of Humanity. In a letter to *The Times* on 30 August 1900 he defended the Memorial Committee's work and pressed his case for a national place of burial since the abbey was getting crowded. I am indebted to Professor M.S. Vogeler for this information.

295

for a bust against the pillar besides Longfellow, and Ruskin is worth 3 Longfellows. I incline to the dark arch near Wordsworth. All the sites are dark. And I almost come round to the idea of an architectural niche – perhaps copied from one of his favourite pieces, with an inscription and low relief.[288]

Eventually a site was selected in the South Transept, above the bust of Sir Walter Scott, and, in opposition to Harrison's suggestion, in the queer corner by the intolerable Argyll Mausoleum. The true disciples of Ruskin's teaching – he described the abbey monuments as ignoble incoherent fillings of the aisles – must have considered it the final insult that the memorial is almost tucked away behind the Duke of Argyll.

Edward Onslow Ford was asked if he would execute the memorial. Replying to E.T. Cook, he wrote

> *Paris, 24 June 1900.* I am much obliged for your letter and I shall be very pleased to accept the commission to execute the memorial to Ruskin for Westminster Abbey, but I very much fear my work here will not allow me to leave for London before Thursday and if you could possibly arrange for the meeting to take place on Friday or Saturday I can promise either day. [Discussion ensued regarding the form and cost of the memorial.] In reply to the question put the other day, I would be very glad if the question of the beard in the medallion of Ruskin might be left open until I have had an opportunity of trying the effect. The price will be about two hundred and fifty pounds.

Cook replied on 16 July accepting these suggestions and the price and asking for the design to be submitted to the committee before work commenced. A leaflet was printed and distributed stating what had been done by the committee. It announced that £500 to £600 would probably be needed and proposed that the amount should be raised privately among Ruskin's friends first, without issuing a general appeal.

The proposal did not meet with universal approval. On 8 August Lady Burne-Jones, one of Ruskin's oldest friends, wrote to the committee:

> It is with regret that I am obliged to answer with a direct negative to the appeal I have received from you to join in the project for placing in Westminster Abbey a memorial to one of England's greatest men and most faithful teachers – but personal regard for members of your committee would be no excuse for hesitation. The reason of my refusal is that, to me, it is clearly a scheme that Ruskin would have condemned, as a continuation of the system which has already defaced the incomparable walls of the Abbey with modern incongruities. That this special memorial should be a good work of art does not seem to me to make it more allowable, for its mere presence would sanction every monument that has been or may hereafter be, according to the caprice of the moment, placed in this majestic relic of Time. It would be contrary to all I have gathered from the teaching of John Ruskin and William Morris, or to the strong influence of my husband if I helped in any scheme that would do this. I will venture to ask you in Ruskin's own name, Gentlemen, not to accept the responsibility'.

Sixteen days later there was a paragraph in the *Daily News* saying that Octavia Hill had written urging reconsideration of the scheme. 'To place anything in Westminster Abbey to the memory of one whose whole teaching was against modern tampering with ancient buildings seems to be a strange anomaly'. She advocated the preservation of some ancient building or the saving of some place of natural beauty as being more appropriate. 'Surely, the continuance of the work of a friend and teacher is better than a monument'.

288 The quoted correspondence relating to the Memorial is in the Whitehouse Collection, RF L 66.

But undeterred by these views the committee went ahead with its plans and on 28 November 1901 Ford wrote to Cook: 'The Ruskin memorial is finished and can be fixed at any time, if you or any other members of the committee would like to see it here before I send it to the Abbey I shall be pleased to see you. My fee, two hundred and fifty guineas, is now due'.

At about the same time that Ford accepted the commission for the medallion he was attacked by a dangerous form of heart disease. He was in precarious health for about a year, and within a month of writing to tell Cook the medallion was finished, he died from pneumonia. At the beginning of 1902 a notice was sent to subscribers announcing that the work was completed and was to be unveiled by Mrs Severn on Saturday, 8 February, the anniversary of Ruskin's birth. There was to be no ceremony but subscribers were invited to attend. The notice also presented the balance sheet and announced 'As the funds in hand admitted of it, the Committee decided to have the Memorial photographed before it left the artist's studio, and to send a copy to each subscriber.

Balance Sheet

Subscriptions:	£504	11s
Memorial	£263	10s
Abbey fee	201	1s
Cost of fixing	5	

The portrait shows Ruskin's head and shoulders, the head in profile looking to the right. The whole is based on the Elliott and Fry photograph taken in 1867 (No. 86). The border to the medallion is formed of a wreath of olive leaves with the dates 1819 and 1900 set at the top and bottom. The name IOHN RVSKIN is cut in cameo on either side of the head.

At least one cast was made from the medallion, which Mrs Onslow Ford lent to the Ruskin exhibition at Manchester in 1904. Collingwood, who

296

surely must have know the details of Ruskin's face better than most people, was not happy with the likeness on the medallion. When he saw the cast at Manchester he wrote in his catalogue

> R's eyes were deep set – these are weak & shallow – his brows particularly square – not formless; the forehead here is low & bulging at top – R's merely went up into his hair. The nostril was large & septum of nose deep – quite lost here. But the worst point is the mouth, which has no faintest resemblance to nature. It is a great pity Ruskin is recorded in Westminster Abbey by a head which is not even a caricature of him.

It is interesting to note that after Ford's death, a memorial obelisk was set up to him in St John's Wood, bearing his portrait in profile by Lucchesi, the sculptor of the Friar's Crag Ruskin Memorial.

No. 296 is Alan Turvey's copy in clay and mixed media of Ford's original, based on the subscribers' photograph.

297 Bust by Isaac Broome, 1901

Soon after Isaac Broome had painted his portrait of Ruskin (No. 290), he made the present bust in order to try to create an interest in the arts and crafts in Ruskin, Tennessee. He probably used one of the 1880s Barraud photographs as his model – possibly the one on which he had based his portrait. Like the portrait, the bust is now lost, but it is reproduced here from Broome's book, *The last days of the Ruskin Co-operative Association*.

297

298 Bust by Henry Charles Fehr (1867–1940), 1901

298

298

Reference has been made above (Nos. 37–38, 40) to Ruskin's involvement with the Working Men's College in Red Lion Square and to his local Camberwell Working Men's Institute. Growing from the latter was the South London Working Men's College. This was begun in 1868, appropriately by William Rossiter who himself had attended classes at Red Lion Square. The South London Art Gallery in Peckham Road, S.E.5 grew from the South London Working Men's College. That was established by Rossiter in 1891. The adjoining Camberwell School of Art opened five years later.

In 1902 one of the rooms of the South London Art Gallery was named the Ruskin Gallery. It was dedicated to Ruskin's memory by J. Passmore Edwards, the Gallery's benefactor. Passmore Edwards had also commissioned, and presented to the Gallery, the present marble bust of Ruskin by Henry Fehr. The plinth bears a small brass plate lettered 'John Ruskin 1819–1900. Presented by J. Passmore Edwards'.

Fehr had exhibited his 'Rescue of Andromeda' at the Royal Academy in 1893. He was encouraged by Lord Leighton to have it cast in bronze and it was subsequently bought for the nation through the Chantry Bequest. It now stands outside the Tate Gallery. Two other examples of his statuary were erected in 1903 in City Square, Leeds.

299 Relief plaque by Julia Bracken, 1901

Eileen Boris[289] has described the extensive influence of Ruskin and Morris on craftsmanship in America at the turn of the century and after. The Industrial Art League was incorporated in 1899. Associated with the League was the Bohemia Guild in Chicago, a prominent member of which was the sculptor Julia Bracken. The Guild ran a School of Industrial Art and Handicraft, and beneath plaques carved by Bracken of Carlyle, Ruskin and Morris, it developed into a gathering place for those individuals dedicated to 'the great industrial prophets'.

Incised into the background of the Ruskin plaque, the portrait on which is based on the Hollyer 'Datur hora quieti' photograph (No. 261), are the works 'Life without Labor is guilt. Labor without art is brutality.'[290]

299

289 Eileen Boris, *Art and Labor. Ruskin, Morris and the Craftsman Ideal in America* (Philadelphia: Temple University Press, 1986).

290 Based on Ruskin's words in the third 1870 Oxford lecture, 'The Relation of Art to Morals' (*Works* XX, p. 93), 'Life without industry is guilt and industry without art is brutality.'.

Caricatures by Max Beerbohm, 1904–36

300 Rossetti's Garden, c.1904

304 Rossetti introduces Ruskin to Fanny Cornforth, 1916

308 'Shades of Rossetti, Ruskin, Swinburne, Pater and Whistler', c.1931

309 'If they were flourishing in this our day', 1936

300

308

Ruskin is included in at least four of Max Beerbohm's caricatures. In the earliest, No. 300, he stands top hat in hand in the right corner of Rossetti's garden at 16 Cheyne Walk watching with amazement while Rossetti sketches Fanny Cornforth, Burne-Jones shows a flower to a kangaroo, and William Morris reads aloud to no one in particular, watched by Holman Hunt and a pelican. Others in the caricature are Swinburne, Whistler, Watts-Dunton, Meredith and Hall Caine.

In the next Max caricature (No. 304) drawn in 1916, Rossetti introduces Ruskin to Fanny Cornforth while Elizabeth Siddall watches from her portrait on the wall.

Ruskin is the central of the five figures in No. 308, 'wondering that so much space has been devoted to this other later Romantic – and whether even he is the "Last" one'. The 'later Romantic' is W.B. Yeats and the caricature was possibly inspired by Yeats's poem 'Coole Park and Ballylee, 1931'. The last verse begins

> We were the last romantics – chose for them
> Traditional sanctity and loveliness.

Max's last Ruskin caricature, No. 309, appeared in the *Manchester Guardian* on 13 March 1936. Captioned 'If they were flourishing in this our day' the caricature shows a group of Victorians – Gladstone, Tennyson, Carlyle, Whistler, Rossetti, Swinburne and others – clad in modern dress and shorn of their hirsute decoration. Ruskin looks a sorry figure with his ill-fitting suit and vacant expression.

304

309

301 Relief Panel incorporating the figure of Ruskin, by Herbert Hampton, 1907

301

The monument to Queen Victoria in Dalton Square, Lancaster, is an impressive piece. The 12 feet high bronze figure of the Queen stands on a granite pedestal supported by bronze lions at its corners. In turn this stands on a base of Furness limestone, on the four sides of which are bronze panels of life-sized figures of eminent Victorians. The whole memorial stands 36' 7" high and was the work of the sculptor Herbert Hampton.

Lord Ashton, who had property and businesses in Lancaster, had offered the memorial to the town in February 1901. It was completed and set in position in 1907; at the same time the surrounding Dalton Square was 'improved'. The total cost of £14,000 was paid by Lord Ashton. Meanwhile, Lord Ashton was also defraying the cost – £155,000 – of the new Town Hall which was being built on one side of the square, and which was opened in December 1909.

The bronze panel on the third side of the memorial includes the figure of Prince Albert, who accompanied the Queen to Lancaster in 1851. He is flanked by twelve of his contemporaries who were leading figures in the Arts. They include Sir Henry Irving, Lord Tennyson, Sir Arthur Sullivan, Lord Leighton and G.F. Watts. Ruskin stands directly behind Prince Albert's chair and is flanked by Turner and, ironically, Millais.

302 Imaginative portrait of Ruskin as Mark Alston, by E.C. Gillespy, 1908

Catherine Morley, in her important work on Ruskin and his Guild of St George[291] explains how one would-be Companion of the Guild was Jessica Cavendish Bentinck. She had married Sir Tatton Sykes, Bt., in 1874 and had commissioned the Bunney painting of St. Mark's (No. 134B) in the same year. Her baby son Mark (to become the sixth baronet) was born in 1879 and soon afterwards both mother and son were baptised as Catholics. Twenty years later she obtained a judicial separation from her husband.

Jessica Sykes had supported the Guild, but for some reason she never became a Companion. She wrote the story of her connection with the Guild and Ruskin in a novel, *Mark Alston* (1908), by C.A.J. Sykes. In her book, Mark Alston, art critic and social and economic theorist, is clearly intended for Ruskin, while the author appears as Portia Bulstrode. Alston and Bulstrode originally met in the house of Rawdon Brown in Venice.

In the novel, Jessica Sykes describes a meeting of the League of St Michael (obviously the Guild of St George) at Alston's house. (The Guild of St George never actually met at Brantwood.)

The book contains an illustration by E.C. Gillespy of the meeting of the League which shows Alston (Ruskin) with a group of people. Morley suggests that Alston is in conversation with Oscar Wilde, while the figure with folded arms to the left could be James Reddie Anderson and the second from the right could be Burne-Jones.

The illustration is of course purely notional and the figure of Mark Alston bears little resemblance to Ruskin.

302

291 Catherine W. Morley, *John Ruskin: Late Work 1870–1890* (New York: Garland Publishing, 1984), pp. 223-25.

303 c.1910 John Ruskin, head and shoulders, based on an earlier photograph, by Frank Reginald Dickinson (1874–1961)

310 1946 John Ruskin, incorporated into a re-working of Raphael's 'Death of Ananias', by Frank R. Dickinson

303

Frank Dickinson was an artist, designer, craftsman and commercial draughtsman who was imbued with the artistic and social ideals of the Arts and Crafts Movement. As a young man Dickinson was drawn to Carshalton in Surrey by Ruskin's praise of the area. He managed to buy a plot of land, and began to draw plans for his ideal house, as well as beginning to make the furniture for his home. In October 1902, with the help of one of his brothers and a labourer, Dickinson began to work on the house. He hired a bricklayer and within three months the main structure was finished. From February 1903 Dickinson and his fiancée worked on the interior and by the time of their marriage on 28 March 1904 they were able to move into the house, Little Holland House, 40 Beeches Avenue, Carshalton.

Dickinson, who had left school at thirteen, was employed as shop boy for an organ builder who encouraged him to attend art classes. His drawing master introduced him to the work and teaching of Morris, Carlyle and Ruskin. Later, when building and decorating his house, Dickinson carved a portrait of Ruskin, based on a photograph, painted it, and set it into the panelled dado of his living room (No. 303). Beneath the image appears the quotation[292] in which Ruskin explained the conditions on which the Guild of St George would hold land:

> We will try to make some small piece of English ground beautiful peaceful & fruitful. We will have no steam-engines upon it & no railroads. We will have no untended or unthought of creatures on it, none wretched but the sick, none idle but the dead. We will have no liberty upon it; but instant obedience to known law & appointed person; no equality upon it; but recognition of every betterness that we can find & reprobation of every worseness.

Dickinson's attraction to Ruskin continued unabated and he was to incorporate the figure of Ruskin into a late painting. This was his 1946 re-working of Raphael's 'Death of Ananias' in a style reminiscent of Stanley Spencer. In his unpublished autobiography Dickinson explained that his painting 'was first inspired by Raphael's cartoon of the same subject which I used to study at the South Kensington Art Museum, which was designed with several others for tapestries which now furnish the Vatican in Rome'. The painting illustrates the story of Ananias which is told in *Acts* V. The new converts agreed to share everything equally, but Ananias sold some land and kept back some of the proceeds. When challenged by Peter and John he was told he had not only cheated his fellows, but had lied to God – and he 'fell down and gave up the ghost'.

In his re-working of the original Raphael, Dickinson has introduced some of the great historical figures who had advocated some of these same

292 *Fors Clavigera* Letter 5, May 1871; *Works* XXXVII, p. 96.

310

principles – Plato, Sir Thomas More, Ruskin, Morris, Shaw, Marx, Lenin, and others. In the foreground Dickinson introduces portraits of his family and himself. Not surprisingly Dickinson was a Companion of the Guild of St George, and Ruskin appears in the painting, to the right side of the dias, receiving a donation from a female figure, perhaps intended as a gift to the Guild.

The painting, in its hand-made frame, was accepted for the Royal Academy's 1946 exhibition, but much to Dickinson's disappointment, it was never hung.

305 Bust by Barbara Crystal Collingwood, 1919, Study

306 Bust by Barbara Crystal Collingwood, 1919, Large version

Another posthumous sculpture of Ruskin was made in 1919, the centenary of his birth, by Barbara Collingwood. The sculptor, later Mrs Oscar Gnosspelius, was the daughter of W.G. Collingwood and a member of a very talented family. Miss Collingwood had, of course, seen Ruskin on many occasions, and she based her likeness on memory and photographs.

Ruskin is depicted in old age, with long flowing hair and beard. His deep penetrating eyes look straight ahead from under their bushy brows. Like her father, the sculptor has portrayed the teacher rather than the old man of the late Severn portraits. The bust was modelled at Lanehead.

It was Miss Collingwood's intention that the finished work should be a large bust. No. 305 is the 11 inches high study for the finished bust. This study was No. 430 in the Ruskin Centenary Exhibition. Plaster casts were made from it for Miss Collingwood, but her work book, which I have examined through the kindness of her daughter Miss Jane Gnosspelius, does not record how many. Miss Gnosspelius suggests that it was probably 12 or 18, but I am inclined to the former number. The work book records eight casts sold in 1919 at two guineas each. They were bought by Mrs Holt (2), Mrs G. Holt, Mrs Severn, Mrs Puncheon, Canon Rawnsley, Mr Marsden and Mrs Jemson. The cast

305

306

bought by Mrs Severn was lot 104 in the Brantwood sale and was bought for 22 s. for the Whitehouse Collection. Canon Rawnsley's copy is now in the Armitt Library, Grasmere. In the mid 1950s, when I was allowed to examine the contents of Lanehead, I found three more casts (one broken), and the 'study' in the cellar. Miss Gnosspelius gave one of these casts to Brantwood. At the same time she gave the study, No. 305, which is modelled in plaster and has a bronze finish, to me for my own collection.

The larger bust (No. 306) was exhibited by the artist at the 1919 exhibition at Coniston and must have been bought by the Coniston Museum during the course of, or immediately after, the exhibition because it appears in the catalogue of the Centenary Exhibition at the Royal Academy as being lent by the Museum. The price paid for the bust was ten guineas. It is still in the Museum, with Barbara Collingwood's companion study of her father.

307 Portrait medallion by Michel de Tarnowski (b.1870), 1925

Ruskin first visited Chamouni (as he always spelled it) in 1833. He wrote of it then, when he was fourteen: 'There is not another scene like Chamouni in all Switzerland'. He returned there very often and throughout his life it remained one of his favourite places in Europe. He planned to live near Chamouni at one time, and he made many drawings of the mountains and even individual rocks there, which he loved. 'Please give my love to the big old stone under the Breven, a quarter of a mile above the village, unless they've blasted it up for hotels', he wrote to a friend in 1879.

When in the 1920s it was decided to make a memorial to Ruskin at Chamouni, this stone was chosen as the site. Michel de Tarnowski, a sculptor born in Nice in 1870, was commissioned to sculpt a bronze portrait medallion (the likeness based on a photograph) which was set onto the stone, now known as the 'Pierre à Ruskin'.

Paul Payot, one-time mayor of Chamouni, was the moving force behind the plan, and in his address[293] at the unveiling of the memorial on 6 September 1925 he outlined Ruskin's association with the district and his descriptions of it. To add an international character to the ceremony, which was attended by a number of English visitors, the unveiling ceremony was performed by Ignace H.

307

Figure 18

293 The speech is printed in P. Payot *Ruskin and the English at Chamonix*, (Bonneville: Plancher, 1938), pp. 5-7.

Paderewski, the concert pianist and later President of Poland. Paderewski outlined Ruskin's life and work and told of his desire to reach the humblest people so that they could see the beauties of Art and Architecture.[294] The medallion is inscribed:

John Ruskin. Ce monument offert par les admirateurs de Ruskin à la Ville de Chamonix a été inauguré le 19 7 1925 sous le presidence de M.Lavaivre, Maire assisté de M.Payot Recteur de l'Université et de M.H. de Noussanne.

The revival of interest

The first half of the twentieth century took little interest in Ruskin. J. Howard Whitehouse and a few other dedicated followers kept his name alive, but Ruskin was largely forgotten. The Brantwood dispersal sales in 1930–31, following the death of Arthur Severn, attracted a little publicity. Indignation was registered in 1933 when R.H. Wilenski's *John Ruskin* was published, and again in 1947 on the publication of Admiral James's *Order of Release*. But it was not until the mid-1950s that there was a resurgence of interest. This lack of interest is reflected in the catalogue of portraits and caricatures. As already discussed, barely a handful of publications appeared until the early 1960s. Helen Viljoen's forty years of research had resulted in her *Ruskin's Scottish Heritage* (1956). Van Burd had begun to publish a series of important articles. The Oxford edition of the *Diaries* had appeared between 1956 and 1959. John Bradley's edition of *Ruskin's Letters from Venice* appeared in 1955. Modern Ruskin scholarship had begun, and with it came a new phase in Ruskin portraiture.

Some, like Richard Butterworth's little bust (No. 312) and Phyllis Arnold's silhouette (No. 313) were made with the intention of duplicating them for sale, principally at Brantwood which, by now, was beginning to attract more visitors. A mould was to be made from the little bust (No. 312) and casts were to be made in laminated resin and Coniston stone dust. The bust was based on the Uhlrich engraving (No. 146) and the Lucchesi (No. 292–93) and Ford (No. 295) medallions – but the mould was never made and the scheme died.

Phyllis Arnold, a professional silhouettist of Bangor, N. Ireland, drew a number of silhouettes of Ruskin (No. 313) around 1972. The likeness was based on the Lucchesi bronze and they were framed in black and gold-leaf box frames, 6" x 5" with a black oval mount (opening 4" x 3"). The framed silhouettes sold at £4.95, but I have no record of how many were made. I only know of my own and Dyke Benjamin's, which are both slightly different.

311

A number of caricatures drawn in the 1960s to 1980s were commissioned to accompany newspaper reviews or articles (for example No. 318 illustrated Diane Johnson's review of Van Burd's *John Ruskin and Rose La Touche* in 1980). Three of David

294 Details from a lecture by Paderewski's secretary, Miss Libke, in H.W. Witmer (ed.), *The Ruskin Art Club: Twelve More Years in Retrospect* (Los Angeles: Ruskin Art Club, 1970), p. 99.

P.Arnold.
John Ruskin
1819-1900

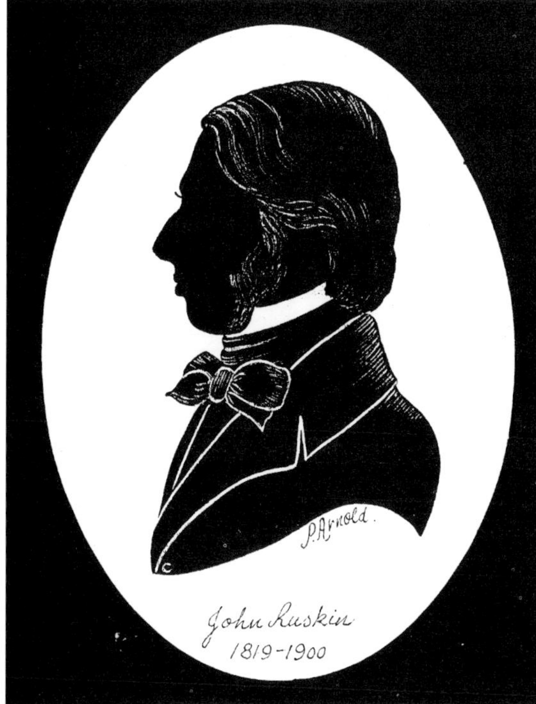

313

Levine's drawings were published in the *New York Review of Books*, a fourth is in the Ashmolean's collection (No. 319). Levine, son of a New York garment manufacturer, had begun drawing cartoons by the age of ten in 1936. He was always concerned with the quality and correctness of draughtsmanship and had a sure command of line.

David E. Smith, an art historian as well as a caricaturist, who is interested in Ruskin's work and ideas, has produced two drawings. No. 320 shows

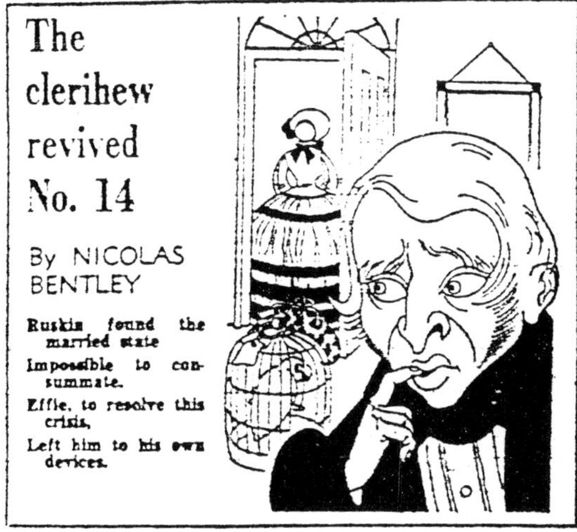

The clerihew revived No. 14
By NICOLAS BENTLEY
Ruskin found the married state
Impossible to consummate.
Effie, to resolve this crisis,
Left him to his own devices.

315

TRUTH

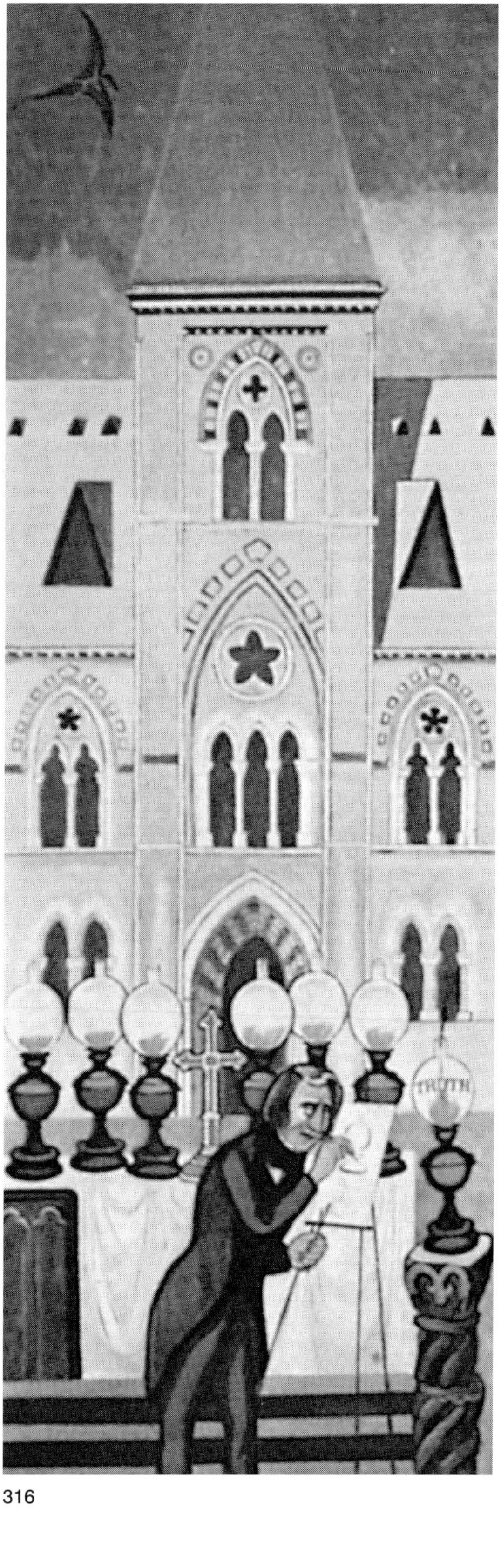

316

317

318

Ruskin in the pose of lecturer; it was drawn to illustrate David Piper's review of Tim Hilton's *John Ruskin: The early years* (1985), in the *Guardian*. His other caricature, (No. 321), was published in Edward Abelson's book *Misalliance* (1989). Smith describes the *Misalliance* caricature as 'not one of my best';[295] it shows Ruskin admiring the Glenfinlas portrait (No. 26) while at his side, Millais embraces Effie.

319

The Bromley caricature (No. 322) is a robotic affair showing Ruskin (is it *really* Ruskin?) surrounded by bulky volumes and seated at a computer keyboard. It accompanied Martin Mulligan's article in the *Financial Times* which partly concerned the then-proposed CD-ROM of the Ruskin *Library Edition* and the translation of the Ruskin archive into electronic analogues.

Chris Orr's series of etchings (No. 314) was begun in 1972, but as the title page explains, 'This is a work of fiction and in no way purports to accurately illustrate the life or times of John Ruskin. The real subject is perhaps myself'.

In May 1974 Ruskin appeared in 'The Clerihew revived, No. 14' by Nicolas Bentley (No. 315).

Ruskin found the married state
Impossible to consummate.
Effie, to resolve this crisis,
Left him to his own devices.

295 In a letter to myself, 18 June 1997.

320

The clerihew was accompanied by a caricature.

In the same year Edward Bawden (1903–89) included Ruskin in his 40 feet long mural in Blackwell's bookshop in Oxford's Broad Street, which depicts the university through the centuries. Ruskin is shown standing in front of the Oxford Museum; he is flanked by seven lamps – six are on an altar behind him while the seventh, labelled 'Truth' stands on a pedestal to be drawn by him (No. 316).

Peter Cross's caricature of Ruskin (No. 323) was reproduced as the frontispiece to *The Illustrators. The British Art of Illustration 1780-1966*, the catalogue for Chris Beetles's 1996 exhibition. The original belongs to his son Alexander, a Tottenham

321

322

Hotspurs enthusiast. It shows Ruskin dressed in 'Spurs 'strip' clutching a football labelled 'Præterita'. The stripes on the shirt are labelled 'The Anatomy of Mountains', and he wears two badges, that of 'Chris Beetles Ltd' and 'Leaf Monuments F.C.'

In sculpting her bust of Ruskin (No. 324) Mary Catterall followed Downey's photograph of Ruskin seated in Rossetti's chair (No. 70), but added to it what she understood of Ruskin's character. The bust, which can be cast in an edition of up to ten, was made to be included in the sculptor's 1998 summer exhibition in Holy Trinity Church, Sloane Street. Designed by J.D. Sedding, and with its east window designed by Burne-Jones and made by Morris & Co., the church is described as 'The Cathedral of the Arts and Crafts Movement'. Bishop Michael Marshall, Assistant Bishop in London, has created exhibition space at the west end of the church. When he invited Dr Catterall to exhibit in 1998 she thought it appropriate to include a study of Ruskin, together with one of William Morris, with her work.

324

Appropriately the latest in the long series of portrayals of Ruskin put him back into Venice and the world of the great Venetian artists. This series of drawings by Geoffrey Appleton (No. 325) illustrates a book by Michelle Lovric published in America in September 1999. *Carpaccio's Cat* is set in Venice during Ruskin's visit of 1876–77 when so much of his time was occupied by studying and copying Carpaccio's *St Ursula*. The story tells of Ruskin's Venetian adventures with a spectral cat. The author wrote[296] 'This is an illustrated book for adults: a sort of magical art-mystery tour'. One or two initial drawings were made for the book by Ian Andrews. (See plates 36 and 37.)

The most recent likeness of Ruskin which I have seen is that drawn in 1999 by Tullio Pericoli (No. 326), an artist working for *L'Indice dei Libri del Mese*. It was drawn to illustrate Donata Levi's review of the new translation into Italian of the five volumes of *Modern Painters*.

325/1

* * * *

Ruskin had told Spielmann[297] that he 'liked to be flattered, both by pen and pencil, so it can be done prettily and in good taste'. He had told him 'in a sweeping sort of way ... he was dissatisfied with all that had been done of him, and

296 Michelle Lovric to JSD, 9 February 1998.
297 *Spielmann II*, p. 123.

325/16

329

the truer and more candid they were, the less he cared for them.

In this amazingly varied range of over 330 portraits, photographs, busts and caricatures, drawn from life and after, over a period of one hundred and seventy-seven years, we are given a remarkable insight into the appearance of one of the greatest Victorians, and into how very many artists saw him. There must even be *something* here to the subject's liking!

326

330

Chapter V
Catalogue of Portraits

(Size is given in inches, height before width)

Principal abbreviations:

Spielmann I – M.H. Spielmann: 'The Portraits of John Ruskin I', *Magazine of Art*, January 1891, pp. 73-79

Spielmann II – M.H. Spielmann: 'The Portraits of John Ruskin – (concluded)' *Magazine of Art*, February 1891, pp. 121-26

Works Cat. – Catalogue of Portraits, *Works* XXXVIII, pp. 207-13

Dearden I – J.S. Dearden: 'Some Portraits of John Ruskin', *Apollo*, December 1960, pp. 190-95

Dearden II – J.S. Dearden: 'Further Portraits of John Ruskin', *Apollo*, June 1961, pp. 171-78

As modern Ruskin scholarship has developed, reproductions of Ruskin portraits have proliferated in the many books and articles which have appeared. Not all such reproductions are listed.

1 1822 **Portrait by James Northcote, R.A.** Life-sized, full length with dog; oil on canvas, 48½ x 39½.
REPRODUCED: *Spielmann I*, p. 73; Spielmann: *John Ruskin*, p. 19; *Bookman*, Oct. 1908, p. 18; *Works* XXXV, pl.ii; and elsewhere
EXHIBITED: Coniston 1919 (2); London 1919 (180); Albright Art Gallery, Buffalo, N.Y., 1950 (*Dramatics' Choice*, p. 49)
Works Cat.: 1
PROVENANCE: Commissioned by J.J. Ruskin; John Ruskin; Severn family; sold at Sotheby's 20 May 1931 (125); Vokins; Theodore Leavitt; sold in 1951 to H.B. Yotnakparian of New York; sold at Sotheby's 18 Nov. 1987 (57); *National Portrait Gallery*, (bought with grants from the National Heritage Memorial Fund and The National Art-Collections Fund, to go on permanent loan to *Brantwood*).

2 **Portrait by James Northcote.** Reduced copy of No. 1 by Arthur Severn or W.G. Collingwood; wash, 8 x 10; inscribed on reverse: John Ruskin aged 3½ (after Northcote) W.G. Collingwood, Lane Head, Coniston, Lancashire.
REPRODUCED: *Graphic* 27 Jan. 1900, p. 113; *Bookman*, March 1900, p. 169; Pengelly: *John Ruskin* (2nd ed. only), p. 17
Works Cat.: 1
PROVENANCE: Joan Severn; *Ruskin Museum, Coniston*

3 **Portrait by James Northcote.** Reduced copy of No. 1; watercolour, 15 x 12.
PROVENANCE: Bought at a sale in Kirkby Lonsdale about 1975 by *Mrs Bibby.*

4 c. 1822 **Silhouette by unknown artist**; full length, wearing a large hat, and with a dog. Black paper cut out and laid on white paper, 6⅞ x 6¼ (irregular). Inscribed by Joan Severn: Di Pa as a child, certified by himself. Further inscribed by F.J. Sharp: Portrait of John Ruskin. The above writing is in the hand of Mrs A. Severn; by F.J. Sharp on reverse of mount: Silhouette Portrait of John Ruskin. The inscription 'Di Pa' etc is in the writing of Mrs Arthur Severn

(Joan Ruskin Severn). This is the first known, portrait of Ruskin.
REPRODUCED: *Dearden II*, p. 171; Burd: *Ruskin Family Letters* 1973, I, pl. xiv; Spear: *Dreams of an English Eden*, 1894, p. 20.
EXHIBITED: Ruskin and his circle 1964 (26); Queens College, New York 1965 (IV, 1).
PROVENANCE: John Ruskin; Severn family; bought privately prior to 1931 Brantwood sale by T.H. Telford; F.J. Sharp; H.G. Viljoen; *Pierpont Morgan Library* (Acc. No. 1974.49 (Viljoen)).

5 1823 **Fancy portrait by James Northcote, R.A., 'The Sylvan Doctor' or 'The Infant Bacchus'**. Full length with satyr; oil on canvas, 50 x 40; signed and dated.
REPRODUCED: *Spielmann I*, 74, Spielmann: *John Ruskin*, p. 23; *Bookman*, Oct. 1908, p. 18
EXHIBITED: Coniston 1919 (3); London 1919 (94),
Works Cat.: 2
PROVENANCE: Bought by J.J. Ruskin; John Ruskin; Severn family sold at Sotheby's, 20 May 1931 (124); Parkin; *untraced*

6 **Fancy portrait by James Northcote. Reduced copy of No. 5 by Arthur Severn or W.G. Collingwood**; wash, 8 x 10; inscribed on reverse: The Thorn in the Foot.
REPRODUCED: *Bookman* March 1900, p. 171
PROVENANCE: Joan Severn; *Ruskin Museum, Coniston*

7 **Imaginative portrait of Ruskin sketching, as a small boy, by Arthur Severn**; watercolour, $5^{3}/_{4}$ x $9^{1}/_{2}$
REPRODUCED: Dearden (ed.), *Iteriad*, p. 32
EXHIBITED: John Ruskin e le Alpi 1990 (4)
PROVENANCE: Bought from B.F. Stevens & Brown, 25 Sept. 1933 by J.H. Whitehouse; *Whitehouse Collection* (RF 526)

8 1836 **Miniature by A.E. Chalon**; watercolour, $1^{3}/_{4}$ x $1^{1}/_{4}$, in leather case $2^{1}/_{2}$ x $2^{1}/_{4}$. Old label: Miniature by A.E. Chalon R.A., London 1836
PROVENANCE: Bought, perhaps in Manchester area about 1950, by G.W. Kippax; *Private collection*.

9 1841 **Sketch by Constantin Roesler Franz for No. 10**; 5 January; chalk.
PROVENANCE: *untraced*

10 1841 **Cameo by Constantin Roesler Franz**; head and shoulders looking left, cut in pink and white shell, enclosed in a leather case. 5 January
REPRODUCED: *Works* XXXV, pl. xiiia (engraved by H.S. Uhlrich); *Dearden I*, p. 191; Gere and Munn: *Artists' Jewellery*, p. 123
EXHIBITED: Coniston 1919 (225); London 1919 (15); Ruskin and his circle 1964 (27); Artists' Jewellery 1989 (166); Ruskin and Tuscany 1993 (1)
Works Cat.: 3
PROVENANCE: Commissioned by J.J. Ruskin; John Ruskin; Severn family; F.J. Sharp; *Whitehouse Collection* (RF 721)

11 1841 **Cameo by Constantin Roesler Franz**; a second version.
PROVENANCE: Commission by J.J. Ruskin; Mrs Thomas Hayes; by descent to Mrs Vandeleur (in 1960)

12 1841 **Cameo by Constantin Roesler Franz**; a third version.
PROVENANCE: Commission by J.J. Ruskin; probably given to a friend of the family; *untraced*

13 **Cameo, after No. 10, designed by Ryuzo Mikimoto and made by the Mikimoto Company**, c. 1930
Several bronze casts seem to have been made.
PROVENANCE: Commissioned by Ryuzo Mikimoto; Y. Mikimoto; *Mikimoto family*

14 c.1841 **Portrait by Thomas Richmond**. Three-quarter length, standing and holding gloves, hat and stick on stone bench beside him. Oil on canvas, 13¼ x 10¼
Two old labels on back of frame:
(1) John Ruskin purchased at Brighton in 1884
(2) Portrait of Ruskin by Thos. Richmond/Mr Warren [?]
EXHIBITED: Ruskin in love 1976 (9); Bembridge 1987 (1)
REPRODUCED: Dearden (ed.), *A Tour to the Lakes in Cumberland* 1990, frontis.
Works Cat.: 4
PROVENANCE: In Brighton 1884; William Ward (in 1912); Mrs van Buren Emmons; given in May 1967 to the Ruskin Galleries; *Whitehouse Collection* (RF 421)

15 1843 **Portrait by George Richmond, 'The Author of *Modern Painters*'**, Full-length, seated at a desk. Watercolour, 27½ x 17½
REPRODUCED: *Spielmann I*, p. 76; Spielmann: *John Ruskin*, p. 45; Collingwood: *Life and Work of John Ruskin* I, p. 108; *Works* III, frontis.; *Bookman* Oct. 1908, cover; Cook: *Life of John Ruskin* I, frontis.; Leon: *Ruskin, the great Victorian*, p. 74; Links (ed.), *Stones of Venice*, jacket; Dearden: *John Ruskin*, p. 2; and elsewhere
EXHIBITED: Royal Academy 1843 (1061); Coniston 1900 (75); Royal Watercolour Society 1901 (325); Fine Art Society 1907 (99); Coniston 1919 (44); London 1919 (70)
Works Cat.: 5 (where dated 1842)
PROVENANCE: J.J. Ruskin; John Ruskin; Severn family; sold Sotheby's 20 May 1931 (30); C.E. Goodspeed; *now believed to have been destroyed*.

16 c.1843 **Miniature by unknown artist**. Body-colour on ivory, 2⅛ x 1¾ (oval)
REPRODUCED: Hunt: *The Wider Sea. A Life of John Ruskin* 1982, pl.4c.
PROVENANCE: Pitt-Heath Collection; probably acquired by 10th Earl of Scarbrough; by descent to the present Earl of Scarbrough; *Guild of St George*.

17 1845 **Portrait with Auguste Gendron and ?Eugène-Paul Dieudonné, by Johann-Ludwig-Rudolph Durheim**. Three figures, heads and shoulders, Ruskin in centre. Oil on paper, laid onto wooden panel, 10 x 5½.
REPRODUCED: Clegg & Tucker: *Ruskin and Tuscany* 1993 (14)
PROVENANCE: Paul Lindt; bought by the Gottfried Keller Foundation in 1898 and deposited in the *Berner Kunstmuseum*.

18 c.1846 **Silhouette portrait**. Head and shoulders looking left. Cut out of black paper and pasted onto white card, 4½ x 3, features brushed in with gold ink; inscribed John Ruskin.
REPRODUCED: *Bulletin of the John Rylands Library*, Vol. 51, No. 2, Spring 1969, pl. II
EXHIBITED: John Ruskin e le Alpi 1990 (105); Ruskin and Tuscany 1993 (41)
PROVENANCE: Mrs Joan Hoare; *Whitehouse Collection* (RF 30)

19 1853 **Sketch of John and Effie Ruskin standing in a gondola, by John Everett Millais**; before summer. Pencil, 18½ x 12
REPRODUCED: *Apollo*, March 1968, p. 192
EXHIBITED: Louisville 1978, (51)
PROVENANCE: Sir Henry Acland; by descent to Sir William Acland; sold 1965 with aid of grant from Virtue-Tebbs Fund, to *Ashmolean Museum*

20 1853 **Portrait by John Everett Millais**, between 22 and 29 June. Head and shoulders; pencil on white paper with touches of brown on hair, eyebrows, eyes, tie and chin; signed with monogram and dated 1853, 13¼ x 10¼
REPRODUCED: *Works* XXXVI, pl. A; Evans: *John Ruskin*, frontis.; *Dearden I*, p. 191
EXHIBITED: Proust and his Times, Wildenstein 1955; British Portraits, Royal Academy 1956-57 (739); Ruskin and his circle 1964 (28); Ruskin a Verona 1966 (79); Central School of Arts and Crafts 1969 (1); Louisville 1978 (52); Brantwood 1979 (25); John Ruskin (Arts Council) 1983 (1); Maas Gallery 1991 (33); John Ruskin and Victorian Art, Japan 1993 (199); National

Portrait Gallery 1999, *Millais: Portraits* (14)
Works Cat.: 6
PROVENANCE: Given by the artist to Lady Trevelyan; Trevelyan family; sold at Christie's, 25 May 1951 (27); *Whitehouse Collection* (RF 356)

21 1853 **Crossing the border, by William Millais**; a sketch of the party from Wallington, *en route* for Scotland, 30 June.
REPRODUCED: J.G. Millais: *Life and Letters of Sir John Everett Millais* I, p. 195; Lutyens: *Millais and the Ruskins*, p. 53
PROVENANCE: Mrs George Hodgkinson (in 1899); *untraced*

22 1853 **Sheet of studies – John Ruskin and William Millais standing in the river at Glenfinlas, by John Everett Millais**, 9 July. Pen and brown ink, $7^{3}/_{8}$ x 9
REPRODUCED: Christie's Catalogue, 14 Nov. 1967, p. 39; Lutyens & Warner: *Rainy days at Brig o'Turk* 1983, p.19.
PROVENANCE: By descent to E.G. Millais; sold at Christie's, 14 Nov. 1967 (143) to Sawyer; Mrs Patrick Gibson; Agnew; *Bolton Museum*

23 1853 **Ascent of Ben Ledi, Ruskin in the distance, by John Everett Millais**, 10 July. Pen and brown ink, $7^{1}/_{4}$ x $9^{1}/_{8}$, signed with monogram, inscribed and dated 1853.
REPRODUCED: *Apollo*, April 1967, p. 247, Christie's *Catalogue*, 14 Nov. 1967; Lutyens & Warner: *Rainy Days at Brig o'Turk* 1983, p.64
PROVENANCE: by descent to E.G. Millais; sold at Christie's 14 Nov. 1967 (142, 650 gns.); Agnew; *Private collector*

24 1853 **A wet day's pastime; Ruskin and William Millais playing battledore, by John Everett Millais**, 25 July. Pen and brown ink, 10 x 8, signed with monogram, inscribed and dated 1853.
REPRODUCED: J.G. Millais: *Life and Letters of Sir John Everett Millais* I, p. 203 (where Ruskin is inaccurately identified as Sir Thomas Acland); Lutyens: *Millais and the Ruskins* 1967, p. 35; Lutyens & Warner: *Rainy Days at Brig o'Turk*, 1983, p. 39
PROVENANCE: W.E.F. Macmillan; presented in 1939 to *The Athenæum Club*

25 1853 **Sketch for the Glenfinlas portrait of John Ruskin, by John Everett Millais**, 28 July. Pencil on blue paper, $7^{1}/_{4}$ x 5. Inscribed on reverse by Henry Acland: The first sketch of J.E. Millais – Picture of John Ruskin . done in the bed of the stream at B of Turk. Thursday July 28th 1853
REPRODUCED: *Apollo*, April 1967, p. 251; Lutyens & Warner: *Rainy Days at Brig o'Turk* 1983, p. 9
EXHIBITED: National Portrait Gallery 1999, *Millais: Portraits* (24)
PROVENANCE: Sir Henry Acland; by descent to Sir William Acland; sold in 1965 with aid of grant from the Virtue -Tebbs Bequest Fund to *Ashmolean Museum*

26 1853 **Portrait of John Ruskin, standing by the stream at Glenfinlas, by John Everett Millais**, 28 July – autumn 1854. Oil on canvas, 31 x $26^{1}/_{4}$ (arched top), signed with monogram and dated 1854
REPRODUCED: *Magazine of Art*, 1891; *Works* XII, frontis; Spielmann: *John Ruskin*, p. 59; Wedmore: *Turner and Ruskin*, I, p. 1; *Bookman*, Oct. 1908, p. 23; Williams-Ellis: *Tragedy of John Ruskin*, p. 170; James: *Order of Release*, p. 244; *Sunday Express*, 18 Jan. 1948; *Illustrated London News*, 7 Feb. 1948; Quennell: *John Ruskin, a portrait of a prophet*, p. 65; Leon: *Ruskin, the great Victorian*, p. 184; Evans: *John Ruskin*, p. 193: Evans: *Lamp of Beauty*, frontis; *Dearden II*, p. 172: Lutyens: *Millais and the Ruskins*, frontis; Millais *Catalogue*, Royal Academy 1967, pl.17; *Apollo*, April 1867, p. 247; Lutyens & Warner: *Rainy Days at Brig o'Turk* 1983, p.9; Grieve: Ruskin and Millais at Glenfinlas, *Burlington* April 1996; and elsewhere
EXHIBITED: Fine Art Society 1884, Grosvenor Gallery 1886, *Millais* (12); Birmingham 1891 (231); Royal Academy 1898, *Millais* (55); Glasgow 1901 (327); Whitechapel 1901 (15); *British Art* (551); Birmingham 1947 (59); Royal Academy 1956-57, *British Portraits* (440);

Nottingham 1959 (47); Ruskin and his circle 1964 (29); Royal Academy 1967, *Millais* (420); The Pre-Raphaelites 1984 (56); 'Sir Geoffrey Agnew: Dealer and Connoisseur' Agnews 1988; National Portrait Gallery 1999, *Millais: Portraits* (23)
Works Cat.: 7
PROVENANCE: Commissioned by J.J. Ruskin, 1853. Bought 1854 £350; given by John Ruskin to Sir Henry Acland c.1871; by descent to Sir William Acland; sold at Christie's, 16 July 1965 (96, 24,000 gns.); Agnew; *Private collector*

27 **Statue, based on No. 26, by K. Kitaji**, 1950 or 1930. Plaster, 20" high, including base; signed on base, Kitaji 1950 [or 1930]
PROVENANCE: Commissioned by R. Mikimoto; *Mikimoto family*

28 **A Cat in frock coat, with hat and stick, standing at the side of Glen Finlas; 'Ruskin (Millais)' by Susan Herbert**, 1991. Body-colour, 15¼ x 13, signed on front and inscribed on reverse with title.
REPRODUCED: Herbert: *Diary of a Victorian Cat,* 1991, p. 63; Brunori & Crowley: *The Illustrators. The British Art of Illustration* 1780–1996, p. 252.
EXHIBITED: Chris Beetles Gallery 1996 (492)
PROVENANCE: *Chris Beetles*

29 1853 **Cruel Treatment of a Master to his Pupil, sketch of John and Effie Ruskin and J.E. Millais, by John Everett Millais**. Pen and brown ink, 7½ x 8¼, signed with monogram, inscribed and dated July 31st, 1853
REPRODUCED: Lutyens: *Millais and the Ruskins*, p. 146; Lutyens & Warner: *Rainy Days at Brig o'Turk* 1983, p.50
EXHIBITED: Millais, Southampton 1996 (88)
PROVENANCE: by descent to *Sir Geoffroy Millais*

30 1853 **Awey-ye goo, sketch of John Ruskin, John and William Millais and Effie, by John Everett Millais**. Pen and brown ink, 7¼ x 8¼ (irregular), signed with monogram, inscribed and dated July 31st 1853
REPRODUCED: J.G. Millais: *Life and Letters of Sir John Everett Millais* I, p. 218; Lutyens: *Millais and the Ruskins*, p. 211; Lutyens & Warner: *Rainy Days at Brig o'Turk* 1983, p.49
PROVENANCE: by descent to E.G. Millais; sold at Christie's, 14 Nov. 1967 (145, 320 gns.); Sawyer; *Private Collector*

31 1853 **Kirk. Effie and John Ruskin and J.E. Millais in church at Loch Achray**. Pen and brown ink, 7 x 9, signed with monogram, inscribed and dated July 31st 1853
REPRODUCED: Lutyens and Warner: *Rainy Days at Brig o'Turk* 1983, p.47
EXHIBITED: Millais, 1967 (303)
PROVENANCE: J.G. & G. Millais; sold at Christie's, 24 Feb. 1908 (90); Agnew; J.R. Holliday who bequeathed it in 1927 to *Tate Gallery*

32 1853 **Two Masters and their Pupils, sketch of Millais and Effie Ruskin, by John Everett Millais**, ?4 August. Pen and brown ink, 7¼ x 9¼, signed with monogram, inscribed and dated 1853. Top right hand corner, which once bore a sketch of Ruskin, cut away.
REPRODUCED: Christie's *Catalogue*, 14 Nov. 1967; *Apollo*, March 1968, p. 194; Lutyens & Warner: *Rainy Days at Brig o'Turk* 1983, p.53
PROVENANCE: by descent to E.G. Millais; sold Christie's 14 Nov. 1967 (144, 350 gns.); Baskett; Sir John Witt; his sale at Sotheby's, 19 Feb. 1987 (170); *untraced*

33 1853 **The Scottish Bog exercise, sketch of Ruskin, John Millais and a ghillie, by John Everett Millais**. Pen and brown ink, 6¾ x 4½, signed with monogram and inscribed.
REPRODUCED: Lutyens & Warner: *Rainy Days at Brig o'Turk* 1983, p.69
EXHIBITED: Millais 1967 (312); Millais, Southampton 1996 (90)
PROVENANCE: by descent to *Sir Geoffroy Millais*

34 1853 **Getting Mama up a Ben, sketch of Ruskin, Effie and others, by John Everett Millais**. Pen and brown ink, 7 x 4½, signed with monogram and inscribed.
REPRODUCED: Lutyens & Warner: *Rainy Days at Brig o'Turk* 1983, p.82
EXHIBITED: Millais 1967 (308)
PROVENANCE: by descent to *Sir Geoffroy Millais*

35 1854 **Portrait of John Ruskin, by John Everett Millais**, 17 January. Head and shoulders looking left. Pencil and some watercolour, 11 x 10, signed with monogram and dated 1854 Jany 17
REPRODUCED: Engraved (plate 14 x 8¾) probably by George Allen. Several proofs exist, but probably never published; *Ruskin's Backgrounds, Friendships*, exhibition catalogue, 1965, frontis; Lutyens: *Millais and the Ruskins*, p. 163; *New York Times* 22 May 1977, p. 29; G. Millais: *Sir John Everett Millais* 1979, p. 55; Hunt: *The Wider Sea* 1982, p1. 4d.
Works Cat.: 8
EXHIBITED: Fogg Art Museum 1909-10 (16); Queen's College Library, New York 1965 (V, 5), Pierpont Morgan Library 1977; National Portrait Gallery 1999, *Millais: Portraits* (28)
PROVENANCE: Drawn for J.J. Ruskin; John Ruskin; Joan Severn; F.J. Sharp; H.G. Viljoen; *Pierpont Morgan Library* (1974.49.3)

36 1856 **Caricature by Edward Coley Burne-Jones**, in letter to Cormell Price, January
PROVENANCE: *untraced*

37 1856 **Photograph, looking half right, watch-chain wrapped round jacket button, by William Jeffreys**.
REPRODUCED: Attwell: *Thoughts from Ruskin*; E.T. Cook: Ruskin and his books, *Strand Magazine* XXIV, No. 144, Dec. 1902, p. 710; *Works* XXXVI, frontis.; K. Clark: *Ruskin Today*, jacket; R. Shaw: *Relevance of Ruskin* 1988, frontis.
Works Cat.: 9

38 1856 **Photograph, facing camera, by William Jeffreys**
REPRODUCED: Llewelyn Davis: *Working Men's College*, 70; Trevelyan: *A Pre-Raphaelite Circle*, 96

39 c. 1856 **Portrait head and shoulders, full face, perhaps by Henry Swan**
PROVENANCE: Given by Henry Swan to Charles Green; sold by him in 1915 to Mr Winder; his gift to Charles Howarth; offered by Mrs Howarth to Graves Art Gallery, Sheffield, 1980; *untraced*

40 c. 1856? **Caricature of Ruskin leading a group of artists, by William J. Hodgson**. Pencil, 7 x 4 (irregular). Inscribed: 'J.R. and his followers. We all believe what our leader says; we account him infallible, every word that he says whether it be sense or nonsense has some deep and hidden meaning in it'; and in another hand, 'Drawn by Willie Hodgson'.
PROVENANCE: Arthur Mackmurdo; by descent to Elinor Pugh; given by her in the 1950s to *William Morris Gallery*

41 1857 **Portrait studies by George Richmond**, head and shoulders, and a separate study of head, for No. 43. Red and black chalk on pale blue paper, watermark Britannia, 12⅞ x 8⅛
PROVENANCE: Henry Yates Thompson; by descent to Sir Christopher Chancellor C.M.G.; Christie's 19 March 1985 (40); *Tom Lindsay*

42 1857 **Portrait study by George Richmond**, head and shoulders. Black chalk on grey paper over earlier drawing in red chalk, 7¾ x 6⅛
PROVENANCE: Henry Yates Thompson; by descent to Sir Christopher Chancellor C.M.G.; Christie's 19 March 1985 (40); *Tom Lindsay*

43 1857 **Portrait by George Richmond**, 24 February – 28 March. Head and shoulders, full face, head resting on hand. Coloured chalk, 22 x 17, signed and dated.
REPRODUCED: Engraving by F. Holl published by Smith Elder, 15 June 1858, 14 x 10¼; Ruskin: *Selections* 1861, frontis.; *Spielmann I*, p. 77, Spielmann: *John Ruskin*, p. 79

(reproduced photographically); *Works* XVI, frontis.; *Eclectic Magazine*, Vol. 69, 1867, p. 513
EXHIBITED: Royal Academy 1857 (737); Coniston 1919 (103); London 1919 (59)
Works Cat.: 13
PROVENANCE: Commissioned by J.J. Ruskin, February 1857 (£42); John Ruskin; Joan Severn; sold at Sotheby's, 20 May 1931 (29, £33); Stevens & Brown; C.E. Goodspeed; *Presumed destroyed in Goodspeed's fire*

44 ?1857 **Portrait by George Richmond**, head only, full face. Chalk, 17 x 14
REPRODUCED: *Works* XXXVI, pl. C; *Bookman*, Feb. 1919, 157; Whitehouse: *Ruskin Centenary Addresses*, frontis.; Whitehouse: *Ruskin and Brantwood*, p. 6; Whitehouse: *Ruskin the Painter*, frontis.; Whitehouse: *Vindication of Ruskin*, frontis.; Arts Council exhibition catalogue 1954, cover; *Dearden II*, p. 173
EXHIBITED: Coniston 1919 (103); Whitworth 1989 (1)
Works Cat.: 14
PROVENANCE: Purchased from the artist's executors in 1896 by *National Portrait Gallery* (1058)

45 c.1857 **Miniature by Samuel John Stump**
PROVENANCE: S.J. Pegg of Leicester (in 1919); *untraced*

46 1857 **Caricature: 'A Nightmare' by Frederick Sandys**, in which Ruskin is portrayed as the ass.
REPRODUCED: Published by Smith Elder & Co., 4 May 1857, as a zinco-engraving, $13^1/_4$ x $19^1/_4$; J.G. Millais: *Life and Letters and Sir John Everett Millais*, I, p. 321; *Graphic*, 27 March 1900; *Bookman*, March 1900, p. 179
Works Cat.: listed on p. 213
PROVENANCE: *untraced* (There are two sheets of studies of bridle and armour, from the Fairfax Murray Collection now in the Birmingham City Museum and Art Gallery).

47 1857 **Portrait with Louisa Stewart-MacKenzie, by William Bell Scott**, 15-21 July. Watercolour, 14 x 10, inscribed John Ruskin and Miss Stuart MacKenzie. Wallington – July 1864 W.B.S. Etching with a lithographic pen by way of giving a lesson in Drawing.
REPRODUCED: *National Trust*, No. 22, p. 15, Spring 1975; J.D. Hunt: *The Wider Sea* 1982, pl.14b; D. Levi and P. Tucker: *Ruskin didata* 1997, cover
PROVENANCE: By descent to Miss E.M. Courtney-Boyd; *National Trust, Wallington*

48 c.1857 **Portrait by Thomas Richmond**, head, life sized. Oil.
Works Cat.: 10
PROVENANCE: John Ruskin Richmond, the artist's son and Ruskin's god-son (in 1912); G.H. Wollaston; *untraced*

49 c.1857 **Portrait by Thomas Richmond**, head. Watercolour sketch for no. 50
Works Cat.: 12
PROVENANCE: Mrs G.H. Wollaston (in 1912); *untraced*

50 c.1857 **Portrait by Thomas Richmond**, head. Oil
Works Cat.: 11
PROVENANCE: Mrs G.H. Wollaston (in 1912); *untraced*

51 c.1860 **Caricature by James Smetham**, showing Ruskin with little eyes at the ends of funnels.
PROVENANCE: By descent to the artist's daughter, Helen Hutton; James Hutton; *untraced*

52 c.1860 **The Choice of Paris: An Idyll, by Florence Anne Claxton**, in which Ruskin appears as a portrait on a wall. Watercolour heightened with gum arabic and gold paint, $12^3/_4$ x $16^1/_2$
EXHIBITED: This is a watercolour version of the oil shown at the Portland Gallery, 1860
PROVENANCE: Sotheby 20 June 1989 (28); *Victoria & Albert Museum*

53 1860 **Sketch of Ruskin and Mary Severn working in the National Gallery, by Ann Mary Severn**, 15 September. Inscribed: Nat. Gallery 15 Sep 60 JR works at Bacchus's nose – MS dashes impudently at Titian's blue hills.
REPRODUCED: Birkenhead: *Illustrious Friends*, p. 140
PROVENANCE: By descent to *Lady Juliet Townsend*

54 1861 **Sketch of the outside of his mouth, by John Ruskin**, March. Pencil. Inscribed by John Ruskin Richmond: Drawn by John Ruskin from his own mouth March 1861. Enclosed in an envelope inscribed in same hand: A Drawing by John Ruskin of his own mouth (March 1861) J.R.R.
PROVENANCE: By descent to H.W. Wollaston; sold in 1961 to *Pierpont Morgan Library* (MA 2159)

55 1861 **Portrait by Dante Gabriel Rossetti**; head and shoulders, full face. Red crayon, 19 x 13¼; signed with monogram and dated 1861.
REPRODUCED: *Works* XXXVI, pl. B.; Poole: *Oxford Portraits*, I, p. 202; Leon: *Ruskin the Great Victorian*, p. 220; *Dearden II*, p. 172
EXHIBITED: BFAC 1883 (134)
Works Cat.: 15
PROVENANCE: C.J. Pocock of Brighton; Christie's, 14 May 1891 (608, £5 10s.); presented in 1891 by Malcolm McClean to *Ashmolean Museum*

56 c.1861 **Caricature sketch by Dante Gabriel Rossetti**, three quarter-length, facing left. Brown ink on grey paper, 4½ x 2½. Inscribed on reverse by William Michael Rossetti: I consider that this sketch is by my Brother. Am not sure as to the person represented, but inclined to think that it is Ruskin. Face something like, and figure more especially. W.M.R.
REPRODUCED: J.C. Troxell: *The Three Rossettis* 1927, p.28
EXHIBITED: Pierpont Morgan Library 1996 'Being William Morris'
PROVENANCE: Janet Camp Troxell; *Mark Samuels Lasner*

57 **Head only, by Henry Treffrey Dunn**; Ruskin appears as one of the crowd in a panel depicting part of the legend of St George. Painted about 1895 but depicting Ruskin about 1861. Oil on panel of Jacobean cupboard, head about 1" high.
REPRODUCED: Pedrick: *Life with Rossetti*, p. 182
PROVENANCE: ?A.C. Swinburne; Theodore Watts-Dunton; Mrs Watts-Dunton; bought from her sale at The Pines, 1939, by Lady Mander; *Wightwick Manor*

58 1861 **Portrait of himself**, head and shoulders, looking right. Watercolour touched with body-colour over pencil, 6¼ x 4½. Inscribed by Joan Severn on old mount: John Ruskin – by himself – given by him to me, J.R.S.
REPRODUCED: Collingwood: *Life and Work of John Ruskin*, I, frontis., (where signature has been added); Collingwood: *Life of John Ruskin*, frontis.; Pengelly: *John Ruskin*, frontis.; *Bookman*, March 1900, p. 177; *Works* XVII, frontis.; *Bookman*, Oct. 1908 coloured supplement; Leon: *Ruskin, the Great Victorian*, frontis.; Evans & Whitehouse: *Diaries of John Ruskin* I, frontis.; *Dearden II*, p. 174; Burd: *John Ruskin and Rose La Touche* 1980, p. 48
EXHIBITED: Royal Watercolour Society, *Ruskin* 1901 (404); Manchester, *Ruskin* 1904 (363); Coniston 1919 (109); London 1919 (128); Ruskin and his circle 1964 (31); New York 1996 (16)
Works Cat.: 16
PROVENANCE: John Ruskin; given to Joan Severn in 1860s; Violet Severn; F.J. Sharp; bought in 1959 by *Pierpont Morgan Library* (1959.22)

59 **Copy of No. 58 by W.H. Caffyn**, signed and inscribed 'after J. Ruskin about 1856'. Pencil, 10 x 8
PROVENANCE: James Ellis; given in 1991 to *R.M. Sawyer*

60 **Copy of No. 58, perhaps by W.G.Collingwood**. Watercolour
PROVENANCE: Mr & Mrs W.G. Collingwood; given to *Ruskin Museum, Coniston* (Con RM 1989.602)

61 1862 **Photograph by Lombardi**, leaning on the back of a chair, looking half left.
REPRODUCED: *Gentlewoman*, 28 Jan. 1900
Works Cat.: 17

62 1862 **Photograph by (Caldesi) Lombardi**, leaning on back of chair, looking ahead

63 1862 **Photograph by (Caldesi) Lombardi**, head and shoulders, eyes looking down

64 1862 **Photograph by (Caldesi) Lombardi**, head and shoulders, eyes looking ahead

65 1863 **Photograph with Dante Gabriel Rossetti and William Bell Scott, Ruskin in centre of group, by William Downey**, 29 June
REPRODUCED: A Grand old Photographer, Some Reminiscences of Mr William Downey, Royal Photographer, *Pall Mall Budget*, 15 Jan. 1891; *Works* XXVI, pl. 18; Gosse: *English Literature* IV, p. 347; Doughty: *Rossetti*; Quennell: *John Ruskin*, p. 209; Bell & Gernsheim: *Those impossible English*; Pedrick: *Life with Rossetti*, p. 70 (omitting W.B. Scott); Burd: Ruskin, Rossetti and William Bell Scott: a second arrangement, *Philological Quarterly*, XLVIII, No. 1, Jan. 1969, pl. 1; *Dearden*: John Ruskin, p. 27
Works Cat.: 18
Negative: By descent to W.E. Downey; sold in 1948 to Radio Times Hulton Picture Library

66 **Copy of Ruskin and Rossetti, from No. 65, on a sheet of sketches by Max Beerbohm**. Pencil and some ink and wash.
REPRODUCED: M. Beerbohm: *Rossetti and his circle* 1987
PROVENANCE: *Princeton University Library* (Robert J. Taylor Collection)

67 1863 **Photograph with Dante Gabriel Rossetti and William Bell Scott, Ruskin on right of group, by William Downey**, 29 June
REPRODUCED: Cook: Ruskin and his books, an Interview with his Publisher, *Strand Magazine* XXIV, No. 144, Dec. 1902, p. 710; Burd: Ruskin, Rossetti and William Bell Scott: a second arrangement, *Philological Quarterly* XLVIII, No. 1, Jan. 1969, pl. 2; Trevelyan: *A Pre-Raphaelite Circle*, p. 128
Provenance of prints: Brantwood, F.J. Sharp; H.G. Viljoen; *V.A. Burd*. Another print in *National Portrait Gallery*

68 **Cartoon, Ruskin and the Hinksey Diggers, figure of Ruskin based on No. 67, by Douglas Percy Bliss**, inscribed: The Gospel of Labour: Professor Ruskin takes a class out to make roads. Watercolour and body-colour over pencil, 9 x 11
PROVENANCE: Abbott & Holder; bought in 1980 by *Whitehouse Collection*

69 1863 **Photograph with Dante Gabriel Rossetti and William Bell Scott, Ruskin on right of group, by William Downey**, 29 June
Provenance of print: S.C. Cockerell; *Virginia Surtees*

70 1863 **Photograph of Ruskin seated in Rossetti's chair, by William Downey**, 29 June
REPRODUCED: (engraving of head and shoulders) Baillie: *John Ruskin* 1882; Angeli: *Pre-Raphaelite Twilight*; Burd: Ruskin, Rossetti and William Bell Scott: a second arrangement, *Philological Quarterly* XLVIII, No. 1, Jan. 1969, pl. 3; Hewison: *New Approaches to Ruskin 1981*, jacket; Maas: *John Ruskin and his circle* 1991, (24)
Works Cat.: 19
Negative: By descent to W.E. Downey; sold in 1948 to Radio Times Hulton Picture Library; destroyed because of deterioration, c.1950

71 **Portrait of Ruskin by Thomas Scott**. Engraving 'on large plate paper' advertised on the back cover of Edmund J. Baillie's *John Ruskin* 1882 may merely be a better quality print of the engraving after No. 70 which was used as frontispiece to that work (see above).

72 **Portrait of Ruskin by Alfred Bryan**, head and shoulders only, after No. 70. Engraving, $7^{1}/_{8}$ x $5^{1}/_{2}$, signed with initials
Provenance: Goodspeed Ruskin Collection, *Wellesley College*

73 1864 **Bust, by Alexander Munro**, February
Works Cat.: 20
Provenance: *untraced*

74 1864 **Sketch portrait by Samuel Laurence**, signed, and also signed by Ruskin. Black, white and red chalk on green tinted paper, 13 x $19^{1}/_{2}$
Provenance: Sotheby 11 Nov. 1979 (31); *Robert Flynn Johnson*

75 1864 **Portrait by Samuel Laurence**, head and shoulders, Spring. Charcoal on grey paper, $15^{3}/_{4}$ x $11^{1}/_{2}$
Reproduced: Whitehouse: *Solitary Warrior*, frontis. and jacket; Whitehouse: *Ruskin and Brantwood*, p. 8; Whitehouse: *Vindication of Ruskin*, p. 49; Evans: *John Ruskin*, p. 304; *Dearden I*, p. 192
Exhibited: London 1919 (249)
Provenance: John Lane; Mrs John Lane; sold at Sotheby's 7 July 1927; J.H. Whitehouse; *Whitehouse Collection* (RF 305)

76 1864 **Portrait sketch by T. Henderson**, head and shoulders looking left, 12 December. Pen and ink on white paper, $2^{3}/_{4}$ x $2^{3}/_{4}$, inscribed: John Ruskin by T. Henderson 1864 Dec. 12
Reproduced: *Dearden I*, 192
Exhibited: Ruskin and his circle 1964 (32)
Provenance: sold by Stevens and Brown (5 March 1954, 2 gns.) to *Whitehouse Collection* (RF 236)

77 1866 **Portrait outlines, by Constance Hilliard**, 29 June. Ink, $5^{1}/_{4}$ x $1^{1}/_{2}$
Provenance: in C. Hilliard's Diary; *Alan Cole*

78 c.1866 **Portrait by Edward Coley Burne-Jones**, 'drawing'.
Provenance: 'Commissioned' by C.E. Norton through Ruskin, but never finished, and *probably destroyed*

79 c.1866 **Portrait of himself**, head, full face. Pen and ink on white paper, $7^{1}/_{4}$ x 6
Reproduced: Invitation to Private View, Arts Council Ruskin Exhibition, 1960; *Dearden I*, 193; Dearden (ed.), *Iteriad*, 32; Dearden: *John Ruskin e le Alpi* 1990, 6; Dearden: *Ruskin Bembridge and Brantwood* 1994, 54
Exhibited: Arts Council 1960, Aldeburgh, Colchester and London (26); Verona 1966 (80); London 1969 (9); Kendal 1969 (2); Rye 1970 (50); Oxford 1970 (3); Arts Council John Ruskin 1983 (3); Thornbury 1983 (1); John Ruskin e le Alpi 1990 (35)
Provenance: Perhaps given to Dr & Mrs John Simon; sold Sotheby with a group of letters from John James Ruskin to Mrs Simon; *Whitehouse Collection* (RF 1507)

80 1867 **Sketch by himself**, of the side of his mouth, in a letter to his dentist, A. Woodhouse, 19 January.
Provenance: *Pierpont Morgan Library* (MA 2228)

81 1867 **Photograph by Elliott & Fry**, head and shoulders, full face
Reproduced: *Bookman* Oct. 1908, 21; there is an unsigned engraving after the photograph ($5^{1}/_{2}$ x $5^{1}/_{4}$) in the Goodspeed Ruskin Collection at Wellesley College
Works Cat.: 21 (but not reproduced as described)

82 **Portrait after No. 81 reproduced in sepia on a cream china Copeland plate with gold border**. Potted in 1881 and first distributed in March and November 1882
PROVENANCE: an example in collection of *John Yates*

83 **Portrait by Stephen Chesters**, after No. 81, painted on porcelain
PROVENANCE: By descent to the great, great grandson of the artist, *David Harté*

84 1867 **Photograph by Elliott & Fry**, same pose as no. 81, but lips parted

85 **Miniature**, possibly after No. 84, on ivory, 3 x $2\frac{1}{2}$
PROVENANCE: W.W. Winkworth; Maas Gallery; *Victoria Andros*

86 1867 **Photograph by Elliott and Fry**, side face
REPRODUCED: *Works* XXVII, frontis., where misdated 1876; there is an unsigned engraving, $4\frac{1}{4}$ x 3 (oval), and a reversed engraving by T. Johnson, $9\frac{3}{8}$ x $7\frac{1}{2}$, after this photograph in the Goodspeed Ruskin Collection at Wellesley College. The photograph was also reproduced lithographically in an elaborate border, by Vincent Brooks Day & Son, 1879, $8\frac{1}{2}$ x $6\frac{1}{2}$; *Bookman* Oct. 1908, 17,
Works Cat.: 23

87 **Sketch by (?)Arthur Severn**, after No. 86. Pencil on white card, 6 x $7\frac{3}{4}$
REPRODUCED: *Dearden I*, 193
PROVENANCE: *Whitehouse Collection* (RF 528)

88 **Copy by J.C. Barry Lindsay** of No. 86. Pencil, $3\frac{3}{4}$ x $2\frac{1}{4}$, signed J.C. Barry Lindsay
PROVENANCE: M.H. Spielmann; *Whitehouse Collection* (RF 309)

89 **Miniature by J.C. Barry**, after No. 86, not before 1893. Body-colour on ivory, 3 x 2. Old label on back of frame: Professor Ruskin LLD, DCL / J.C. Barry / [?] Preford Place / Larches St / Sparkbrooke
PROVENANCE: Miscellaneous sale at Cartmel; *Whitehouse Collection*

90 **Etching by S. Haydon**, based on No. 86 (but reversed), plate size $7\frac{3}{4}$ x 5
Works Cat.: 24
PROVENANCE: Print in *Whitehouse Collection*

91 **Relief, perhaps by William Calder Marshall**, probably based on No. 86. Cream wax, oval $6\frac{1}{4}$ high, signed with W.M. monogram and dated '83 [?]
EXHIBITED: John Ruskin and his circle, Maas Gallery 1991 (36)
PROVENANCE: E. Cemlyn-Jones; Christie 5 Oct. 1976 (16); Blair; Maas Gallery; bought by a group of friends in appreciation of the work of The Lord Lloyd of Kilgerran and presented to *Brantwood*

92 **Watermark on sheet of notepaper**; outline portrait based on No. 86. Folded sheet, 7 x $4\frac{3}{8}$. Watermark 'Ruskin Linen' on [p. 1] and outline portrait $4\frac{1}{2}$ x 3 on [p.3]
PROVENANCE: F.J. Sharp; given about 1947 to *J.S. Dearden*

93 1867 (second sitting) **Photograph by Elliott and Fry**, head and shoulders, full face looking slightly left
REPRODUCED: *Letters of John Ruskin to Charles Eliot Norton*, I, frontis.
Works Cat.: 22

94 1867 (second sitting) **Photograph by Elliott and Fry**, as No. 93 but looking ahead
REPRODUCED: engrave by J.A. O'Neill for *New Electric Magazine*; Charles Cox's *Catalogue* V, Spring 1976

95 1868 **Caricature**: Nature and Art, respectfully dedicated to Matilda Griggs, in which Ruskin is represented fondling two calves
REPRODUCED: *Judy*, 29 Jan. 1868
Works Cat.: Listed on p.213
PROVENANCE: original *untraced*

96 1868 **Caricature**, unsigned, showing Ruskin as a police constable (Number A1) in the act of moving on other figures. ?November
Reproduced as a print, 1868; T.J. Johnstone: *Ruskin for Rector, The Edinburgh Rectorial Election of 1868*, 1980, p.6
PROVENANCE: original *untraced*. Print in *Edinburgh University Library* (MS ref DA)

97 1869 **Photograph by Elliott and Fry**, head and shoulders, full face
REPRODUCED: *Bookman*, March 1900, 180; Lutyens: *The Ruskins and the Grays*, p. 51

98 1869 **Photograph by Elliott and Fry**, as No. 97, but head turned fractionally to the right

99 1869 **Photograph by Elliott and Fry**, as above, full face, looking up slightly
REPRODUCED: Quennell: *John Ruskin, portrait of a prophet*, p. 112; Birkenhead: *Illustrious Friends*, p. 172; Surtees: *Sublime and Instructive* 1972, p. 14; anonymous photolithograhic reproduction, 9 7/8 x 7, in Goodspeed Ruskin collection at Wellesley College Library, in South London Art Gallery, and in National Portrait Gallery Archive, reproduced in *Cassell's National Portrait Gallery*, and in *Ruskin and Early Victorian Camberwell* 1981

100 1869 **Photograph by Elliott and Fry**, as above, head and shoulders, looking intently ahead, forehead creased.
REPRODUCED: Froude: *Carlyle*, c.1980
PROVENANCE: Carlyle Album No. 4, *Butler Library, Columbia University*

101 1869 **Photograph by Elliott and Fry**, as above, seated, three-quarter length, looking ahead
PROVENANCE: Carlyle Album No. 4, *Butler Library, Columbia University*

102 1869 **Photograph by Elliott and Fry**, as above, seated, three-quarter length, looking right
PROVENANCE: Carlyle Album No. 4, *Butler Library, Columbia University*

103 **Portrait by Henry Matthew Brock R.I.**, based on No. 99, head and shoulders in a garden setting, ? c.1930
REPRODUCED: Dust jacket of Ruskin: *Sesame & Lilies*, Blackie & Son, n.d.
EXHIBITED: Chris Beetles Gallery, The Illustrators, 1996 (80) and reproduced in catalogue
PROVENANCE: *Chris Beetles*

104 1870 **Imaginative portrait by Alan Sorrell**, 1953, of Ruskin delivering his Inaugural Lecture at Oxford, 8 February 1870. Guache, 9 3/4 x 13 1/2. A tablet on the frame reads: Rhodes, seated beside the rostrum, hears Ruskin lecture in the Sheldonian Theatre. He was lastingly influenced by Ruskin's pronouncement that England's high destiny was to found colonies 'as fast and as far as she is able'.
REPRODUCED: *Illustrated London News*, 18 July 1953, pp. 86-87
PROVENANCE: *Rhodes Memorial Museum and Commonwealth Centre* (acquired 1953)

105 **Working sketch for No. 104, by Alan Sorrell**, pencil, 3 1/2 high
PROVENANCE: *Mrs Elizabeth Sorrell*

106 c.1870–75 **Anonymous sketch**, half length, facing right. Pen and ink, 6 x 4 1/4 (oval)
REPRODUCED: J.D. Hunt: *The Wider Sea* 1982 pl. 23b; J.L. Spear: *Dreams of an English Eden* 1984, p. 179
PROVENANCE: Sotheby 29 May 1956; John Schroder; sold in 1956 to *Pierpont Morgan Library* (MA 1748)

107 1872 **Sketch by Adriano Ceciono**. Head and shoulders looking left. Pencil, 5 x $4^{1}/_{2}$, inscribed John Ruskin
REPRODUCED: Vanity Fair, National Portrait Gallery Exhibition catalogue, 1976, p.23; J.D. Hunt: *The Wider Sea* 1982, pl.23c
PROVENANCE: Gabinetto dei Desegni e delli Stampe, *Uffizi Gallery, Florence* (1174-75)

108 1872 **Sketch by Adriano Cecioni**. Head and shoulders looking left. Pencil, $5^{3}/_{4}$ x $4^{1}/_{2}$
PROVENANCE: Gabinetto dei Desegni e delli Stampe, *Uffizi Gallery, Florence* (1174-75)

109 1872 **Caricature by Adriano Cecioni**, full length, facing left. Watercolour, 12 x 7
REPRODUCED: *Vanity Fair*, 17 Feb. 1872, with text on reverse by 'Jehu Junior' (Thomas Gibson Bowles); National Portrait Gallery exhibition cat. 1976, p. 23; Dearden: *John Ruskin, an illustrated life* 1981, cover; Merrill: *A pot of paint* 1992, p. 45; and elsewhere
Works Cat.: 26 (where wrongly ascribed to F. Waddy)
PROVENANCE: *Vanity Fair* sale at Christie's, 5-8 March 1912 (669); *South London Art Gallery*

110 1872 **Caricature by Edward Linley Sambourne**, Visions of Burlington House, sixth of May, in which Ruskin is depicted fleeing from the crowd, tearing his hair
REPRODUCED: *Punch*, 11 May 1872
Works Cat.: Listed on p. 213
PROVENANCE: original *untraced*

111 1872 **Caricature by F. Waddy**, of Ruskin as the Angel of Light hovering over London
REPRODUCED: *Once a Week*, 25 May 1872; *Cartoon Men of the Day* 1873; *Glasgow Evening Times* 31 Dec. 1904; *Listener* 7 Feb. 1972. Redrawn showing Ruskin above the Oxford Museum for cover of Dearden: *John Ruskin* 1973.
Works Cat.: 31 (where wrongly dated as 22 May 1874). The listing on p.213 of *Works Cat.* for *Once a Week* refers to the present caricature.
PROVENANCE: original *untraced*

112 1872 **Photograph of Ruskin with Joan and Arthur Severn, Mrs and Constance Hilliard and Albert Goodwin**, probably taken in Venice, June-July
REPRODUCED: Dearden: The Ruskin circle on tour in Italy in 1872, *Connoisseur*, April 1972, p. 240; Clegg and Tucker: *Ruskin and Tuscany* 1993, p. 114
PROVENANCE: (only known prints) by descent to *John and Sarah Bunney*; *Brantwood* (formerly Kate Raven's)

113 **Portrait by Charles Herbert Moore**, head and shoulders, looking half right, based on No. 112. Watercolour, 8 x $5^{3}/_{4}$
REPRODUCED: Mather: *Charles Herbert Moore, Landscape Painter*, pl. 34; Leith: *A Quiet Devotion* 1996, p. 6
PROVENANCE: Given by the artist to C.E. Norton; by descent to the Misses Sara, Elizabeth and Margaret Norton, who presented it to the *Fogg Art Museum, Harvard University* (1919.1)

114 1873 **Portrait of himself**, January. Head, full face. Watercolour, 14 x 10, inscribed by Joan Severn, Di Pa by himself
REPRODUCED: Rosenberg: *The Darkening Glass*, frontis. and jacket; *Dearden II*, p. 174; Burd: *John Ruskin and Rose La Touche* 1980, p. 81; and elsewhere
EXHIBITED: Ruskin and his circle 1964 (34), reproduced as catalogue frontispiece and on poster; British Landscape Drawings and Watercolours, Brussels 1994 (95)
PROVENANCE: Joan Severn; Violet Severn; F.J. Sharp; Mrs M. Holmes; sold to *Pierpont Morgan Library* (1959.23)

115 1873 **Photograph by Frank Meadow Sutcliffe**, sitting on the ground near a wall at Brantwood, autumn
REPRODUCED: Dearden: *Facets of Ruskin* 1970, frontis.; Barnes: *Ruskin in Sheffield* 1985, p. 8
Negative in possession of *Sutcliffe Gallery, Whitby*

116 1874 **Portrait by himself**, Spring. Head and shoulders, full face. Pencil on white paper, 10 x 8. Inscribed by C.E. Norton (on recto): J. Ruskin (se ipsum) del. (and on verso): J. Ruskin. His own drawing of himself, 1873 or 4. C.E.N. Not a good likeness.
REPRODUCED: Whitehouse: *Ruskin Centenary Letters*, frontis. (where its inscription has been moved from its true position on the left, to a central point below the portrait); Gosse: *English Literature* IV, p. 289; Gosse *Modern English Literature*, p. 356: *Dearden I*, p. 193; Walton: *The Drawings of John Ruskin*, p. 111, and elsewhere
EXHIBITED: London 1919 (319); Ruskin and his circle 1964 (35); Lancaster 1979 (46); Arts Council 1983 (4)
Works Cat.: 27 (note that *Works Cat.* 25 is also the present portrait, included in that catalogue in error)
PROVENANCE: John Ruskin; given to Charles Eliot Norton; sold at Christie's, May 1919; *Whitehouse Collection* (RF 991)

117 1874 **Portrait by himself**, Spring. Head, full face. Watercolour, 14³/₄ x 9³/₄
REPRODUCED: Evans & Whitehouse: *Diaries of John Ruskin* II, frontis. (where inaccurately described as being in the Fogg Art Museum); Hewison: *John Ruskin, the argument of the eye*, pl. 2 and jacket; *Connoisseur* Feb. 1976; F. Kirchhoff: John Ruskin 1984, frontis.
EXHIBITED: Ruskin Exhibition in memory of Charles Eliot Norton, Fogg Art Museum 1909-10; Salander-O'Reilly Galleries, New York 1996 (24)
PROVENANCE: John Ruskin; given to C.E. Norton; C.E. Goodspeed, presented in 1920 to *Wellesley College Library*

118 1874 **Caricature**: Ruskin and Realism, a caricature of the Hinksey Diggers
REPRODUCED: *Fun*, 18 April 1874
Works Cat.: Listed on p. 213
PROVENANCE: original *untraced*

119 1874 **Caricature portrait by INO**, 'No XVI, Great Guns of Oxford, President of the Amateur Landscape Gardening Society'. Watercolour, 20³/₄ x 13¹/₂
REPRODUCED: Photographs of the drawing were sold at the time by Shrimptons of Oxford; *Catalogue* of the Ruskin College exhibit at Franco-British Exhibition 1908; *Bookman* October 1908, p. 33; Dearden: *John Ruskin*, p. 35
EXHIBITED: Franco-British Exhibition 1908, Ruskin College exhibit (12)
Works Cat.: 30
PROVENANCE: *Ruskin College, Oxford*

120 1874 **Self-portrait as St Francis**; a copy by Ruskin of Cimabue's St Francis, at Assisi, June-July. Watercolour and pencil, 18³/₈ x 23¹/₄, inscribed 'JR. Assisi, 1874 to C.E.N. 1st Jul. 83'
REPRODUCED: *Gazette of the Grolier Club*, No. 28/29, June/December 1978; J.L. Spear: *Dreams of an English Eden* 1984, frontis.; V.A. Burd (ed.), *Christmas Story* 1990, p. 102
EXHIBITED: New York 1965 (I, 4 – as a colour transparency); Grolier Club 1978 (53)
Works Cat.: Unlisted as portrait but included in the Catalogue of Drawings, *Works* XXXVIII, No. 491
PROVENANCE: Given to C.E. Norton, 1 July 1883; given by Norton's daughter to Professor Sydney Ross; c.1978 given by Ross to *R.Dyke Benjamin*

121 1874 **Sketch of Ruskin lecturing, by a *Vanity Fair* artist**, December
PROVENANCE: *untraced*

122 1875 **Photograph by Charles Lutwidge Dodgson**, sitting in an armchair, looking at the camera, 6 March
REPRODUCED: S.D. Collingwood: *Life and Letters of Lewis Carroll*, p. 158; *Works* XXXVIII, p. 217
Works Cat.: 29
Dodgson's negative number: 2309

123 1875 **Photograph by Charles Lutwidge Dodgson**, full face, head resting on hand, 3 June

REPRODUCED: *Thought-Treasures from the Works of John Ruskin*, n.d. frontis. (where acknowledged to the Stereoscopic Company)

124 **Portrait by Charles Herbert Moore**, based on No. 123, c.1877. Oil, $8\frac{3}{4}$ x $6\frac{1}{8}$

PROVENANCE: *Fogg Art Museum, Harvard University* (Meta & Paul J. Sachs Collection 317.1930)

125 1875 **Plaster medallion by Charles Ashmore**, probably based on a photograph

Works Cat.: 32

PROVENANCE: Mr Downing of Birmingham (in 1891); *untraced*

126 1876 **Cartoon by Edward Linley Sambourne**, Lady of the Lake Loquitur, in which Ruskin is portrayed as a knight smashing up the railway in the Lake District

REPRODUCED: *Punch* 5 Feb. 1876

Works Cat.: Listed on p. 213

PROVENANCE: original *untraced*

127 1876 **Cartoon by T.C.**, Playing with edged tools, in which Ruskin is depicted as Saint Rusty turning his back on an industrial town

REPRODUCED: *Fun* 29 March 1876

Works Cat.: Listed on p. 213

PROVENANCE: original *untraced*

128 1876 **Portrait by Arthur Severn**, seated at a table at Brantwood with Sara Anderson, Laurence Hilliard and Joan Severn, June. Watercolour and body-colour, $5\frac{7}{10}$ x $8\frac{9}{10}$

REPRODUCED: Dearden, *Ruskin Bembridge and Brantwood* 1994, p. 201

PROVENANCE: Bought from Brantwood c.1930 by Haddon C. Adams; bequeathed in 1971 to *Whitehouse Collection* (RF 527)

129-130 ?1876 **Two sketches by Laurence Jermyn Hilliard**, of Ruskin at his wood chopping, ?23 June. Pen and ink, $6\frac{1}{4}$ x $4\frac{1}{2}$ and $6\frac{1}{4}$ x $4\frac{1}{4}$, both mounted onto one sheet which is inscribed by Alexander Wedderburn, Two caricatures of Ruskin at his wood-chopping at Brantwood at which he wore a very frock coat. By his secretary L. Hilliard. On his way to the wood. Pausing to look at the view.

PROVENANCE: *Bodleian Library, Oxford* (MS Eng. misc c.249)

131 1876 **Portrait by 'Pilotell' (Georges Labadie)**, head and shoulders looking left (reversed). Dry-point etching, plate size 6 x $4\frac{1}{4}$.

REPRODUCED: Etching published by Noséda of the Strand, in a series of portraits of notabilities; *Spielmann I*, p. 79; Spielmann: *John Ruskin*, p. 105

Works Cat.: 33

PROVENANCE: original sketch *untraced*

132 1877 **Portrait by Charles Fairfax Murray**, head and shoulders, full-face, April. Watercolour with some body-colour, and pencil, $18\frac{3}{4}$ x $12\frac{1}{4}$, inscribed on reverse, John Ruskin s.m. circa 1875 aet. 56

REPRODUCED: R. Hewison: *Ruskin a Venezia* 1983, p. 54

EXHIBITED: Ruskin and Venice, Louisville 1978 (85); Venezia nell Ottocento, Venice 1983-84 (108)

Works Cat.: unlisted

PROVENANCE: Paul Oppé (bought in March 1921; D.L.T. Oppé (1081 (d)), sold in 1996 to *Tate Gallery* (T10251)

133 1877 **Bust by Countess Isabel Curtis-Chomeley in Birmani**

PROVENANCE: J. Ruskin; *untraced*

134A 1877–78 **Portrait by John Wharlton Bunney** of Ruskin with himself and his wife standing in the Piazza, Venice. Oil, signed, dated and numbered 180
PROVENANCE: Commissioned by Lt Col. A. Ellis; *untraced*

134B 1877–79 **Copy of No. 134A by J.W. Bunney**. Watercolour, 19½ x 36, signed and dated, Venice 1877-9/189
EXHIBITED: Perhaps The Fine Art Society 'Venice', 1883 (97)
PROVENANCE: Commissioned by Lady Sykes; by descent to *Sir Tatton Sykes, Bt.*

135 ?1877 **Portrait by Edward William Andrews**. 'small studies from which the larger work was produced'
Works Cat.: see 34
PROVENANCE: *untraced*

136 ?1877 **Portrait by Edward William Andrews**. Chalk, life-size
Exhibition: Royal Academy 1877 (1265)
Works Cat.: 34
PROVENANCE: *untraced*

137 c.1877 **Portrait by Arthur Severn**, full length. Watercolour.
Works Cat.: 35
PROVENANCE: *untraced*

138 1877 **Caricature by Reginald Blomfield**, of Ruskin blowing two trumpets. Brown ink over pencil, 10⅞ x 9, inscribed A Modern Art Professor
PROVENANCE: Warren Howell; *Pierpont Morgan Library* (1984.35)

139 1877 **Bust by Benjamin Creswick**, based on photographs. Modelled in plaster
EXHIBITED: Sheffield Society of Artists 1877 (222)
Works Cat.: unlisted
PROVENANCE: *untraced* (casts were advertised, which are also untraced)

140 1877 **Bust by Benjamin Creswick**, September. Modelled in plaster, 13" high including base
REPRODUCED: Collingwood: *Life and Work of John Ruskin* II, p. 103 (according to *Works Cat.*: 37 is partly based on this bust); Collingwood: *Ruskin Relics* p. 157; *Works* XXX pl. iii
EXHIBITED: Sheffield Society of Artists 1878 (1267); Coniston 1900 (following 366)
Works Cat.: 36
PROVENANCE: Presented to Prince Leopold in 1879; presumably returned to Brantwood on the death of the Prince in 1884; Brantwood sale 1931 (587); bought by Stevens and Brown (£1) for J.H. Whitehouse; *Whitehouse Collection* (RF R 89)
A number of casts were made (offered in 1878 exhibition at 1 guinea each)
1 Dr Kendall; *Coniston Museum* (exhibited London 1919 (429))
2 Sir Henry Acland; *untraced* (Spielmann say that a 'duplicate was executed for Sir Henry Acland'; this was probably a cast.
3 John E. Fowler; by descent to Holda Fowler; Peter Wardle; given by him to *C.C. Quayle*
4 Mrs Harley; *Peter Wardle* (this is in terracotta and is dated 1887; it probably indicates a second casting)
5 J.E. Phythian (exhibited, Manchester 1904 (541)); by descent to Dr Mabel Tylecote: *untraced*

141 1878 **Caricature by Alfred Bryan**. Men of the Day – Mr John Ruskin
REPRODUCED: *Hornet*, 20 March 1878, Vol. 12, p. 712
Works Cat.: Listed on p. 213
PROVENANCE: original *untraced*

142 1878 **Cartoon by Edward Linley Sambourne**, An Appeal to Law, in which Ruskin is portrayed as the Old Pelican in the Art Wilderness
REPRODUCED: *Punch*, 7 Dec. 1878; L. Merrill, *Pot of Paint* 1992, p. 253
Works Cat.: Listed on p. 213
PROVENANCE: original *untraced*

143 1878 **Caricature** in which Ruskin is depicted as a blackbird hovering above the washing line where J.A.McN. Whistler hangs out his canvases to dry
REPRODUCED: *Funny Folk*, 28 December 1878; L. Merrill, *Pot of Paint* 1992, p. 104
Works Cat.: unlisted
PROVENANCE: original *untraced*

144 1878 **Cartoon by 'G. Pipeshank'** in which Ruskin is portrayed as one of the modern pilgrims journeying to 'Ye Shrine of St Nicotinus'
REPRODUCED: *The Plenipotent Key to Cope's Correct Card of the Peerless Pilgrimage to Saint Nicotinus of the Holy Herb*, 1878, frontis.
Works Cat.: Listed on p. 213
PROVENANCE: original *untraced*

145 1879 **Photograph by J. Lund of Coniston**, of Ruskin and others on the ice off Brantwood, January/February
PROVENANCE: Only known print in *Whitehouse Collection* (Adams Bequest)

146 1879 **Portrait by Heinrich S. Uhlrich**, head and shoulders, full face. Wood engraving, engraved surface 13 x 10
REPRODUCED: Originally published in *The Graphic* 5 July 1879, with words at top: Supplement to the Graphic July 5, 1879, and at foot: John Ruskin. Frontispiece to Vol. XIX; it has also been reprinted on better quality paper with a facsimile of Ruskin's commendary note at foot; *Works* XX, frontis.; Dearden: *Ruskin Bembridge and Brantwood* 1994, p. 45; Ruskin: *Præterita* (ed. A.J.C. Cockshut, Whitehouse Series) 1994, jacket
Works Cat.: 38

147 1879 **Statue by Joseph Edgar Boehm**, November. Full length, modelled in clay. Referred to in the Subscription Appeal, 27 May 1880. This model was not used for Boehm's final work and presumably was subsequently destroyed.

148 1879 **Bust by Joseph Edgar Boehm**, November, head and shoulders, probably modelled in clay, 19 inches high; overall height with *en suite* plinth, 23½"
PROVENANCE: *untraced*, but probably destroyed after a mould was made from which two terracotta casts were made:
1 REPRODUCED: N. Penny: *Catalogue of European Sculpture in the Ashmolean Museum* 1992, III, p. 12; R. Hewison: *Ruskin in Oxford* 1996, p. 49.
EXHIBITED: It seems probable that *this* cast was exhibited in the Turner Gallery of the University Galleries, Oxford, 1880; Pre-Raphaelites in Oxford, Japan 1987 (58); Ruskin and Oxford 1996 (1)
PROVENANCE: Sir Henry Acland; Dr T.D. Acland; T.W.G. Acland, who presented it in 1932 to *Ashmolean Museum* (Penny 449)
2 EXHIBITED: It seems likely that this was the second cast which was exhibited at the Royal Academy in 1880 (1635)
PROVENANCE: *untraced*

149 1879–80 **Bust by Joseph Edgar Boehm**, head and shoulders modelled in marble, 19½" high; overall height with plinth, 25", incised on right shoulder, J.E. Boehm fecit, and inlaid in black on front of plinth, Ruskin
REPRODUCED: Cook: *Studies in Ruskin* 1890, frontis.; *Bookman*, March 1900, p. 186; *Works* XXI, p. ixx; Hewison: *Ruskin and Oxford* 1996, p. 51

EXHIBITED: *Ruskin and Oxford* 1996 (2)
Works Cat.: 39
PROVENANCE: Commissioned by *The Ruskin Drawing School, Oxford*
Casts were made, are incised in plinth John Ruskin, and are located at:
1 Bought from the Trustees of the sculptor immediately after his death in 1890 by William White and presented by him in 1892 to *The Guild of St George*
2 Earl of Carlisle; presented by him in 1896 to *National Portrait Gallery* (1053) (incised on back: Sir Joseph Edgar Boehm 1881)
REPRODUCED: *Spielmann II*, p. 121; Spielmann: *John Ruskin* 1900, p. 141
3 National Gallery of Victoria, given in 1943 to *Geelong Art Gallery Inc.* Incised on left shoulder, Boehm Sculpt. (Cast not in bronze as mentioned by Penny (op.cit.), but in a dark plaster composition.

150 1881 **Caricature of Sir J.E. Boehm contemplating his bust of Ruskin, by 'Spy' (Sir Leslie Ward)**
REPRODUCED: *Vanity Fair*, Vol. 25, 51, 22 January 1881; Blackwood: *London's Immortals* 1989, p. 265
PROVENANCE: original *untraced*

151 **'Bust of John Ruskin in the Ruskin School of Drawing' by Douglas Pittuck** (b. 1911). Oil on card, $6^{5}/_{8}$ x $4^{5}/_{8}$
PROVENANCE: given by the artist in 1948 to Albert Rutherston; bought by M.C. Ezra; given in 1981 to *Ashmolean Museum* (1981.562)

152 1879 **Portrait by Hubert von Herkomer**, November, head and shoulders. Original sketch for No. 153, pencil
PROVENANCE: Inscription on reverse is said to record that this 'original drawing by Herkomer (was) purchased at auction in 1904'; *untraced collector in Bombay*

153 1879 **Portrait by Hubert von Herkomer**, November, head and shoulders, full face. Watercolour, 29 x 19, signed
REPRODUCED: Engraved ($15^{6}/_{10}$ x $11^{7}/_{10}$) by the artist and published by The Fine Art Society 18809; *Harper's Magazine*, March 1980, p. 581; *Spielmann II*, p. 125; *Works* XXXVII, pl. viii; *Manchester Guardian*, 8 Feb. 1919; Mills: *Life and Letters of Sir Hubert Herkomer*, p. 108; Grierson: *The English Bible* , p. 41; Leon; *Ruskin, the Great Victorian*, p. 514; *Dearden II*, p. 175; Viljoen: *The Brantwood Diary*, 207; *Apollo*, April 1974, p. 268
EXHIBITED: Grosvenor Gallery 1881
Works Cat.: 40
PROVENANCE: Presented in 1903 by the artist to the *National Portrait Gallery* (13360)

154 **Portrait of John Ruskin by Herbert Johnson Harvey** (1884–1928) after No 153. pastel and conte, 18 x 12, signed H.J. Harvey (with initials in monogram)
PROVENANCE: *Ruskin Museum, Coniston* (ConRM 1989.792)

155 1880 **Cartoon by Edward Linley Sambourne**, The Morris Dance round St Mark's in which Ruskin is depicted as one of the dancers
REPRODUCED: *Punch*, 10 Jan. 1880
Works Cat.: Listed on p. 213
PROVENANCE: original *untraced*

156 1880 **Cartoon by unknown artist**, following Ruskin's lecture, A caution to snakes
REPRODUCED: *London Figaro*, 24 Mar. 1880
Works Cat.: Listed on p. 213
PROVENANCE: original *untraced*

157 1880 **Cartoon by Hancock**, A concert by the Powers, depicting Ruskin with Gladstone and Disraeli
REPRODUCED: *Moonshine*, 23 Oct. 1880
Works Cat.: Listed on p.213
PROVENANCE: original *untraced*

158 c. 1880 **Caricatures probably by Alfred Bryan**, a sheet of sketches, unsigned but inscribed with numerous notes. Ink and watercolour, 16 x $11^{1}/_{2}$
PROVENANCE: *William A. Stewart*

159 1880 **Caricature by Alfred Bryan**: Mr Ruskin. The Complete Letter-writer in spite of himself. Signed with initials.
REPRODUCED: probably *Hornet* or *Moonshine*, but untraced
PROVENANCE: original *untraced*

160 1880 **Caricature by Edward Linley Sambourne**, Punch's Fancy Portraits – No 12. Mr Ruskin
REPRODUCED: *Punch*, 18 Dec. 1880
Works Cat.: Listed on p.213 (where dated in error 12 Dec.)
PROVENANCE: original *untraced*

161 1881 **Sketch by himself**, showing himself and a group of people climbing a hillside, 15 September. Pen and ink on a sheet of Brantwood notepaper, $4^{1}/_{2}$ x 7
PROVENANCE: Webling family; by descent to Ruskin Watts; presented by him to Brantwood; *Whitehouse Collection* (RF B XIX)

162 1881 **Drawing of the façade of The Fine Art Society, Ruskin in conversation with Whistler on pavement, by T. Raffles Davison**, pen and ink
REPRODUCED: *British Architect* 16 Dec. 1881; Fine Art Society: *FAS100* 1976, fig B; Dearden: *John Ruskin and the Alps* 1991, p. 27; and elsewhere
PROVENANCE: *The Fine Art Society*

163 **Drawing by T. Raffles Davison**, sepia
EXHIBITED: Manchester 1904 (368)
PROVENANCE: W.E.A. Axon (1904); *untraced*

164 1881 **Bust by G. Atkinson**, December, head and shoulders. Modelled in clay or plaster, 11" high
Works Cat.: 42
PROVENANCE: *untraced*

165 1881 **Bust by G. Atkinson**, head and shoulders. Terra-cotta cast of No. 127, by Jabez Thompson, 12" high.
PROVENANCE:
1 Alexander Macdonald; Miss J.K. Macdonald; bequeathed with her house, c.1930 to Society of Oxford Home Students, which became *St Anne's College, Oxford* (Incised on reverse: John Ruskin/Modelled at Brantwood 1881/by G. Atkinson/Published by Jabez Thompson/ Northwich/Registered [and number] 36)
2 Given by a Welsh builder to John Challinor, who gave it in 1967 to *Whitehouse Collection* (RF R 90) (Stamped on reverse: Ruskin/Jabez Thompson/Northwich)
3 J. Thornton; by descent to his grandson J.S.D. Thornton, bookseller of Oxford; *Whitehouse Collection, Brantwood* (incised as (1) above but numbered 12)
4 The Fine Art Society, Edinburgh, 1987; a Scottish dealer; Joanna Barnes Fine Arts, sold in 1996 to *Abbot Hall Art Gallery, Kendal* (incised as (1) but numbered 22)
5 *Whitehouse Collection, Brantwood*, (numbered 23).
Copies, cast by Tony Flood from one of the Brantwood busts, have been made for sale at Brantwood. Up to May 1993 some thirteen had been made. They are numbered separately to the originals.

166 1882 **Portrait with Laurence Hilliard posing as Ruskin by William Gershom Collingwood**, February, full length, seated at the winter table in the Brantwood study, watercolour, 29³/₄ x 19¹/₂, signed and dated W.G. Collingwood Brantwood 1882
REPRODUCED: As a colour plate with descriptive text on reverse, by W. Holmes of Ulverston, 1902 (3s 6d); *Picture Post*, 21 Sept. 1944; *Dearden II*, p. 176; Blunt: *Cockerell*, p. 48; Dearden: *John Ruskin and the Ruskin Museum at Coniston*, p. 1; and elsewhere
EXHIBITED: Coniston 1900 (205); London 1919 (250); Ruskin and his circle 1964 (36); Whitworth 1989 (31)
Works Cat.: 43
PROVENANCE: W.G. Collingwood; *Ruskin Museum, Coniston*

167 1893 **Portrait by W.G. Collingwood**, copied from No. 166, pencil and watercolour heightened with white, 10³/₄ x 16³/₄, signed and dated W.G. Collingwood 1893
EXHIBITED: Whitworth 1989 (32)
PROVENANCE: Christie's 26 April 1988; *Private Collection*

168 1883 **Portrait by Ethel Webling**, head only, February-March. Silver point drawing
REPRODUCED: P. Webling: *A Sketch of John Ruskin*, [1914] frontis.; P. Webling: *Peggy, the Story of One Score Years and Ten*, p. 446; *The Bookman*, Dec. 1914
PROVENANCE: *untraced*

169 1882 **Caricature by Alfred Bryan**, Days with Celebrities 46 – Mr Ruskin, signed with initials
REPRODUCED: *Moonshine*, 6 May 1882
Works Cat.: Listed on p. 213
PROVENANCE: original *untraced*

170 1882 **Portrait by Valentine Cameron Princep**, head and shoulders, full face. Oil, 5¹/₂ x 3¹/₂, on ivory composition
REPRODUCED: *Dearden II*, p. 176
EXHIBITED: Arts Council 1954 (John Ruskin, 41); Pre-Raphaelites in Oxford, Japan 1987 (14)
PROVENANCE: Fine Art Society; sold in 1934 to *Ashmolean Museum, Oxford*

171 1882 **Photograph by Elliott & Fry**, head and shoulders, full face
REPRODUCED: *Works* XXIX, frontis.; engraving 'Done for F. Parsons, The 'Morris' Studio, Boston, U.S.A. Copyright 1903', 10 x 7 (in Wellesley Colln); *Bookman* March 1908, 28; and elsewhere, frequently
Works Cat.: 44

172 **Portrait based on No. 171, by Phoebe Traquair**, 1885-86, in one of a series of lunettes surrounding the panel depicting the Three Divine Powers
REPRODUCED: Elizabeth Cumming: *Phoebe Anna Traquair* 1993, p. 14
PROVENANCE: Part of mural, south walls of Mortuary Chapel, *Royal Hospital for Sick Children, Edinburgh*

173 **Portrait based on No. 171, by M. Ethel Jameson**, pen and ink, signed with initials
REPRODUCED: M.E. Jameson: *A Bibliographical contribution to the study of John Ruskin* 1901, frontis.
PROVENANCE: original *untraced*

174 **Portrait by Isabella Jay**, head and shoulders, full face, based on No. 171, c. 1882. Pastel, 15 x 11
REPRODUCED: *Dearden I*, p. 194
PROVENANCE: Bequeathed by the artist in 1919 to J.H. Whitehouse; *Whitehouse Collection* (RF 738)

175 **Bust by Roland Morris**, 1882-87, based on No. 171, manufactured by Robinson & Leadbetter. Parian ware, $7\frac{1}{2}$" high; some copies have an additional plinth bringing the overall height up to $11\frac{1}{2}$". Impressed with the name RUSKIN on the front of the plinth and with the makers' monogram R&L on reverse of right shoulder.
REPRODUCED: P. Atterbury (ed.), *The Parian Phenomenon* 1989, p. 233
Provenance; *Whitehouse Collection, Brantwood*; *Whitehouse Collection, Lancaster* (RF R113); *J.S. Dearden*; *Mikimoto Collection*; *R. Smith*; *Stephen Wildman* (two latter are the smaller brown version)

176 **Bust by K. Kitaji**, c.1931, based on No. 175. Bronze, $7\frac{3}{4}$" high, J. Ruskin cut into plinth
PROVENANCE: Probably commissioned by R. Mikimoto; *Mikimoto Colln.* (There is a plaster cast of the bust also in the Mikimoto collection, and a photograph overprinted '1931.1.10 by Kitaji'

177 **Portrait, head and shoulders, by Herbert Cole**, based on No. 171. Pen and ink, $3\frac{7}{8}$ x $2\frac{7}{8}$ on card $5\frac{1}{2}$ x $3\frac{3}{4}$, signed with initials
PROVENANCE: J.M. Dent & Co.; Ian Hodgkins Cat 33 no 238, 1990; *J.J. Challem*

178 1882 **Photograph by H.R. Barraud**, head and shoulders, head turned to left

179 1882 **Photograph by H.R. Barraud**, head and shoulders, full face
REPRODUCED: Supplement to *Bookman*, Oct. 1908; engraving by T. Johnson, $6\frac{3}{4}$ x $5\frac{3}{8}$ in Wellesley Collection

180 **Portrait by T.H. Stephenson**, after No. 179. Oil on canvas, $23\frac{1}{2}$ x $17\frac{1}{4}$
PROVENANCE: Possibly commissioned by Edward Woolgar; given by his step-daughter, Mrs Inman, to Brantwood; *Whitehouse Collection* (RF (802))

181 **Portrait by Joseph Simpson**, after No. 179
REPRODUCED: Drinkwater (ed.), *Outline of Literature* (c.1920), p. 556
PROVENANCE: original *untraced*

182 **Portrait based on No. 179**
REPRODUCED: Photograph in National Portrait Gallery Archive endorsed 'Presented by Plimpton 1933'
PROVENANCE: original *untraced*

183 **Portrait based on No. 179**. Pen and ink
REPRODUCED: *Sheffield Weekly Telegraph*; *Sheffield Illustrated II*, 1885
PROVENANCE: original *untraced*

184 **Bust, based on No. 179 manufactured by Carlton China**. Cast in Parian ware and mounted on a porcelain plinth painted with imaginary coat of arms of Coniston. Bust $3\frac{1}{4}$" high, overall, 5"; stamped across back of shoulders, John Ruskin
PROVENANCE: *J.S. Dearden*; *R. Smith*; *R. Williams*; *Mikimoto Collection*
In the 1970s Mr Williams produced some casts of the bust without its plinth of which there is one in the *Whitehouse Collection*.

185 1882 **Photograph by H.R. Barraud**, head and shoulders, full face, eyes looking right
REPRODUCED: engraving by T.A. Butler, $6\frac{3}{4}$ x $4\frac{7}{8}$, at Wellesley

186 **Portrait, full face, by Henry H. Sands**, based on No. 185. Oil on board, 9 x 6
PROVENANCE: (information from old label): Commissioned by Howard S. Pearson; at his death given by his daughter to 'K.H.' Sept. 1923; Bonham 17 Nov. 1994 (137); *Whitehouse Collection*.

187 1882 **Photograph by H.R. Barraud**, head and shoulders, full face turned slightly right
REPRODUCED: Collingwood: *Life and Work of John Ruskin*, II, p. 215
Works Cat.: 48

188 1882 **Photograph by Elliott & Fry** (second sitting), 9 August, head and shoulders, full face, head tilted to left
REPRODUCED: Supplement to *Bookman*, Feb. 1919; engraving omitting top coat by C. Lewis, 7¼ x 5⅛ at Wellesley

189 **Portrait by Harrison Ruskin Fowler**, based on No. 188, after February 1919. Beaten copper relief, probably 8½ x 4, signed with monogram HRF
Reproduced from a pencil drawing by Harrison Fowler of the relief in E.H Scott: *Ruskin's Guild of St George* 1931, frontis.
PROVENANCE: by descent to the artist's daughter, Holda Fowler; *untraced*

190 1882 **Photograph by Elliott & Fry** (second sitting), 9 August, head and shoulders, looking half right
REPRODUCED: frequently, including *Spielmann II*, p. 123; Spielmann: *John Ruskin* 1900, p. 157 (where attributed to Barraud)
Works Cat.: 46

191 1882 **Portrait by William Gershom Collingwood**, 18 August (misdated 1884). Pencil, inscribed in ink by Ruskin, J.R. in contemplation of a mediaeval Town (Troyes). Drawn by G. Collingwood. 18 August 1884
REPRODUCED: Hunt: *The Wider Sea* 1982, pl.28a
PROVENANCE: Given by the artist to Ruskin, and by him probably to C.E. Norton; by descent to Miss Elizabeth Norton; in album sold by her in 1944 to *Beinecke Library, Yale University*

192 1882 **Caricature, with W.G. Collingwood and Frank Randal**, by Charles Randal. Pen and ink, 3½ x 4½ (at top of sheet 7⅛ x 4½) inscribed and dated 'Modern Artists' N.B. The third artist will arrive in a few minutes by the train in the background. Charles Randal Del et Invt. Sept. 7. 1882
REPRODUCED: John Gibbens: 'My dear Aunt', *Oldie*, Jan. 1996, p. 33
PROVENANCE: Part of letter from the artist to his sister Fanny Randal, 8 September 1882; by descent to Miss Evelyn Sage; Abbott & Holder List 303 (285) March 1996; *Guild of St George*

193 1883 **Portrait by Dugald Sutherland McColl**, 9 March, three-quarter length, standing at a lecturer's desk. Pencil, 5 x 3, inscribed (?later): Ruskin's opening lecture 1882
REPRODUCED: *Times* 5 Mar. 1932; *Studio* CXXXII, no. 645, Dec. 1946, p. 179
EXHIBITED: Ruskin and his circle 1964 (37)
PROVENANCE: Presented in April 1932 by the artist to *The Ruskin Drawing School, Oxford*

194 **Copy by Alan Sorrell of No. 193**. Pencil, 3" high, inscribed: John Ruskin lecturing at Oxford by D.S. MacColl
PROVENANCE: *Mrs Elizabeth Sorrell*

195 1883 **Medallion by Clement Emptmeyer**
EXHIBITED: Royal Academy (Ruskin and Carlyle) 1883 (1662)
Works Cat.: 55
PROVENANCE: *untraced*

196 1884 **Portrait by Kate Greenaway**, February. Drawing, never completed
Works Cat.: 48a
PROVENANCE: *untraced*

197 1884 **Portrait by unidentified artist**. Pencil, 5⅞ x 4¾ (sight), signed with monogram, inscribed and dated, John Ruskin at the London Institute Feb. 11th 1883 [sic] 5.45pm
PROVENANCE: Kendal antique dealer; *Whitehouse Collection, Brantwood*

198 1884 **Portrait, head and study of eyes, study for No. 199, by Theodore Blake Wirgman**. Pencil and light brown wash heightened with white, $10^{1}/_{4}$ x $5^{1}/_{8}$
Reproduced: J.D. Hunt: *The Wider Sea* 1982, frontis.
Provenance: William Drummond; *Pierpont Morgan Library* (1981.27.1)

199 1884 **Portrait by Theodore Blake Wirgman**, ?February, three-quarter length, seated in his study at Herne Hill. Pencil, $10^{1}/_{2}$ x $13^{1}/_{2}$, signed T. Blake Wirgman, Herne Hill
Reproduced: *Graphic*, 3 April 1886; *Harper's Bazar* XIX, No. 17, p. 276; *Bookman* March 1900, p. 190; *Dearden II*, p. 177; *Spectator* 24 July 1971; J.D. Hunt: *The Wider Sea* 1982, pl.4g (reproduced from *The Graphic*); Dearden: *John Ruskin's Camberwell* 1990, frontis.; Merrill: *Pot of Paint* 1992, p. 278
Works Cat.: 49
Provenance: *The Graphic*; sold at Christie's; M.H. Spielmann, who gave it in 1939 to the *National Portrait Gallery* (3035)

200 1884 **Bust by Conrad Dressler**, head and shoulders, modelled in clay or plaster, 16" high
Works Cat.: 50
Provenance: *untraced*

201 **Bust by Conrad Dressler**. Plaster cast of No. 200, 16" high (on square plinth, overall 22"), signed and dated 1885
Exhibited: London 1919 (234)
Provenance: J. Ruskin; Joan Severn; sold at Sotheby's 8 May 1931 (61); H.H. Silbert who presented it in November 1932 to Hendon Library; *now lost*

202 **Bust by Conrad Dressler**. Plaster cast of No. 200, 16" high (on round plinth) dated 1892
Reproduced: *Spielmann II*, 124; Spielmann: *John Ruskin* 1900, p. 170; M. Cole: *Whitelands College, The History* 1982, p. 21
Provenance: *Whitelands College*

203 **Bust by Conrad Dressler**. Plaster cast of No. 200, 22" overall, dated 1903
Provenance: Thomas Thornton, presented on 12 March 1904 to Ruskin Memorial Hall, now *Bournville School of Arts & Crafts*

204 **Bust by Conrad Dressler**. Terracotta from No. 200, 16" high (on square plinth) dated 1885
Reproduced: *Graphic* 27 Jan. 1900; Collins: *Sculptures from the Life* (reprint in 1904 of the 1889 exhibition catalogue), cover
Exhibited: New Gallery, summer 1888 (32); Dowdeswell & Dowdeswell, June 1889 (27)
Provenance: Thomas Thornton; presented in 1902 to National Gallery; transferred in 1912 to *Tate Gallery* (2242)

205 **Bust by Conrad Dressler**, head only. Terracotta from No. 200, 16" high, (on square terracotta plinth, overall $18^{1}/_{2}$" high), signed and dated 1887
Provenance: ? Mr Bunn; Sotheby's Belgravia 23 Nov. 1982 (233) unsold; *untraced*

206 **Bust by Conrad Dressler**. Based on No. 200; modelled in terracotta-coloured plaster, on round plinth, 10" overall. Signed and dated 1888
Provenance: John Ruskin; said to have been given by him – or the Severn family – to) Rathbone family (pencil name on base, H.F. Rathbone); *John Hutchinson*, c.1986

207 **Bust by Conrad Dressler**. Bronze casts from No. 206, $6^{1}/_{2}$" high (excluding square base)
Reproduced: *The Artist*, March 1900
Works Cat.: 51 (inaccurately listed as the Bournville cast)
Provenance:
1 M.H. Spielmann, presented by the artist; *untraced*
2 Arthur Jones, presented in 1924 to the *National Portrait Gallery* (2030)

208 c.1884 **Portrait by William Gershom Collingwood**, as a design for the seal of the Ruskin Society of Liverpool, head looking left
REPRODUCED: Engraved by Hugh Allen, 1 1/8 x 7/8
EXHIBITED: engraving exhibited at Manchester 1904 (417)
Works Cat.: 41 (where inaccurately dated c. 1879)
PROVENANCE: original *untraced*

209 1884 **Fancy Portrait by T.G.** – The Pleasures of England
REPRODUCED: *Fun* Dec. 1884
PROVENANCE: original *untraced*

210 1885 **Photograph by H.R. Barraud**, three-quarter length, leaning on a tree, eyes looking right, May-June

211 1885 **Photograph by H.R. Barraud**, three-quarter length, leaning on tree, full face

212 1885 **Photograph by H.R. Barraud**, three-quarter length, leaning on a tree, body facing slightly left
REPRODUCED: *Bookman* March 1900, 191; Pengelly: *John Ruskin* (2nd ed. only) p. 120
Works Cat.: 53

213 1885 **Photograph by H.R. Barraud**, head and shoulders, profile looking left

214 **Portrait by unknown artist**, based on No. 213. Watercolour on white card, 5 1/2 x 4 1/4
REPRODUCED: *Dearden I*, p. 194
PROVENANCE: *Whitehouse Collection* (RF B XV)

215 1885 **Photograph by H.R. Barraud**, head and shoulders, head turned slightly left
REPRODUCED: *Bookman*, March 1900, 189

216 1885 **Photograph by H.R. Barraud**, seated at table, head on hand
REPRODUCED: *Works* XXXIV, frontis.; *Bookman*, Oct. 1908, 28
Works Cat.: 47

217 1885 **Photograph by H.R. Barraud**, seated at a table, writing, full face

218 **Engraving by W. Burton**, c.1889, after No. 217
REPRODUCED: Collingwood: *John Ruskin, a biographical outline*, frontis.; separate proofs of this engraving were also issued

219 1885 **Photograph by H.R. Barraud**, seated at a table, writing
REPRODUCED: *Bookman*, March 1900, p. 192 (where parts of the chair and table are painted in); R. Maas: *John Ruskin and his circle* 1991, p. 26

220 1885 **Photograph by H.R. Barraud**, seated in an upright chair by table
REPRODUCED: *Bookman*, March 1900, p. 191
Works Cat.: 54

221 1885 **Photograph by Green Bros. of Grasmere**, leaning against a wall at Brantwood
REPRODUCED: *Works* XXXVII, frontis.; Abraham: *Some Portraits of the Lake Poets*, p. 47; *Times Literary Supplement*, 11 Feb. 1972
Works Cat.: 52

222 1886 **Caricature**: Mr Ruskin has been complaining that he can find no books about the shrimp ...
Reproduced in unidentified journal
PROVENANCE: original *untraced*

223 1887 **Caricature of Ruskin as the Gauche-hen, by L.T.(?)**
REPRODUCED: *Punch* June 1887
PROVENANCE: original *untraced*

224 1887 **Portrait by Henry Jamyn Brooks**, painted in 1889, full length, partly obscured, in large group at Private View of 'Old Masters' exhibition at Royal Academy, 30 December 1887. Oil, 60 x 160 (Ruskin's head 1 4/5" high)
PROVENANCE: Deposited on loan by the artist in 1909 and presented in 1919 to the *National Portrait Gallery* (1833)

225 1888 **Miniature by Ethel Webling**, head only. On ivory, oval 4 x 3 1/4
REPRODUCED: *Dearden II*, p. 177
EXHIBITED: Royal Academy 1888 (1546)
Works Cat.: 56
PROVENANCE: Given by the artist to her nephew, *Ruskin Watts*

226 1888 **A pair of caricatures by 'Kuklos'**: 'John Ruskin sees a cyclist!' and 'A cyclist sees John Ruskin'
Reproduced in unidentified journal
PROVENANCE: original *untraced*

227 1888 **Caricature by F.C.G.** in the New Gallery of Portraiture
REPRODUCED: *Pall Mall Gazette*, 21 April 1888
PROVENANCE: original *untraced*

228 1888 **Portrait by Edward Robert Hughes**, 24 April, full length, seated, in the South Kensington Museum. Pencil on white paper, 7 x 4; inscribed and dated: John Ruskin SKM Ap 24 1888 E.R. Hughes
REPRODUCED: *Dearden I*, p. 194
PROVENANCE: Given by the artist in 1902 to Sidney Morse; bought 11 March 1952 by J.H. Whitehouse; *Whitehouse Collection* (RF 245)

229 c.1889 **Portrait in stained glass, made in the glass works at Youghal, Ireland**
Works Cat.: Listed on p. 213
PROVENANCE: Commissioned by Robert Day F.S.A. and presented to Cork High School for Girls; *untraced*

230 1890 **Imaginative portrait of Ruskin standing in Brantwood study, probably based on a photograph and A. Macdonald's painting of the room**
REPRODUCED: *Cassell's Saturday Journal*, 12 April 1890, p. 681; *Literature*, 24 Aug. 1901, p. 174
Works Cat.: 68
PROVENANCE: original *untraced*

231 1891 **Caricature**: Ariel's Album. Fifty First Portrait John Ruskin M.A., LL.D.
REPRODUCED: unidentified newspaper cutting dated 28 Feb. 1891
PROVENANCE: original *untraced*

232 1891 **Photograph, probably by Lund of Coniston**, with Joan Severn in Jumping Jenny, Arthur Severn standing in his boat beyond, Summer
REPRODUCED: Birkenhead: *Illustrious Friends*, 1965, p. 300

233 1891 **Photograph, probably by Lund of Coniston**, with Joan Severn in Jumping Jenny, Arthur Severn sitting in his boat beyond, Summer

234 1891 **Photograph, probably by Lund of Coniston**, in Jumping Jenny, to left, with Arthur Severn in his boat, centre, Summer

235 1892 **Photograph by Captain Walker**, with Joan Severn, standing near waterfall steps at Brantwood, Spring
REPRODUCED: as a drawing in Collingwood: *Life and Work of John Ruskin*, II, p. 244
Works Cat.: 57

236 1892 **Caricature of Ruskin standing on Whistler's head, by Phil May**, January
REPRODUCED: *Pick-me-up*, 9 January 1892; L. Merrill: *Pot of Paint* 1992, p. 58
PROVENANCE: original *untraced*

237 1892 **Photograph, standing against a leafy wall, wearing hat, by J. McClelland**, Summer

238 1892 **Photograph, standing by leafy wall, holding hat, with Joan Severn, by J. McClelland**, Summer

239 1893 **Photograph by Sarah Angelina Acland**, seated in a basket chair, 1 August
REPRODUCED: *Bookman*, March 1900, 193; D. Measham: *John Ruskin, the last chapter* 1989, p. 3
Works Cat.: 59

240 **Portrait by B.C. Leeming**, 1901, based on No. 239. Ink, 12¼ x 10¼, signed and dated: B.C. Leeming 01
PROVENANCE: F.J. Sharp; *J.S. Dearden*

241 1893 **Photograph by Sarah Angelina Acland**, seated in a basket chair, with Sir Henry Acland, 1 August
REPRODUCED: Acland & Ruskin: *The Oxford Museum* 1893, p. xxv; Atlay: *Sir Henry Wentworth Acland, Bart.*, p. 476; *Works* XXXV, pl. A; *Country Life*, 23 Nov. 1972
Works Cat.: 58

242 1893 **Photograph by Sarah Angelina Acland**, seated in a basket chair, with Sir Henry Acland and Joan Severn, 1 August
REPRODUCED: Birkenhead: *Illustrious Friends*, p. 300

243 1893 **Photograph by J. McClelland**, on curved wooden garden seat, looking left, August

244 1893 **Photograph by J. McClelland**, on curved wooden garden seat, looking right, August

245 1893 **Photograph by J. McClelland**, on curved wooden garden seat, Joan Severn with sun shade standing right, August

246 1893 **Photograph by J. McClelland**, on curved wooden garden seat, with Joan Severn, August

247 1893 **Photograph by J. McClelland**, seated in study arm chair, fingers on chin, August

248 1893 **Caricature by John Wallace**, depicting Ruskin as St George, Autumn
REPRODUCED: *John Ruskin on himself and things in general*, (Cope's, 1893), cover
PROVENANCE: original *untraced*

249 1893 **Fancy Portrait by John Wallace**, standing in a gondola with Venice in the background, Autumn
REPRODUCED: *John Ruskin on himself and things in general*, (Cope's, 1893), frontis.
PROVENANCE: original *untraced*

250 1893 **Fancy Portrait by John Wallace**, showing Ruskin seated in front of Brantwood, Autumn
REPRODUCED: *John Ruskin on himself and things in general*, (Cope's, 1893), title page
PROVENANCE: original *untraced*

251 c.1893 **Sheet of sketches by Gutzon Borglum**, showing Ruskin's head and shoulders, right hand supporting head, and left hand, gripping arm of chair. Pencil, 6 1/3 x 3 3/4
PROVENANCE: By descent to the artist's son, *Lincoln Borglum*

252 c.1893 **Sketch by Gutzon Borglum**, full face head only. Pencil, 7 x 5
PROVENANCE: By descent to the artist's son, *Lincoln Borglum*

253 c.1893 **Sketch by Gutzon Borglum**, full length, standing. Pencil, 14 1/2 x 11
PROVENANCE: By descent to the artist's son, *Lincoln Borglum*

254 c.1893 **Statue by Gutzon Borglum**, made in 1903-4, seated in arm chair, right hand on book. Bronze, 15" high x 12" long
REPRODUCED: *Studio* XL, No. 167, Feb. 1907, p. 35; *Scribner's Magazine*, Dec. 1917, LXII, No. 6, p. 745; W. Price: *Gutzon Borglum, Artist & Patriot*, p. 62; Rhode Island School of Design exhibition cat, p. 111
EXHIBITED: (The Classical Spirit in American Portraiture) 1976 (48, lent by Met. Mus. of Art)
PROVENANCE: Casts:
1 Rhode Island School of Design (acquired 1929; sold New York 1949); *untraced*
2 George G. Booth, given in 1919 to *Detroit Institute of Art* (cast dated 1903)
3 *Warrel Howell* (bought c.1955)
4 David Peel (in 1965) signed on reverse Gutzon Borglum 1903 – copyrighted 1905 Gutzon Borglum No. 3; *untraced*
5 *Metropolitan Museum of Art, New York* (acquired in 1906, signed and dated 1904)
6 Kerrison Preston; Sotheby's, 20 April 1968, lot 125; *Mrs Naughton*

255 **Bust, head and shoulders, by Kotaro Takamura**, based on No. 254, 1906-1907. Bronze, 5" high
REPRODUCED: *Kindai-no-Bijutsu*, No. 7, Nov. 1971, p. 41; Prof. Goto (ed.), *Ruskin and Morris*, Great Books of the World Series, Tokyo 1971, p. 44; K. Anazawa *et al.* (eds.), *Kotaro Takamura's Whole Scuptural Works*, Tokyo 1973, p. 171
PROVENANCE:
1 By descent to the sculptor's nephew, *Tadashi Takamura*
2 Perhaps bought from the sculptor in Italy by R. Mikimoto; *Mikimoto Collection* (incised on base: Copied from Mr G. Borglum)
3 Mrs Homma, gift to *J.S. Dearden*
4 There are two further bronzes and a plaster cast in the *Mikimoto Collection*
5 Copy after No. 255 in bronzed plaster, 12" high, *Mikimoto Collection*

256 **Model of Ruskin's left hand, by Gutzon Borglum**, 1903-1904. Bronze, 3" long, incised on cuff, Borglum, and under the hand, Hand of Ruskin
PROVENANCE: a number of casts were given by Gutzon Borglum to his friends; *untraced*
Plaster cast made by Lincoln Borglum for *J.S. Dearden*

257 1894 **Photograph by C.P. MacCarthy**, head and shoulders, full face, sitting in Brantwood study, May
Works Cat.: 59a
Reproduced as a postcard

258 1894 **Photograph by Frederick Hollyer**, seated against a wall, with W. Holman Hunt, September
REPRODUCED: *The Sphere*, 6 July 1901; D Measham: *John Ruskin, the last chapter* 1989, p. 2; R. Maas: *Ruskin and his circle* 1991, p. 26

259 1894 **Photograph by Frederick Hollyer**, seated against a wall, with Joan Severn, September
REPRODUCED: Birkenhead: *Illustrious Friends*, p. 332

260 1894 **Photograph by Frederick Hollyer**, seated against a wall, by himself, September

261 1894 **Photograph by Frederick Hollyer**, seated in Brantwood study, profile, looking left, September
REPRODUCED: *Works* XXXV, frontis. (where called Datur hora quieti, and dated 1896); *St George* II, frontis.
Works Cat.: 60

262 **Portrait, based on No. 261, by Garschagen**. Oil on canvas, 35¾" x 31¼", signed and dated (bottom right) 1902
PROVENANCE: by descent to *F.J.H. Rutgers van der Loeff*

263 1894 **Photograph by Frederick Hollyer**, seated in Brantwood study, full face, September
REPRODUCED: Meynell: *Friends of a Lifetime*, p. 60

264 1895 **Photograph by ?P. Baxter**, group on ice off Brantwood, Joan Severn standing and ?J. McClelland in background, 14 February
REPRODUCED: *Picture Post*, 23 Sept. 1944; *Country Life* 2 Feb. 1978, pp. 272-73, fig.1

265 1895 **Photograph by John McClelland**, group on ice off Brantwood, Joan Severn standing, Baxter on tricycle to right, 14 February
REPRODUCED: *Country Life*, 2 Feb. 1978, fig. 2

266 1895 **Photograph by John McClelland**, group on ice off Brantwood, Joan Severn seated, 14 February
REPRODUCED: Birkenhead: *Illustrious Friends*, p. 301; *Country Life*, 2 Feb. 1978, fig. 3; B. Hanson: *Brantwood* 1992, p. 32; Brantwood Christmas Card 1997 (with inaccurate caption)

267 1895 **Photograph by John McClelland**, standing, three quarter length, in overcoat and fur gloves, 14 February
REPRODUCED: *Bookman*, March 1900, p. 173; *Country Life*, 2 Feb. 1978, fig. 5; Dearden: *John Ruskin e le Alpi* 1990, p. 11
Works Cat.: 61 (where wrongly dated 1897)

268 1895 **Photograph by John McClelland**, standing in snow with P. Baxter and Bramble (who moved), 14 February
REPRODUCED: Wilenski: *John Ruskin*, p. 178 (where wrongly dated 1893)

269 1895 **Photograph by John McClelland**, standing in snow with P. Baxter and Bramble (who did not move), 14 February
REPRODUCED: *Country Life* 2 Feb. 1978, fig. 4

270 1895 **Photograph by John McClelland**, sitting in basket chair outside study window, with walking stick, 14 February
REPRODUCED: R. Sawyer (ed.), *The Island from within* 1990, p. 50

271 1895 **Photograph by John McClelland**, sitting in basket chair outside study window, without walking stick, 14 February

272 1897 **Portrait of William Gershom Collingwood**, head and shoulders, January/ February. Oil, 23¾ x 19¾, inscribed (at top): John Ruskin ætatis-anno lxxviii, [at foot] W.G. Collingwood 1897, [and on reverse] John Ruskin / AD MDCCCXCVII / by W.G. Collingwood / Coniston / (This is the original study / painted from the life at / Brantwood)
REPRODUCED: in colour on p. 3 of a 'Seasons Greetings' folder from Antoinette and Warren Howell
EXHIBITED: Liverpool; Whitechapel ?1900; Coniston 1900 (279a); Coniston 1919 (213); London 1919 (105)

Works Cat.: 66
PROVENANCE: By descent to the artist's daughter, Mrs Dora Altounyan; sold by her executors at Sotheby's 16 Feb. 1966 (£150); C.J. Sawyer; Warren Howell; given, c.1985 to *Pierpont Morgan Library*

273 1897 **Portrait by William Gershom Collingwood**, three quarter length, seated, 29 January. Oil, 29 x 26½, inscribed W.G. Collingwood / Brantwood / Jan. 29 1897
REPRODUCED: *Dearden II*, p. 178
EXHIBITED: Royal Society of British Artists
Works Cat.: 65
PROVENANCE: *Ruskin Museum, Coniston*

274 **Portrait after No. 273, by Bryan Thorpe**, embroidered, cross stitch, 13" x 11", 1996
PROVENANCE: made for *Alan Turvey*

275 1897 **Portrait by William Gershom Collingwood**, three quarter length, seated, 19 February. Oil, 35½ x 28¼, inscribed W.G. Collingwood / Brantwood Feby 19 1897
REPRODUCED: *Dearden I*, p. 195; Dearden: *Ruskin, Bembridge and Brantwood* 1994, p. 65
EXHIBITED: John Ruskin and Victorian Art, Japan 1993 (241)
PROVENANCE: J. Ruskin; Severn family; sold at Brantwood sale 28 July 1931 (83, £24) to Mrs C.D. Cooper; presented by her to Brantwood, 1939-40; *Whitehouse Collection* (RF 163)

276 1897 **Portrait by Arthur Severn**, half length, seated. Watercolour, 14 x 10¼, signed and dated, Arthur Severn 1897
REPRODUCED: *Dearden I*, p. 195; Dearden: *The Professor*, frontis.; Kendal exhib. cat. 1969
EXHIBITED: Manchester 1904 (95); London 1919 (236); Bembridge 1959 (14); Kendal 1969 (1); Maas Gallery, London, 1991 (40); John Ruskin and Victorian Art, Japan, 1993 (226)
Works Cat.: 64
PROVENANCE: The drawing was finished immediately after Ruskin's death in 1900, for Robert E. Cunliffe; J.H. Whitehouse; *Whitehouse Collection* (RF 529)

277 1898–99 **Portrait by Arthur Severn**, half length, seated. Oil 23 x 19, signed and dated, Arthur Severn 1898-9
REPRODUCED: Wedmore: *Turner and Ruskin* II [iv]; *Works* XXXVIII, frontis.
EXHIBITED: Keswick 1909 (87); Coniston 1919 (212); London 1919 (160)
Works Cat.: 63
PROVENANCE: Arthur Severn; *Ruskin Museum, Coniston*

278 1897 **Photograph by John McClelland**, seated in study, full face, hands visible, 17 July
REPRODUCED: *Scribner's Magazine*, Dec. 1898; *Bookman*, Dec. 1899, supplement; *Bookman* March 1900, p. 194
Works Cat.: 62

279 1897 **Photograph by John McClelland**, seated in study, full face, hands invisible, 17 July

280 1898 **Photograph by John McClelland**, sitting in wheel chair at Brantwood front door, 25 July (Sitting A)
REPRODUCED: Viljoen: *Ruskin's Backgrounds, Friendships and Interests*, New York exhibition catalogue 1965, p. 2

281 1898 **Photograph by John McClelland**, sitting in wheel chair at Brantwood front door with Joan Severn seated, 25 July (Sitting A)

282 1898 **Photograph by John McClelland**, sitting in wheel chair at Brantwood front door with Joan Severn standing, 25 July (Sitting A)

283 1898 **Photograph by John McClelland**, sitting on a garden bench, with Bramble, July (Sitting B)

284 1898 **Photograph by John McClelland**, sitting on a garden bench with Joan Severn, July (Sitting B)

285 1898 **Photograph by John McClelland**, standing holding open sunshade, with Joan Severn, July (Sitting C)

286 1898 **Photograph by John McClelland**, relaxing in study arm chair, July (Sitting D)

287 1898 **Photograph by John McClelland**, sitting in study arm chair, three quarter length, July (Sitting D)

288 1898 **Photograph by John McClelland**, sitting in study arm chair, Joan Severn standing behind, July (Sitting D)

289 1899 **Portrait by C. Hertschel**, after an earlier photograph. Pen and ink, $9\frac{1}{8}$ x $7\frac{5}{8}$
Reproduced: *Daily Chronicle* 8 Feb. 1899 (to illustrate article by H.W. Nevinson); *Daily Chronicle* 22 Feb. 1900
Provenance: with Manning Gallery in 1966; Christie's 12 Dec. 1967 (102, 28gns.); Sawyer; *untraced*

290 1899 **Portrait, life-sized, by Isaac Broome**, 'based on his latest photograph'
Provenance: *untraced*

291 1900 **Portrait by W. Small from a sketch by A. Cox**, face only, lying in coffin in Coniston Church, 24 January
Reproduced: *The Graphic* 3 Feb. 1900, p. 142
Provenance: *untraced*

292 1900 **Portrait medallion 'as he appeared in the seventies' by A.C. Lucchesi**. Bronze, $18\frac{3}{4}$ diameter
Reproduced: Rawnsley: Ruskin and the English Lake district, p. 208, Dearden (ed.), *Iteriad*, p. 49
Works Cat.: 67
Provenance: Set into a monolith of Borrowdale stone, *Friar's Crag, Derwentwater*
Casts in bronzed plaster:
1 H.D. Rawnsley; given by Mrs Rawnsley to *Whitehouse Collection* (RF R 87)
2 *Ruskin Museum, Coniston* (exhibited London 1919 (294))
3 *Corpus Christi College, Oxford* (now lost)

293 1900 **Portrait medallion by A.C. Lucchesi**. Bronze, $3\frac{1}{4}$" diameter, possibly casts of the original model for No. 292
Provenance:
1 H.D. Rawnsley; *Whitehouse Collection* (plaster cast in collection of *J.S. Dearden*)
2 *Ruskin Museum, Coniston*
3 *Roy Davids Ltd*. (Cat.IV, 117, 1998)

294 1901 **Portrait medallion designed by Messrs Farmer and Brindley**, February. Marble, approximately 60" x 30"
Provenance: The medallion forms the upper part of the Ruskin memorial Tablet in *St Paul's Church, Herne Hill*

295 1901 **Portrait medallion as he appeared about 1867, by Edward Onslow Ford**. Bronze
Reproduced: A photograph was issued to subscribers; *St George* VI, frontis.
Exhibited: A plaster cast was lent by Mrs Ford to Manchester 1904 (542)
Provenance: *Poet's Corner, Westminster Abbey*. Plaster cast *untraced*

296 **Portrait medallion, after No 295, by Alan Turvey**, Clay, mixed media, finished in acrylic bronze, 14" dia., 1996

297 1901 **Bust by Isaac Broome**
REPRODUCED: Broome: *The last days of the Ruskin Co-operative Association*
PROVENANCE: *untraced*

298 1901 **Bust by Henry C. Fehr**, based on an earlier photograph. Marble, 33½ high x 21 x 14
PROVENANCE: commissioned by J. Passmore Edwards for the Ruskin Gallery of *South London Art Gallery*

299 1901 **Relief plaque by Julia Bracken**, generally based on photographs
REPRODUCED: E. Boris: *Art and Labor. Ruskin, Morris and the Craftsman Ideal in America* 1986, p. 24
PROVENANCE: *Chicago Historical Society*

300 c. 1904 **Caricature by Max Beerbohm** of a group, including Ruskin, in D.G. Rossetti's garden at 16 Cheyne Walk. Watercolour over pencil, pen and ink, 7⅞ x 12½
REPRODUCED: Beerbohm: *The Poet's Corner* 1922; Ayrton & Turner: *Aspects of British Art*, p. 235; Pedrick: *Life with Rossetti*, pl.15; Times, 1 Jan. 1972; Beerbohm: *Rossetti and his circle*, ed. N.J. Hall, 1987, suppl.pl.3
Exhibition: Carfax Gallery, London, 1904; British Watercolours from Birmingham, Tokyo 1992 (7); Visions of Love and Life, New York & Birmingham 1995 (118)
Hart Davis No. 1272
PROVENANCE: Miss Gladys Curry ?; Langton Gallery; *Birmingham City Art Gallery* (P2'81)

301 1907 **Relief panel by Herbert Hampton**, including the figure of Ruskin. Bronze.
PROVENANCE: *Queen Victoria Monument, Dalton Square, Lancaster*

302 1908 **Imaginative portrait of Ruskin as Mark Alston, by E.C. Gillespy**
REPRODUCED: C.A.J. Sykes: *Mark Alston* 1908; C.W. Morley: *John Ruskin Late work 1870-1890* 1984, p. 339
PROVENANCE: original *untraced*

303 c. 1910 **Portrait, based on a photograph, by Frank Reginald Dickinson**. Wooden panel, carved and painted
PROVENANCE: set into the panelled dado of the living room of Little Holland House, 40 Beeches Avenue Carshalton, Surrey. By descent to Gerard Dickinson; *London Borough of Sutton*

304 1916 **Caricature by Max Beerbohm** – Rossetti introduces Ruskin to Fanny Cornforth. Watercolour and pencil, 13 x 9¾; inscribed and signed: Max 1916 Miss Cornforth: 'Oh, very pleased to meet Mr Ruskin, I'm sure'.
REPRODUCED: Beerbohm: *Rossetti and his circle* 1922; Beerbohm: *Rossetti and his circle*, ed. N.J. Hall, 1987, pl. 7
EXHIBITED: Royal Academy (Rossetti) 1973 (373)
Hart Davis No. 1272
PROVENANCE: *Tate Gallery* (5391(5))

305 1919 **Bust by Barbara Crystal Collingwood**, head and shoulders, modelled in plaster and finished in bronze, 11" high (study for No. 306)
EXHIBITED: London 1919 (530)
PROVENANCE: By descent to the artist's daughter Janet Gnosspelius, who gave it to *J.S. Dearden*
Plaster casts: *Whitehouse Collection* (RF R82 & R 88); *Armitt Library, Ambleside*

306 1919 **Bust by Barbara Crystal Collingwood**, head and shoulders, modelled in plaster, 22" high (excluding base)
REPRODUCED: R.G. Collingwood: *Ruskin's Philosophy* 1922
EXHIBITED: Coniston 1919 (218); London 1919 (235)
PROVENANCE: Bought by the *Ruskin Museum, Coniston* in 1919

307 1925 **Portrait medallion by Michel de Tarnowski**, 'The Pierre à Ruskin'. Bronze, 30" diameter
REPRODUCED: Payot: *Ruskin et les anglais a Chamonix* 1938, p. 2; Walton: Seven Ruskin Drawings in the Fogg Art Museum, *Harvard Library Bulletin* XIV, No. 2, Spring 1960, pl. viic
PROVENANCE: *Set onto a boulder at Chamonix*

308 c.1931 **Caricature by Max Beerbohm**, 'Shades of Rossetti, Ruskin, Swinburne, Pater and Whistler, wondering that so much space has been devoted to this other later Romantic – and whether even he is the 'Last One'. Pencil on brown paper, 8¼x 5½
REPRODUCED: Mayfield: *Swinburneiana*, (back cover)
Hart Davis No. 1829
PROVENANCE: Bought from the artist's collection at Rapallo by G.F. Sims (his catalogue No. 53 (48)); bought in May 1962 by *John S. Mayfield*

309 1936 **Caricature by Max Beerbohm**. 'If they were flourishing in this our day'; group includes Ruskin
REPRODUCED: *Manchester Guardian* 13 March 1936; Ayrton & Turner: *Aspects of British Art*, p. 235
Hart Davis No. 595
PROVENANCE: *untraced*

310 1946 **Portrait of Ruskin incorporated into re-working of Raphael's 'Death of Ananias', by Frank R. Dickinson**, signed and dated
EXHIBITED: accepted for but finally not hung in the Royal Academy Summer Exhibition 1946
PROVENANCE: By descent to Gerard Dickinson; *London Borough of Sutton*, at 40 Beeches Avenue, Carshalton, Surrey

311 1964 **Caricature by David Levine**, of Ruskin verbally assisting Turner with a Watercolour
REPRODUCED: Updike: *Pens and Needles: Literary Caricatures by David Levine* 1964, p. 111; New York Review of Books, c.1969
PROVENANCE: *untraced*

312 1971 **Bust by Richard Frederick Butterworth**, based on photographs, December. Modelled in 'Plastertone', c. 4" high
PROVENANCE: *Collection of the sculptor*

313 1972 **Portrait silhouette by Phyllis Arnold**, loosely based on No. 292. Black ink heightened with white, oval, 4 x 3
REPRODUCED: *Gazette of the Grolier Club*, N.S. 28/9, June/December 1978, cover
EXHIBITED: Grolier Club 'Ruskin observed' 1978 (42)
PROVENANCE:
1 *J.S. Dearden*
2 *R. Dyke Benjamin*

314 1972–76 **A series of ten etchings by Chris Orr**, and a watercolour re-worked from another plate, 1976, depicting the artist's impression of Ruskin's life.
1 Title page (on which only Ruskin's hat and stick appear)
2 Ruskin's Room
3 A Chump at Oxford
4 'Was that John?'
5 The Needles

6 Deaf in Venice
7 Life at Herne Hill
8 Rain, Shuttlecock and Stolen Kisses
9 The Angels of Boulogne
10 Ice Age, The Last Lecture
11 Ruskin and Effie arrive in Venice

Reproduced: as a set of etchings, 16½ x 10½, 75 prints per image (except the title plate, only available with a complete set, 10 x 10¾; Orr & Hewison: *Chris Orr's John Ruskin* (for which the 11th plate was re-worked as cover)
Exhibited: Bear Lane Gallery, Oxford, Dec. 1972; Thumb Gallery, London, June 1976

315 1974 **Caricature** of Ruskin in 'Clerihew No. 14'
Reproduced: *Sunday Telegraph* 5 May 1974

316 1974 **Caricature of Ruskin drawing Seven Lamps, in mural depicting Oxford University through the centuries, by Edward Bawden**. Mural, 7' 6" x 40'
Provenance: Mural above the steps leading into the Norrington Room, *B.H. Blackwell Ltd, Broad Street, Oxford*

317 1978 **Caricature by David Levine**, head and shoulders, full face. Pen and ink, 12 x 8½, signed and dated
Reproduced: *New York Review*
Provenance: *David Levine*

318 1980 **Caricature by David Levine**, whole figure, full face, with Rose La Touche. Pen and ink, 11 x 6½, signed and dated
Reproduced: *New York Review* 15 May 1980
Provenance: *David Levine*

319 1985 **Caricature by David Levine**, full face, seated at a table, with sketchbook and palette. Pen and ink over pencil, 13¾ x 11, signed and dated
Provenance: *Ashmolean Museum*, (E690(iii))

320 1985 **Caricature by David Smith**, standing at a desk. Ink on Academy Board, 15 x 11, signed and dated
Reproduced: *Guardian* 23 May 1985
Provenance: *Alan Turvey*

321 1989 **Caricature by David Smith**, with Millais and Effie Ruskin, looking at Millais's Glenfinlas portrait
Reproduced: Edward Abelson: *Misalliance: Disastrous and Bizarre Literary Love Lives* 1989
Provenance: *untraced*

322 1995 **Caricature by Bromley**, surrounded by books, seated at a computer keyboard, signed
Reproduced: *Financial Times* 6 February 1995
Provenance: *untraced*

323 1996 **Caricature by Peter Cross**, as a football player. Watercolour, body-colour and pencil, 5½ x 4½, signed with initials and with various labels
Reproduced: B. Brunori & T. Crowley: *The Illustrators* 1996, frontis.
Exhibited: Chris Beetles, The Illustrators 1996
Provenance: C. Beetles; *Alexander Beetles*

324 1998 **Bust, head and shoulders based on No. 70, by Mary Catterall**. Bronze resin, 16¾" high
Exhibited: Holy Trinity Church, Sloane Street, S.W.1, Summer 1998
Provenance: *the artist*

325 1998 **A series of illustrations by Geoffrey Appleton** for Michelle Lovric's book *Carpaccio's Cat*, New York: Artisan 1999. Only the illustrations containing an image of Ruskin are listed here. The listing is taken from the artist's brief, and thus may vary slightly in the finished book.

1	pp.6-7	Ruskin, head and shoulders, holding a copy of *Stones of Venice*
2	20	Ruskin comparing a locket of Rose La Touche's hair with Carpaccio's painting of St Ursula
3	21	Ruskin running past the cat which sits on the steps of S. Maria della Salute
4	22-23	Ruskin sitting in the traghetto
5	24-25	Ruskin at the Piazetta, cat rubbing round his legs, boy selling rotten figs in front of Ducal Palace
6	26-27	Ruskin at the Piazza S. Marco, with the basilica, campanile and piazza behind
7	28	Two vignettes: Ruskin looking at the orchestra at Caffé Florian, one with cat, one without
8	29	Two vignettes: Ruskin passing 'Drunkenness of Noah' angle of Ducal Palace; Ruskin walking past the other side of bridge
9	30-31	Vignette, cat preceding Ruskin to Scuola di S. Giorgio degli Schiavoni
10	32	Ruskin studying Carpaccio's St George
11	33	Ruskin writing in front of Carpaccio's St George
12	34	Carpaccio's St Ursula's bedroom, with Ruskin in bed instead of St Ursula
13	35	Ruskin looking at Carpaccio's St Ursula
14	35	Ruskin and his sketch of Rose La Touche
15	36-37	Ruskin looking into a bead shop window
16	38-39	Ruskin with Carpaccio's 'Two Venetian Ladies with their Pets' and 'The Languid Knight' from the St Ursula cycle
17	39	Ruskin and the cat
18	42	Ruskin at a cafe drinking coffee
19	41	Ruskin at the fish market
20	42-43	Ruskin in gondola passing Ca d'Oro
21	42-43	Ruskin running through the arches
22	46-47	Ruskin standing on balcony, Rose's face imprinted on the moon
23	48-49	Ruskin in pose of Carpaccio's St Augustine
24	50-51	Ruskin holding hat, coat-tails flying
25	50-51	Ruskin emerging from La Fenice steps
26	52-53	Ruskin looking at the cat, his cravat awry
27	57	Ruskin and the cat walking along a calle towards Scuola di S. Giogio degli Schiavoni
28	60	Ruskin and the cat outside a derelict doorway
29	61	Ruskin blowing dust off a picture of Carpaccio and the cat
30	62	Ruskin holding the picture of Carpaccio

326 1999 **Portrait, based on earlier likenesses, by Tullio Pericoli,** pencil, signed.
REPRODUCED: *L'Indice dei Libri del Mese,* May 1999

Addenda

327 1880s **Study of Ruskin, head and shoulders, half profile, by George Howard**. Pencil, 4½ x 3¼
PROVENANCE: By descent to *The Castle Howard Collection*

328 1880s **Study of Ruskin's head in profile, by George Howard**. Pencil, 4½ x 3¼
PROVENANCE: By descent to *The Castle Howard Collection*

George James Howard (1843–1911) was a skilled amateur painter and patron of the arts. He was friendly with many of the leading figures in the art world of his day – Browning, Tennyson, Lord Leighton – and particularly with Burne-Jones and Morris. He commissioned paintings from Burne-Jones, and Morris & Co. decorated his London home at 1 Palace Green which had been designed for him by Philip Webb. Howard first met Burne-Jones in the mid-1860s and the Burne-Joneses and Morrises stayed with the Howards at their home at Naworth Castle on several occasions. Although I can find no record of Howard meeting Ruskin, they clearly did so. Howard was *au fait* with Ruskin's work, and he helped continue one aspect of this work, with others, by commissioning T.M. Rooke to make records of ancient buildings. George Howard was a Liberal M.P. and succeeded as the 9th Earl of Carlisle in 1889. On 15 April 1890 the Earl of Carlisle opened the Guild of St George's new Ruskin Museum at Meersbrook Park, Sheffield. In his address he explained that while he had not been associated with Ruskin in any of his life's work, 'he was proud to think that he knew him, yet he could not claim that old friendship which would enable him to speak as Sir Henry Acland had done'.[1] He had, however, known most of the men whose work was represented in the Guild's collection, and had sat with them while they worked at their pictures now in the gallery.[2]

329 1880s **Bust of Ruskin**, based on a photograph, as finial to a coffee spoon
PROVENANCE: *Ruskin Museum, Coniston*

330 1897-8 **Head of Ruskin**, full face, based on a photograph of the 1880s, sculpted onto a roof corbel
PROVENANCE: *Abbotsholme School Chapel, Rocester*

Cecil Reddie (1858–1932) was a member of the Fellowship of the New Life (founded 1882) which promoted the founding of experimental schools. The utopian tradition is clear in their assertion that 'all schools ought to be communities, miniature commonwealths or states, as they were in the Middle Ages'. His membership and beliefs led him to found Abbotsholme School near Rocester, between Ashbourne and Uttoxeter, on the Derbyshire-Staffordshire borders, in 1889. Reddie was a friend of Edward Carpenter and an admirer of the Arts and Crafts Movement. C.R. Ashbee made or designed much of the furniture. The chapel was built by William Sugden of Leek in 1897–98. Nine roof corbels are carved with the heads of figures admired by Reddie, including, of course, Ruskin.

DATES NOT KNOWN

331 **Bas relief by Alexander Stirling Calder**, head. Cast in plaster, bronze finish, 19½ x 32
PROVENANCE: Fielding Stilson; given to *Ruskin Art Club of Los Angeles* (badly damaged in an earthquake.

332 **Portrait by George T. Tobin** 'of Ruskin in old age' almost certainly drawing from a photograph. Reproduction (unseen) in *Wellesley Collection*.

1 *Igdrasil*, Supplement, May 1890, p. xiii.
2 *Igdrasil*, Supplement, May 1890, pp. xv-xvi.

Bibliography

Abelson, Edward, *Misalliance* (London: Macdonald, 1989).

Acland, Henry W., and John Ruskin, *The Oxford Museum* (London: George Allen, 1893).

Anazawa, K., *et al.*, *Kotaro Takamura's Whole Sculptural Works* (Tokyo: Rikuyosha, 1973).

Angeli, Helen Rossetti, *Pre-Raphaelite Twilight: The Story of Charles Augustus Howell* (London: Richards Press, 1954).

Anon, *The Plenipotent Key to Cope's Correct Card of the Peerless Pilgrimage to Saint Nicotinus of the Holy Herb* (Liverpool: Cope's Tobacco Plant, 1878).

—*John Ruskin on Himself and Things in General* (Liverpool: Cope's, 1893).

—'A Memory of John Ruskin' (*Picture Post*, 23 Sept.1944, pp. 18-19).

—*FAS100* (London: The Fine Art Society, 1976).

Atlay, J.B., *Sir Henry Wentworth Acland, Bart., A Memoir* (London: Smith, Elder, 1903).

Atterbury, Paul, *The Parian Phenomenon* (Shepton Beauchamp: Richard Dennis, 1989).

Attwell, Henry, *Thoughts from Ruskin* (London: George Allen, 1900).

Ayrton, M, and W.J.R. Turner (eds.), *Aspects of British Art* (6 vols.; London: Collins, 1947).

Baillie, Edmund J., *John Ruskin: Aspects of his Thoughts and Teachings* (London: John Pearce, 1882).

Barnes, Janet, *Ruskin in Sheffield* (Sheffield: Sheffield Arts Department, 1985).

Bassin, Ethel, *The Old Songs of Skye: Frances Tolmie and Her Circle* (ed.Derek Bowman; London: Routledge & Kegan Paul, 1977).

Beerbohm, Max, *The Poet's Corner* (London: William Heinemann, 1904).

—*Rossetti and his Circle* (London: William Heinemann, 1922).

—*Rossetti and his Circle* (introduction by N. John Hall; New Haven: Yale University Press, 1987).

Beeching, H.C., 'A Memorial Address Delivered in St Paul's Church, Herne Hill, February, 1901, on the Occasion of the Unveiling of a Memorial to John Ruskin by Mr Holman Hunt' (*St George*, IV, Oct.1901, pp. 275-80).

Benjamin, R.Dyke, 'Ruskin Observed' (*Gazette of the Grolier Club*, N.S. 28-29, June-Dec.1978, pp. 3-56).

Benson, Arthur Christopher, *Ruskin; A Study in Personality* (London: Smith, Elder, a re-issue, 1913).

—*Memories and Friends* (London: John Murray, 1924).

Birkenhead, Sheila, *Illustrious Friends; The Story of Joseph Severn and his son Arthur* (London: Hamish Hamilton, 1965).

Blomfield, Reginald, *Memoirs of an Architect* (London: Macmillan, 1932).

Blunt, Wilfred, *Cockerell: Sydney Carlyle Cockerell, Friend of William Morris and Director of the Fitzwilliam Museum, Cambridge* (London: Hamish Hamilton, 1964).

Bookman, Ruskin Memorial Number (March 1900).

Bookman, Ruskin Double Number (October 1908).

Boris, Eileen, *Art and Labor: Ruskin, Morris, and the Craftsman Ideal in America* (Philadelphia: Temple University Press, 1986).

Bradley, John Lewis, *Ruskin's Letters from Venice 1851–1852* (New Haven: Yale University Press, 1955).

Bradley, John Lewis, and Ian Ousby, *The Correspondence of John Ruskin and Charles Eliot Norton* (Cambridge: Cambridge University Press, 1987).

Brinton, Selwyn, 'American Sculptors of To-day' (*Studio*, Feb. 1907, pp. 34-42).

Broome, Isaac, *The Last Days of the Ruskin Co-operative Association* (Chicago: C.H.Kerr, 1902).

Browning, Oscar, 'Personal Recollections of John Ruskin: A Lecture Delivered before the Ruskin Union, December 12th, 1902' (*St George*, VI, 1903, pp.134-43).

Brunori, Bénédicte, and Teresa Crowley, *The Illustrators: The British Art of Illustration 1780–1996* (London: Chris Beetles, 1996).

Bryson, John, *Dante Gabriel Rossetti and Jane Morris: Their Correspondence* (Oxford: Clarendon Press, 1976).

Burd, Van Akin, 'Ruskin, Rossetti and William Bell Scott: A Second Arrangement' (*Philological Quarterly*, XLVIII, 1, Jan. 1969, pp. 102-107).

Burd, Van Akin (ed.), *The Winnington Letters: John Ruskin's Correspondence with Margaret Alexis Bell and the Children at Winnington Hall* (London: George Allen & Unwin, 1969).

—*The Ruskin Family Letters: The Correspondence of John James Ruskin, His Wife, and Their Son, John, 1801–1843* (2 vols.; Ithaca: Cornell University Press, 1973).

—*John Ruskin and Rose La Touche: Her Unpublished Diaries of 1861 and 1867* (Oxford: Clarendon Press, 1979).

—*Christmas Story: John Ruskin's Venetian Letters of 1876–1877* (Newark, N.J.: University of Delaware Press, 1990).

B[urne]-J[ones], G[eorgiana], *Memorials of Edward Burne-Jones* (2 vols.; London: Macmillan, 1904).

Caine, Hall, *Recollections of Rossetti* (London: Elliot Stock, 1882).

Clark, Kenneth, *Ruskin Today* (London: John Murray, 1964).

Clegg, Jeanne, and Paul Tucker, *Ruskin and Tuscany* (Sheffield: Ruskin Gallery in association with Lund Humphries, 1993).

Clubbe, John (ed.), *Froude's Life of Carlyle* (London: John Murray, 1979).

Cohen, Morton N., *Lewis Carroll: A Biography* (London: Macmillan, 1995).

Cole, Malcolm, *Whitelands College: The History* (London: Whitelands College, 1982).

Collingwood, R.G., *Ruskin's Philosophy: An Address Delivered at the Ruskin Centenary Conference, Coniston, August 8th, 1919* (Kendal: Titus Wilson & Sons, 1922).

Collingwood, S.D., *Life and Letters of Lewis Carroll* (London: Fisher Unwin, 1898).

Collingwood, W.G., *The Life and Work of John Ruskin* (2 vols.; London: Methuen, 1st edn, 1893).

—*The Life of John Ruskin* (London: Methuen, 1900).

—*Ruskin Relics* (London: Isbister, 1903).

Colvin, Sidney, *Memories and Notes of Persons and Places* (London: Edwin Arnold, 1921).

Cook, E.T., *Studies in Ruskin: Some Aspects of the Work and Teaching of John Ruskin* (Orpington: George Allen, 1890).

—'Ruskin and his Books: An Interview with his Publisher' (*Strand Magazine*, XXIV 144, Dec.1902, pp. 709-19).

—*The Life of John Ruskin* (2 vols.; London: George Allen, 1911).

Cook, E.T., and Alexander Wedderburn (ed.), *The Library Edition of the Works of John Ruskin* (39 vols.; London: George Allen, 1903–12), referred to as *Works*.

Crane, Walter, *An Artist's Reminiscences* (London: Methuen, 1907).

Cumming, Elizabeth, *Phoebe Anna Traquair* (Edinburgh: Scottish National Portrait Gallery, 1993).

Dale, J.A., and L.T. Dodd, 'Ruskin Hall, Oxford' (*St George*, II, 1899, pp. 94-105).

Davis, J.Llewelyn, *The Working Men's College, 1854–1904* (London: Macmillan, 1904).

Dearden, James S., 'Some Portraits of John Ruskin' (*Apollo*, Dec. 1960, pp. 190-95) referred to as *Dearden I*.

—'Further Portraits of John Ruskin' (*Apollo*, June 1961, pp. 171-78) referred to as *Dearden II*.

—'The Ruskin Galleries at Bembridge School, Isle of Wight' (*Bulletin of the John Rylands Library*, LI, 2, Spring 1969, pp. 310-47).

—*John Ruskin and The Ruskin Museum at Coniston* (Coniston: Ruskin Museum, 1969; 2nd edn, 1975).

—*Facets of Ruskin: Some Sesquicentennial Studies* (London: Charles Skilton, 1970).

—'The Ruskin Circle in Italy in 1872' (*Connoisseur*, 179, 722, April 1972, pp. 240-45).

—*John Ruskin: An Illustrated Life 1819–1900* (Aylesbury: Shire Publications, 1973).

—'John Ruskin on Ice' (*Country Life*, CLXIII, No.4204, 2 Feb. 1978; pp. 272-73).

—*John Ruskin: An Illustrated Life 1819–1900* (Coniston: The Brantwood Trust, 1981).

—*John Ruskin's Camberwell* (St Albans: Brentham Press for The Guild of St George, 1990).

—'J. Howard Whitehouse and the Ruskin Galleries at Bembridge School', in Roger Sawyer (ed.), *The Island from Within* (Bembridge: Robook, 1990, pp. 50-54).

—*John Ruskin e le Alpi* (Turin: Museo Nazionale della Montagna, 1990).

—*John Ruskin and the Alps* (Lancaster University for The Fine Art Society, 1991).

—*Ruskin, Bembridge and Brantwood: The Growth of the Whitehouse Collection* (Keele: Ryburn Publishing, 1994).

Dearden, James S. (ed.), *The Professor: Arthur Severn's Memoir of John Ruskin* (London: George Allen & Unwin, 1967).

—*A Tour to the Lakes in Cumberland: John Ruskin's Diary for 1830* (Aldershot: Scolar Press, 1990).

Doughty, Oswald, *Rossetti* (New Haven: Yale University Press, 1949).

Downey, William, 'A Grand Old Photographer: Some Reminiscences of Mr William Downey, Royal Photographer' (*Pall Mall Budget*, 15 Jan. 1891).

Drinkwater, John, *The Outline of Literature* (London: George Newnes 1923–24).

Evans, Joan, *John Ruskin* (London: Jonathan Cape, 1954).

Evans, Joan (ed.), *The Lamp of Beauty: Writings on Art by John Ruskin* (London: Phaidon Press, 1959).

Evans, Joan, and John Howard Whitehouse (ed.), *The Diaries of John Ruskin* (3 vols.; Oxford: Clarendon Press, 1956–59).

Fowler, L.N., 'Phrenological Description of Mr John Ruskin' (*The Phrenological Magazine*, I, June 1880, pp. 169-72).

Fredeman, W.E., 'Pre-Raphaelites in Caricature' (*Burlington Magazine* CII, Dec.1960, pp. 523-29).

Gere, Charlotte, and Munn, Geoffrey, *Artists' Jewellery: Pre-Raphaelite to Arts and Crafts* (Woodbridge: Antique Collectors' Club, 1989).

Gibbens, John, 'My dear Aunt' (*Oldie*, Jan. 1996, p. 33).

Goss, Edmund, *English Literature* (4 vols.; New York, 1935).

Graham, J.W., 'John Ruskin at Home' (*Proceedings of Warrington Literary and Philosophical Society*, 1897).

Graphic, The, Ruskin Memorial Number (3 Feb. 1900).

Green, Roger Lancelyn (ed.), *The Diaries of Lewis Carroll* (2 vols.; London: Cassell, 1953).

Grierson, Sir Herbert, *The English Bible* (Britain in Pictures Series; London: William Collins, 1943).

Grieve, Alastair, 'Ruskin and Millais at Glenfinlas' (*Burlington Magazine*, April 1996, pp. 228-34).

Grylls, Rosalie Glynn, *Portrait of Rossetti* (London: Macdonald, 1964).

Hanson, Bruce, *Brantwood: John Ruskin's Home 1872–1900* (Coniston: Brantwood Trust, 1992).

Hayman, John (ed.), *John Ruskin: Letters from the Continent 1858* (Toronto: University of Toronto Press, 1982).

Herbert, Susan, *Diary of a Victorian Cat* (London: Thames & Hudson, 1991).

Hewison, Robert, *John Ruskin: The Argument of the Eye* (London: Thames & Hudson, 1976).

—*Chris Orr's John Ruskin* (London: Signford, 1976).

—*Art and Society: Ruskin in Sheffield 1876* (London: Brentham Press for The Guild of St George, 1979).

—*Ruskin a Venezia: Ruskin in Venice* (Venice: The British Centre, 1983).

—*Ruskin and Oxford: The Art of Education* (Oxford: Clarendon Press, 1996).

Hewison, Robert (ed.), *New Approaches to Ruskin: Thirteen Essays* (London: Routledge & Kegan Paul, 1981).

Hilton, Tim, *John Ruskin: The Early Years 1819–1859* (New Haven: Yale University Press, 1985).

Hubbard, Elbert, *Little Journeys to the Homes of Good Men and Great – John Ruskin* (New York: G.P. Putman's Sons, 1895).

Hudson, Derek, *Mumby: Man of Two Worlds* (London: Abacus, 1974).

Hunt, John Dixon, *The Wider Sea: A Life of John Ruskin* (London: J.M. Dent & Sons, 1982).

Hunt, William Holman, *Pre-Raphaelitism and The Pre-Raphaelite Brotherhood* (2 vols.; London: Macmillan, 1905).

Image, Selwyn, 'Some Personal Recollections of John Ruskin: A Paper Read before The Ruskin Union, June 25th, 1903' (*St George*, VI, 1903, pp. 287-301).

James, Sir William (ed.), *The Order of Release: The Story of John Ruskin, Effie Gray and John Everett Millais Told for the First Time in their Unpublished Letters* (London: John Murray, 1947).

Jameson, M. Ethel, *A Bibliographical Contribution to the Study of John Ruskin* (Cambridge, MA: Riverside Press, 1901).

Johnstone, T.J., 'Ruskin for Rector: The Edinburgh Rectorial Election of 1868' (*Carlyle Pamphlets* 2, *The Carlyle Newsletter*, n.d.).

Kirchhoff, Frederick, *John Ruskin* (Boston: Twayne Publishers, 1984).

Kitchin, G.W., *Ruskin in Oxford and Other Studies* (London: John Murray, 1903).

Leith, Royal W., *A Quiet Devotion: The Life and Work of Henry Roderick Newman* (New York: The Jordan-Volpe Gallery, 1996).

Leon, Derrick, *Ruskin: The Great Victorian* (London: Routledge & Kegan Paul, 1949).

Levi, Donata, and Tucker, Paul, *Ruskin didata: Il disegno tra disciplina e diletto* (Venice: Marsilio, 1997).

Lovric, Michelle, *Carpaccio's Cat* (New York: Artisan, 1999).

Lutyens, Mary, 'Portraits of Effie' (*Apollo*, March 1968, pp. 190-97).

—'Where Did Ruskin Sleep?' (*TLS*, 2 Jan. 1969, p. 19).

Lutyens, Mary (ed.), *Effie in Venice: Unpublished Letters of Mrs John Ruskin Written from Venice between 1849–1852* (London: John Murray, 1965).

—*Millais and the Ruskins* (London: John Murray, 1967).

—*The Ruskins and The Grays* (London: John Murray, 1972).

Lutyens, Mary, and Malcolm Warner, *Rainy Days at Brig o'Turk: The Highland Sketchbooks of John Everett Millais 1853* (Westerham: Dalrymple Press, 1983).

[Maas, Rupert], *John Ruskin and his Circle* (London: Maas Gallery, 1991).

Marwick, William (ed.), *The Ruskin Reading Guild Journal* (12 monthly parts; Orpington: George Allen, *et al.*, 1889).

Marwick, William, and Kineton Parkes (ed.), *Igdrasil: The Journal of The Ruskin Reading Guild. A Magazine of Literature, Art, and Social Philosophy* (3 vols.; London: George Allen, 1890–1902).

Mather, Frank Jewett, Jr, *Charles Herbert Moore: Landscape Painter* (Princeton: Princeton University Press, 1957).

Measham, Donald, *John Ruskin, The Last Chapter: A Study of John Ruskin's Autobiography Praeterita* (Sheffield: Arts Department, 1989).

Merrill, Linda, *A Pot of Paint, Aesthetics on Trial in Whistler v. Ruskin* (Washington: Smithsonian Institution Press, 1992).

Meynell, Viola (ed.), *Friends of a Lifetime: Letters to Sydney Carlyle Cockerell* (London: Jonathan Cape, 1940).

Millais, John Guille, *The Life and Letters of Sir John Everett Millais: President of The Royal Academy* (2 vols.; London: Methuen, 1899).

Mill, John Saxon, *Life of Sir Edward Cook, K.B.E., A Biography* (London: Constable, 1921).

—*Life and Letters of Sir Hubert Herkomer, C.V.O., R.A.: A Study in Struggle and Success* (London: Hutchinson, 1923).

Morley, Catherine W., *John Ruskin: Late Work 1870–1890; The Museum and Guild of St George: An Educational Experiment* (New York: Garland Publishing, 1984).

Nevinson, Henry W., 'Some Memories of Ruskin', in Whitehouse, J. Howard (ed.), *Ruskin the Prophet and Other Centenary Studies* (London: George Allen & Unwin, 1920), pp. 147-57.

Norton, C.E. (ed.), *Letters of John Ruskin to Charles Eliot Norton* (2 vols.; Boston and New York: Houghton Mifflin, 1904).

Norton, Sara, and M.A. DeWolfe Howe (ed.), *Letters to Charles Eliot Norton* (2 vols., Boston and New York: Houghton Mifflin, 1913).

Payot, Paul, *Ruskin et les anglais à Chamonix* (Bonneville: Plancher, 1938).

Pedrick, Gale, *Life with Rossetti* (London: Macdonald, 1964).

Penny, N., *Catalogue of European Sculpture in the Ashmolean Museum* (Oxford: Clarendon Press, 1992).

Poole, Mrs Reginald, *Catalogue of Portraits: The University Colleges, City and County of Oxford* (3 vols.; Oxford: Clarendon Press, 1912–25).

Potter, Beatrix, *Appley Dapply's Nursery Rhymes* (London: Frederick Warne, 1917).

Price, A. Willadene, *Gutzon Borglum, Artist and Patriot* (Chicago: Rand McNally, 1962).

Quennell, Peter, *John Ruskin: The Portrait of a Prophet* (London: Collins, 1949).

Rawnsley, H.D., *Ruskin and the English Lakes* (Glasgow: James MacLehose & Sons, 1901).

Read, Benedict, and Joanna Barnes, *Pre-Raphaelite Sculpture: Nature and Imagination in British Sculpture 1848–1914* (London: Lund Humphries, 1991).

Richmond, Sir W.B., 'Ruskin as I knew him' (*St George*, V, 1902, pp. 285-303).

Rosenberg, John D., *The Darkening Glass: A Portrait of Ruskin's Genius* (New York: Columbia University Press, 1961).

Rossetti, W.M., *Some Reminiscences of William Michael Rossetti* (2 vols.; London: Brown, Langham, 1906).

Ruskin, John, *Two Letters Concerning 'Notes on the Construction of Sheepfolds' Addressed to The Rev.F.D.Maurice, M.A. in 1851* (London: T.J.Wise, 1890).

—*The Stones of Venice* (ed. J.G. Links; London: Collins, 1960).

Ruskin, John, *Iteriad or Three Weeks among the Lakes* (ed. James S. Dearden; Newcastle upon Tyne: Frank Graham, 1967).

—*Praeterita* (ed. A.O.J. Cockshut; The Whitehouse Edition of John Ruskin; Keele: Ryburn Publishing, 1994).

Scott, Edith Hope, *Ruskin's Guild of St George* (London: Methuen, 1931).

Shapiro, Harold I. (ed.), *Ruskin in Italy: Letters to his Parents 1845* (Oxford: Clarendon Press, 1972).

Shaw, Roy, *The Relevance of Ruskin* (St Albans: Brentham Press for The Guild of St George, 1988).

Shiga, Naoya (ed.), *Shirakaba* (Tokyo, 1910).

Smetham, James, 'Modern Sacred Art in England' (*The London Review*, XVIII, 1862, pp. 68-70).

Spear, Jeffrey L., *Dreams of an English Eden: Ruskin and his Tradition in Social Criticism* (New York: Columbia University Press, 1984).

Spielmann, M.H., 'The Portraits of John Ruskin – I' (*Magazine of Art*, Jan. 1891, pp. 73-79), referred to as '*Spielmann I*'.

—'The Portraits of John Ruskin – (Concluded)' (*Magazine of Art*, Feb. 1891, pp. 121-26), referred to as '*Spielmann II*'.

—*John Ruskin* (London: Cassell, 1900).

Spielmann, M.H., and G.S. Layard, *Kate Greenaway* (London: A. & C. Black, 1905).
Stirling, A.M.W., *The Richmond Papers* (London: Heinemann, 1926).
Surtees, Virginia, *The Paintings and Drawings of Dante Gabriel Rossetti (1828–1882): A Catalogue of Raisonné* (2 vols.; Oxford: Clarendon Press, 1971).
Surtees, Virginia (ed.), *Sublime and Instructive: Letters from John Ruskin to Louisa, Marchioness of Waterford, Anna Blunden and Ellen Heaton* (London: Michael Joseph, 1972).
—*Reflections of a Friendship: John Ruskin's Letters to Pauline Trevelyan 1848–1866* (London: George Allen & Unwin, 1979).
—*The Diaries of George Price Boyce* (Norwich: Real World, 1980).
Sutcliffe, F.M., 'A Day's Sunshine at Brantwood' (*The Amateur Photographer*, 9 Feb. 1900, pp. 107-108).
—'Photographer to John Ruskin' (*Photographic Journal*, June 1931, p. 255).
Swett, Lucia Gray, *John Ruskin's Letters to Francesca and Memoirs of the Alexanders* (Boston: Lothrop, Lee and Shephard, 1931).
Takamura, Kotaro, 'Mr Gutzon Borglum, American Sculptor' (*Shin-cho* (*New Tide*), June 1917, p. 207).
Talbot, Fanny, *A Visit to Brantwood* (Bembridge: The Ruskin Association, 1980).
Trevelyan, Raleigh, *A Pre-Raphaelite Circle* (London: Chatto & Windus, 1978).
Troxell, J.C., *The Three Rossettis* (Boston: Harvard University Press, 1937).
Unwin, Rayner (ed.), *The Gulf of Years: Letters from John Ruskin to Kathleen Olander* (London: George Allen & Unwin, 1953).
Viljoen, Helen Gill, *Ruskin's Scottish Heritage: A Prelude* (Urbana: University of Illinois Press, 1956).
Viljoen, Helen Gill (ed.), *The Brantwood Diary of John Ruskin Together with Selected Related Letters and Sketches of Persons Mentioned* (New Haven: Yale University Press, 1971).
Wakefield, Mary, 'Brantwood, Coniston, John Ruskin's Home' (*Murray's Magazine*, VIII, Nov.1890, pp. 587-606).
Walton, Paul H., 'Seven Ruskin Drawings in the Fogg Art Museum' (*Harvard Library Bulletin*, XIV, 2, Spring 1960, pp. 265-82).
—*The Drawings of John Ruskin* (Oxford: Clarendon Press, 1972).
Ward, William C. (ed.), *John Ruskin's Letters to William Ward: With a Short Biography of William Ward* (Boston: Marshall Jones, 1922).
Wardle, Peter, and Cedric Quayle, *Ruskin and Bewdley* (St Albans: Brentham Press for The Guild of St George, 1989).
Watts, M.S., *George Frederick Watts: The Annals of an Artist's Life* (3 vols.; London: Macmillan, 1912).
Webling, Peggy, *A Sketch of John Ruskin* (London: Published by the author, 1914).
—*Peggy: The Story of One Score Years and Ten* (London: Hutchinson, n.d.).
Wedmore, Frederick, *Turner and Ruskin: An Exposition of the Works of Turner from the Writings of Ruskin* (2 vols.; London: George Allen, 1900).
Whitehouse, J. Howard, *Ruskin and Brantwood: An Account of the Exhibition Rooms* (Cambridge: Ruskin Society, 1937).
—*Ruskin the Painter and his Works at Bembridge* (London: Oxford University Press, 1938).
—*Vindication of Ruskin* (London: George Allen & Unwin, 1950).
Whitehouse, J. Howard (ed.), *John Ruskin: Letters Written on the Occasion of the Centenary of his Birth 1919* (Oxford: University Press for the Ruskin Centenary Council, 1919).
—*Ruskin Centenary Addresses 8 February 1919* (London: Oxford University Press, 1919).
—*The Solitary Warrior: New Letters by Ruskin* (London: George Allen & Unwin, 1929).
Wilenski, R.H., *John Ruskin: An Introduction to Further Study of his Life and Work* (London: Faber and Faber, 1933).
Williams, W. Smith (ed.), *Selections from the Writings of John Ruskin* (London: Smith, Elder, 1861).
Williams-Ellis, Amabel, *John Ruskin* (Life and Letters Series; London: Jonathan Cape, 1933).
Wise, Thomas J. (ed.), *Letters on Art and Literature by John Ruskin* (London: Privately Printed, 1894).
—*Letters from John Ruskin to Rev. J.P. Faunthorpe, M.A.* (2 vols.; London: Privately Printed, 1895–96).
—*Letters from John Ruskin to Frederick J. Furnivall, M.A., Hon. Dr. Phil. and Other Correspondents* (London: Privately Printed, 1897).
Witmer, Helen Williams, *The Ruskin Art Club: Twelve More Years in Retrospect, 1948–1960* (Los Angeles: Ruskin Art Club, 1970).
Wyndham, G. (ed.), *Letters to M.G. & H.G.* (Privately Printed, 1903).

Principal Ruskin Exhibitions

1900	(21 July–8 Sept.)	Coniston Institute
1901	(4 Feb.–2 Mar.)	London: Royal Society of Painters in Watercolours
1904	(23 Mar.–)	Manchester City Art Gallery
1904	(Mar.–Apr.)	London: The Fine Art Society
1919	(21 July–20 Sept.)	Coniston Institute, 'Ruskin Centenary Exhibition'
1919	(1 Oct.–22 Nov.)	London: Royal Academy, 'Ruskin Centenary Exhibition'
1954	(10 July–18 Jan.)	Arts Council Travelling Exhibition, Hull, Kendal, Bristol, Norwich, Cardiff, Newcastle, Plymouth and London (Leighton House)
1960	(11 June–24 Aug.)	Arts Council Travelling Exhibition, Aldeburgh, Colchester and London
1964	(17 Jan.–15 Feb.)	Arts Council; London: Arts Council Gallery, 'Ruskin and his circle'
1965	(Jan.–Feb.)	New York: Queens College Library 'Ruskin's Backgrounds, Friendships and Interests...'
1966	(Oct.–Nov.)	Verona: Museo di Castelvecchio, 'Ruskin a Verona'
1969	(8 Feb.)	London: 12 Hobart Place, 'Sesquicentennial Exhibition'
1969	(26 July–Oct.)	Kendal: Abbot Hall; Sheffield: Graves Art Gallery
1969	(21–30 Oct.)	London: Central School of Art & Design, 'Ruskin and Venice'
1970	(27 Mar.–25 April)	Rye Art Gallery
1970	(11–22 Nov.)	Oxford: Corpus Christi College
1972	(15–16 Sept.)	London: 9 Upper Belgrave St, 'Pictures, Books and Letters from the Adams Bequest'
1973	(18 Apr.–12 May)	Portsmouth: City Museum and Art Gallery, 'The European Scene, Drawings by John Ruskin'
1977	(13 Feb.–)	Oundle School
1977	(July)	New York: Pierpont Morgan Library
1978	(16 Oct.–19 Nov.)	Louisville: J.B. Speed Art Museum, 'Ruskin and Venice'
1979	(19 Jan.–4 Mar.)	Cambridge, Mass.: Fogg Art Museum
1983	(25 May–13 Nov.)	Arts Council Travelling Exhibition, 'John Ruskin', Sheffield, Liverpool, Kendal and Oxford
1989	(6 Apr.–10 Sept.)	Manchester: Whitworth Art Gallery; Bath: Holburne Museum; London: Bankside Gallery. 'Ruskin and the English Watercolour'
1989	(1 Dec.–5 Apr. 1991)	Basle: Historisches Museum; Schaffhausen: Museum zu Allerheiligen; Lucerne: Kunstmuseum; Sion: Musées Cantonaux du Valais; Turin: Museo Nazionale della Montagna; London: The Fine Art Society, 'Ruskin and the Alps'
1993	(8 Jan.–12 June)	London: Accademia Italiana: Sheffield: Ruskin Gallery; Lucca: Fondazione Ragghianti, 'Ruskin and Tuscany'
1993	(25 Feb.–15 Aug.)	Tokyo: Isetan Museum; Kurume: Ishibashi Museum; Naru Sogo Museum of Art; Utsunomiya: Tochigi Prefectural Museum; 'John Ruskin and Victorian art'
1993	(15 Mar. –)	Phoenix Art Museum, 'John Ruskin and the Victorian Eye'
1996	(21 May–24 Nov.)	Oxford: Ashmolean Museum; Sheffield: Mappin Art Gallery, 'Ruskin and Oxford, the Art of Education'
1996	(5–28 Sept.)	New York: Salander-O'Reilly Galleries

Index to the Catalogue of Portraits

(Numbers shown are the Portrait Catalogue Numbers)

Index

(Note: This index should be used in conjunction with the Index to Portraits.)